LEGAL AND FINANCIAL ASPECTS OF EQUIPMENT LEASING TRANSACTIONS

RICHARD M. CONTINO

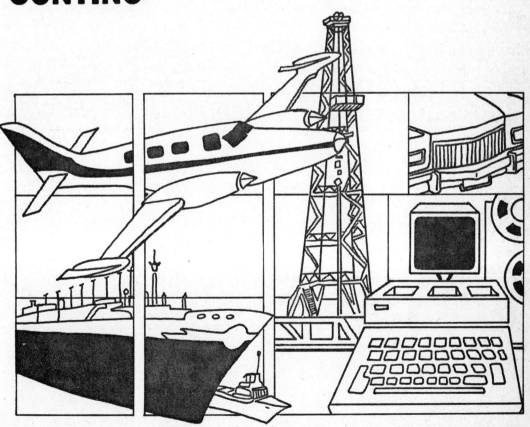

Prentice-Hall, Inc.

Englewood Cliffs, N.J.

51351

Prentice-Hall International, Inc., *London*
Prentice-Hall of Australia, Pty. Ltd., *Sydney*
Prentice-Hall of Canada, Ltd., *Toronto*
Prentice-Hall of India Private Ltd., *New Delhi*
Prentice-Hall of Japan, Inc., *Tokyo*
Prentice-Hall of Southeast Asia Pte. Ltd., *Singapore*
Whitehall Books, Ltd., *Wellington, New Zealand*

© 1979 by

Prentice-Hall, Inc.

Englewood Cliffs, N.J.

This publication is designed to provide accurate and authoritative information in regard to the subject matter covered. It is sold with the understanding that the publisher is not engaged in rendering legal, accounting or other professional service. If legal advice or other expert assistance is required, the services of a competent professional person should be sought.
*—From the Declaration of Principles jointly adopted
by a Committee of the American Bar Association and
a Committee of Publishers and Associations.*

Library of Congress Cataloging in Publication Data

Contino, Richard M.
  Legal and financial aspects of equipment leasing
transactions.

  Includes bibliographical references and index.
  1. Industrial equipment leases--United States.
2. Industrial equipment leases--Taxation--United States.
I. Title.
KF946.C66   343'.73'078   78-10188
ISBN 0-13-528315-9

Printed in the United States of America

Dedication

To Mother, Father, Ronnie, Carol and Mary Kay

ABOUT THE AUTHOR

Richard M. Contino is a practicing attorney and business consultant in New York City. He limits his business exclusively to the area of capital equipment leasing. As a leasing consultant and legal advisor, his services cover the legal, financial and market aspects of capital equipment leasing.

Prior to entering private practice, Mr. Contino held the positions of Marketing Vice President and Eastern Regional Counsel for GATX Leasing Corporation, a major equipment lessor and lease underwriter. Before joining GATX, he practiced corporate law with two major New York City law firms.

The author has lectured at American Management Association seminars and before other professional groups.

Mr. Contino is a member of the Bars of the State of New York, the State of Maryland and the District of Columbia. He is also a member of the American Bar Association and the New York State Bar Association. The author holds an L.L.M. in Corporate Law from New York University Graduate School of Law, a J.D. from the University of Maryland School of Law and a Bachelor of Aeronautical Engineering from Rensselaer Polytechnic Institute.

INTRODUCTION

The purpose of this book is to provide the legal, financial, accounting, and business background essential to successfully evaluate, negotiate, and advise on equipment lease transactions. Capital equipment leasing is one of the most complex forms of financing in existence today. It involves sophisticated concepts often understood only by experts. Many equipment users fail to consider this important alternative when the need for acquiring capital assets arises because of their lack of understanding of the advantages. Even those who do consider it, frequently do not know how to maximize their position.

The equipment lease transaction is analyzed from start to finish. The reader is taken step-by-step through the seven most important aspects of finance leasing—the general market place, the preliminary evaluation stage, the proposal, the documents, the tax issues, the accounting treatment, and the economics. The latest and best techniques for dealing with the complex technical issues are explained. Practical suggestions and insights are offered throughout to enable the reader to gain every advantage and avoid the many legal and financial pitfalls. It addresses, for example, issues such as:

What types of equipment can be leased?
Can individuals act as lessors?
Do bank leasing companies give the most aggressive rates?
When is leasing a poor choice?
What is the best way for a company to solicit lease bids?
Does a proposal letter really commit a lessor?
What should a properly written lease cover?
How can an underwriter protect his fee?
How good is a legal opinion on questionable issues?
When should a leveraged lease be used?
When will a lease meet the IRS requirements?
Can a fixed price purchase option be used?
What are the most effective depreciation methods?
Can the lessee ever claim any of the ownership tax benefits?
What tax and economic risks does a lessor have?
What special risks must a leveraged lease investor consider?

How should a lease be analyzed financially?

What impact do the new lease accounting rules have?

Many prospective lessees do not know how to properly assess the leasing marketplace. As a result they do not find the most favorable deals available. Some lessors, for example, are more suited than others for particular transactions. The various lessors are discussed as well as the pros and cons of dealing with each.

The proposal stage is a critical point in any lease financing arrangement. During this phase the parties establish the business parameters. A prospective lessee will be in his strongest negotiating position. If he takes advantage of some simple techniques recommended by the author, he can, for example, get a "below market" lease rent. A prospective lessor can, on the other hand, gain some valuable advantages at this time by properly structuring his offer.

The documentation phase is another crucial aspect. Here the rights and obligations of the parties are defined. All parties must understand the fundamental concepts that are covered in order to be fully aware of what their risks and obligations will be. For example, a lessor may inadvertantly assume certain State tax payment obligations. These taxes can drastically reduce a lessor's profits. A lessee may also unknowingly assume burdensome obligations. The documents are examined comprehensively to give anyone responsible for negotiating an equipment lease the essentials necessary to avoid the many traps.

Problems often arise because of lack of appreciation for the complex tax issues. Parties spend time and money on transactions that will not be approved by the Internal Revenue Service. The tax issues are identified and suggestions are offered for dealing with the potential risks.

How a lease must be accounted for should always be a foremost consideration. Improper structuring can cause undesirable accounting treatment. In the past the lease accounting requirements have been in doubt. Recently, however, the Financial Accounting Standards Board has promulgated an extensive and complicated set of rules. The rules are summarized and put into a more meaningful context.

The financial side of a lease decision is another key consideration. There are many apparent economic advantages and disadvantages. There are also many which are not so apparent. Lease investors, for example, should be aware that incorrect equipment residual assumptions can wipe out profits. A prospective lessee can end up making the wrong financing decision by using an incorrect method of analysis. The economic advantages and disadvantages as well as the methods of financial analysis are discussed so that a prospective lessor, lessee, lender, or investor can determine what his position is or should be.

An entire chapter is devoted to the specialized field of leveraged leasing, one of the most sophisticated and competitive forms of leasing. Leveraged leasing can produce many unique benefits. There are, however, many dangers. Some lease underwriters, for example, "low ball" rent quotations to eliminate the competition and then later raise the rates. A prospective lease investor can end up making a poor investment by relying on an unrealistic investment analysis.

Time-saving checklists covering all the critical stages and aspects of an equipment lease financing have been included. Examples have been incorporated to illustrate many of the financial points discussed. All the important terms and "buzz" words have been compiled and simply defined for ready access. Finally, selected sample lease documents have been supplied.

In summary, the book gives the reader a complete grasp of the legal, financial, accounting, and business considerations that are necessary to originate, evaluate, and negotiate the most favorably structured capital equipment leasing transaction.

Richard M. Contino

CONTENTS

1

PRIMARY EQUIPMENT LEASING

CONSIDERATIONS

You Can't Get By Without Knowing the Fundamentals • Certain Equipment Can Not Be Economically Leased • Some Lessors Should Be Avoided • There Are Many Advantages—But also Disadvantages • Be Aware and Make the Right Decision.

A. EQUIPMENT LEASING IN TODAY'S MARKETPLACE

The concept of leasing has been around for decades. In the early years most lease arrangements centered around *real estate*. The legal requirements and financial considerations were relatively straightforward. During the 1950's, however, leasing began to emerge as a viable alternative for funding *capital equipment*. Today, the equipment leasing industry plays a major role in the financial community. Virtually any type of equipment can be leased on a variety of terms. There is, however, a drawback—the legal requirements and financial considerations are extremely complex. In fact, many transactions involve concepts which are so sophisticated that even the most experienced people sometimes inadvertently miss points which could cost them or their clients many thousands of dollars.

The increased interest in leasing as an alternate source of funding equipment acquisitions has resulted in a deluge of questions not only from equipment users, but also from the legal and financial community. For example, what are the *real* advantages and disadvantages? How much structuring leeway is there under the new tax rules? What do the new accounting rules mean? How should a lease transaction be analyzed from a financial viewpoint? For these and many other questions there are no easy answers.

Unfortunately, because of the many variables which can be involved in a lease decision, this book cannot answer all the questions concerning the desirability of entering into a *specific* transaction. The criteria used by one company may be *totally* inappropriate for another company. The reader will, however, be provided with a comprehensive working knowledge of the fundamental tools necessary to intelligently handle *any* lease situation from start to finish. The relevant issues will be clearly identified, simply explained, and fully discussed.

B. WHAT TYPES OF EQUIPMENT CAN BE LEASED?

Any type of equipment *could* be leased. The critical question for a prospective lessee is—*at what cost?* In general, leasing is not an economically competitive way of acquiring equipment unless certain tax advantages are available to the lessor. Consider the following hypothetical situation.

ILLUSTRATIVE EXAMPLE—
THE TAX ADVANTAGE:

Company A wants to acquire the use of a $10,000 truck. It can borrow funds from its bank for five years at the prime rate, assumed for this example to be 10% per year. If Company A were able to borrow 100% of the funds required, its cost to finance the truck would be the cost of the $10,000 loan.

As an alternative, Company A could lease the truck from Company B. Assume Company B also borrowed "at prime" from the same bank and that it would fund the truck purchase entirely from its bank borrowings. If there were no truck ownership tax advantages, the only way it could make a profit would be to charge a lease rate greater than its cost of funds. Therefore, Company A would have to pay something over the prime rate to Company B, a not very attractive arrangement.

Although the above example is admittedly oversimplified and not completely realistic, it is used to make the point—*leasing may not make any economic sense unless there are ownership tax benefits which can be claimed by a lessor.* Fortunately, there are tax advantages which are available to an equipment owner, such as depreciation and investment tax credit, which provide tax savings. These tax savings are taken into consideration by a prospective lessor when calculating the rent to be charged.

OBSERVATION:

Generally speaking, the greater the tax benefits attributable to a particular type of property, the more likelihood it can be attractively lease financed.

Equipment which technically qualifies as "section 38 property" under the Internal Revenue Code is ideally suited to lease financing because of the favorable tax benefits, such as accelerated depreciation and investment tax credit benefits, which are available to its owner. "Section 38 property" is basically tangible moveable *personal* property, as distinguished from real property or fixtures. Trucks, automobiles, tractors, aircraft, tugboats, barges, oil rigs, and computers are common examples. Lease transactions involving this type of property can be structured so they make economic sense for both lessors *and* lessees.

C. WHO LEASES EQUIPMENT?

Any user of equipment *could* be a potential lessee. For example, for many reasons both personal and business, individuals lease equipment. For an equally wide range of reasons businesses—whether corporations, partnerships, or other entities—lease equipment. Leasing is not, however, advisable for *every* equipment user. In general, those that lease typically do so to avoid certain business or equipment risks, to solve certain business or equipment problems, or to maximize their cash resources. Those that do not lease, do not based upon a variety of considerations which vary with each situation. The fundamental considerations which must be factored into each lease decision will be discussed later on in this chapter.

D. SOURCES OF LEASE FINANCING—BASIC TO PICKING THE BEST IS KNOWING HOW THEY OPERATE

Without knowing the actual *scope* of the lessor market, a prospective lessee will not be able to find the best potential deal available. As the reader will see from the following discussion, equipment lessors run the gamut from individuals to banks to non-bank companies. From a practical viewpoint, there are too many lessors to consider inviting *every one* to submit a bid. Therefore, a prospective lessee can never be *absolutely* certain it will find the *most* favorable deal *possible* in the market. However, by selecting a meaningful cross section of potential lessors, the chances can be significantly increased. The key to such a selection is understanding what each type has to offer, including any unusual positive or negative attributes.

For discussion purposes it is useful to separate the lessor group into five basic categories: individuals, independent leasing companies, lease brokers, captive leasing companies, and banks. In this way certain unique aspects can be isolated. In practice, however, it is not as clear cut and it is sometimes hard to decide in what category a particular lessor may fit. For example, some independent finance leasing companies also act as lease brokers.

1. Individuals Have Limited but Competitive Appeal

Although high tax bracket individuals can be competitive as lessors of equipment, they are not a primary factor in the lessor market because of certain restrictions on their ability to claim the investment tax credit available under the Internal Revenue Code. As a result, they are at a disadvantage when competing in the greater number of transactions against a lessor who can claim the investment tax credit. When, however, they are entitled to claim the credit, they can be extremely competitive. Very simply, this is because when they are not precluded from claiming the same tax benefits as any other type of lessor, their higher income tax bracket allows them to take greater advantage of the benefits. By getting a greater percentage tax saving they can charge a relatively lower rent and still get a comparable return.

ILLUSTRATIVE EXAMPLE—
THE HIGH TAX BRACKET ADVANTAGE:

Consider two prospective lessors, Individual A and Company B. Both want to earn the same overall return on their lease investment. Who will be the most competitive under the following assumptions?

Individual A Income Tax Rate	70%
Company B Income Tax Rate	50%
Available Lease Tax Loss	$1,000

It is easy to see that Individual A would save $700 in taxes (70% x $1000) through a $1000 tax loss and Company B would save $500 in taxes (50% x $1000) through the same tax loss. Individual A, therefore, has a $200 cash advantage over Company B. Because of this, Individual A will be able to offer a lower rent and still get the same investment return.

A WORD OF CAUTION:

A prospective lessee considering using an individual-type lessor must look at more than the rent advantage. For example, there may be a potential risk that a Federal income tax lien imposed on the individual could result in the attachment of the equipment under lease. In addition, individuals can be somewhat more arbitrary to deal with when variances from the terms of the lease are required.

2. Independent Leasing Companies—
Good but Watch the Cost

The independent, or non-bank, leasing companies are a major source of equipment lease financing. Because leasing is usually their principal source of revenue, they have to be extremely aggressive and, in some cases, are willing to "bend the rules" for the benefit of a lessee in order to win a transaction. For example, some will give a lessee the right to purchase the equipment at a predetermined fixed price when the lease ends—a practice prohibited under the IRS lease guidelines.

The independent leasing companies can be put into two categories. The first category consists of firms which do nothing more than provide money. That is, the only service they offer is to the purchasing and leasing of the desired equipment. The second category consists of those which offer equipment-related, nonfinancial services, such as maintenance and repair services, in addition to asset funding.

a. Some Act Only as "Lenders"

Millions of dollars of capital equipment is financed each year by lessors referred to as "finance leasing companies," or "financial" lessors. They operate in much the same manner as banks or other financing companies. They do not maintain an inventory of equipment but rather purchase specific equipment for lease to a specific lessee. No other services are provided. In other words, when the equipment arrives and is ready for lease, they pay for it, take title, and lease it to the equipment user. They do not, for example, get involved with the ordering or handling of the equipment, this is taken care of by the prospective lessee.

Typically, the leases written by finance leasing companies run for 70% to 80% of the equipment's useful life and, as such, are commonly referred to as "finance" leases. The total amounts due under such leases, including the rents payable and the equipment residual value, are usually sufficient to provide the lessor with a full return of his equipment investment and a profit. If the transaction is leveraged with third-party debt, the rents will also generally be enough to cover the full repayment of the debt. Many finance leases are "net" to the lessee. That is, substantially all the equipment ownership responsibilities, such as maintenance, taxes, and insurance, must be assumed by the lessee.

How do the rental rates offered by a typical finance leasing company compare to those which may be offered by a high tax bracket individual-type lessor? They will probably be higher. Financial lessors are generally corporations and, as such, are subject to a lower Federal income tax rate, currently a 48% maximum. Even considering they may also be subject to state and city income taxes, their overall, or "effective," tax rate will generally not exceed 54%. This is as compared to an individual whose tax rate may be in the 70% area. As the reader will recall, the *lower* the tax rate the *less* the tax saving benefit. Therefore, the financial lessor cannot "earn" as much from the same available tax benefits and will have to charge more to keep his return respectable.

With the lower tax bracket "disadvantage," can finance lessors successfully compete against high tax bracket individual-type lessors? Yes. The greater percentage of major equipment lease transactions involve investment tax credit eligible equipment where the lessor is asked to retain the credit. Because an individual's ability to claim investment credit is severely limited, he cannot effectively compete rate-wise against a corporate-type lessor who can take advantage of the credit. This is true *even though he is in a higher tax bracket*. As a result, many equipment lease transactions are completely out of the reach of the individual-type lessors.

ILLUSTRATIVE EXAMPLE—
ITC CAN MAKE THE DIFFERENCE:

Lessor A, a wealthy individual, and Lessor B, a corporation, are both asked by Company C to submit a lease quotation on a small industrial crane it wants to lease. The crane will be delivered and ready for lease on January 1, 19X0. The question is whether Lessor A can effectively compete with Lessor B. Lessor A cannot claim the investment tax credit. Lessor B can claim the credit. The facts are as follows:

Lease term	10 years
Crane economic useful life	12 years
Cost	$10,000
First year expenses (including depreciation)	$ 2,000
First year rent income	$ 1,000
10% Investment tax credit (10% × $10,000)	$ 1,000
Lessor A's income tax rate	70%
Lessor B's income tax rate	50%

For simplicity, only the first year's relative position will be compared. Although Lessor A cannot claim the investment tax credit, it can take greater advantage of the first year tax loss of $1000 (rent income − expenses = $1000 − $2000 = $1000) because of its higher tax rate. Will this offset its inability to claim the investment credit?

Lessor A's first year tax savings from the transaction's tax loss is $700 (70% $\times$ $1000). Lessor B's tax savings from the same tax loss is only $500 (50% $\times$ $1000). Its investment credit tax savings, however, is $1000 (10% $\times$ $10,000). Therefore, Lessor B has a tax savings "advantage" in the first year over Lessor A of $800 ($1500 — $700) to work with. This will give Lessor B a distinct edge.

Another competitive advantage many finance leasing companies have over individual-type lessors is that they have an organized marketing staff actively looking for business. Individuals, on the other hand, generally rely on brokers to find transactions for them. As a result, they frequently do not even see lease situations in which they could be competitive.

b. Some Work Only with Certain Equipment or Industries

Certain independent leasing companies, often referred to as "specialized," or "service," lessors, provide nonfinancial equipment related services in addition to pure equipment financing. For example, they may supply services such as equipment maintenance, repair, or purchasing, or may offer operational or design advice.

Specialized lessors typically limit their activity to a single type of equipment, such as computers, or to a single type of industry, such as the mining industry. The intense experience gained through the specialization enables them to reduce many leasing risks. For example, they are usually very familiar with the used equipment market because of their continual activity in the area. This enables them to more effectively handle equipment when it comes off lease, which in turn reduces their re-leasing or sale risks. Because of their facility with used equipment they can offer attractive lease termination or equipment exchange privileges.

OBSERVATION:

Many feel that product specialization creates less downside exposure for a lessor than industry specialization. That is, there is a greater likelihood that an industry specialized lessor would suffer more if his industry hit hard times than an equipment specialized lessor would if one of the industries in which its equipment was used hit hard times. Logically, this seems to make sense.

The leases typically written by specialized lessors are nonpayout in nature and, as a result, have much shorter lease terms than finance leases. If a lease is nonpayout in nature, the lessor will not recoup his entire equipment investment during the first lease term and, therefore, he must continue to re-lease the equipment at the end in order to make his investment pay off. If the equipment unexpectedly becomes obsolete, he will undoubtedly incur a loss.

When is it most appropriate for a prospective lessee to consider bringing in a specialized lessor? There are three situations. One is when services related to the equipment are offered which the prospective lessee needs and cannot provide, such as specialized maintenance or repair services. The second is when the equipment may have a high risk of obsolescence or other unusual market characteristics, such as computer equipment. The last situation is when the prospective lessee's industry is in a down cycle. In the latter two situations, the lessor's product or industry knowledge will enable him to take a more aggressive approach and, thereby, offer a more attractive lease proposal. For example, a computer lessor with a strong equipment re-marketing capability has little difficulty offering short term nonpayout leases or long-term leases with very attractive early termination privileges. He will rely on his re-marketing expertise to protect his investment. A pure financial lessor, on the other hand, does not usually have a strong re-marketing capability and is generally unwilling to take these types of investment risks. When, for example, a prospective lessee insists on a right to terminate the lease early, he may require a substantial premium to be paid if the right is exercised in order to make sure his equipment residual risk is at a minimum.

RECOMMENDATIONS:

I. A prospective lessee considering leasing equipment which it may want to turn back early in the lease should carefully review any premium charged by a nonspecialized lessor for early termination. Even though the rents are somewhat lower than a specialized lessor's, the cost to terminate may be considerably higher—thereby possibly offsetting the lower rent advantage.

II. If early termination privileges are not critical and if long term usage is likely, an underwritten leveraged finance lease transaction should be considered—even though the equipment is normally the type handled by a specialized lessor. If the lease terms are equal, a leveraged finance lease transaction should offer a lower rent.

3. Lease Brokers Can Provide Some Real Benefits

Lease brokers, also referred to as "lease underwriters" or "syndicators," play a major role in the leasing industry. Basically, they "package" lease transactions for the account of third parties. That is, they match up prospective lessees with prospective lessor-investors. They charge a fee for their service, which usually ranges from 3/4% to 8% of the total cost of the equipment leased and which is usually paid by the lessor-investors.

In order to put the lease broker's role into perspective, it is helpful to understand how a broker normally operates. Generally, his involvement in a transaction is the direct result of "cold calling." That is, he blindly contacts all types of equipment users to determine whether there are any leasing needs. If there are, he will attempt to define the rough parameters through discussions with the prospective lessee. Before going any further, the broker may perform a credit check on the prospective lessee in order to make sure the "credit" is marketable. If there do not seem to be any problems, he will formulate a concise lease structure, including rental rate, and offer it to the equipment user, generally through a formal proposal letter. If the user finds the proposed arrangement acceptable, the broker then proceeds to "firm up" prospective lessor-investors, commonly referred to as *equity participants*. If the transaction is to be leveraged with third-party debt, a *leveraged* lease, he may also put out feelers for prospective lenders, commonly referred to as *debt participants*. Usually, however, the debt side is handled by an investment banker. Once the equity and debt participants have been found, the broker proceeds to shepherd the transaction through documentation to completion.

Although generally a lease underwriter acts exclusively as a broker, he may, in a limited number of situations, invest some of his own funds in the equipment along with other third-party lessor-investors and, thereby, become a part owner. He may do this, for example, because he feels it will add credibility to the investment and enable him to more readily "sell" the lease transaction to potential investors.

One of the most valuable services a broker offers is advice as to current lease rates, overall structure, and documentation. Because he is continually "in the equity market" he will know where to find the most competitive and *realistic* equity participants. He cannot earn his fee unless he is awarded the transaction and he will not win unless his offer is the best. Thus, a good broker will always be looking for the most aggressive "equity sources."

RECOMMENDATION:

In general, a prospective lessee considering a finance lease arrangement should always invite a good cross section of brokers to quote, in addition to "regular" lessors. Because of their ability to find aggressive equity participants, lease brokers will add a new dimension to the bidding environment.

4. Captive Leasing Companies Are Sometimes Hard to Beat

In increasing numbers, equipment manufacturers are setting up their own leasing companies, generally referred to as "captive" leasing companies, to service their customers. Although the purpose is usually to offer lease financing on equipment made by an affiliated company, some also participate directly or as a broker in unrelated equipment transactions. For example, some may be willing to purchase and lease equipment manufactured by an unassociated company.

A captive leasing company competing to lease its affiliated company's equipment can be hard to beat. It has, in effect, the consolidated corporation's equipment profit margin to work with in addition to the tax benefits and residual value of the equipment. Since the primary reason for a captive leasing company's existence is generally to assist in marketing its affiliated company's equipment, it usually works on a lower financing profit than other types of lessors. This coupled with its knowledge of the equipment's potential residual value can result in very attractive rents for a lessee.

RECOMMENDATION:

A prospective lessee should always inquire whether the manufacturer of the equipment under consideration has a captive leasing company. If so, it should definitely be requested to submit a lease quotation.

5. Banks—Competitive When They Want to Be

Banks, particularly national banks, to a greater or lesser extent are actively involved in equipment leasing. Their interest usually centers around net finance lease arrangements because these provide the least risk and most similarity to their lending activity.

In the past banks have generally taken a more conservative approach in structuring lease transactions than independent leasing companies. For example, they have been less inclined to take aggressive equipment residual value positions. On the other hand, their cost of funds is in many cases lower than that of non-bank leasing companies. This frequently enables them to make up for other conservative pricing criteria.

The bank lessors do not always seem to price transactions consistently with competing non-bank lessors. That is, they are at times unusually competitive and at other times way out of line. This may in part be due to the fact that they are not as dependent on their leasing activity for revenues as many non-bank leasing companies are and, therefore, can afford to hold out for better rates. Periodically, however, they go on major drives for lease business. At these times they can be extremely rate aggressive, and because of this it is always a good idea for a prospective lessee to invite a select few into the bidding.

In the past, many bank lessors operated with a limited lease marketing staff. As a result the transactions they saw were fundamentally limited to those coming in through existing customers or lease brokers. Today, however, an increasing number of bank lessors appear to be establishing stronger marketing organizations and, as a group, will undoubtedly become more of a factor in the marketplace in the not too distant future.

It is worth mentioning that banks directly participate in the leasing market in another major way. They frequently act as lenders in leveraged lease transactions.

E. ARE THERE ANY REAL DIFFERENCES AMONG THE COMMON TYPES OF LEASES?

There are significant differences among the various types of leases. Unfortunately, the industry jargon used to label the different types is sometimes less than precise. The problem is further compounded by the fact that many hybrid arrangements are surfacing which are crossing over the lines of the "standard" descriptive terminology. Once the fundamental characteristics are understood, however, the confusion can be eliminated.

For discussion purposes it will be helpful to separate all equipment leases into two main categories: financial leases and operating leases. The *financial,* or "finance," lease typically represents a long term lease commitment in which the sum of the rents due will approximate the purchase cost of the asset. As such, therefore, decisions to enter into a financial lease should be part of a company's financial, as opposed to operating, policy considerations. All leases not fitting within the financial lease category can be put into the *operating* lease category. Operating leases involve shorter term financial commitments and, therefore, decisions as to their use can come within the scope of a company's operating policy.

Within the two categories described in the preceding paragraph there are a number of basic variations: leveraged leases, non-leveraged leases, and service leases. These variations are sometimes incorrectly considered to be separate *types* of leases rather than what they are, descriptive *forms* of the basic types. For example, finance leases can be leveraged leases or non-leveraged leases. Service leases can be financial in nature or operating in nature. They will, however, be treated individually in order to give the reader a working perspective.

The following chart was designed to assist the reader in gaining a general overview of some fundamental lease characteristics. It is not by any means an all-inclusive summary.

	Lease Term	Typical Type of Transaction	Comments
Finance Lease	Substantial Portion Of Asset's Economic Life	Underwritten and Direct Lessor	Payout-type Lease
Net Finance Lease	Substantial Portion Of Asset's Economic Life	Underwritten and Direct Lessor	Payout-type Lease. Lessee Has Basically All Ownership Responsibilities.
Leveraged Lease	Usually, Substantial Portion Of Asset's Economic Life	Underwritten	Usually Net Finance Lease
Nonleveraged Lease	Hours to Substantial Portion Of Asset's Economic Life	Direct Lessor	Any Lease Where No Third-Party Debt Involved
Operating Lease	Hours to Years	Direct Lessor	Usually Nonpayout With Nonfinancial Services Supplied

1. The Finance Lease

Finance leases are a common type of equipment lease. They are considered long term leases since the primary lease terms usually run for most of the equipment's useful life. Typically, the total cash flow over the term—from rents, tax shelter, and equipment residual value—will be sufficient to pay back the lessor's investment, take care of his administrative expenses, pay off any debt obligations and commissions, and provide a profit. Because they are entered into by lessors as long-term financial commitments, lessee early termination privileges are not freely granted. When they are, the lessor usually imposes a substantial prepayment penalty which will assure the return of his investment and a profit, at least up to the date of termination.

A finance lease is similar to a loan in that the lessor, like a lender, is only involved in the asset funding. In keeping with its financial nature, it is usually a "net" lease. That is, all the fundamental ownership responsibilities, such as maintaining and repairing the equipment, paying for the necessary insurance, and taking care of property, use, and sales taxes, are placed upon the lessee. The lessor's only basic responsibilities are to pay for the equipment, lease it to the lessee for the agreed-upon term, and not interfere with its use.

Since the term of a finance lease runs for most of the equipment's useful life, the risk of obsolescence is shifted to the lessee to the extent the lessor's assumed residual value turns out to be accurate. For example, if a lessor computes the rent based upon a zero equipment residual value at the end of the lease term, the lessor has no residual value risk and, therefore, no obsolescence risk. This, of course, presumes there is no risk of premature equipment return as a result, for instance, of a default on the part of the lessee. As a practical matter, however, a lessor must generally use a residual value greater than zero in order to be price competitive. The risk of obsolescence would then be on the lessor to the extent of the value estimated. If his profit is dependent on the anticipated residual value, the greater the risk of obsolescence the greater the chance the transaction will turn out to be unprofitable.

One of a financial lessor's principal concerns is the protection of his investment in the event of a lease default or an equipment casualty. Toward this end, provisions are usually included in his leases in order to make him "whole" if any of these events occur. From a casualty loss standpoint, an agreed-upon set of values is usually incorporated which will, in effect, guarantee the lessor a return of his investment, reimburse him for any tax benefit losses, and assure him of at least some of his profit. These "stipulated loss values" are also sometimes used as a measure of lease default damages, although there are other methods.

Finance leases frequently contain a "hell or high water" rent commitment. Under this type of obligation, a lessee is required to *unconditionally* pay the full rent when due. He is not permitted to make any deduction even though he has a legitimate claim against the lessor for money owed. This is not as bad as it sounds for a lessee, since he can still bring a lawsuit against the lessor for any claims.

A "hell or high water" rent commitment increases a lessor's chances of getting a lender to loan him part of the equipment cost on a nonrecourse basis and, thereby, attractively "leverage" his investment. The nonrecourse loan is a loan in which the lender agrees to look only to the lessee and the equipment for repayment. The reason a lender is willing to do this is because he does not have to worry about any lessor-lessee disputes causing a rent withholding by the lessee.

2. The Operating Lease

Leases which are not considered financial in nature, those that are written for a short period of time in relation to the equipment's useful life, are categorized as *operating* leases. Operating leases typically run anywhere from a few months to a few years in duration, although some are as short as a few hours. A good example of this type of lease is an office copying machine lease.

Since the lease terms are relatively short, it is not generally possible for a lessor to earn much of his equipment investment back through the rents from one lease transaction. Therefore, he must either sell or re-lease the equipment on attractive terms in order to come out ahead. The danger to an operating lessor, of course, is that the market value of the equipment will be inadequate to allow him to sell or re-lease it on economically favorable terms. In other words, he has the risk of equipment obsolescence. As a result, such a lessor will attempt to earn his money back faster to lessen his investment exposure by charging a rent premium.

Because of the short available lease terms, operating leases can be a convenient way for a company to acquire equipment needed only for a limited period of time. Their attractiveness in these situations is further enhanced by the fact that they can usually be cancelled on short notice. This is important, for example, if a lessee discovers that better equipment is available or that the equipment is not needed for as long as anticipated. Computer equipment is a good example of the type of equipment which users frequently lease under operating leases because of the constant evolution of more efficient models.

3. The Leveraged Lease

A *leveraged* lease is one in which the lessor has borrowed as a part of the lease transaction a percentage, usually 70% to 80%, of the equipment's cost from a bank or other lender. Since the lessor has only put up a small percentage of the cost of the equipment, his investment is said to be *leveraged* because his return is based upon 100% of the cost. Leveraging generally enables a lessor to provide a lessee with relatively lower rents while at the same time maintaining his return. Frequently, finance leases are structured as leveraged leases.

The debt used to leverage a lease transaction is usually nonrecourse debt. That is, the lender has no recourse against the *lessor* for nonpayment of the loan. He can only look to the rental stream, the lessee, and the value of the equipment for its repayment. In such an arrangement, the lessor has to assign to the lender its rights under the lease, including the right to the rental payments. The lender is also given a mortgage on the equipment as security for the repayment of the loan.

OBSERVATIONS:

I. Although a lessor has no repayment obligation to a nonrecourse lender if the lessee defaults, he is in a secondary position. His right to get his outstanding "equity" investment back is generally subordinated to the repayment rights of the lender.

II. Leveraged leases can be attractive tax shelter investments. If the tax rules are adhered to, a lessor-investor typically has available fast depreciation write-offs, investment tax credit, and debt interest deductions. Since his investment is small compared to the equipment's cost and since the depreciation and investment credit benefits are based upon 100% of the cost, the economics can be favorable.

4. The Non-Leveraged Lease

A non-leveraged lease, also referred to as an "unleveraged" or "straight" lease, is one in which the lessor puts up 100% of the equipment purchase price from his own funds. Many leases entered into by leasing companies are non-leveraged leases.

A distinct advantage in using a non-leveraged lease is that there are usually only two principals involved, the lessee and the lessor. Because of the limited number of parties, the mechanics of putting together a transaction are simpler. The result can be a significant saving in time and documentation costs, such as legal fees. One disadvantage for a lessee, however, is the fact that the rent is usually higher than it would be if the lease were leveraged.

5. The Service Lease

Leases in which the lessor assumes equipment ownership responsibilities, such as maintenance, repair, insurance, record keeping, or payment of property taxes, in addition to providing the asset financing, are usually called "service" leases or, if appropriate, "maintenance" leases. Since they are generally operating-type, as opposed to finance-type, leases, the lease terms are usually relatively short.

F. SHOULD EVERY COMPANY WITH CAPITAL EQUIPMENT NEEDS LEASE?

Leasing is not always the best way for a company to acquire the use of equipment it needs. There are many good reasons why a company might lease and they may or may not be purely financial. There are also some real disadvantages to leasing. Unfortunately, there are no easy answers for a company confronted with the decision of whether or not to lease certain equipment. In order to make a proper lease decision, each company must weigh *all* the advantages and disadvantages together in *each* situation.

This, of course, can only be done if the various pros and cons have been adequately identified. The material in this section will provide the reader with the basic considerations essential to a comprehensive evaluation.

1. Leasing Can Solve Some Specific Problems

There is absolutely no doubt that leasing *can* be an attractive way of acquiring equipment in certain situations. There are many reasons why an equipment user will decide to lease. The fundamental ones will now be discussed.

a. Obsolescence Concerns and Limited Use Needs

Companies frequently lease equipment which they feel is likely to become obsolete before the end of its actual life. Certain high technology equipment, such as computer equipment, usually fits within this category because new generations of more efficient models are continually being developed which quickly outdate their predecessors.

As a practical matter as long as the equipment does its job does it really matter whether there is better equipment available? In some situations it does. For example, the more efficient an item of manufacturing equipment is, the lower the production costs may be. It is conceivable, therefore, that a company would have to acquire a new model before the old model has been written off in order to insure its price competitive position in the market. If a company had purchased rather than leased the equipment, the overall cost of replacing it could be expensive. If the market value of the old equipment, for example, was significantly less than its book value at the time of replacement, the company could be confronted with a potentially undesirable book loss in addition to the replacement cash outlay.

OBSERVATION:

A lessor also runs the risk of financial loss through equipment obsolescence. Therefore, in order to protect himself he will undoubtedly build a premium into his lease rate in order to compensate for the risk. A prospective lessee may be willing to pay the premium as a form of insurance against a loss through obsolescence. Of course, if the equipment does not become obsolete the increased rate will have reduced his profits.

RECOMMENDATIONS:

I. Since it is impossible to absolutely determine whether equipment will become obsolete, the obsolescence risk issue can cause a real dilemma. Evaluating the past history of the type of equipment under consideration can be of some assistance in predicting trends. In addition, estimating the materiality of the impact on profits if the equipment was not replaced until it was written off, even though it became obsolete, can also be useful.

II. If the obsolescence risk is small, a company anticipating leasing equipment for most of its economic life may be better off entering into a longer finance lease, with a right to terminate, rather than a shorter operating lease. The longer leases tend to have less of a rent premium for the risk. If the equipment does not in fact become obsolete, the firm may very well come out ahead.

If equipment is only needed for a limited period of time, leasing can be an effective way of acquiring its use. It eliminates the re-marketing risks an owner would have at the end of a period of short use and it also permits a more defined estimate of the effective cost of using the equipment. For example, public utilities sometimes build their own power plants and must acquire certain specialized construction equipment to do the job. Once the plant is finished the equipment may be of no further use, but it may still have many years of useful life left. If it cannot be sold for a reasonable price, the overall cost of its use can be high. Leasing removes the re-sale risk and, in addition, allows them to determine in advance the total effective usage cost.

b. Possible Off-Balance Sheet Benefits?

In the "old days" many companies leased equipment instead of taking out long-term loans to buy equipment in order to avoid burdening their balance sheet with long-term debt liabilities. The lease, regardless of its duration, was basically treated as an operating expense. As a result, a company's profit to fixed asset ratios were improved which, in turn, generally permitted a greater bank borrowing capability. Today, the circumstances have changed. Regardless of whether significant lease obligations have to be recorded on the balance sheet or not, sophisticated lenders factor them into their evaluation of a company's financial condition. In addition, and certainly most important, the new accounting rules have effectively eliminated the traditional "off balance sheet" benefit in most situations.

c. An Alternate Source of Funding

Companies who would otherwise have little reason to lease sometimes do so merely to preserve their existing funds or bank lines for alternate uses. This is true even though purchasing the equipment may be more favorable from an analytical point of view than leasing. The absence of a "down payment," in effect "100% financing," can assist high growth rate companies in maximizing the use of their funds. In other words, it can help expand the total source of available money. This is particularly attractive in periods of tight bank money.

OBSERVATION:

Putting together a lease financing can require less red tape and time than a loan transaction. There are situations in which the documentation time and expense that could be saved can make up for a lower interest cost. This is particularly true when the cost of the equipment involved is relatively small.

d. Lack of Necessary Technical or Administrative Services

Leasing can be a convenient way for companies not having the staff or expertise to attend to specialized equipment needs to acquire the necessary technical or administrative services. Through "service" leases these companies can avoid tying up time and manpower in activities which are outside of their normal operations. There is, of course, generally a charge for the nonfinancial services supplied. The charge is usually "built into" the rent. Typically, lessors of office equipment, trucks, automobiles, and rail cars offer some form of nonfinancial services as a supplement to their financing. For example, rail car lessors frequently offer maintenance services.

e. Borrowing Problems

Companies with bank borrowing problems may have an easier time getting leasing companies to fund their equipment needs. The financial requirements imposed by leasing companies are usually less stringent than those imposed by traditional lenders. Typically, they are more inclined to accept greater credit risks because they have the security of actually owning the equipment. In addition, their familiarity with the used equipment rental and sale markets enables them to handle default situations more easily than conventional lenders.

Frequently companies with financial problems can acquire equipment on a more economical basis through leasing than through other available alternatives. This is not to say, of course, that leasing companies will provide equipment financing to a company regardless of its financial condition. There still has to be a reasonable assurance that the company will be able to meet the lease payments.

f. Inability to Use Tax Benefits

It is not uncommon for a company to find itself in a situation in which it cannot use the tax benefits which would result from equipment ownership. It may, for example, have an excess of accumulated tax benefits or insufficient earnings, either due to poor performance or to major acquisitions, which have used up its tax bill. Such a company can *indirectly* take advantage of most of the ownership tax benefits through leasing. Since a lessor takes these tax benefits into account when calculating the transaction's economic return, he, in effect, passes these benefits through in the form of a relatively lower rent.

OBSERVATION:

A lessor will not pass 100% of the equipment ownership tax benefits on to a lessee through rental charge concessions. He will make a "profit" on these benefits by adjusting the rent to only reflect a *partial* recognition. The rent adjustments vary with each lessor and each situation.

If a company can use *some* of the ownership tax benefits, is there any way a lessee can claim part of the benefits *directly*? Yes. Under Section 48(d) of the Internal Revenue Code, a lessor can elect to treat the lessee as the purchaser of the equipment *for investment tax credit purposes.* By so doing, the lessee can claim the investment credit directly. Only the depreciation tax benefits are given up. The rent charge will, of course, be higher to account for the lessor's relinquishment of the investment credit to the lessee, but the overall effective cost should be lower than in transactions in which the lessor retains the credit.

RECOMMENDATION:

If the overall effective cost to a prospective lessee in an investment tax credit "pass through" situation is not lower than in a situation in which it is not, the prospective lessor should be asked to explain why it is not.

g. Capital Budget Restrictions

Decisions to lease equipment are sometimes made to avoid capital budget restrictions. A manager may have to get prior approvals for capital equipment purchases above a certain amount. The approvals may be virtually impossible to get. If the equipment is leased, he may be able to account for the rental payments as an operating expense (even though the lease represents a long-term financing similar to a capital expenditure) to get around the approval problem. In this way he may also be able to maximize his capital budget.

RECOMMENDATION:

Top management should prescribe certain rules in this area to avoid budget end running, particularly with finance leases. Long-term equipment leases can have a significant negative future impact on a company's earnings, particularly when cutbacks are necessary. Therefore, certain reasonable lease commitment restrictions should be formulated.

2. There Can Be Some Prime Disadvantages

Although leasing has many advantages for an equipment user, there are also some real disadvantages. In order to make a well balanced evaluation, the basic negative factors must be considered.

a. Residual "Upside" Is Lost

Generally, when a company leases equipment, it loses the opportunity to benefit from any favorable re-sale market that may exist when the use is over. For this reason companies experienced with the potential residual market values of certain equipment refuse to lease. By purchasing the equipment they will have the benefit of any windfall gain, "residual upside," resulting from a market price in excess of its depreciated value. For example, through inflation or buyer demand, a ten year old river barge may still be worth what it originally cost.

Lessees are frequently given an option to purchase the equipment at the *end* of the lease term for its fair market value. If the fair market value turns out to be high, the purchase price coupled with the rent paid can result in a very expensive transaction. In such a situation, the lessee would undoubtedly have been better off if it had originally purchased the asset. The problem is there is no way of telling what the future value is going to be. There is, however, one way for a prospective lessee to limit his cost exposure in the event he feels it is likely he will want to buy the equipment at the end of the term and, in addition, share in any residual upside—a fixed price purchase option. Under such an option a lessee would have the right to purchase the equipment at the end of the lease at a fixed price, say 25% of cost, which was agreed upon at the time the lease was entered into. If the equipment's market value at the end was high, say 75% of cost, the lessee has the option of taking advantage of the favorable market by purchasing it for 25% of cost and selling it for 75% of cost. There are, however, two problems with fixed price purchase options. First, not all lessors are willing to grant them and give up their residual upside. Second, the Internal Revenue Service can refuse to issue a favorable Revenue Ruling on a transaction in which such a right exists. This is not to say, however, that the transaction will not qualify as a true tax lease. Many tax attorneys feel a properly structured fixed price purchase option can withstand an IRS challenge.

RECOMMENDATION:

If a prospective lessor is willing to grant a fixed price purchase right at say 35% of cost, the prospective lessee should request that it be at 35% of cost or fair market value, *whichever is less.* In this way if the market value at the time of exercise is lower than the fixed price, the lessee will not have to pay more than the equipment is worth if a purchase is necessary.

Frequently, a prospective lessee's concern over the loss of residual value upside is more emotional than practical. The potential loss must always be kept in the proper *economic* perspective. This can be done by attempting to put a realistic value on it by, for example, bringing in a qualified appraiser to give an opinion as to what the equipment is likely to be worth in the future.

ILLUSTRATIVE EXAMPLE— A RESIDUAL PERSPECTIVE:

Company A is considering whether to lease or purchase a heavy duty crane. Company A's financial vice president recommends that it be leased; however, the operational vice president feels that it should be bought because of its potentially favorable market value at the end of the period of use. The facts are as follows:

Crane Cost	$3,000,000
Lease Term	20 years
Depreciated Book Value At End of 20 Years	$ 300,000

If the market value of the crane is estimated to be $500,000 at the end of the lease term, Company A would lose the chance at a $200,000 upside gain ($500,000 − $300,000) if it leased the equipment.

What if, however, the potential "loss" is considered in terms of "today" dollars? The present value of such a "loss" 20 years out, computed using an annual discount rate of 10%, is approximately $30,000. Compared to the original cost of $3,000,000 and considering the fact that the upside gain may not materialize, the residual concern may be overstated, particularly if any down payment which would have been required in a purchase was put to productive use.

b. It Can Be Expensive

Generally speaking, *tax-paying* companies with *favorable* borrowing capabilities will find leasing equipment more expensive than purchasing it. Logically this makes sense because in many cases a lessor's cost of borrowing funds will, at best, be equal to that of a company who, for example, can borrow at the prime bank lending rate. This coupled with the fact that a lessor will figure in his overhead and a profit in the rent computation, it is likely that leasing will come out costing more. Of course, this may not be the case for companies on the other end who cannot use the tax benefits or who have poor borrowing power. Companies falling in between the extremes have the toughest decision. Unfortunately, there are no easy answers. Each case must be evaluated on its own. The *cost* of borrowing as well as the *capability* of borrowing must be considered.

OBSERVATION:

When evaluating whether to lease or to purchase equipment, a company must carefully evaluate the *real* cost of borrowed funds. For example, a high compensating balance requirement can easily increase the effective cost of a bank loan. As this type of collateral loan cost increases, the attractiveness of leasing usually increases.

c. Equipment Control May Be Limited

When a lease ends, a lessee's right to continue to use the equipment ends. This can create a problem for an equipment user if suitable replacement equipment is not readily available and the lessor refuses to re-lease or sell it to the lessee. Purchase or renewal options theoretically eliminate this risk. From a practical standpoint, however, when a third party owns the equipment there is no guarantee he will abide by the terms of the options voluntarily. In addition, there is always the possibility, although remote, that a lessor will interfere with the lessee's right to use the equipment *during* the lease term even though he may have no legal right to do so. Having the legal right of continued use may be of little consequence to a lessee when equipment essential to its continued operations becomes unavailable.

G. THERE ARE CERTAIN KEY SITUATIONS WHEN LEASING SHOULD BE CONSIDERED

There are certain times when leasing is a solid contender against alternate methods of equipment financing. They are:

1. If a company must pay high interest rates for money borrowed, leasing can be an economically attractive equipment funding alternative. Companies whose credit dictates high borrowing rates, however, may also dictate high leasing rates. A lessor must offset the increased credit risks by increased returns. The cost of leasing, however, will probably not increase proportionately as high as the cost of borrowing.

2. A company which cannot use a significant part or all of the equipment ownership tax benefits may come out ahead by leasing. This, of course, assumes the tax benefits can be used by the leasing company and the benefits are passed through in the form of a relatively lower rental rate.

3. Leasing is desirable when the equipment involved has unusual service problems which cannot be handled by a company internally, due, for example, to the technical nature of the equipment or the company's inadequate staffing.

4. If implicit lease interest rates are about the same as debt interest rates and there are significant ancillary costs to borrowing, such as high compensating balances or commitment fees, leasing should be considered.

H. THE DISASTER OF POOR LEASE STRUCTURING

There are many ways of financing the acquisition of necessary capital equipment besides leasing, such as through conditional sale, mortgage, or loan financing arrangements. The tax treatments of the alternative methods are quite different than that of a lease transaction. When a transaction qualifies as a true lease for income tax purposes, the lessee may deduct the rental payments as an operating expense and the lessor may claim all the equipment ownership tax benefits, such as investment tax credit and depreciation. If the transaction does not qualify, the "lessee" will not be able to deduct the rental payments as an operating expense and the "lessor" will lose the ownership tax benefits. For example, if the "lease" were classified as a loan, the "lessee" would be deemed the equipment owner and the "lessor" deemed the lender. In this type of situation, if the "lessee" cannot use any ownership tax benefits and if the "lessor" must have them in order for the transaction to make economic sense, everybody loses!

I. A WHEN-TO-LEASE CHECKLIST

A company should consider leasing when one or more of the following factors exist:

1. There Is a High Risk That Equipment Will Become Obsolete Before the End of Its Useful Life.
2. The Equipment Will Be Needed Only for a Short Period of Time.
3. It Is Desirable to Use Existing Lines of Bank Credit for Purposes Other Than Funding Certain Equipment.
4. It Is Desirable to Maximize Available Capital Resources.
5. Technical, Administrative, or Other Nonfinancial, Equipment Related Services Which Are Not Internally Available Can Be Easily Secured from a Leasing Company.
6. High Interest Rates Must Be Paid for Borrowed Money.
7. The Tax Benefits Resulting from the Equipment Ownership Cannot Be Used.
8. The Equipment Will Have a Poor Market Value at the End of Its Term of Use.

J. A PROSPECTIVE LESSEE CHECKLIST FOR APPROACHING THE LESSOR MARKET

1. Can the Equipment Be Leased, i.e., Will It Qualify as Section 38 Property under the Internal Revenue Code?
2. What Basic Type of Lease Arrangement Is to Be Considered?
   a. Non-Leveraged Finance Lease
      (1) Net Lease
   b. Leveraged Finance Lease
      (1) Net Lease
   c. Operating Lease
      (1) Long-Term
      (2) Short-Term
      (3) Nonfinancial Services Required.
3. What Potential "Sources" of Lease Financing Will Be Invited to Submit Lease Quotations?
   a. High Tax Bracket Individuals.
   b. Independent Non-Bank Leasing Companies
      (1) Finance Lessors
      (2) Specialized Lessors
   c. Banks

    d. Captive Leasing Companies

    e. Lease Brokers

4. If a High Tax Bracket Individual Is under Consideration There May Be a Potential Problem Unless the Transaction Involves:

    a. Used Equipment.

    b. An Investment Tax Credit Pass Through to the Lessee.

    c. A Lease Term Less Than Half the Equipment's Useful Life and the First Year Operating Expenses in Excess of 15% of the Rent Income.

5. If an Independent Non-Bank Leasing Company Is under Consideration:

    a. Does It Have a Good Reputation in the Financial Community?

    b. Have Other Existing Lessees Been Contacted to Determine How Difficult It May Be to Deal With?

    c. Is Its Financial Condition Sufficient to Insure Adequate and Timely Funding?

    d. Will the Equipment Be Funded Entirely from the Lessor's Own Funds.

    e. If Equipment Related Nonfinancial Services Will Be Supplied, Does It Have an Adequate Staff and Facilities to Supply These Services on a Timely Basis?

    f. How Tough Is the Lessor's Lease Documentation? A Form of Lease Should Be Reviewed.

6. If the Prospective Lessee's "Regular" Bank Will Be Involved, Will the Lease Restrict Its Future Loan Availability?

7. If a Lease Broker Is under Consideration:

    a. How Many Similar Transactions Has He Completed in the Last Three Years?

    b. What Do Other Companies Who Have Used His Service Say About His Method of Operation and His Ability to Follow Through on a Proposed Transaction?

    c. Are There Any Banks or Other Prospective Lessor-Investors Who Should Not Be Approached by the Broker?

2

THE PROPOSAL STAGE—
WHERE THE LEASING DEAL IS MADE

The Proposal Stage Is Critical • The Terms and the Tone of the Deal Are Established Here • A Lessee Has Unparalleled Leverage If Handled Properly • An Unsuspecting Lessor Can Lose Many Points.

A. WHAT IS THE BEST WAY FOR A PROSPECTIVE LESSEE TO "GO OUT FOR" LEASE BIDS?

Many prospective lessees approach the leasing market place in an inefficient and disorganized manner. As a result, they not only end up paying thousands of dollars more rent than necessary, but they also miss getting many benefits which are typically available.

How does a prospective lessee get the best lease deal? To begin with, by "shopping the market." That is, by inviting a meaningful cross section of potential lessors and underwriters to submit lease quotations. A good cross section, however, is not the complete answer. *How* that cross section is requested to bid is also an essential element. Informal written or verbal requests are definitely a mistake. They usually result in responses that are not only confusing but also incapable of being compared. The best approach is a well thought out and comprehensive written *request-for-bids* letter, commonly referred to as a "bid letter." By using this type of letter the bidders are better able to accurately assess the transaction and respond with a minimum of dialogue and time. No one appreciates the benefits of a good bid letter more than the individual who has not used one and has had to tediously field many repetitious telephone calls about the basic facts.

The use of a bid letter will help assure that the responses will be on a uniform and, thereby, comparable basis. Nothing can be more frustrating, for example, than receiving five proposals, each with a different rental payment mode—quarterly, in advance; semi-annually, in arrears; semi-annually, in advance; monthly, in arrears; and monthly, in advance. Since it may be difficult, if not impossible, to make a meaningful comparison, requotes on a specified payment basis will be necessary. This wastes valuable time.

A well-thought-out bid letter will cause everyone concerned on the lessee's side to think through what they need or would like out of the transaction. There is less chance that an important request will be overlooked. It should go without saying that if a particular benefit is not requested, it will probably not be offered.

What issues should be covered in a good bid letter? It should address the same basic subjects which would be covered in a well-drafted *proposal* letter. Section C of this chapter will examine the terms of a typical proposal letter. It may be helpful, however, to point out that at a bare minimum a bid letter should cover the following twenty issues:

- The type of equipment and the manufacturer.

- The number of units of equipment which will be involved.

- The aggregate cost and per unit cost of the equipment.

- When the equipment delivery is anticipated.

- The type of lease desired, i.e., net financial lease, service lease, etc.

- The lease term and any renewal periods desired.

- The rental payment mode, i.e., monthly, quarterly, semi-annually, or annually—in advance or in arrears.

- The extent of any acceptable tax indemnifications.

- Whether the equipment will be self-insured.

- What options are required.

- A request for appropriate casualty and termination values.

- Who will have the responsibility for the transaction's fees and expenses.

- Whether a tax ruling is necessary or desirable.

- Whether it is acceptable for a favorable tax ruling to be a prerequisite to the execution of the lease documents.

- Whether a favorable tax ruling should relieve any tax indemnification obligations assumed.

- The deadline for the submission of lease quotations.

- When the transaction will be awarded.

- Whether underwriting bids are acceptable.

- If underwriting proposals are permitted, whether the bids may be on a "firm" or "best efforts" basis.

- Potential equity participants and lenders who may be unacceptable if the transaction is to be underwritten.

A sample request-for-bids letter has been included in the Appendix for further reference. In addition, a bid letter drafting checklist has been included in Section H of this chapter.

B. IS A FORMAL LEASE PROPOSAL NECESSARY?

Before answering the question of whether a formal lease proposal is necessary, it might be a good idea to explain what a "lease proposal" is. Simply, it is an offer by a prospective lessor to lease, or in the case of an underwriter to arrange the lease of, specified equipment. It outlines the major "business" points of a proposed transaction, such as the lease term and the rent, and in many cases also identifies certain critical tax obligations which the lessee will have to assume, such as tax loss protection. Generally, the lease proposal, if written, is done in letter form and is commonly referred to as a *proposal letter*.

Should a formal written proposal be a part of every lease transaction? Yes. Not only does it serve as a valuable guide for the parties, including their lawyers, when documenting the transaction, but it keeps points which may be essential to the viability of the financing, such as tax indemnification commitments, from being "forgotten."

RECOMMENDATIONS:

I. A prospective lessee has a considerable amount of negotiating leverage during the bidding stage, particularly if more than one bidder is involved. The loss of one will not jeopardize the transaction and they know it. Therefore, the time to press for the tough concessions is *before the transaction is awarded.* Prospective lessors are sometimes willing to concede points just to win the deal. Once the transaction has been awarded, the winning bidder is in a stronger negotiating position merely by virtue of the fact that the other bidders are no longer involved.

II. A prospective lessee should plan adequate lead time between a lease award and the equipment delivery. In this way, if a prospective lessor becomes unreasonable after the award, there may still be time to go elsewhere for the financing. If this is not possible and the prospective lessor starts to "get tough," some balance can be put back into the negotiations by letting it be known that because of the problems a decision to purchase is under consideration.

III. From a prospective lessor's viewpoint the faster it can get a prospective lessee to "sign off" on a proposal letter the less likely a "problem" request will be made. Once the lease documentation has begun, particularly if there are near-term deliveries, a prospective lessor's negotiating position is improved. Psychologically, a prospective lessee is more reluctant to start over with new people once the document negotiations have started.

C. WHAT ESSENTIAL ISSUES MUST BE COVERED IN A PROPOSAL LETTER?

The lease "deal" should be outlined in the proposal letter. The letter does not have to cover every detail, but it should set the framework for the overall lease arrangement. In order to do this, however, the parties must know what points should be covered.

RECOMMENDATION:

If an important point comes up after a proposal letter has been agreed upon, but before the lease documentation has begun, consideration should be given to amending the letter to include the point.

Typically, an *underwritten leveraged* lease situation will involve the most complex form of lease proposal. Proposals relating to *non-underwritten* transactions, although usually somewhat simpler, generally contain most of the same basic elements. By understanding the more complex transaction format, the others will fall into place and, therefore, the following discussion will be centered on issues which should be addressed in an underwritten leveraged lease proposal.

Several proposal letters have been included in the Appendix. The first is typical of that used by a leasing company acting on its own behalf, a non-underwritten transaction, and the second is typical of that used by an underwriter acting on behalf of prospective third-party lessors. They both cover the major topics which should be identified and can be used as a guide when drafting or reviewing a lease proposal. Since there can be many variables in a particular transaction, however, they should only be used for reference purposes. It may be helpful to review them before reading further in order to put the following discussion into a good overall perspective.

1. What Is the Offer?

What is actually being offered by a lease proposal must be clearly defined and understood. For example, is it a direct offer by a prospective lessor to *lease* the equipment to the prospective lessee or is it an offer by an underwriter to *arrange* the lease financing of the equipment for the prospective lessee. In the latter case, the underwriter may or may not have a specific third-party lessor in mind. Even if he does, the name usually will not be disclosed in the proposal in order to protect his position as a broker.

ILLUSTRATIVE LANGUAGE—
LESSOR DESIGNATION:

An unknown or undisclosed Lessor may be described by an underwriter in the following manner:

"The lessor will be a trustee acting as owner trustee pursuant to an owner's trust for the benefit of one or more corporate investors."

As the reader will note very little has been stated other than the ownership *structure*.

In a non-underwritten transaction, the prospective lessor will make an offer directly *as principal* to lease the equipment to the prospective lessee. For example:

"ABC Leasing Company will purchase and lease to XYZ Company the equipment designated in this proposal under the terms and conditions specified herein."

As the reader might suspect, a prospective lessee dealing with an underwriter who does not have a specific lessor prospect in mind at the time of the award runs the risk that he will be unable to find one. However, intelligent handling can minimize the risk. This will be discussed later on.

RECOMMENDATIONS:

I. In an underwriting situation, a prospective lessee is in a better position if he does not make an award to a particular underwriter until he has disclosed the prospective lessor *and* someone with authority to represent such lessor has been contacted to confirm their interest. If there is going to be a problem, the time to find out is when the remaining bidders are still in the picture.

II. An underwriter should make sure his proposal is only an offer to *arrange* the proposed financing, unless of course he is prepared to step in as lessor in the event a third-party investor cannot be found.

III. It is always advisable for an underwriter to have a prospective lessor in mind when submitting a proposal, in case the prospective lessee insists on talking to him before making the award.

There are many types of offer combinations. For example, a direct lessor could offer to lease finance the equipment entirely from its own funds or partly from its own funds and partly from a nonrecourse loan. The latter arrangement is a simple form of *leveraged* lease. On the other hand, an underwriter may offer to put together a leveraged lease using one or more lessor-investors and one or more third-party lenders. In addition, an underwriter may propose to bring in a "single source" investor to act as lessor, such as a regional bank, who would pay for the equipment entirely from its own funds.

Each variation has certain advantages and disadvantages. For instance, a prospective lessee with a near-term equipment delivery situation may be well advised to limit its consideration to a direct lessor transaction. Dealing with one party directly will lessen the risk that the financing cannot be done within the short time frame. If there is plenty of time, the best approach may be to pursue a syndicated leveraged lease transaction. This type of transaction will certainly be more involved, but it will usually provide the best rental rate for a prospective lessee.

Since the amount of lead time available before the equipment will be delivered may dictate the type of transaction which can be considered, it is essential that all parties keep this aspect in mind. Table 2-1 can be used as a *general* guide when planning the timing of a proposed lease financing.

TABLE 2-1			
RECOMMENDED TRANSACTION LEAD TIME			
Type of Transaction	Anticipated Number of Lessor-Investors	Anticipated Number of Lenders	Recommended Lead Time[1] (Months)
Underwritten Leveraged Lease	Two or more	Two or more	Six
Underwritten Leveraged Lease	Two or more	One	Six
Underwritten Leveraged Lease	One	Two or more	Five
Underwritten Leveraged Lease	One	One	Four
Underwritten Single Investor[2]	One	0	Three
Direct Lease[3]	One	One or more	Three
Direct Lease	One	0	Two

[1]*Lead time* is defined as the time between the due date of the proposals and the first equipment delivery. The estimates assume an allowable proposal analysis time of one month.

[2]An *underwritten single investor* transaction is defined as one in which the underwriter brings in only one lessor-investor who puts up 100% of the funds required.

[3]A *direct lease* transaction is defined as one in which the prospective lessee will deal directly with the prospective lessor.

2. The Basis of the Offer—an Unsuspecting Trap

Typically, a lease underwriter will state in his proposal whether the offer is made on a "best efforts" or on a "firm" basis. A best efforts proposal is nothing more than an offer to *try* to arrange the lease financing on the stated terms and conditions. There are no guarantees of performance and the underwriter is generally not liable to the prospective lessee if he cannot perform.

ILLUSTRATIVE LANGUAGE—
"BEST EFFORTS" COMMITMENT

"ABC Leasing Company proposes to use its *best efforts* to arrange an equipment lease according to the terms and conditions set forth in this proposal."

Generally, underwriters favor best efforts bid situations because they don't have to spend any time trying to find a prospective lessor until they know the transaction is theirs. Many prospective lessees, however, are uncomfortable with best efforts proposals because valuable documentation time can be lost if the underwriter has trouble finding a lessor. The longer a transaction remains unsold and the more it is "shopped," the greater the danger it will not be sold as proposed. Prospective lessors-investors become suspicious when a transaction has been around the market for a while and may refuse to consider it *for that reason alone.*

RECOMMENDATION:

A *best efforts* underwriting bid may result in a slightly more attractive rate to a prospective lessee than a *firm* underwriting bid. When prospective lessors must make a firm commitment to do a transaction before it is actually awarded, they do not seem to stretch as much rate-wise as when confronted with an awarded deal which they know they can have if they accept the terms. Therefore, if a prospective lessee has adequate lead time, a best efforts underwriting should be considered. If the winning underwriter cannot perform quickly, the prospective lessee can move on to the underwriter in second place without creating a timing problem.

A *firm* underwriting bid is simply just that. The underwriter states that he *can* deliver the financing under the proposed terms and conditions.

ILLUSTRATIVE LANGUAGE—
FIRM COMMITMENT:

"ABC Leasing Company proposes to arrange *on a firm commitment basis* an equipment lease for XYZ Inc. according to the terms and conditions set forth in this proposal."

In the typical firm bid situation the underwriter will have secured a formal commitment from a prospective lessor to do the transaction as proposed prior to the submission of the proposal to the prospective lessee. There are situations, however, in which an underwriter will firmly commit to do the transaction even though he does not have any lessor prospects in mind. In other words, the underwriter agrees to purchase and lease the equipment *himself* if he cannot broker it. This type of arrangement can be risky for a prospective lessee because an unsuccessful underwriter-lessor may later look for any excuse to justify a way out. For example, offers conditioned upon mutually satisfactory lease documentation may provide an underwriter with an opportunity to create a document "disagreement" and, thereby, a basis to refuse to go forward.

RECOMMENDATIONS:

I. A prospective underwriter should be very cautious in "backing" a proposal. Unless it can actually follow through in the event the transaction cannot be placed, it may be confronted with a lawsuit.

II. Prospective lessees should investigate interesting bids "backed" by an underwriter to make sure the underwriter has the financial wherewithal to stand behind the transaction.

If the offer is made directly by a prospective lessor instead of an underwriter, the situation will be different. Since the prospective lessor will typically use its own money to fund the transaction, the offer will in that sense be "firm."

ILLUSTRATIVE LANGUAGE—
DIRECT COMMITMENT:

"ABC Leasing Company, as lessor, offers to purchase and lease to XYZ Inc. the equipment described below under the stated terms and conditions."

3. The Equipment and Its Cost Must Be Agreed Upon

The *type, quantity,* and *cost* of equipment to be leased are fundamental proposal stage considerations. The *quality* of the equipment can also be meaningful, particularly when a "residual sensitive" lessor is involved. Residual sensitive lessors are those who, because of their equipment experience and knowledge, are willing to factor aggressive equipment residual value assumptions into their rent determinations. Aggressive residual value assumptions translate into very attractive rent quotations.

RECOMMENDATION:

Prospective lessors should carefully analyze what the proposed equipment could be worth at the end of a lease. Many treat this area lightly and end up assuming unrealistically low values. As a result, their potential rate competitiveness is reduced.

The total equipment cost should be identified. Frequently, a prospective lessor will put a limit on, or "cap," the amount of money he is willing to commit to a transaction. For example, he may agree to purchase and lease an oil tanker at a cost *not to exceed* $40,000,000. Without a cap, he runs the risk that unexpected cost escalations will cause him to invest more than he is comfortable with. A total cost deviation may give a prospective lessor who no longer finds the transaction desirable an excuse to back out if there is only one item. If there are a number of items, a prospective lessee may be able to exclude a few to stay within the limit.

RECOMMENDATION:

A prospective lessee entering into a lease agreement covering equipment to be delivered in the future should make sure the lessor's cost commitment is adequate. For example, will it cover any allowable manufacturer price escalations? If there is a problem with determining an exact price, a dollar cushion can be built into the estimate. A word of caution, however, if a fee has been imposed by the prospective lessor for the failure to use all of the funds committed (commonly referred to as a *non-utilization* fee). A prospective lessee should be careful not to build in an excessive cushion because any fee paid on the excess will increase the effective cost of the financing.

4. Who Is Going to Be Responsible for the Rent?

The answer to the question of who will be responsible for the rent seems easy. The lessee, of course. Sometime, however, the *real* lessee is not actually identified during the proposal stage. If this happens, not only will time and money be lost, but the entire financing can be jeopardized if the discovery is not made until the last minute. For example, the bidders may have inadvertently been given the impression that the lessee will be XYZ Inc. XYZ Inc. may, in fact, want its subsidiary to be the named lessee because the equipment is to be acquired for the subsidiary's use. If the subsidiary is a viable legal entity on its own and its financial condition can support the lease obligations, there may be no problem. If this is not the case, and if the credit review and approval was based upon the financial statements of XYZ Inc., the parent company, a reassessment will be necessary. If this was not discovered until well into the lease negotiations, there may not be enough time to make any necessary adjustments. For example, getting a parent company's guarantee of the lease obligations at the last minute, can be difficult, if not impossible, to obtain.

5. How Is the Rent to Be Paid?

One of the most crucial factors to be covered in the proposal stage is the rent program—that is, how much rent will be due and how it is to be paid. For example, a five year lease may provide for twenty consecutive, level, quarterly payments, in arrears, each payment to equal 3.0000% of the equipment cost, commencing as of the start of the primary lease term.

When a leveraged lease proposal is involved, there is usually a complication. The leveraged debt is generally not secured until *after* the award because it wouldn't be practical to spend the time and money necessary until there is a deal. The rent computation, however, depends upon the debt interest rate. How then does an underwriter compute the rent? By using an *assumed* per annum interest rate. In other words, the underwriter determines what economic return is required based upon an assumed interest rate and calculates his rent accordingly. If it actually varies from that which was assumed, the underwriter should have the option of making a rent adjustment in order to protect his return. The debt assumption should, therefore, be stated in the proposal.

ILLUSTRATIVE LANGUAGE—
RENT ADJUSTMENT:

"Lessee shall make twenty consecutive, level, quarterly payments, in arrears, each equal to 3.0000% of equipment cost commencing on January 1, 19XX. The rental percentage factor is based on the assumption that the interest rate on the leveraged debt will be 8½% per annum. If the interest rate is other than 8½% the rental factor will be adjusted, upward or downward, accordingly so that Lessor's return shall be maintained."

ILLUSTRATIVE EXAMPLE—
THE NEED FOR A RENT ADJUSTMENT CLAUSE:

Company B proposes to lease to Company A a $10,000 item of mining equipment. The transaction will be leveraged with 80% debt at an assumed interest rate of 6% per annum. The terms are as follows:

Lease term	10 years
Loan term	10 years
Annual rent	$1,200
Annual debt service (level, in arrears)	
($8,000 @ 6%)	$1,087

The annual rent will cover the annual debt service by $113 ($1,200 − $1,087). Assume that when Company B goes into the debt market the best available annual interest rate is 10%. The annual debt service, assuming level payments, will be approximately $1,302. In this case not only will the increased debt service expense erode the lessor's return, but the lessor will have to invest an additional $102 per year ($1302 − $1,200) to make up for the "shortfall."

RECOMMENDATIONS:

I. If a prospective lessor has the right to protect his return by adjusting rents *upward* if the actual debt interest rate is higher than assumed, a prospective lessee should require a *downward* rent adjustment if it comes in lower than assumed.

II. A prospective lessee should determine what criteria will be used by a prospective lessor to make any rent adjustment so the accuracy of the calculation can be independently confirmed.

III. Any time a rental adjustment is permitted, the parties should also provide for appropriate adjustments in values that relate to the rent, such as casualty and termination values.

6. The Length of Permissible Use Is a Major Consideration

How long the lease will run is as important a consideration as is how much rent must be paid. Therefore, the *lease term* should be agreed upon and specified in the proposal. When many items of equipment will be involved, frequently more than one lease term will be called for. In such a situation, the proposal should clearly allocate which equipment goes under what term.

The basic lease period frequently involves a main lease term, generally referred to as the *primary term*, and an interim lease term, generally referred to as the *interim term*. The interim term covers the period from the time the equipment is accepted for lease to the start of the primary term and is commonly provided for when many items of equipment are involved and deliveries are scattered over many months. By consolidating the start of the primary lease terms to, for example, calendar quarters the rent payment and processing mechanics are simplified.

ILLUSTRATIVE EXAMPLE—THE INTERIM
TECHNIQUE FOR RENT CONSOLIDATION

Company B wants to lease 100 trucks from Company A. The trucks will be delivered over a 12 month period at a rate of 10 trucks per month. Company B wants to pay the lease rent in quarterly, in arrears, payments. Company A proposes this solution:

1. There shall be four primary lease terms starting as follows:
    a. First Primary Term - April 1, 19X0
    b. Second Primary Term - July 1, 19X0
    c. Third Primary Term - October 1, 19X0
    d. Fourth Primary Term - January 1, 19X1

2. All trucks delivered and accepted for lease in the calendar quarter preceding the nearest primary term start date shall be on interim lease until the start date, at which time the primary term shall begin for such trucks.

Without the interim arrangement Company A could end up with as many as 100 different primary lease term start dates and, therefore, *100 different rental payment dates.*

7. Any Credit Support for the Lease Obligations Should Be Identified

If it is determined that a prospective lessee is not financially strong enough to support a particular lease financing, some form of credit support will be necessary. This area should be fully discussed and a solution agreed upon during the proposal stage.

In the event credit support is required, prospective lessors prefer to get a *full and unconditional guarantee* of *all* the lease obligations from a creditworthy entity, such as a parent company, a bank, or, possibly, an underwriter. There are many other acceptable forms of credit support in addition to a full and unconditional guarantee, such as a manufacturer's deficiency guarantee or a "take or pay" contract assignment. Different forms may be acceptable in different situations. An experienced leasing company or underwriter should be able to offer some viable alternatives to meet the needs of a particular transaction.

RECOMMENDATION:

If a lease is proposed with a corporate subsidiary and credit support is required, the parent company should pursue a structure which will have the least impact on its future borrowing capabilities. For example, an assignment of a "take or pay" contract between the subsidiary and an outside entity may have little impact on the parent company whereas a full, unconditional guarantee could have a substantial impact.

8. The Structure of the Owning Entity Is Important

The actual *form* of the equipment owning entity can be important. For example, will the lessor be a trust, a partnership, a corporation, or an individual. Therefore, this should be decided early in the proposal stage.

From both a tax and liability viewpoint the form of ownership structure will be of greatest concern to prospective lessor-investors, particularly when two or more are brought together to act as the "lessor." Usually a structure which will permit a direct flow-through of all the available tax benefits as well as a shield against direct liability in the event of a lawsuit is what will be desired.

RECOMMENDATION:

Trust arrangements can be a useful equipment ownership structure for prospective lessor-investors. If set up properly it is generally agreed that they will be treated, for tax purposes, as a partnership and, for liability purposes, as a corporation.

The form of ownership vehicle can also be important to a prospective lessee. For example, if the equipment ownership is not centralized in a multiple lessor-investor situation, the lessee may have to deal individually with each investor throughout the lease. Separate pro-rated rent checks may have to be issued and separate consents may have to be obtained if a lease variance is necessary. This can be a substantial inconvenience.

RECOMMENDATION:

In a multiple lessor-investor situation, a prospective lessee should insist that there be a single representative with the authority to handle the day-to-day issues. A lessor trust arrangement is one way to meet this need.

9. Any Debt Arrangement Should Be Disclosed

If a leveraged lease will be proposed, the debt arrangement should be outlined in the proposal letter. For example, who will find the debt, the repayment schedule, the anticipated per annum interest charge, the anticipated principal amount as a percentage of equipment cost, the form of lender representative, and whether the debt will be recourse or nonrecourse to the lessor. A five year debt structure may be as follows:

ILLUSTRATIVE LANGUAGE—
DEBT STRUCTURE:

"ABC Leasing Company (ABC), or an investment banker acceptable to the lessee and to ABC, shall arrange for the private placement of a note ("Indebtedness") to be issued by the lessor for a principal amount of approximately 80% of the total cost of the equipment to certain institutional investors (Lenders). The Lenders may be represented by an indenture trustee or agent bank.

"This proposal assumes that the Indebtedness shall be amortized in twenty payments of principal and interest at 8½% per annum, payable quarterly, in arrears, over five years. The Indebtedness shall be secured by an assignment of the lease and a security interest in the equipment but otherwise shall be without recourse to the lessor. Any variance from the debt assumptions, other than interest rate which is provided for in the rent adjustment clause, will relieve the offeror from his commitment hereunder, if so elected."

By stating the debt structure as provided above, the offeror has room to back away if there is a variance which would affect the economics, such as the debt term or the principal amount. An interest rate variance can be handled simply through a rent adjustment provision and, therefore, a prospective lessor does not usually need to be able to get out of his commitment if the interest rate varies.

RECOMMENDATION:

In a leveraged lease financing, a prospective lessee should require the right to be able to exclude any potential lender. For example, it may not be wise for any of its "line" banks to become involved because of potential future borrowing restrictions. In addition, some lenders are notoriously difficult to deal with and they should be brought in only as a last resort.

DOCUMENTATION SUGGESTION:

Many documents used in a leveraged transaction will be subject to lender approval. Some lenders can be difficult to negotiate with and slow in responding. To avoid last minute problems, the relevant papers should be sent to them as soon as possible and monitored carefully as to their review progress.

Who will handle the debt placement and who must pay the placement fee are issues which should be addressed. An underwriter, for example, will usually pay most of the costs involved in an underwritten transaction, including any debt placement fee. If the underwriter places the debt himself, he will save the debt placement fee and, thereby, increase his profit. If he is not regularly in the debt market, however, he may not find the best available interest rate. In addition, if any interest rate increase over that assumed can be passed on through a rent adjustment provision, there may be little incentive for him to make sure he has found a truly rock-bottom rate.

RECOMMENDATIONS:

I. A prospective lessee should insist upon having the right to veto anyone designated to place the debt on a leveraged transaction to insure a good selection will be made. In addition, a prospective lessee should be able to reject any interest rate that it deems unfavorable if the increased rate can be passed on through an upward rent adjustment.

II. If a prospective lessor or underwriter must pay the debt placement fee, he should have an equal say in the selection of the party who will place the debt. This will prevent him from being "stuck" with an inappropriately high placement fee.

10. Certain Tax Aspects May Dictate a Narrow Equipment Delivery Time Frame

When an offer is made well in advance of equipment deliveries, a proposal frequently specifies that the equipment *must* be delivered between certain dates. If any equipment is delivered before or after the designated dates, the prospective lessor may refuse to finance the equipment. For example, the following type of clause may appear in a proposal letter:

ILLUSTRATIVE LANGUAGE—
LESSOR'S TIME FRAME:

"Delivery of the equipment will take place on or after January 1, 19X0 but no later than June 30, 19X0. The lessor shall have no obligation with respect to deliveries occuring before or after such dates."

How important are the delivery dates? In many cases, *very* important. They determine when the equipment will be ready for lease and, therefore, when the ownership tax benefits, such as depreciation, can be claimed by the lessor. When these tax benefits will be available can be a critical factor in determining the lessor's economics. For example, a prospective lessor may commit to lease certain equipment provided it delivers *after* his current tax year because he cannot use the tax benefits in the current year. In addition, such a commitment may only extend to the midpoint of the following year because of the depreciation assumptions used in pricing the transaction. The timing of deliveries can also be important to a prospective lessor in anticipating his cash needs for funding the equipment purchases.

When a long term lease commitment involving many items of equipment is involved, there is a greater risk to a prospective lessee of late deliveries and, therefore, a greater risk that equipment will be excluded. A commitment period time cushion is one solution. That is, having the lease commitment run, for example, six months more than the last expected delivery. The longer the commitment period, however, the more likely it is that a prospective lessor will impose a fee for holding the funds available. Such a fee is commonly referred to as a commitment fee and is usually based upon a percentage of equipment cost. For example, a lessor may charge a fee equal to ½ of 1% of the total funds committed. Generally, lessors are willing to hold funds available for up to twelve months without charging a commitment fee.

RECOMMENDATION:

A commitment fee should be included in a prospective lessee's cost-to-lease computation. A transaction with a lower rent and a commitment fee may be less attractive than one with a slightly higher rent and no fee. *This is not, however, always the case and, therefore, a prospective lessee should not automatically exclude a proposal just because it involves a commitment fee.*

11. It Is Important to Designate the Equipment Location

Where the leased equipment is to be located can be significant for many reasons. Security interest filings which a lessor deems necessary to protect its ownership interest against creditors of a lessee cannot generally be made without knowing the location. The availability of certain tax benefits will depend on where the equipment will be used. For example, a lessor will not be able to claim investment tax credit on certain equipment used outside of the United States.

Underwriters sometimes overlook the psychological benefits that location can have on their sales effort. Certain lessor-investors may be more willing to participate in situations involving equipment used in their local area. For example, if the equipment is to be used in the state of Maryland by a division of a California corporation, Maryland regional banks may be interested because of the possibility of doing future business with a company they normally may not be involved with.

12. Additional Rights Should Be Spelled Out

There are certain rights, or "options," which are frequently a part of a lease transaction. If they are considered important to either party they should be outlined in the proposal letter. For example, a lessee commonly has the right to purchase the equipment, or renew the lease, under certain conditions at the end of the primary lease term. Such a proposal letter provision might be as follows:

ILLUSTRATIVE LANGUAGE—
PURCHASE AND RENEWAL OPTIONS:

At the end of the primary lease term the lessee may (with one hundred eighty days written notice prior to the end of such term):

a. Renew the lease with respect to the equipment for an amount equal to its then fair market rental value, or

b. Purchase the equipment for a price equal to its then fair market value.

RECOMMENDATION:

From a lessee's viewpoint, a purchase option should not only be exercisable at the end of the main lease term but also at the end of each renewal term. In addition, the renewal term rights should adequately cover potential periods of extended use.

A "right of first refusal" option is used at times as an alternative to the standard purchase or renewal options. Basically, a first refusal option gives the lessee the right to purchase or renew the equipment under the same terms as offered by an unrelated third party. A typical proposal letter clause might be written as follows:

ILLUSTRATIVE LANGUAGE—
RIGHT OF FIRST REFUSAL:

"At the end of the primary lease term, the lessee will have a right of first refusal as to any sale or re-lease of the equipment."

OBSERVATION:

A right of first refusal may create a potential problem for a lessee. It is conceivable that a competitor would bid for equipment essential to a lessee's operations merely to attempt to interfere with its business.

Prospective lessees sometimes find that it is important to have the right to terminate a lease before the end of its *primary* term. Such a right is commonly referred to as an "early termination option" and allows the lessee to prematurely end the lease as to any equipment which becomes obsolete or surplus to its needs. Lessors typically do not like to grant termination rights since they cut off future earnings on a transaction. Therefore, when granted, the lessee is usually required to pay a substantial premium, commonly referred to as a "termination value," if it is exercised.

ILLUSTRATIVE LANGUAGE—
TERMINATION RIGHT:

"At the expiration of each year during the primary lease term, the lessee shall have the right at its option to terminate the lease. The lessee will be required to give the lessor ninety days prior written notice of its intention to terminate and, during the period from giving notice until the termination date, the lessee shall use its best efforts to obtain bids from unaffiliated third parties for the purchase of the equipment. On the termination date, the lessor shall sell the equipment for cash for the highest bid received. The total proceeds of such sale shall be retained by the lessor and the lessee will pay to the lessor the difference, if any, by which the sales proceeds are less than the appropriate termination value indicated on the attached schedule."

RECOMMENDATION:

If a prospective lessor is willing to grant a termination right, the prospective lessee should make sure that the termination *values* along with the *right* are incorporated into the lease proposal. These values are not standard and can vary significantly depending on the competition and the lessors. Too many times the values are not seen until after the award and sometimes only a few weeks before the anticipated closing. If they turn out to be excessive, it may be too late to go elsewhere for the financing.

In some situations prospective lessors want the right to be able to force a lessee to buy the equipment at the end of the lease. This type of right is commonly referred to as a "put" and should, as with the other options, be identified in the proposal. Because, however, of potential tax problems, puts are not generally used.

13. What Happens if There Is an Equipment Loss?

The basic financial responsibilities of a lessee in the event of an equipment casualty loss should be identified. For example, a finance lessor will typically require the lessee to pay a predetermined amount of money, typically referred to as the "casualty value," if a casualty loss occurs. Casualty values are usually calculated to protect a lessor's equipment investment and, as with termination values, can be arbitrary. Prospective lessees should, therefore, review them *before* awarding the deal and, if satisfactory, make sure they are incorporated into the proposal letter.

RECOMMENDATION:

Lessees required to insure equipment against casualty losses for the benefit of the lessor should consider having the right to have any insurance proceeds received by the lessor credited against any casualty value due.

14. The Relevant Tax Assumptions and the Responsibility for Their Loss Shoud Be Identified

In determining what rent to charge, a prospective lessor generally anticipates receiving certain tax benefits, such as investment tax credit and depreciation. These assumed tax benefits are usually critical to the economics of the transaction.

ILLUSTRATIVE EXAMPLE—
THE IMPORTANCE OF TAX BENEFITS:

Company A and Company C propose to jointly lease a $1,000,000 tank barge to Company B for 10 years. The barge will be used to carry a highly dangerous chemical. Company A and Company C will each be a 50% partner. The investment tax credit will be passed through to Company B. For the first year of the lease the facts are:

First Year Annual Rent	$120,000
First Year Depreciation	$200,000
Company A and C's Tax Rate	50%

Because of the potential liability in the event of an accident, Company A and C decide to act through a trust arrangement. They anticipate that the trust will receive partnership-type tax treatment. In other words, Company A and C as the beneficial owners of the equipment will be able to *directly* claim on their tax returns any tax loss resulting from the transaction. Assuming there are no other expenses, the transaction would produce a tax shelter, or loss, of $80,000 for the first year.

Revenues	$120,000
Expenses (depreciation)	−$200,000
Net Profit (loss)	$(80,000)

With partnership treatment Company A and Company C may each claim $40,000, ½ of the "partnership" loss, against their other income. This loss would save each $20,000 (50% x $40,000) in taxes. If instead the IRS held that the trust was to be treated as a corporation for tax purposes, the excess write-off would not flow through to Company A and Company C. The "shelter" would, therefore, be lost. If the transaction were competitively structured to begin with, it would more than likely no longer be economically viable for Company A and Company C.

Because of the adverse impact the loss of anticipated tax benefits can have for tax orientated lessors, they frequently want lessees to indemnify them against any loss of expected tax benefits. Lessees, however, do not like to do so. As a result, the indemnification issue can be troublesome. Therefore, each side should discuss the tax loss responsibilities at the proposal stage to insure they can find, in concept, an acceptable arrangement.

Although the tax assumptions can vary with each situation, the following are representative, in a general manner, of those typically found in a finance lease:

- In the event a trust, or a partnership, will be established to act as the lessor, such entity will receive partnership treatment for Federal income tax purposes.

- The lease will qualify as a "true" lease for Federal income tax purposes.

- The owning entity will qualify as the owner, lessor, and, if the equipment contemplated is new equipment, "original user." (Original user status is generally necessary to enable a lessor to claim the maximum depreciation and investment tax credit benefits available to an equipment owner.)

- The most accelerated form of depreciation will be available. (The specific method of depreciation will be identified. For example, the lessor may anticipate using the 200% declining balance method when new equipment is involved.)

- The lessor will be able to depreciate the equipment over a prescribed period of time.

- The lessor will be entitled to a designated minimum number of months of depreciation for the initial year of the lease term.

- If the transaction will involve "outside" debt (a leveraged transaction), the deductibility for Federal income tax purposes of the annual debt interest charge will be anticipated.

- If the transaction involves certain aircraft or vessels and is a "foreign source transaction," i.e., predominant equipment use outside of the United States, the lessor may assume that he will have the ability to make a domestic source income election.

- If the lessor intends to claim any available investment tax credit, this intention and the amount will be stated.

15. What Happens if the Tax Laws Change?

A change in the tax laws can affect the lessor's economic return in a tax-orientated lease. Changes, for example, in the tax laws affecting the investment tax credit percentage; the ADR depreciation life, if ADR is elected; the method of depreciation; or the current Federal income tax rate can have a substantial *positive or negative* impact.

ILLUSTRATIVE EXAMPLE—
THE CHANGE IN TAX LAW RISK:

Company A contracts on April 1, 19X0 to lease a truck to Company B under the following facts:

Truck cost	$10,000
Investment tax credit percentage	10%
Delivery date	June 1, 19X0

Under the 10% investment credit, Company A would have a first year *credit* against its Federal income tax (a savings) of $1,000 (10% x $10,000).

Assume that on April 2, 19X0 the investment tax credit percentage is changed to 5% for all equipment delivered on or after June 1, 19X0. The first year tax credit would then be only $500 (5% x $10,000). Clearly, the transaction has become less attractive. If the annual rent charged the lessee cannot be appropriately adjusted, the transaction will not be as "profitable."

If, on the other hand, the investment tax credit percentage went to 20%, the lessor would be able to claim a $2000 credit (20% x $10,000). Certainly a more desirable situation *for the lessor*.

But, what about the lessee?
In the 5% case the lessee gets a good deal. The transaction has been priced assuming a 10% investment credit rate with the result that the rent is lower than if the credit percentage had only been 5%. The lower the tax saving the more the rent must be increased to get the same return. In the 20% case, the lessee only received through the rent the benefit of a 10% credit. If the lessor's computation had been based on a 20% credit, it could have lowered the rent to the lessee anticipating a greater return through the tax saving.

As the above example illustrates, both parties can be affected directly or indirectly by a change in the tax laws.

Is there a way to equitably handle the change in tax law risk? Yes, the rent can be quoted subject to an appropriate adjustment to reflect any tax law change affecting the lessor's expected economic return. The parties may agree, for example, that the rent shall be adjusted so that the lessor's net return shall be maintained.

> RECOMMENDATION:
>
> The particular parameter which is to serve as a guide for the rent adjustment should be defined to prevent a calculation disagreement. "Net return," for example, may mean different things to different people. If a lessee does not know how to check an adjustment it may pay more than necessary if the lessor tries to squeeze a little higher return. By the same token, a lessee may incorrectly object to a legitimate adjustment.

16. Will a Tax Ruling Be Involved?

Whether a tax ruling will be involved can be an important proposal-stage consideration. In many cases, lessors like to have the Internal Revenue Service confirm the various tax assumptions through a Revenue Ruling. Sometimes a tax ruling will play a special role in the transaction. For example, a favorable ruling may be a prerequisite to the lessor's obligation to enter into the transaction. A lessor may be willing to release a lessee from certain indemnification obligations on tax assumptions "blessed" by the Service in their ruling.

> ILLUSTRATIVE LANGUAGE—
> THE USE OF A REVENUE RULING:
>
> "The lessor plans to obtain a private Internal Revenue Service Ruling with respect to the assumptions stated in this proposal letter. The lessee shall agree to indemnify the lessor for the tax assumptions which are the subject of the ruling request. Such indemnity shall remain in effect until a favorable ruling has been obtained on each of these points."

17. Who Has the Expense Responsibility for the Transaction?

Who is responsible for the various transaction expenses should be decided early. Many non-underwritten transactions involve only one prospective lessor and one prospective lessee. The primary expense is legal fees and the party incurring the expense usually pays for it. In an underwritten transaction this is not usually the case. Because this type of transaction can involve many parties,—equity participants, lenders, trustees, and the underwriter—a variety of substantial expenses may be incurred. For example:

- Fees and disbursements of special counsel for the lenders and their representative.

- Acceptance and annual fees of the lenders' representative—usually found in a trust arrangement.

- Fees and disbursements of special counsel for the equity participants and their representative.

- Acceptance and annual fees of the equity participants' representative—usually found in a trust arrangement.

- Fees and disbursements related to the filing for a Revenue Ruling.

- Documentation expenses, such as reproduction and printing expenses.

- Fees related to the placement of the debt.

The expense allocation is usually not as much of a problem as the reader might suspect. Typically, an underwriter will pay substantially all of the expenses. An underwriter may, however, "cap" these expenses by agreeing to pay only up to a specified percentage, usually around ¾ to 1¼%, of equipment cost, the excess to be paid by the lessee. Since an underwriter makes his money by charging the equity investors a set fee for bringing them the transaction, the more he can limit his expense responsibility the less he has to worry about fees and expenses eroding his profit. In a competitive market, however, many underwriters are willing, particularly if pushed a little, to assume the *entire* expense responsibility.

ILLUSTRATIVE EXAMPLE—
THE UNDERWRITER EXPENSE PROBLEM:

Company A, an underwriter, arranged for Company C and Company D to participate as the sole equity investors in the leveraged lease financing of one ocean-going tugboat to be leased to Company B. Company C and D agreed to pay Company A a brokerage fee equal to 2% of the equipment's cost for bringing in the transaction. As a condition of the transaction award, Company A had to commit to Company B that it would not have to pay any expenses, except for Company B's counsel fees. At the closing the following costs were incurred:

Tugboat cost	$6,000,000
Fees for the lender's counsel	20,000
Counsel fees for Company C & D	50,000
Counsel fees for Company A	2,000
Counsel fees for Company B	35,000
Printing expenses	21,000

What does Company A's profit picture look like?

Company A's "gross" fee from the transaction is $120,000 (2% x $6,000,000). All fees and expenses, excluding Company B's counsel fees, total $93,000 ($20,000 + $50,000 + $2,000 + $21,000). Therefore, Company A "nets" $27,000 ($120,000 − $93,000). If Company A had a 1% "cap" its expense responsibility would have been limited to $60,000 (1% x $6,000,000) and it would have made $60,000 ($120,000 − $60,000) instead of $27,000.

The difficult expense question is who must pay what expenses if a proposed underwritten transaction collapses! There are two things that can be counted on—the lenders and the prospective lessor-investors will not want to have any responsibility if the transaction does not go through. Who's left? The underwriter and the prospective lessee. Some underwriters attempt to put the responsibility for *all* expenses incurred in such a situation on the prospective lessee by inserting an appropriate clause in the proposal letter. Typically, the clause provides that the prospective lessee must pay if the transaction is not consummated *for any reason whatsoever*. This can be a dangerous position for a prospective lessee, particularly when the underwriter may be the reason the transaction failed.

RECOMMENDATION:

The expenses in a major underwritten lease financing can be substantial. For example, it is not unheard of for the legal fees and other expenses in a complicated $10,000,000 leveraged lease financing to run $200,000 to $400,000. Therefore, underwriters and prospective lessees should each carefully evaluate their potential expense exposure and clearly define the responsibilities *in all events*.

18. What Type of Lease Will It Be?

The type of lease which will be involved is certainly a basic issue which must be brought out during the proposal discussions. There are many types, each having different responsibilities for the lessor and the lessee. Without fully understanding what the equipment related expense obligations will be, for example, the overall costs cannot be properly assessed. Many equipment lease transactions involve net finance lease arrangements. Under this type, the lessee must pay all fixed expenses relating to the equipment during the lease term; such as maintenance, insurance, and certain taxes. It can be an expensive surprise, for instance, for a lessee to discover after the equipment is on lease that he must pay a substantial sales tax.

D. WHEN DO THE PARTIES HAVE A DEAL?

A lease transaction does not come into existence until there has been an *offer* and the offer has been *accepted*. Do the parties have a deal when a proposal letter has been signed by both parties? Yes and no. Generally, all they have at that point is an agreement to *see* if they *can* work out a deal. Initially, this seems to go against basic contract law—that is, once an offer has been made and accepted the parties have a contract. The problem lies in that usually the offer, and sometimes the acceptance, is *qualified*. In other words, conditions are imposed which must be satisfied *after* all parties have signed the lease proposal. Typical "conditions," for example, are:

- Necessary governmental or regulatory approvals, licenses, or authorizations.

- Favorable opinions of counsel.

- The effective placement of the debt, in the case of a leveraged lease.

- Acceptable financial covenants, such as a minimum debt-to-equity ratio.

- Favorable opinions of officers of the prospective lessee as to its business or financial condition.

- Satisfactory current audited financial statements.

- Mutually satisfactory documentation.

- Formal transaction approvals by the prospective equity participants and lenders.

- A minimum dollar participation of equity and debt participants.

- A detailed equipment list.

- Favorable equipment appraisals justifying the lease term and the equipment residual value.

The "satisfactory documentation" condition gives each side the most latitude to find justification to back out if they so desire. That is, unless the parties can reach agreement on each term and condition contained in the lease documents, they don't have to go through with the transaction. As the reader might suspect, this condition leaves a lot of room for some wide open discussions on issues not even anticpated in the proposal stage, such as whether the lessee should pay for the return of the equipment to *any* location designated by the lessor.

Although a fully accepted proposal letter may have only a qualified bond on all parties, it does outline a business intent. A good lawyer *may* be able to build a substantial case if one side backs out, particularly if financial obligations have been incurred on the other side. It would, however, be a difficult situation to deal with if one party refused to go forward.

E. HOW DOES A PROSPECTIVE LESSEE ACCEPT AN OFFER?

A prospective lessee generally "accepts" an offer by acknowledging his willingness to proceed on the basis of the terms presented. If the offer is submitted in the form of a written proposal it can be accepted by an appropriate officer signing his acceptance directly on the letter or in a separate writing properly referencing the proposal letter. Any acceptance condition should be clearly a part of the acceptance and identified as such. For example, if the acceptance is made by signing in a designated space on a proposal letter, the condition should precede the signature.

RECOMMENDATION:

If a proposal letter is used, a prospective lessee should "accept" directly on the proposal letter not in a separate writing, particularly if the acceptance is conditioned. Separate papers can easily be lost or misplaced.

F. WHAT ARE THE PROSPECTIVE <u>LESSEE'S</u> OBLIGATIONS AFTER A PROPOSAL IS ACCEPTED?

A fully accepted proposal may have no more than a psychological hold on the transaction because of various stated conditions, such as mutually satisfactory documentation, which are usually imposed. Therefore, except for any obligation to pick up the expenses of a collapsed transaction, the prospective lessee's obligations may be minimal or nonexistent at the time of the proposal acceptance. As a result, prospective lessors may be unable to require a prospective lessee to go through with a transaction or even recover damages for his failure to proceed.

RECOMMENDATION:

Inasmuch as a prospective lessee's obligations to go forward *may* be nonexistent after the acceptance of the offer, prospective lessors and underwriters should make sure transactions are quickly and efficiently completed.

G. WHAT ARE THE PROSPECTIVE LESSOR'S OBLIGATIONS AFTER A PROPOSAL IS ACCEPTED?

Since there are usually many conditions contained in a lease proposal which must be satisfied in the future, the offeror's obligations at the time the prospective lessee accepts the proposal will probably be very limited. For example, if the offer is conditioned upon acceptable documentation, a prospective lessor may have no trouble finding "unacceptable" points and walking away from the transaction. Of course, there may be an ethical obligation to go forward, but this will be of little value to a prospective lessee when left standing at the last minute without the essential financing.

RECOMMENDATION:

If a proposal is conditioned on certain lessor committee approvals, a prospective lessee should request written verification once the approvals have been given. Psychologically, this will bring the prospective lessor further into the transaction.

H. A REQUEST-FOR-BIDS LETTER CHECKLIST

There are certain topics which should be covered in a comprehensive request-for-bids letter. The following topic checklist will assist a prospective lessee in its preparation.

1. Equipment Description.
    a. What Type Will Be Involved?
    b. Who Is the Manufacturer?
    c. What Is the Model?
    d. How Many Units Will Be Involved?
2. Equipment Cost
    a. What Is the Total Cost Involved?
    b. What Is the Cost Per Item?
    c. Is the Cost Per Item Fixed?
        (1) If Not, What Is the Probable Cost Escalation?

3. Equipment Payment
   a. When Must the Equipment Be Paid For?
   b. Must the Entire Purchase Price Be Paid at Once?
4. Equipment Delivery.
   a. What Is the Anticipated Delivery Date?
   b. How Long Should the Lease Commitment Run Past the Last Anticipated Delivery Date?
5. Equipment Location.
   a. Where Will the Equipment Be Located?
      (1) At the Lease Inception.
      (2) During the Lease Term?
6. Equipment Lease.
   a. What Type of Lease Is Desired?
      (1) Net Finance Lease.
      (2) Service Lease.
      (3) Other.
7. Lease Period.
   a. How Long Must the Lease Run?
   b. Will an Interim Lease Period Be Acceptable?
      (1) If So, What Is the Latest Date on Which the Primary Term Can Begin.
   c. How Long a Renewal Period Is Desired.
   d. How Will the Renewal Right Be Structured? For Example, Five One-Year Periods, One Five-Year Period, Etc.
8. Rent Program.
   a. When Should The Rent Be Payable?
      (1) Annually.
      (2) Semi-annually.
      (3) Quarterly.
      (4) Monthly.
      (5) Other.
   b. Should The Payments Be "In Advance" or "In Arrears"?
   c. If There Is an Interim Period, How Should the Interim Rent Be Structured?
      (1) Based on the Primary Rent. For Example, The Daily Equivalent of the Primary Rent.
      (2) Based on the Long-Term Debt Interest Rate.
      (3) Other.
   d. If There Will Be a Renewal Period, How Should the Renewal Rent Be Structured?
      (1) Fixed.
      (2) Fair Rental Value.
9. Options.
   a. What Type Of Options Are Desired?
      (1) Fair Market Value Purchase Right.
      (2) Fixed Price Purchase Right.

        (3) Fair Market Rental Value Renewal Right.

        (4) Fixed Price Renewal Right.

        (5) Right of First Refusal.

        (6) Termination Right.

        (7) Other.

    b. Is a Right of First Refusal Specifically Unacceptable?

10. Casualty and Termination Values.

    a. If a Termination Right Is Required, Will the Termination Values Be a Primary Factor in the Lease Decision?

    b. Must the Termination and Casualty Values Be Submitted at the Time of the Proposal?

11. Maintenance and Repair.

    a. Who Will Have the Equipment Maintenance and Repair Obligations?

12. Tax Indemnifications.

    a. What Tax Indemnifications Will Be Acceptable, if Any?

13. Insurance.

    a. Is the Right of Self-Insurance Desired?

14. Taxes.

    a. What Taxes Will Be Assumed?

        (1) Sales.

        (2) Rental.

        (3) Other.

15. Transaction Expenses.

    a. What Expenses Other Than Lessee's Legal Fees, if Any, Will Be Assumed if the Transaction Is Completed?*

        (1) Counsel Fees for Any Lenders and Their Representative.

        (2) Acceptance and Annual Fees of Any Lenders' Representative (Trust Arrangement).

        (3) Counsel Fees for the Lessor-Investors and Any Representative.

        (4) Acceptance and Annual Fees of Any Lessor-Investors' Representative (Trust Arrangement).

        (5) Revenue Ruling Fees.

        (6) Documentation Expenses.

        (7) Debt Placement Fee.

        (8) Other.

    b. What Expenses, if Any, Will Be Assumed if the Transaction Collapses?

16. Tax Ruling.

    a. Is A Revenue Ruling Necessary or Desirable?

*Usually only a concern in underwritten transactions.

   b. Can a Favorable Revenue Ruling Be a Prerequisite to Any
      of Lessor's Obligations.
   c. Should a Revenue Ruling Relieve Any Tax Indemnification
      Obligations?
17. Submission Date.
   a. What Is the Latest Date on Which the Proposal Can Be
      Submitted?
18. Award Date.
   a. On What Date Will the Transaction Be Awarded?
19. Type of Proposals.
   a. Is an Underwritten Transaction Acceptable? If so:
      (1) Will "Best Efforts" or "Firm" Proposals Be Accepted?
          cepted?
      (2) Is a Leveraged or Single Source Transacton Pre-
          ferred?
   b. If "Best Efforts" Proposals Are Acceptable, How Long
      After the Award Will the Underwriter Have To Firm Up the
      Prospective Lessor-Investors and Any Lenders?
20. Prospective Lessors—Underwritten Transaction.
   a. Are Any Prospective Lessor-Investors Not to Be
      Approached?

I. A PROPOSAL STAGE CHECKLIST FOR THE LESSOR

There are certain fundamental issues which a prospective lessor
should address during the proposal stage. The following checklist
will serve as a guide in identifying these issues and in preparing a
proposal letter.

1. The Offer.
   a. Will an Underwritten or Direct Lessor Proposal Be
      Involved?
   b. If an Underwritten Offer Is Involved:
      (1) Will It Be on A "Best Efforts" or "Firm" Basis?
      (2) Must There Be More Than One Equity Participant?
      (3) If It Can Be on a "Best Efforts" Basis, Is There Any
          Deadline When the Equity Participants Must Give
          Their Formal Commitment?
      (4) Will the Transaction Be Leveraged with Third-Party
          Debt?
2. The Lessee.
   a. Has the Lessee Been Accurately Identified?
   b. Has the Lessee's Financial Condition Been Reviewed?

3. Credit Support.
   a. Can the Lessee's Financial Condition Support the Entire Lease Obligation?
   b. If the Lessee's "Credit" Is Not Sufficient, Are There Additional Credit Support Alternatives Available?
      (1) Parent Company Guarantee.
      (2) Affiliated Company Guarantee.
      (3) Unrelated Third-Party Guarantee.
      (4) Deficiency Guarantee.
      (5) Bank Support.
      (6) Other.
   c. If Credit Support Is Necessary, Has the Financial Condition of the Entity Giving the Support Been Reviewed?
4. The Equipment Description.
   a. What Type Will Be Involved?
   b. Who Is the Manufacturer?
   c. What Is the Model?
   d. How Many Units Will Be Involved?
5. The Equipment Cost.
   a. What Is the Total Cost Involved?
   b. What Is the Cost Per Item?
   c. Is the Cost Per Item Fixed?
      (1) If Not, What Is the Probable Cost Escalation?
6. The Equipment Delivery.
   a. What Is the Anticipated Delivery Date?
   b. Must the Lease Commitment Run Past the Anticipated Delivery Date? If So, for How Long?
      (1) Will a Fee Be Charged for the Commitment to Lease Future Delivered Equipment?
7. The Equipment Location.
   a. Where Will the Equipment Be Located?
      (1) At the Lease Inception?
      (2) During the Lease Term?
8. The Rent Program.
   a. What Is the Primary Rent Payment Program Structure?
      (1) Will the Rent Be Payable "In Advance" or "In Arrears"?
      (2) Will the Rent Be Payable Annually, Semi-Annually, Quarterly, Monthly, or Other?
   b. Will Interim Rent Be Involved? If so,
      (1) Will It Be Based Upon the Primary Rent, the Long-Term Debt Interest Rate (if Leveraged), or Other?
      (2) When Will the Payments Be Due?
9. The Term of the Lease.
   a. How Long Will the Lease Run?
      (1) Primary Lease Term.

        (2) Renewal Period?
- b. Will an Interim Lease Term Be Involved? If so,
  - (1) When Will the Interim Term Lease Term Start?
  - (2) When Will the Primary Lease Term Start?

10. The Lessor
    - a. How Will the Equipment Be Owned?
      - (1) Directly?
      - (2) Indirectly Through a Partnership, Trust, or Corporation?
    - b. Will the Ownership Structure Satisfy Any Tax and Liability Criteria?
      - (1) Flow-Through of Tax Benefits.
      - (2) Corporate-Like Liability Protection.
      - (3) Other.

11. The Debt—if the Transaction Is Leveraged.
    - a. What Is the Loan Repayment Program?
      - (1) "In Advance" or "In Arrears"?
      - (2) Will the Debt Service Be Payable Annually, Semi-Annually, Quarterly, Monthly, Or Other?
    - b. Who Will Be Responsible for Arranging for the Placement of the Debt?
    - c. Will the Rent Be Quoted on the Basis of an Assumed Debt Principal Amount, Per Annum Interest Charge, Etc.
      - (1) If so, Will the Rent Quoted Be Subject to Adjustment if Other Than Assumed?
    - d. If the Rent Is Subject to a Debt Assumption Adjustment, What Adjustment Criteria Will Be Used?
      - (1) After-Tax Yield.
      - (2) Cash Flow.
      - (3) Net Return.
      - (4) Other.
    - e. Who Will Be Responsible for Fees Related to the Debt?
      - (1) Placement Fee.
      - (2) Lender's Commitment Fee.
      - (3) Other.

12. Options.
    - a. What Special Rights Will the Lessee Have?
      - (1) Fixed Price Purchase Right.
      - (2) Fair Market Value Purchase Right.
      - (3) Fixed Price Renewal Right.
      - (4) Fair Market Rental Value Renewal Right.
      - (5) Termination Right.
      - (6) Other.
    - b. What Special Rights Will the Lessor Have?
      - (1) Fixed Price Sale Right.
      - (2) Fixed Price Renewal Right.

(3) Termination Right.

(4) Other.

13. Casualty Loss.

    a. What Financial Responsibilities Will the Lessee Have in the Event of a Casualty Loss?

14. Casualty and Termination Values.

    a. What Amounts Are to Be Used?

15. Tax Aspects.

    a. What Are the Relevant Tax Assumptions?

       (1) Partnership-Type Tax Treatment.

       (2) Original User, Owner, and Lessor.

       (3) Depreciation.

          (a) Facts and Circumstances Method.

          (b) Asset Depreciation Range System Method.

          (c) Percentage Annual Write-Off.

          (d) Minimum Number of Months of First Year Write-Off.

          (e) Depreciation Amount.

          (f) Salvage Value.

       (4) Investment Tax Credit.

          (a) To the Lessor.

          (b) To the Lessee.

       (5) Deductibility of Third-Party Debt Interest.

       (6) Domestic Source Income Election.

       (7) True Lease Treatment for Federal Income Tax Purposes.

       (8) Other.

    b. What Tax Assumptions, if Any, Will the Lessee Have to Indemnify the Lessor For in the Event of Loss or Inability to Claim?

    c. If There Are Lessee Tax Indemnifications, What Events Which Result in Tax Benefit Unavailability Will Trigger an Indemnification Payment?

       (1) Any Reason.

       (2) Acts or Omissions of Lessee.

       (3) Acts or Omissions of Lessor.

       (4) Change in Law.

       (5) Other.

    d. If the Investment Tax Credit Has Been "Passed Through" to the Lessee, Will the Lessor Indemnify the Lessee Against the *Lessee's* Loss or Inability to Claim the Credit as a Result of the Lessor's Acts or Omissions?

16. Tax Ruling.

    a. Will A Tax Ruling Be Involved?

    b. If so, Will A *Favorable* Ruling:

       (1) Relieve the Lessee from Any Tax Indemnifications?

      (2) Be a Prerequisite to the Lessor's Obligation to Lease The Equipment.

17. Transaction Expenses.
    a. Who Must Pay for the Expenses If:
       (1) The Transaction Goes Through Without Problems?
       (2) The Transaction Collapeses Before the Lease Documents Are Executed?
       (3) The Transaction Collapses After the Lease Documents Are Executed but Before the Equipment Is Delivered?
18. Type of Lease.
    a. What Type of Lease Will Be Involved?
       (1) Net Finance Lease?
       (2) Service Lease?
       (3) Other?
19. Conditions.
    a. What Conditions Must Be Satisfied Before the Lessor Is Committed?
       (1) Governmental or Regulatory Approvals.
       (2) Licenses or Authorizations.
       (3) Favorable Opinions of Counsel.
       (4) Maintenance or Achievement of Certain Financial Tests.
       (5) Lessee Officer Certificates as to Business or Financial Condition.
       (6) Satisfactory Audited Financial Statements.
       (7) Acceptable Documentation.
       (8) Approvals by Prospective Lessor or Equity Participants.
       (9) Minimum Dollar Participation by Equity And Debt Participants.
       (10) Favorable Equipment Appraisals Justifying Lease Term and Residual Value.
       (11) Other.
20. Form of Proposal.
    a. Will a Written Proposal Be Used? If so,
       (1) How Should Acceptance Be Acknowledged?
21. Submission and Award Dates.
    a. When Is the Latest Date on Which the Proposal Can Be Submitted?
    b. What Is the Anticipated Transaction Award Date?
       (1) Is There Adequate Time to Do the Deal?
22. Offer Termination Date.
    a. How Long Will the Prospective Lessee Have to Accept the Offer?

3

GUIDELINES FOR DRAFTING AND
ANALYZING THE LEASE DOCUMENT

**What Is a Lease • What Essential Protections Must a Lessor Build In
•What Lessees Have to Know—and Usually Don't • The Many Hidden
Dangers—How to Successfully Handle Them.**

A. WHAT IS THE CENTRAL PURPOSE OF A LEASE?

Although a lease agreement can involve many complex, highly
technical, and sometimes overwhelming concepts, its central purpose is
very simple. It defines a contractual arrangement in which an owner of
property sells the *right to use* the property to another *for a period of time.*
The property owner, or lessor, retains title to the property subject to any
purchase rights which the user, or lessee, may have negotiated.

A lease is to be distinguished from a conditional sale, an outright sale,
or a mortgage type of transaction. In a *conditional sale* transaction the
property owner sells the *property*, not its *use,* to another. At the time of sale,
title to the property is not transferred to the purchaser but rather is retained
by the seller as security for the performance of any conditions attached to
the sale. Possession, however, is transferred. A seller may, for example,
agree to let a buyer pay for the property in installments over a period of
time. In this case payment in full is a condition which must be satisfied
before the buyer has the right to receive title. In an *outright sale,* the
property owner unconditionally transfers the property, *including title,* to
the purchaser and, at the same time, the purchaser pays the seller the full
purchase price. In a *mortgage* situation, a purchaser of property borrows
from a third-party lender some or all of the money necessary to buy the
property. The lender, or mortgagee, as security for the repayment of its
loan, requires the borrower, or mortgagor, to give it a security interest
(mortgage) in the property. The borrower has possession of and title to the
property subject to the lender's *right* to claim the property in the event of a
loan default.

B. ARE THERE ANY REAL DIFFERENCES AMONG THE COMMON FORMS OF LEASES?

Typically, lease agreements follow the same fundamental structure. People sometimes think the three common *format* variances—the standard lease, the master lease, and the custom lease—imply certain differences in the basic concepts included. They do not. The categories are merely descriptive of the *mechanical* nature of the lease. This will become clearer in the following discussion.

1. The Standard Lease

Lessors, particularly in small transactions and "vendor" programs, frequently use a "standard" preprinted lease. The form has "fill in" blanks for those aspects, such as rent, which typically vary with each transaction. Although this type of lease format can be "tailored" to meet certain required variations, it is difficult to incorporate too many and still come out with a readable document. The real advantage to using a preprinted lease is that it permits the expenses involved in documenting a transaction, such as legal fees, to be kept to a minimum. The form nature eliminates extensive drafting and also discourages heavy negotiation. This is particularly attractive in small dollar lease transactions where excessive documentation expenses could easily turn what started out to be an economically viable transaction into one that is not. The greater the expenses, the less the profit to a lessor and the greater the overall cost to a lessee.

RECOMMENDATION:

I. The estimated costs involved in *documenting* a lease should always be considered in determining the economic attractiveness of a transaction, *both* by the prospective lessor and the prospective lessee. Documentation expenses can be the same regardless of the dollar amount of equipment involved. A $10,000 legal fee may be reasonable for a $500,000 transaction but it will not be for a $20,000 transaction.

2. The Master Lease

A lease which is set up to permit future delivered equipment to be easily added is commonly referred to as a *master lease*. The future equipment may or may not be identified at the time the lease is signed.

A master lease is arranged in two parts. The main, or "boiler plate," portion contains the provisions which will not vary from transaction to transaction, such as basic representations, warranties, tax obligations, and maintenance responsibilities. The second part, sometimes called the "schedule," contains the items which will vary, such as equipment type, rent, and options. A schedule may run only two to three pages long, whereas the main portion may be forty to fifty pages in length. The advantage to using a master lease format is that the parties can document future transactions with a minimum amount of time and expense by merely adding a schedule containing the relevant information.

> OBSERVATION:
>
> A lessor with a *master lease* "in place" with a particular company has a competitive advantage over other prospective lessors in any new bidding situation. Because documenting new equipment additions is simpler than negotiating an entire new lease agreement, companies with master leases frequently go out of their way to let an existing lessor win, such as giving him the chance to match a lower proposal.

3. The Custom Lease

There are many times when a lease arrangement will involve a great number of aspects unique to the particular transaction. In these cases, it is usually not practical, or even possible, to consider using a preprinted form and a lease must be specifically drafted "from scratch." Leases of this nature are often referred to as *custom leases* and are frequently found in major equipment lease transactions.

C. WHAT SHOULD A PROPERLY WRITTEN LEASE COVER?

It is absolutely essential for all parties involved in a lease transaction to have a thorough understanding of the basic concepts contained in the lease document. All too often competent, but inexperienced, individuals are taken advantage of by the opposition because they are unaware of the legal, financial, or practical aspects of what goes into a lease. The intent of the following discussion is to identify and explain the various issues which should be covered in a major equipment lease and, where appropriate, to offer the most effective ways for them to be handled—whether from the viewpoint of a lessee or a lessor. It will center around a *net finance* lease because it is generally the most comprehensive and complex form. Mastering this type will enable an individual to deal with virtually *any* kind of equipment lease.

A sample net finance lease has been included in the Appendix. The reader is urged to glance through it before reading further to get an overview of what is to be discussed.

RECOMMENDATION:

It is advisable for the party drafting a lengthy lease document to incorporate an index containing all the topic headings and page
numbers. Valuable time can be saved during the negotiation
process by being able to readily locate relevant provisions.

1. The Parties Should Be Properly Identified

Every lease should begin by clearly stating the full legal name of the
lessor and the lessee, the jurisdiction in which each is organized, and the
mailing address of their principal places of business. In this way there can
be little dispute as who is intended to be bound by the contract.

ILLUSTRATIVE LANGUAGE—
THE PROPER NAME DESIGNATIONS:

"This lease made as of the 25th day of February, 19XX, by and
between ARROW CORPORATION, a Delaware corporation, having
its principal place of business at 200 Curtis Street, Zenia, Ohio
(hereinafter called "Lessor") and THE HARRIS CORPORATION, a
Missouri corporation, having its principal place of business at 100
Barkley Street, St. Louis, Missouri (hereinafter called "Lessee")"

RECOMMENDATION:

Corporations sometimes lease equipment to be used exclusively by
one of their divisions. When such a division has been organized as a
"profit center" they frequently want it to be the named "Lessee." If
the division is merely a "bookkeeping" entity with no legal standing
of its own, this can be a problem. An "officer" of the division signing
in his divisional capacity can not bind the division since it does not
legally exist. The officer may be bound in his individual capacity but
this will usually be of little value unless he is wealthy in his own right.
If the "division" is in fact a corporate subsidiary this problem will not
be present because it will have a separate legal existence. A
prospective lessor should, therefore, make sure that the lessee entity has been properly identified and is capable of being legally
bound in the capacity indicated in the lease.

2. It Is Helpful to Include a Factual Summary

It is always good form for the lease document to summarize at the out-
set the basic facts surrounding the transaction. Such a summary is particularly useful for future reference by individuals who were not involved
at the time the lease was negotiated. For example, describing an equipment
purchase contract which the lessee had entered into prior to the lease

transaction and which was assigned to the lessor as part of the transaction. The factual summary is usually incorporated into what are referred to as "whereas" clauses.

Although not always necessary, it is also good form to spell out the *consideration* for the lease, generally stated as the mutual obligations of the lessor and the lessee under the agreement. This is usually done in a "Now, Therefore" clause following the "Whereas" section.

> ILLUSTRATIVE LANGUAGE—
> A FACTUAL SUMMARY:
>
> "Whereas, pursuant to a purchase agreement (the "Purchase Agreement") dated January 2, 19X7 between White Aircraft Corporation (the "Manufacturer"), a Delaware corporation, and the Lessee, the Manufacturer has agreed to manufacture and sell to the Lessee, and the Lessee has agreed to purchase from the Manufacturer, one White Model A-14 aircraft, which is to be financed pursuant to this Lease; and
>
> "Whereas, the Lessee and the Lessor will enter into an assignment of the Purchase Agreement simultaneously with the execution of this Lease whereby the Lessee assigns to the Lessor all of the Lessee's rights and interests under the Purchase Agreement, except to the extent reserved therein;
>
> "Now, Therefore, in consideration of the mutual agreements contained in this Lease, the parties hereto agree as follows:"

3. The Key Terms Should Be Defined

The fundamental terms used repeatedly in the lease agreement which have special meaning should all be defined in one section, preferably at the beginning of the document. For example, terms such as "fair market purchase value," "fair market rental value," "manufacturer," "purchase contract," "stipulated loss value," and "termination value" will usually have certain meanings in a particular transaction and must be pinned down. Using such a definition section has a number of benefits. It makes the text cleaner to read, permits the parties to more readily locate definitions, and lessens the risk that an important term will accidentally be left undefined.

4. The Mechanics of Adding Future Delivered Equipment Should Be Agreed Upon

It is not uncommon for a lease agreement to be entered into before the equipment to be covered is delivered. The agreement may, for example, represent a lease line of credit in which the lessor commits to provide lease funding for certain equipment to be delivered over a twelve month period. The prospective lessee may just be uneasy and insist upon negotiating and executing the agreement well in advance of delivery in order to make sure no insurmountable problems will arise before it is too late to find another lessor. On the other hand, an equally anxious prospective lessor may want to proceed as quickly as possible to lessen any risk of the prospective lessee changing its mind.

When a lease transaction is documented before the equipment is delivered, the parties must prescribe a method for putting the equipment under lease when it arrives. Usually the arrangement is for the lessee to notify the lessor in writing of the delivery of the equipment and its acceptability for lease. The notification usually takes the form of what is sometimes referred to as an "acceptance supplement," which is nothing more than a written statement which lists the equipment delivered and states that it has been accepted for lease as of a specified date. If the equipment conforms to the agreement, the lessor automatically puts it on lease.

a. How a Lessor Can Protect Against a Lessee Walking Away Free

When a lease relates to future delivered equipment, the lessee's obligation to lease the equipment must be clearly spelled out. For example, if a prospective lessor wants a prospective lessee to be bound to lease the prescribed equipment when it is delivered, the lease should state this precisely. If this is not done, a prospective lessee may decide at the last minute to buy the equipment or lease it from another lessor.

Frequently, ambiguous equipment acceptance provisions create problems. For example, an acceptance provision might state that "the lessee *may* accept the equipment when delivered by executing the appropriate acceptance supplement." Although the intent goes to the method of acceptance and not *whether* the lessee may or may not elect to lease the equipment, it could imply that the lessee has an option of whether to lease. Of course if this is the arrangement, there is no problem. If it is not and the lessee walks away unexpectedly, a lessor would have lost the opportunity of pursuing alternative uses for the money allocated during the commitment period. The moral is—if there is to be a firm lease obligation, the word *may* should be replaced with *shall* and the provision should read: "the lessee *shall* accept the equipment. . .".

b. A Lessor Can Make Money Even if a Lessee Walks Away

There are two techniques which a lessor committing future funds to a transaction can use to lessen the financial impact of a lessee not leasing specified equipment when it arrives. One is by imposing *a non-utilization fee* and the other is by imposing a *commitment fee*. Generally, the thought of either will make a prospective lessee unhappy; however, they are saleable in certain situations.

The purpose of a non-utilization fee is to compensate a lessor for funds committed to future delivered equipment that remain unused at the end of the commitment period. Usually, the fee is expressed as a percentage of originally estimated equipment cost and is payable in a lump sum at the end of the commitment period. If all or an agreed-upon portion of the funds are used, the lessee owes nothing.

ILLUSTRATIVE EXAMPLE— THE NON-UTILIZATION FEE:

Company A, a leasing company, has agreed to give Company B a lease line of credit for ten river barges. The total cost of the barges will be $1,000,000 and they will be delivered over a twelve month period. Company A, however, has a limited amount of funds available and wants to be sure it will be protected from an opportunity loss if the barges are not delivered or Company B decides not to lease them. Therefore, it imposes a 1% non-utilization fee. If only $400,000 worth of barges are delivered during the commitment period, how much of a fee is due?

Company B would owe Company A $6,000. The amount is calculated by multiplying 1% by the funds remaining unused, $600,000. If none of the equipment was put on lease, Company B would owe $10,000 (1% x $1,000,000). If $1,000,000 worth of equipment was leased, Company B would not owe anything.

A non-utilization fee arrangement has its dangers for a lessee. An unexpectedly high equipment purchase cost (whether from a mistaken estimate or a price escalation) or a delivery delay may give the lessor the right to exclude equipment from the lease. If this happens, a lessee may end up paying a non-utilization fee based on the unused funds remaining at the end of the commitment period. It is not, however, generally considered unreasonable, in cases other than where a lessor could arbitrarily choose not to lease certain agreed-upon equipment when it arrives, for the lessee to bear this type of risk.

RECOMMENDATION:

A prospective lessee confronted with having to agree to a non-utilization fee arrangement can lessen the risk of incorrect cost estimates or delivery delay causing a payment obligation by requesting a commitment percentage leeway. In other words, providing for the fee to be payable only to the extent that, say, greater than 10% of the funds are not used.

The commitment fee approach is a more commonly used compensation technique. Under such an arrangement a lessee must pay a flat fee based upon the total equipment cost involved for the commitment. Generally, the fee is payable at the time the lease is entered into and is expressed as a percentage of total cost. Fees of ⅜ to ½ of 1% of equipment cost are common. Since the commitment fee pays a lessor for holding his funds available, the lessee can freely elect not to put equipment on lease.

OBSERVATION:

In a competitive lease market, non-utilization fees and commitment fees can be extremely difficult for prospective lessors to impose. This is due to the fact that there will always be lessors willing to hold funds available without a fee in order to win business.

c. Certain Minimum Acceptance Requirements Can Cause Problems for a Lessee

When a lease transaction involves many low dollar cost items of equipment to be delivered over a long period of time, a lessor may require a minimum equipment acceptance grouping. For example, a lessee may not be able to accept equipment for lease in aggregate cost groups of less than $100,000. The purpose of the minimum dollar grouping is to reduce the lessor's administrative handling expenses.

An equipment grouping requirement can cause serious problems for a lessee. For example, if the dollar minimum were set high, the lessee may have to manipulate deliveries in order to avoid having equipment sit idle until the specified amount is accumulated. If delivery times cannot be appropriately adjusted, the equipment may have to be stored, a result which may be impractical from a business needs standpoint. If a lessee is obligated to indemnify a lessor for any tax benefits lost, having to let equipment remain idle may also create problems. When equipment ready for use is not immediately put into service, there is a risk it may be deemed technically "used" for depreciation and investment tax credit purposes when it finally goes on lease.

RECOMMENDATION:

When a prospective lessee is confronted with a minimum dollar amount equipment grouping requirement, it is advisable for it to negotiate a "best efforts" qualification. In other words, if after using its best efforts to assemble the required minimum it becomes impractical to do so, it will be permitted to have a smaller amount accepted.

5. The Period of the Lessee's Use Is Fundamental

The length of time the lessee will have the right to use the equipment is as fundamental an issue as how much rent he must pay. The period of permissible use usually involves two segments—(1) a main lease term, generally referred to as the "base lease term," the "primary lease term," or the "initial lease term," and (2) a renewal term. Some transactions also call for an "interim lease term," which runs from the time the equipment becomes subject to lease until the start of a predetermined base term. The interim term concept is frequently used when many items of equipment will go on lease at various times. For example, the base term may start on January 1, 19X0 for all equipment delivering during the prior three month period. By consolidating the start dates of the primary lease terms there will be less administrative work.

> RECOMMENDATION:
>
> Prospective lessees and lessors sometimes fail to pay sufficient attention to their renewal period rights. For example, a prospective lessee may inadvertently be given an open-ended right to renew the lease *indefinitely*. As a result the lessor may be unable to take advantage of a favorable re-sale market at the end of the lease.
>
> From the lessee's viewpoint, the renewal period arrangement is frequently not as flexible as it should be. For example, instead of a right to renew the lease for one four-year period, a program in which the lease could be renewed, at the lessee's option, for four one-year periods, two two-year periods, a three-year period followed by a one-year period, or a one-year period followed by a three-year period is more ideal. This would give the lessee more opportunity to play the rental market, using a shorter renewal period if the rates are high and a longer period if the rates are low. A lessor, of course, has to be careful not to lose too much control because its interest may be opposite to that of the lessee's. For example, in a high rent market the longest possible renewal term may be more desirable.

6. The Rent Payment Structure Must Be Included

When the rent is due and *how much* the lessee must pay are key elements of every lease transaction. These obligations should be clearly set forth in detail in the lease. For example, a 10 year lease transaction may call for rent to be payable in twenty consecutive, level, semi-annual in arrears payments, each payment to be equal to 2% of the total cost of the equipment.

Where the rent is payable, such as at the lessor's place of business; the *form of payment*, such as in immediately available funds; and *when it is to be deemed received by the lessor*, such as when deposited in a U.S. mailbox, are also important issues. Unfortunately, they are sometimes given little attention. Unless they are specified, a lessee runs the risk of a lessor claiming a technical default based on what the lessor deems to be an incorrect or late payment. A lessor, on the other hand, runs the risk of losing interest it could have earned had the rent been paid in a manner which would have permitted an earlier use of the money. For example, having the rent paid in immediately available funds as opposed to by regular check which would take time to clear.

RECOMMENDATION:

Lessees should establish appropriate internal rent payment procedures in order to avoid technical defaults through, for example, accidental late payments. If the rent must be sent to a special P.O.Box number, all individuals responsible for handling the payments should be *separately* advised so that the rent does not instead get sent to the lessor's regular business address.

Frequently, the rent payment is expressed as a percentage of equipment cost, as opposed to a specific dollar amount, particularly when equipment is to be delivered after the lease is signed. By doing this the rent does not have to be recalculated and the lease amended if the purchase price varies from that anticipated. For example, if the annual rent is expressed as 2% of equipment cost, changes in cost will not require a lease rate adjustment. If, on the other hand, the rent is fixed at $2000 per year based upon a $100,000 item of equipment and the price actually turns out to be $105,000 after the lease is executed, a lease amendment would be necessary to incorporate the proper rent.

When the rent is based upon a percentage of equipment cost, the parties sometimes fail to define what may be included, or "capitalized," in the "cost" term. If a prospective lessor has a lot of money available, he may be eager to include as much as possible into the rent computation cost base. For example, he may readily pay for sales taxes, freight charges, and installation costs. If, however, his money supply is limited, he may want to spread his funds over as many different deals as possible. As a result, he will probably be unwilling to include the "extras." Further, when "soft" costs, such as installation costs, are substantial in relation to the raw equipment purchase price, a prospective lessor may not be willing to exceed a certain dollar amount on such costs because to do so would lessen his collateral value protection. For example, if the installation costs were financed by the lessor and they ran 25% of the raw equipment cost, the lessor's collateral position would be diluted. In other words, 25% of the total amount financed would relate to installation charges which would have no re-marketing value.

RECOMMENDATION:

The equipment related cost items which a prospective lessor is willing to finance can vary with each transaction. A prospective lessee should, therefore, define the ground rules in the proposal letter stage in order to eliminate potential misunderstandings or misconceptions.

When a prospective lessor's economic return depends at least in part on anticipated equipment ownership tax benefits, he will want to be able to make rent adjustments if unexpected tax law changes occur which adversely affect his return. For example, he may incorporate a provision which would allow him to adjust the rent so that his *"yield and after-tax cash flows"* are maintained. Instead of a yield and after-tax cash flow, a maintenance of *earnings* or *net return* standard is sometimes used.

RECOMMENDATIONS:

I. A prospective lessor, in addition to being able to make rent adjustments in the event of adverse tax law changes, should also have the ability to make appropriate adjustments to values which are based on the rent, such as termination values or stipulated loss values. Without being able to adjust these rent-related values, the financial integrity of the transaction may not be maintained in the event, for example, of an early termination or a casualty loss.

II. A prospective lessee should always make sure any lessor rent adjustment criterion is clearly defined. Terms such as *yield* or *earnings,* for example, do not have standard meanings and, as a result, can be subject to many interpretations. The exact formula to be used in making any adjustment should be set forth in the lease. This will enable an independent verification of any of the lessor's computations.

III. If a lessor has the right to adjust the rent up in the event of an adverse change in the tax laws in order to compensate for any loss, a lessee should request the right to have the rent adjusted downward if there is a tax law change which is economically *favorable* to the lessor. If, for example, there is an increase in the investment tax credit, the lessee should be entitled to a rent reduction to reflect the added benefit to the lessor.

Although it is not always practical or reasonably necessary to do so, it is sometimes useful for the parties to determine in advance what the rents and rent related values will be when a tax benefit change is likely and put them in the lease agreement. In this way everyone knows how they would stand and any problem can be worked out before a final commitment is made. For example, if the investment credit percentage is 10% when the transaction is negotiated but the parties anticipate it may be changed to 7% before all the equipment is delivered, it would be advisable to incorporate two rental rates, one based upon a 10% investment credit and one based upon a 7% investment credit. The change may actually vary from that expected and, therefore, the formula for making the adjustments should be included as well.

a. A Hell or High Water Condition Sometimes Causes Concern

In many equipment leases, particularly finance leases, the lessee's rent obligation is absolute and unconditional. That is, the rent must be paid in full and on time regardless of any claim the lessee may have against the lessor. The obligation is commonly referred to as a "hell or high water" obligation and at first sight shocks many new prospective lessees. The provision is not as bad as it seems because it does not prevent a lessee from independently bringing a lawsuit against the lessor on any claim.

RECOMMENDATION:

Although not technically necessary, it is good form for a prospective lessee to have a statement inserted in a hell or high water provision to the effect that any rights of action it may have for damages caused by the lessor will exist regardless of the hell or high water rent commitment.

Typically, a lessor incorporates a hell or high water provision when he wants to leverage his investment through the use of a nonrecourse loan. With such a provision, a lender is more likely to lend on a nonrecourse-to-lessor basis because potential claims against the lessor would not affect the rental stream which is being relied on for the loan repayment.

OBSERVATIONS:

I. The use of nonrecourse debt as opposed to recourse debt is the most desirable way for a lessor to leverage a lease transaction. For financial reporting purposes the nonrecourse nature permits a lessor to disregard the loan obligation on its books because the lender may only look to the lessee and the collateral for repayment, not to general funds of the lessor.

II. Sometimes a lessor's general lending banks require hell or high water lease provisions to be included in all leases written by the lessor. The requirement is generally written in the lending agreement and is usually coupled with a right to require an assignment of all of the lessor's rights under each lease, including the right to the rent payments, as an additional form of security for their loans.

7. It Is Advisable for a Lessor to Get Certain Reports

The necessity for the various possible lessee reports depends on each transaction. It is usually advisable, however, for a prospective lessor to at least require financial reports, accident reports, lease conformity reports, equipment location reports, and third-party claim reports. These will enable him to stay on top of a transaction.

a. Financial Reports

One of the best methods for a lessor to monitor a lessee's financial condition during the lease term is to require financial reports, such as current balance sheets and profit and loss statements, to be periodically submitted. With these, a lessor will be in a good position to spot potential financial problems and take whatever early action may be necessary to protect his investment.

RECOMMENDATIONS:

I. A prospective lessor should require quarterly, as well as annual, balance sheets and profit and loss statements. Each should be certified by an independent public accounting firm.

II. A prospective lessee should insure that the time between that period when the information is gathered and when a financial report is due is adequate for its preparation and submission in order to avoid a potential default situation.

b. Accident Reports

A lessor should receive *immediate* notification of *every* significant or potentially significant accident in which his equipment is involved, whether the damage is to the equipment itself or to persons or other property. It is not uncommon, for example, for a lessor to be sued solely on the basis of his ownership interest. Therefore, lessee accident reports are a must. They should be in writing and contain a summary of the incident, including the time, place, and nature of the accident, and the persons and property involved. Reviewing all incidents may be a tedious job, particularly when many items of equipment are on lease, but it can prevent some costly surprises.

RECOMMENDATIONS:

I. When an accident could involve major dollar liability, the lessee should be required to immediately notify the lessor by telephone in addition to submitting a written report. A lessor's early arrival on the scene can produce facts which would otherwise be lost.

II. A prospective lessee should limit his accident notification responsibility to only incidents involving serious accidents. Minor accidents can create an unnecessary volume of paperwork. One approach is to set an estimated damage dollar amount below which notification is not required. The problem with this for a lessor is that the lessee may incorrectly estimate the potential liability and the lessor may not hear about a major claim until it is served with a summons.

c. Lease Conformity Reports

Lessors sometimes require lessees to annually submit an officer's certificate stating whether any events of default under the lease have occurred during the reporting year and whether there were any conditions that could result in an event of default after the lapse of time. If there are any, an appropriate factual summary must accompany the certificate. From a lessor's viewpoint, this type of report can be a good early warning technique. From a lessee's viewpoint, although they are somewhat of a burden, they are useful in avoiding inadvertent lease default situations.

d. Equipment Location Reports.

Requiring a lessee to prepare and submit equipment location reports is frequently advisable and sometimes necessary. Where practical a lessor should periodically inspect the leased equipment, particularly when the lessee has an obligation to maintain it. If the location is known, it is easy to "drop in" to check up on its condition. Reports of this nature may be essential if a lessor intends to keep any security interest or other collateral protection filings up to date. A change in location sometimes necessitates a new filing.

RECOMMENDATIONS:

I. When security interest filings are deemed necessary, the lessee should be required to notify the lessor at least 45 days *prior* to a change of equipment location to allow sufficient time to make any additional filings or amendments to existing filings.

II. Many lessors do not conduct equipment inspections. However, they should be made, particularly when the lessee must maintain the equipment. It is not unheard of for lessees burdened with stringent maintenance requirements to fail to live up to their obligations. Poorly maintained equipment provides poor collateral protection.

e. Third-Party Claim Reports

Theoretically, the fact that a lessor can take his equipment back if the lessee defaults under a lease puts a lessor in a very secure position. However, tax liens or other third-party claims imposed on the equipment, viable or not, can seriously jeopardize this protected position. Therefore, a lessor must be kept informed through third-party claim reports of any events which result, or *could* result, in such an imposition so that he will have the opportunity to best protect his position and equipment.

f. Other Reports

It is always a good idea for a prospective lessor to impose a general reporting requirement. In other words, a lessor should be able to require a lessee to submit reports which are determined to be necessary in the future, even though they were not specifically contemplated when the lease was entered into.

RECOMMENDATION:

Prospective lessees should make sure any general reporting obligation is qualified to the extent that only information relevant to the lease transaction can be requested.

8. The Equipment Maintenance Responsibility Should Be Designed

Depending on the type of lease arrangement involved, the lessor *or* the lessee will have some or all of the responsibility for maintaining the equipment in working order. Net finance leases, for example, put the normal maintenance responsibilities on the lessee. Regardless of the arrangement, however, the maintenance issue should be specifically addressed in the lease. Improperly maintained equipment can easily ruin the economics of a transaction.

The *condition* in which the equipment will have to be maintained is an integral part of the maintenance issue. For example, a lessor may want the lessee to keep the equipment in "good working order, ordinary wear and tear excepted." Standards such as this can create problems because they are somewhat vague. For example, a lessor could claim that the wear and tear on returned equipment was greater than "ordinary" and therefore the lessee must pay for appropriate repairs. On the same basis, the lessee may legitimately feel that it was ordinary. Unfortunately, there are no easy answers. Specific guidelines are difficult to define. Limiting dealings to responsible parties will help considerably.

RECOMMENDATIONS:

I. If a prospective lessee will use equipment in high wear and tear operations and if it is responsible to keep the equipment in "good working condition, ordinary wear and tear excepted," it should consider having the standard qualified because the intended usage may per se cause excessive wear and tear. One solution is to have the obligation limited to ordinary wear and tear *for the use intended by the lessee.*

II. To help protect against a lessor's unwarranted claim for damages due to violations of the maintenance standards imposed, a lessee should institute proper maintenance procedures. One of the best approaches is to make sure any maintenance instructions issued by an equipment manufacturer are followed.

Particular care must be taken when special maintenance will be required. Aircraft maintenance, for example, is governed by regulatory standards put out by the Federal Aviation Administration. Unless they are met, the aircraft may not be permitted to be flown and, in addition, may provide good grounds for a lawsuit in the event of an accident.

RECOMMENDATION:

Expert advice should always be sought in specialized maintenance situations. Parties negotiating lease agreements frequently do not fully appreciate the cost effect of a proposed maintenance arrangement and, as a result, fail to adequately protect themselves.

a. Maintenance Records Are a Good Idea

When a lessee is responsible for equipment maintenance, he should also be required to keep maintenance records and make them available to the lessor. By reviewing these records, a lessor can quickly determine at any time whether the equipment is being properly serviced. Although sometimes a burden for a lessee, good records can be a valuable aid against any erroneous inadequate maintenance allegation raised by a lessor.

RECOMMENDATION:

If the lease agreement permits the lessor **access to maintenance** records, a prospective lessee should limit the access to normal business hours.

b. When Equipment Alterations Will Be Permitted Should Be Agreed Upon

A lessor should have the right to prohibit a lessee from making any equipment alteration not related to normal maintenance. Of particular concern would be those which could adversely affect the equipment's market value, such as, for example, additions which would impair its originally intended use or which could not be removed without so impairing its use. Generally, this is handled by a lessor by making the lessee get its prior written consent to a proposed change.

RECOMMENDATION:

A prospective lessor may want to provide that any device installed on its equipment, whether or not through repair, will become its property if it cannot be removed without impairing the originally intended function or use. On the other hand, a prospective lessee should specifically preserve title to items which it installs at its own expense and which can be removed without causing such an impairment.

9. The Lessor's Ownership Should Be Specifically Protected

There are certain basic possession, use, and operational conditions which may be necessary for a lessor to impose in order to protect its ownership interest in the leased equipment. This section will be devoted to a discussion of the most essential considerations.

a. Certain Filings May Be Essential

There are situations when special filings will be required or conservatively necessary. An aircraft lessor, for example, must make certain filings with the Federal Aviation Administration to protect his ownership position. In some cases it may not be practical for the lessor to handle the filings directly, such as when he does not have the staff to do the job, and the burden can reasonably be put on the lessee for making them. In other situations a lessor should not risk relying on the lessee to take care of the filings, such as when they are deemed necessary to secure the lessor's interest in the equipment against potential third-party creditors of the lessee. Uniform

Commercial Code security interest filings are a good example. If the responsibility was put on the lessee in this case and the filings were not made, the lessor would not have the security protection it wanted. A decision, therefore, to rely on the lessee to take care of any necessary or appropriate filings should be carefully considered, particularly when the lack of fulfillment could result in fines, assessments, or collateral protection problems.

If a lessor feels it must rely on the lessee to make any desired filings, is there a way it can limit its risk? Yes, the lessor can require the lessee to promptly confirm that the designated action has been taken. Obligating a lessee to pay for any out-of-pocket losses incurred will also help, however, it will not compensate the lessor for any distraction from its ongoing business activities resulting from the failure.

b. An Equipment Marking Requirement Is Useful

A lessee should be required to mark the leased equipment with the lessor's name and its principal place of business. Marking the assets has two basic benefits for a lessor. First, it will be of assistance in the event it has to defend against a creditor of the lessee trying to claim the equipment for the *lessee's* unpaid debts. Second, it will enable a lessor to more readily identify his equipment during an inspection trip or in the event a reclaiming action is necessary.

ILLUSTRATIVE LANGUAGE—
OWNERSHIP MARKING:

"White Leasing Corporation, Owner-Lessor, San Francisco, California."

c. Certain Broad Use Prohibitions Are Advisable

A lessee should be prohibited from "using, operating, maintaining, or storing the leased equipment carelessly, improperly, in violation of law, or in a manner other than contemplated by the manufacturer." If, for example, the equipment is damaged by improper handling or storing, or the lessor becomes responsible to a third party for damages caused through any of these actions, it would then have a good basis for making a claim against the lessee.

RECOMMENDATIONS:

I. Because of the scope of some general usage prohibitions, a lessee can easily find itself in technical default for relatively minor violations. A prospective lessee should, therefore, attempt to define the parameters more specifically, such as pinpointing the exact laws with which it must comply.

II. Lessees prohibited from using equipment other than in conformity with the manner contemplated by the manufacturer can unknowingly run into trouble. Frequently, equipment is acquired for a use different than originally built because, for example, nothing else is available. In such a case, a prospective lessee should attempt to get a *use exception*. That is, a specific authorization to use it as necessary.

10. The <u>Lessor</u> Should Require Certain Key Assurances

There are certain key representations which a prospective lessee should be asked to make on matters related to a lease transaction. The representations should be given as true on the date of the execution of the lease document and, where relevant, should also be ongoing during the lease period. The failure of any to be as stated should be specified as grounds for the lessor to declare an event of default under the lease and enable it to get out of its commitments.

a. That the Lessee Is Legally in Existence

Whether or not the lessee is legally in existence can be a crucial issue. The prospective lessor must assure itself through an appropriate lessee representation that the entity it is entering into the lease agreement with, i.e., the prospective lessee, actually exists. A corporate lessee should, for example, be required to represent that it is properly *organized, validly existing,* and in *good standing* under the laws of its state of incorporation and that it is duly authorized to do business in those states where the equipment will be used. If it is not, the lessor may have a difficult time bringing the lessee into court if it becomes necessary to do so. In addition, any lack of proper legal standing may result in a seizure of the equipment by the state authorities. Very simply, the lessor's secured position could be jeopardized.

b. That the Lessee Has the Transactional Authority to Enter into the Lease

It is important for a lessor to have a representation from the lessee that it has been duly authorized to enter into the lease transaction and that the parties executing the lease, by name or official title, have been fully authorized to sign on its behalf. For example, if the lessee is a corporation and it had not been properly empowered by its board of directors to make the lease commitment, a lessor may be unable to enforce the agreement against the corporation. The lessor's only recourse may be against the individual executing the lease "on behalf of the corporation." Since it is unlikely that the signing party, in his individual right, would have enough personal wealth to satisfy any substantive claim, the lessor would be in a precarious position.

OBSERVATION:

It should be remembered that the mere fact that a lessee gives a representation as to a particular point does not mean it is true as stated. If, however, a falsehood is deemed an event of default, the lessor would have the ability to reclaim the equipment.

c. That There Are No Conflicting Agreements

Existing agreements may place restrictions on a prospective lessee's ability to enter into a lease transaction. A bank credit agreement, for example, could prevent the borrower from taking out additional loans without the lender's consent. If "loans" are defined to include lease obligations, the failure to secure the lender's consent would most likely be treated as a loan default. Typically, if there is a loan default, the lender would have the right to demand an immediate repayment of the outstanding money, which in turn could adversely effect a lessee's financial condition. Any lessening of the lessee's financial strength may jeopardize its ability to meet its lease obligations. A lessee should, therefore, be required to represent that by entering into the lease agreement it is not violating any existing credit or other agreements.

d. That All Necessary Regulatory Approvals Have Been Obtained

It may be necessary for a prospective lessee to secure regulatory approval with respect to certain aspects of a lease transaction. For example, a public utility may be required to clear certain lease commitments with the appropriate utility regulatory authority. If they are not cleared, the commitments may be unenforceable. It is essential, therefore, that a lessor get a representation that all necessary regulatory approvals have been obtained or, if none are needed, that no such approvals are required.

RECOMMENDATIONS:

1. Because of the regulatory complexities existing in certain industries, such as the public utility industry, it may be wise for a prospective lessor to independently verify that all necessary regulatory aspects have been complied with, rather than relying

on the lessee's representation or its counsel's opinion. An error will more than likely be a major problem. The fact that the lessor can reclaim the equipment if a misrepresentation is deemed an event of default is not always the best answer. The expense and time involved in getting the equipment back combined with the problem of having to dispose of, for example, 100 heavy duty used trucks at a reasonable price can present serious practical problems. Securing a favorable opinion from independent counsel expert in the area is good but it is not an "ironclad" solution. The safest course of action, if possible, is to get the appropriate regulatory authority to issue a favorable written opinion on the relevant issues.

II. Regulatory approval processes frequently take a substantial period of time. In order to avoid major delays, a prospective lessee should start the process as early as possible so that, if necessary, it will be in a position to deliver the necessary assurances at the lease closing, such as supplying certified copies of any approvals obtained.

e. That There Are No Adverse Proceedings

A lessor would certainly want a representation that there are no pending or threatened legal or administrative proceedings of which the lessor is not aware and which could adversely affect the lessee's operations or financial condition. For example, it is not inconceivable for an impending lawsuit to be potentially serious enough to bankrupt a company. If it comes to a lessor's attention after the lease is signed, a no adverse proceeding representation would allow a lessor to terminate the transaction.

RECOMMENDATIONS:

I. It is sometimes impossible for a prospective lessee to be aware of all threatened lawsuits or similar proceedings, particularly those involving minor incidents. Therefore, a no adverse proceeding representation should be qualified to the effect that there are no proceedings which would have a *material* adverse impact on its operations or financial condition *of which it is aware.*

II. A no adverse proceeding representation, from a lessor's viewpoint, should be broad enough to cover not only the lessee but also its subsidiaries and affiliated companies. Any negative financial impact on a related company could affect the lessee's financial condition.

f. That the Lessee's Financial Statements Are Accurate

Since the lessee's financial condition is a critical consideration in a lessor's credit analysis, the lessor should have a representation that all financial statements delivered to the lessor, including those prepared by the lessee's outside accountants, accurately represent its financial condition. Such a representation should be requested *whether or not the statements have been certified by the lessee's independent accountants.* If, for example, a mistake were made, the lessor could reassess its willingness to continue with the transaction when it is discovered.

11. The <u>Lessee</u> Should Require Certain Key Assurances

All too often *lessees* neglect to have *lessors* provide them with fundamental assurances as to their lease obligations. This may be due to the fact that in many cases lessors essentially do nothing more than supply the financing. Serious consideration, however, should be given to incorporating certain key lessor representations in the lease.

a. That the Lessor Has the Transactional Authority to Lease the Equipment

Even though a prospective lessor presents itself to the public as being in the leasing business, certain external restrictions existing, for example, in a credit agreement may prohibit it from entering into particular types of transactions. In addition, a prospective lessor may have to go through prescribed internal procedures before a lease is in fact an authorized transaction. A violation of any such restrictions or procedures could jeopardize the lessee's right to the continued use of the equipment. Of course, an appropriate representation from a lessor will not *guarantee* there will be no use interference, but it will provide the lessee with another ground on which to base a claim in the event of a problem.

In underwritten transactions the lessor-investors, "equity participants," are frequently not "in the leasing business" per se. Many corporations, for example, invest in leases on an irregular basis, and if a transaction does not have *all* of the appropriate internal approvals, a lessee may have some enforceability problems. In such a case if a lessor backs out, a lessee may try to sue for performance on the basis that the lessor should be held to the contract based on its *apparent* authority to enter into the lease. If a lessor-investor is involved who is not regularly in the leasing market this possible ground may be unavailable. Therefore, it is important in underwritten transactions for a lessee to secure a representation that the transaction has been duly authorized by the lessor-investor.

b. That the Equipment Will Be Paid For

The lease agreement should contain a statement by the lessor, particularly when it is executed in advance of equipment deliveries, that it *will* pay for and lease the agreed upon equipment to the lessee. Of course, a firm commitment will not guarantee that funds will be available, but it will assist in a legal action for damages in the event the lessor does not follow through. Any such commitment by the lessor will, undoubtedly, be subject to the lessee fulfilling certain obligations, such as equipment inspection and acceptance. As long as the conditions are within the lessee's capability they should not be of concern.

RECOMMENDATIONS:

I. A lessor payment commitment representation becomes of particular importance when a prospective lessee is dealing with smaller, less well financed leasing companies. It cannot, however, be relied on exclusively if the dollar amount of the equipment involved is significant, or last minute funding problems could cause a budgeting disruption. Therefore, the reputation and financial background of a prospective lessor should be investigated in order to insure that funding risk is at a minimum. A cheaper rental rate from a lesser known leasing company, or equity participant in the case of an underwritten transaction, will quickly lose its attractiveness if the funds are not available when needed.

II. It is advisable for a lessee to have a representation from the lessor that the equipment will be, and will remain, free of all liens and encumbrances, except those of which the lessee is aware, such as the debt in a leveraged lease. The intent is to attempt to make sure there will be no interference with the lessee's use from third-party creditors of the lessor.

c. That There Will Be No Interference with the Equipment's Use

A lessee's right to the quiet enjoyment and peaceful possession of the equipment during the lease period is a fundamental lessee right, provided, of course, the lessee is not in default under the lease. A prospective lessee should require a representation to that effect.

RECOMMENDATION:

A prospective lessor should limit any quiet enjoyment obligation to that of not "interfering" with the lessee's use, as opposed to stating the lessee will be entitled to quiet enjoyment, in effect a guarantee. If it is not so qualified, a lessor may be liable for damages if an unrelated third party, not claiming directly or indirectly through the lessor, interferes with the lessee's use of the equipment.

12. The Lessor Should Disclaim Certain Product Responsibility

If the lessor is not also the equipment vendor, he will not typically be responsible to the lessee for anything that goes wrong with the equipment. However, to be on the safe side, a lessor should make an appropriate product warranty disclaimer to prevent any possible exposure to a lessee for defects in the equipment's design, suitability, operation, fitness for use, or merchantability. The disclaimer should not cause any concern to a prospective lessee since it can rely on the usual manufacturer's, sub-contractor's, or supplier's product warranties.

13. It Is Advisable for the Lessee to Get An Assignment of Product Warranties

Since in many lease situations the lessor will not supply the equipment, the likelihood of its being responsible for product defects is remote. If this is the case and if the lessee cannot end the lease without a penalty, a defect which reduces the equipment's efficiency or which interferes with its use can be a costly problem. Therefore, a prospective lessee should ask for an assignment of any rights which the prospective lessor would have as equipment owner against any manufacturer, sub-contractor, or supplier during the lease term. If these rights are not assignable because, for example, of a warranty restriction, a lessee should have the power to obligate the lessor to sue on its behalf if it deems it necessary.

RECOMMENDATIONS:

I. If a prospective lessee finds it necessary to have the right to require the prospective lessor to sue in the name of the lessor because, for example, the product warranty rights cannot be assigned, it should be coupled with the right to control the action, including the selection of counsel and the grounds of the lawsuit.

II. If a prospective lessor agrees to allow the prospective lessee to be able to require it to sue on its behalf, it should also specify the extent of its obligation to pay all the legal expenses. Generally, these will be the lessee's responsibility.

14. The Ownership of Equipment Replacements, Additions, and Alterations Should Be Designated

The guidelines for dealing with equipment replacements, additions, and alterations should be clearly established. This includes what consents are necessary, who must or may do them, and which party will have legal title.

A question sometimes arises when the lessee must replace any part necessary for good equipment operation or maintenance as to who owns the replacement. Generally, it is agreed that title will vest in the lessor. What if the change is not necessary for good maintenance or operation, such as when the lessee adds a part to improve the equipment's usefulness to him? Typically, title will remain with the lessee provided the item can be removed without damage to the equipment.

RECOMMENDATION:

A prospective lessor should specifically prohibit a prospective lessee from making any replacements, alterations, or additions which are not required by the lease and which could adversely affect the equipment's fair market value.

15. The Party with the Risk of Loss Should Be Specified

It is not uncommon for the risk of equipment loss, whether due to damage, theft, requisition, or confiscation, to be placed on the lessee. Net finance leases, for example, frequently require the lessee to guarantee that the lessor will receive a minimum amount of money, usually referred to as the "stipulated loss value" or "casualty value," if there is an equipment loss. The stipulated loss value, which decreases as the lease term runs, is calculated so the lessor will not have to report a loss on its books. The obligation basically puts the lessee in the position of ultimate insurer.

RECOMMENDATIONS:

I. Whenever a stipulated loss obligation is imposed, a prospective lessee should:
   (i) request an offset for any insurance proceeds or other awards resulting from the loss, and
   (ii) make sure its obligations, including rent, under the lease as to the affected equipment terminate as of the date of loss.

II. When a stipulated loss provision is incorporated, a prospective lessee should insist upon a clear definition of the term "loss" since it can be susceptible to various interpretations. Generally, unless a *defined* loss has occurred, the rent must continue with the possible result that the lessee would be paying on unusable equipment. Typically, "loss" means destruction to the extent the equipment is no longer usable by the lessee. It is also worth noting that loss for the *use intended* may be somewhat less than *actual total destruction.* Therefore, a prospective lessee should be careful in agreeing to the ground rules.

III. If a prospective lessee will be required to repair equipment damaged by a third party at its own expense, it should insist upon the right to claim any money received, at least up to the costs incurred, from the party causing the damage.

16. Spell Out How Certain General Taxes Will Be Treated

In a typical net financial lease, the lessee will be responsible for paying taxes, such as sales, property, and rental taxes, imposed by any local, state, or Federal taxing authority. A prospective lessee should take into account any tax payment obligations when determining its effective leasing cost. Some taxes can be significant.

RECOMMENDATIONS:

I. Frequently, lease agreements require a lessee to pay equipment related taxes which, by law, the lessor is obligated to pay. If a lessor is improperly assessed by a taxing authority and refuses to institute a proceeding to correct the problem, the lessee may have to pay an incorrect assessment. Therefore, a prospective lessee should request a right to be able to have any tax assessment contested or reviewed.

II. At times a lessee will not be able to contest a tax imposition in its own name and will have negotiated the right to require the lessor to contest it in the lessor's name. In such a situation the lessor should be able to require that the lessee deliver an opinion from its counsel setting forth a legitimate basis for the action before it has the obligation to proceed. It should also be in a position of being able to require the lessee to put up a reasonable amount of money in advance to cover the expenses.

a. Tax Imposition Notifications Are a Must

Each party to a lease agreement should have an obligation to timely notify the other party of the *potential* or *actual* imposition of any taxes or similar assessments on the equipment. This will allow the interested party to be able to participate at the earliest possible time.

17. If a "True" Lease Is Intended, the Document
Should Assure This

Generally speaking, the parties to a lease will want the transaction to be classified as a "true" lease for Federal income tax purposes. It is absolutely essential, therefore, that the lease document be drafted to insure that the desired tax treatment will not be endangered.

If a "lease" does not qualify as a true tax lease, the lessor probably has the greatest exposure. An alternate classification would undoubtedly result in a loss of the ownership tax benefits, such as depreciation and investment tax credit. Because such a loss can turn a favorable transaction into a highly unfavorable one, sophisticated lessors try to build protections into the lease documentation in two basic ways—prohibiting inconsistent actions and filings and requiring tax indemnifications.

a. Inconsistent Actions And Filings Should Be Prohibited.

Lessees should be generally prohibited from taking any action or filing any documents, including income tax returns, which would be inconsistent with the true lease intent. Normally, this is not a problem for lessees since by doing so they could lose their right to deduct the rent charges as an operating expense—usually one reason the transaction was structured as a lease to begin with.

b. Tax Indemnifications—a Way to Protect
A Lessor's Economics

The availability of certain basic equipment ownership Federal income tax benefits, investment tax credit, depreciation, and, in the case of leveraged leases, interest on third-party debt, to a lessor is an essential factor in the economic viability of many types of equipment leases, particularly finance leases. A loss of any one can have a severe adverse impact on the lessor's lease economics. Because of this, lessors attempt to protect themselves against such problems through *tax indemnification* provisions. Typically, these provisions require the lessee to pay the lessor an amount of money which, *after taxes*, will put him in the same economic position as before the loss.

Tax Indemnification provisions can be extremely complex and, in order to properly assess their effect and workability, one must understand how the ownership tax benefits can be lost. Basically, there are three ways. One is through acts or omissions of the *lessor*. Another is through acts or omissions of the *lessee*. The third way is through a *change in law*. Generally, lessors try to put the economic burden of a loss or inability to claim all of the expected tax benefits on the lessees, regardless of the cause. Lessees, however, object to assuming the entire burden and, as a result, a compromise is usually reached.

There is usually little argument that a lessor is justified in making the lessee pay for economic losses which are caused by the lessee. Who should be responsible for losses arising through changes in the tax law is a tougher issue. Typically, which party bears this risk depends on who is in a better negotiating position. In situations where the lease transaction is marginally profitable, a lessor is less inclined to take the risk.

What about tax benefit losses resulting from the lessor's own acts or omissions? It seems that there are few, if any, instances when a lessor could justify imposing the responsibility for any such loss on the lessee. Lessors do, however, sometimes get lessees, particularly inexperienced ones, to assume this risk.

RECOMMENDATIONS:

I. There is one *lessor* tax indemnification area frequently overlooked—the investment tax credit "pass through" situation. That is, when the lessee will be entitled to claim the investment credit on the leased equipment. If the lessee can not claim the credit because, for example, the lessor failed to take the required steps under the Internal Revenue Code to pass it through, its effective cost to lease the equipment would go up significantly. Therefore, the *lessor* should be required to indemnify the *lessee* against any investment credit loss caused by the lessor.

II. A prospective lessor should limit any investment credit indemnity responsibility in a "pass through" situation to its own acts or omissions. It would not be prudent to assume the burden of credit unavailability because of the lessee's own acts or omissions. Although not as clear cut, the change in law risk may also more appropriately belong on the lessee, the party claiming the credit.

(1) A Way for a Lessee to Limit Its Tax Indemnification Risk

A prospective lessee faced with the proposition of having to indemnify a prospective lessor for the loss of or inability to claim any ownership tax advantages, such as the investment tax credit or depreciation benefits, can limit his risk by agreeing to indemnify only for those unavailable due to the lessee's own acts or omissions. By then taking proper precautions, such as insuring that new equipment is not used before it goes on lease, a lessee can virtually eliminate the indemnification payment risk.

RECOMMENDATIONS:

I. If a prospective lessee is successful in getting its tax indemnification responsibility limited to its own acts or omissions, the indemnification provision should be written in a direct manner. In other words, the lessee will indemnify the lessor if, as a result of any of its acts or omissions, the lessor suffers a loss of or inability to claim any or all of the ownership tax benefits. This is as opposed to a provision which states that the lessee will indemnify the lessor for any loss or inability to claim the benefits, except those resulting from acts or omissions of the lessor or changes in law. Although this seems like a fine distinction, it is conceivable that some unforeseen event not fitting within either of the two exclusions could trigger the indemnification.

II. If a prospective lessee cannot limit its tax indemnification exposure to only its acts or omissions, it should at least exclude events which would be within the sole control of the lessor. For example, voluntary dispositions by the lessor, the lessor's failure to timely claim any benefits, and the lessor's failure to have sufficient Federal income tax liability against which to apply any benefits.

(2) The Change In Law Issue Is Tricky

How significant is assuming the risk of tax benefit losses resulting from changes in tax law? To begin with it should be recognized that the "risk" breaks down into a *retroactive* risk and a *prospective* risk. That is, changes which affect equipment already delivered and those which affect equipment arrives or the right to exclude affected equipment. The lessee would then be allowed to exclude the equipment if the rent is too high. Alert prospective lessees usually make sure when a rent adjustment right is given that the lessor will have to make a downward adjustment if there is an increase in the available tax benefits.

OBSERVATION:

Prospective lessees sometimes easily shift the burden of a retroactive change in tax laws to a prospective lessor by arguing that it is a "normal" leasing business risk which a lessor should assume. There is some logic to this position.

What about prospective changes in tax law, those affecting equipment which a lessor has made a commitment to lease but which has not yet been delivered? In this case, the risk does not really have to be assumed by either party. For example, the lessor could be given the right to appropriately adjust the rent upward if there is adverse change in the tax benefits before the equipment arrives or the right to exclude affected equipment. The lessee would then be allowed to exclude the equipment if the rent is too high. Alert prospective lessees usually make sure when a rent adjustment right is given that the lessor will have to make a downward adjustment if there is an increase in the available tax benefits.

RECOMMENDATIONS:

I. Before a prospective lessor agrees to adjust the rents downward if there is an increase in tax benefits affecting future delivered equipment, it should carefully determine whether it can use any increased benefits. If not, a downward adjustment will erode his economic return.

II. As discussed in the above section, the parties, when dealing with the issue of who should bear the risk of a prospective tax law change affecting future delivered equipment, sometimes agree to provide for a rent adjustment as to such equipment and couple it with a mutual exclusionary right if the adjustment is unfavorable. Although the arrangement may be good, certain disadvantages must be considered. A lessor can lose alternate investment opportunities if a lessee excludes equipment at the last minute and a lessee may not have enough time to find substitute lease financing if the lessor exercises its rights.

III. If a prospective lessor excludes equipment under the type of compromise arrangement discussed in Recommendation II above and if a non-utilization fee is imposed based upon any unused dollar commitment, a prospective lessee should ensure that any unused amount excludes the cost of any equipment which is not leased as a result of a lessor's change-in-law exclusion right. If this is not provided for, a lessee will have to pay a fee on funds which remain unused as a result of the lessor's exclusion election.

c. The Tax Loss Payment Formula Should Be Established

When a lease contains a tax indemnification provision the method for determining how much the *indemnifying* party will have to pay the *indemnified* party in the event of a specified loss should be agreed upon. In other words, a tax loss payment formula should be incorporated.

The purpose of tax loss payment formulas is to make the indemnified party "whole" with respect to the loss covered. Typically, these formulas are broad in scope and provide for the payment of an amount of money which, after deduction of all fees, taxes, and/or other charges payable as a result of the indemnification payment, will put the indemnified party in the same economic position as before the loss. In the lessor's case this means his economic return will be maintained. The formulas, however, do sometimes present problems because tax loss measurement can be difficult to translate into a precise and easy to understand format. As a result, in many situations only the most sophisticated tax lawyers can determine their operation and impact.

There are a number of tax loss payment formula structure variations. One common type calls for a loss repayment through a one-time lump-sum payment and another provides for repayment through adjusted remaining rent payments. Many lessors prefer using a lump-sum payment concept when possible because they like to recoup the entire loss as quickly as possible.

ILLUSTRATIVE LANGUAGE—
LUMP SUM PAYMENT

If a final determination is made, by agreement with the Internal Revenue Service or by any final decision (after expiration of time for appeal therefrom of a court of competent jurisdiction [including the United States Tax Court] hereinafter in this Section referred to as a "Final Determination") that the Lessor shall not have or shall lose (by recapture or otherwise) the right to claim, or there shall be disallowed any portion of, the Investment Credit, the Lessee shall pay to the Lessor as liquidated damages (for loss of bargain and not as a penalty) within thirty days of such Final Determination an amount equal to the sum of:

(a) The quotient of (i) the difference between 10 percent of the Capitalized Cost of the Equipment which is not currently deducted in computing taxable income (or the total investment credit previously allowed the Lessor if there has been a previous Final Determination with respect to the Equipment) and the investment credits with respect to the Equipment which are allowed to Lessor (before taking into account any limitation on the amount of such credit based on the income tax liability of the affiliated group with which the Lessor files a consolidated Federal income tax return) divided by (ii) that percentage which is the difference between (A) 100 percent and (B) the sum of (x) the highest effective Federal income tax and/or excess profits tax rate generally applicable to domestic corporations for the taxable year of the Lessor in which such Final Determination is made including therein the effect of any applicable surtax, surcharge and/or any other Federal tax or charge related to net income or excess profits, or related to any tax on net income or excess profits) (hereinafter in this Section referred to as the "Federal Tax Rate"), plus (y) the highest effective generally applicable rate of tax imposed by California on net income and/or excess profits of a California corporation engaged in business solely within the State of California for the taxable year of the Lessor in which such Final Determination is made (including therein the effect of any applicable surtax, surcharge and/or any other California tax or charge related to net income or excess profits or related to any tax on net income or excess profits) multiplied by that percentage which is the difference between 100 percent and the Federal Tax Rate for such year (hereinafter referred to as the "State Tax Rate"), plus

(b) (i) any penalties required to be paid by the Lessor with respect to such Final Determination divided by that percentage which is the difference between (A) 100 percent and (B) the sum of (x) the Federal Tax Rate plus (y) the State Tax Rate and (ii) the amount of any interest required to be so paid, excepting penalties and interest resulting from the Lessor's negligence or failure to act timely.

ILLUSTRATIVE LANGUAGE—
PERIODIC PAYMENT ADJUSTMENT:

If for any reason the Lessor shall lose, or shall not have, or shall lose the right to claim, or shall suffer a disallowance of or shall be required to recapture (any such event being hereinafter called a "Loss"), (1) all or any portion of the 10% investment tax credit presently allowed by Sections 38 and 46 through 50 of the Code for "new section 38 property" with respect to the Lessor's cost of an item or items of equipment leased pursuant to this lease (hereinafter referred to as "Unit" or "Units") or any adjustment of such Lessor's cost of such Units (such investment credit being herein referred to as the "Investment Credit"), or (2) in computing its Federal taxable income or its taxable income for purposes of computing its liability to all states, cities and/or other local authorities for any taxable year (or portion thereof) during which this lease is in effect, all or any portion of depreciation deductions with respect to the Lessor's cost of a Unit or the Units or any adjustment of such Lessor's cost of such Units, based upon and computed upon the basis of: (i) the double-declining balance method of depreciation, switching over to the sum-of-the-years-digits method of depreciation or to the straight-line method as Lessor may prefer, at the appropriate time to secure the maximum depreciation deduction with respect to said Lessor's cost; (ii) a useful life of seven (7) years, and (iii) utilizing a salvage value of no greater than 10% of such Lessor's cost, and in the case of state and local taxes, under the most accelerated method of depreciation allowed by any such state or local taxing authority on the date hereof (such depreciation deductions being herein referred to as the "Depreciation Deduction"), then (A) the rental for the Units shall, on the next succeeding rental payment date after written notice to Lessee by Lessor of payment by Lessor of the tax and interest and/or penalties attributable to such Loss, be increased (any increase to be paid directly to Lessor) to such amount or amounts as shall, in the reasonable opinion of Lessor, after deduction of all fees, taxes and/or other charges required to be paid by Lessor (including any claims or deductions lost by Lessor) in respect of the receipt of all amounts payable by Lessee to Lessor under this Section under the laws of any Federal, state, city or local government or taxing authority in the United States, (hereinafter called "fees, taxes and/or other charges"), cause the Lessor's net return on investment to equal the net return on investment that would have been realized by Lessor if the Lessor had been entitled to utilize all the Depreciation Deduction or Investment Credit; or (B) if payment of the tax and interest and/or penalty attributable to such Loss is made after the final rental payment date hereunder, within 30 days after written notice by Lessor to Lessee of such payment by Lessor, the Lessee shall pay to Lessor such amount which, after the deduction of all fees, taxes and/or other charges, when added to the rental payments made pursuant to this Lease, will cause the Lessor's net return on investment to equal the net return on investment that would have been realized by Lessor if Lessor had been entitled to utilize all the Depreciation Deduction or Investment Credit; and (C), in addition to the applicable foregoing Lessee shall forthwith pay to Lessor the amount which after deduction of all fees, taxes and/or other charges, equals the amount of any interest and/or penalties (including any additions to tax because of underpayment of estimated tax) which may be assessed by the United States of America or any state or local taxing authority against Lessor attributable to the loss of all such portion of the Depreciation Deduction or Investment Credit.

The concept of investment tax credit indemnification is easy to understand. If the investment credit becomes unavailable, the party suffering the loss will have a greater Federal income tax liability than it would have had the benefit not been lost. Calculating the *loss* is straightforward since the investment credit is a dollar-for-dollar offset against Federal income tax liability. Determining the indemnity payment, however, is a little tricky. Should the amount which must be paid be equal to the credit lost? No. The reimbursement payment will be treated as taxable income and, therefore, the investment credit indemnification must take into account the *taxes*, such as Federal income taxes, which the indemnified party will have to pay upon receipt of the payment.

ILLUSTRATIVE EXAMPLE—
TAXES MUST BE TAKEN INTO ACCOUNT:

Company A leased a new $1,000 lathe to Company B. In computing its rental rate, Company A anticipated receiving an investment tax credit equal to 10% of the cost of the lathe. Company A would, therefore, be entitled to a $100 *credit* against its Federal tax bill (10% x $1,000). That is, if Company A's fiscal year Federal tax liability was $300 before taking into account the investment credit, its tax bill would be reduced to $200 after adjusting for the $100 credit. If for some reason Company A is unable to claim or suffers a recapture of the $100 credit, how much then should it be paid to compensate it for the loss? Clearly, since any indemnity money paid by Company B will be treated as taxable income to Company A, Company B should pay enough so that after Company A pays the tax on its receipt it will be in the same position as if it had been entitled to the credit. For simplicity assume Company A to be in the 50% tax paying bracket. Company B would have to pay Company A *$200* so that Company A's *after-tax* reimbursement would equal $100—what it would have saved in taxes if the credit was available.

Developing a formularized liquidated damage approach for depreciation losses is more complex than the investment credit situation. In many cases, the depreciation indemnification payments are incorporated into the remaining rental payments. That is, the future rents are increased by amounts necessary to compensate the lessor for depreciation lost. Frequently, careless or unaware lessees can end up overpaying under many depreciation indemnification provisions because they fail to properly analyze the overall effect of the repayment formula.

Frequently, tax indemnification provisions obligate the lessee to pay the lessor enough money so that the lessor's "net return," or standards of a similar nature, will be the same as before the tax benefit loss. Much to a lessee's detriment, terms such as "net return" all too often go undefined in a lease agreement. Undoubtedly, this is largely due to the fact that many think such terms have specific and unique meanings. This is generally not the case. Net return, for example, could mean total earnings, discounted rate of return, after-tax cash flow, etc. Without a precise definition a lessor could, if an adjustment must be made, take the position that it means whatever will provide the best economics for him at the time. This may result in a higher rent charge to a lessee than might be reasonable under the circumstances. The moral for a lessee is to make sure a reasonable and *understandable* definition of all tax loss economic measuring standards are clearly stated in the lease. In this way the correctness of any adjustment can be independently verified.

RECOMMENDATION:

It is generally in a lessor's best interest to define any indemnification economic measuring criteria, such as net return. Without doing so, there is a greater chance that a lessee will dispute any adjustment and, worse yet, that a court will decide it means something less than economically acceptable to a lessor.

d. The Tax "Loss Date" Should Be Defined

The point in time when a tax indemnification will be triggered by a tax benefit loss is an essential part of the indemnification concept because it determines when the indemnification payment is due. For example, would the lessee become responsible to pay for a tax benefit loss when the lessor discovers the problem or when a court rules on it? In many situations the "loss date" is defined as the time when the tax benefit loss has been established by the final judgment of a court or administrative agency having jurisdiction over the matter.

RECOMMENDATIONS:

I. A prospective lessee should not agree to any provision which obligates it to make any tax indemnification payment until the lessor has actually incurred, or is about to incur, an out-of-pocket expense.

II. A lessor should have the right under a tax indemnification clause to be able to make justifiable tax adjustments without prompting from the Internal Revenue Service and call upon the lessee to pay if it realizes that it may not properly claim a tax benefit. A prospective lessee may rightfully object to being at the lessor's mercy and if so an agreement to rely on the opinion of reputable, *jointly chosen* counsel, or some other similar arrangement where each will have some control, is usually an acceptable compromise.

III. The right to be able to require a lessor to contest any tax claim which will trigger an indemnification payment is valuable for a lessee. Without it, a lessor could decide not to defend against a claim since he will not ultimately have to pay it.

e. There Should Be a Reimbursement Provision For Erroneous Tax Loss Payments

The right to be reimbursed for any money incorrectly paid under a tax indemnification provision is an important concept to include within such an arrangement. Simply, if the tax loss is determined not to exist, the indemnified party should be required to promptly return any money paid.

RECOMMENDATION:

When a lessee has the right to obligate a lessor to contest a tax claim which he is responsible under the lease to pay, he should also have a right to the return of any amount which he has to pay before a final resolution if the lessor, without justification or consent, settles or discontinues the action. The purpose, of course, is to make sure the claim will be fully contested.

18. An Agreement as to How and Where the Equipment Will Be Returned Can Avoid Costly Problems

The condition in which, and the place where, the leased equipment must be returned are important considerations. Overlooking either can be a costly omission for the lessor or the lessee.

Whether or not a lessee has met his return condition obligation as far as the lessor is concerned depends on whether he has maintained a standard of care acceptable to the lessor. If a lessor determines, for example, that the lessee did not properly maintain the equipment, it will insist that the lessee pay for any repairs necessary to restore the equipment. Even if the lessor's claim for repairs is legitimate, a lessee may feel that the maintenance standards were met and dispute payment. Therefore, it is essential for both parties to have the standard of care criteria defined in the lease. The best approach is to set an objective, easy to measure "outside" standard. For example, agreeing that an aircraft under lease will be returned with no less than 50% of remaining engine operation time before the next major overhaul. If an easily measurable criterion is not available, the parties might agree to use an independent equipment appraiser to assess the equipment's condition. If the appraiser will not be specifically named in the lease, a selection method should be established. For example, agreeing to have each party pick an appraiser at the appropriate time. In this case it is usually advisable to further provide that if the two appraisers cannot come to a common agreement, they are to jointly select a third independent appraiser whose opinion will be final and binding.

Where the equipment is to be returned and who shall bear the delivery expense is just as important a consideration as is the condition in which it will be returned. If a lessor, for example, had to unexpectedly pay at the end of a lease for the transportation of 200 trucks from ten of a lessee's plants scattered up and down the East Coast to a central sale point in the Midwest, his profit margin could be noticeably affected. Who pays for what shipping expense generally varies with each transaction. It is not unusual, however, for a lessee to only have to pay for shipping charges to a general transportation shipping point near where the equipment is used.

RECOMMENDATIONS:

I. Prospective lessors without access to inexpensive equipment storage facilities should consider negotiating the right to store equipment on the prospective lessee's premises at the end of a lease until a buyer or new lessee can be found.

II. Prospective lessees must carefully consider the potential expense exposure in agreeing to return equipment to a particular return point, particularly when many items are involved. For example, a trucking pickup location may be much closer and, thereby less expensive, than the nearest railhead. Having the right to choose between alternative return locations may also be advisable. Circumstances can change and it may turn out to be more practical to transport the equipment to, for example, the nearest railhead instead of the nearest truck pickup point.

19. A Lessor Must Be Able to Terminate the Lease or Take Other Protective Action in Certain Cases

If a problem arises which would jeopardize a lessor's rights or interest in the lease or the equipment, the lessor should be in a position to end the lease or take such other action as may be appropriate, such as reclaiming the equipment. The various "problem" situations which would give rise to this type of lessor right should be clearly specified in *every* lease agreement. They are generally referred to as "events of default."

a. Where There Is a Nonpayment of Rent

It is essential for the lessee's failure to pay the rent, when and in the amount due, to be included as an event of default. The payment of the rent is a fundamental obligation and a lessor should expect the fullest attention to it, allowing, perhaps, for a reasonable overdue payment grace period for unavoidable delays.

RECOMMENDATIONS:

I. Prospective lessees are well advised not only to negotiate a reasonable overdue rent payment grace period, but also a lessor notice requirement. For example, providing that the failure to pay rent will not result in an event of default until a period of time, say five days, after the lessee has received written notice of the nonpayment.

II. If a lessor assumes an overdue rent notice obligation as described in Recommendation I, he should make sure the proper controls are instituted to monitor the timeliness of the rent payments.

b. When There Is an Unauthorized Transfer

An unauthorized assignment or transfer of the lease agreement or the equipment by the lessee should be a designated event of default. Generally, a lessor's willingness to enter into a lease transaction depends to a great extent on the quality and reputation of the lessee. If assignments or transfers were freely permitted, the equipment could end up in the hands of an unacceptable third party. A sublease, for example, to someone who intended to use the equipment in a high wear operation could seriously jeopardize the equipment's anticipated residual value. By controlling transfers and assignments a lessor will protect its investment position.

c. When There Is a Failure To Perform An Obligation

A lessor will certainly want to be in a position to declare a lease default if the lessee fails to observe or perform *any* condition or agreement in the lease. Whether or not a court would allow a lessor to actually terminate a lease agreement no matter how minor the failure may be open to discussion; however, the potential threat may keep a lessee in full compliance. Lawsuits are expensive even for the winner.

RECOMMENDATIONS:

I. Many conditions and agreements in a lease may not be fundamental to the essence of the lease transaction, such as the correct marking of the equipment. Therefore, a prospective lessee should attempt to minimize the default risk by requiring that the breach be "material" before it gives rise to a default event.

II. A good way for a lessee to avoid inadvertent lease defaults is to have the lessor obligated to give at least thirty days prior written notice before a default can be declared. Lengthy notice requirements, however, could hinder a lessor's ability to move quickly to protect its equipment and should be carefully considered before being given.

d. When the Lessee Has Made a Material Misrepresentation

A lessee is frequently required to represent certain facts which a lessor deems critical to its decision to enter into the lease. Any misrepresentation of a material nature could subject a lessor to a risk which it would not otherwise have assumed had it known the actual facts. In many cases, for example, a lessor will rely on a statement that there have been no adverse changes in the lessee's financial condition between the date of the latest financial statements and the transaction's closing date. If a lessor discovers the representation was not true after the lease is signed, it should be entitled to declare a default even if the misrepresentation was inadvertent.

e. When the Lessee Is Going Bankrupt

A court order or decree declaring the lessee bankrupt or insolvent; the appointment of a receiver, liquidator, or trustee in bankruptcy for a lessee under any state or Federal law; or any similar action which would expose the leased equipment to a third-party claim or otherwise endanger the lessor's position should be included as events of default. Any voluntary act on the part of a lessee which would lead to any of these events should also permit a lessor to declare a default and pursue his remedies.

20. It Is Useful to Designate the Default Remedies Which Can Be Pursued

It can be helpful to specify what remedies a lessor may pursue if a lessee defaults under a lease. Although doing so will not necessarily guarantee a lessor that a particular action will be permitted if the parties end up in court, it will put a lessee on notice as to what a lessor may have in mind and will weigh against any objection raised by a lessee.

There are many types of default remedies incorporated in lease agreements. Usually they represent nothing more than a common sense approach to dealing with the default issue. The various remedies listed in a lease sometimes overlap but from a lessor's viewpoint it is better to be somewhat redundant than to risk a claim that a certain course of action was waived by implication because it was not included.

a. Court Action

The most obvious default remedy which should be included is a right to bring a court action to require the lessee to perform any breached obligation or to get money damages for the failure to do so. This is the standard type of remedy available in a basic contract action.

b. Termination of the Lease

The right to terminate a lessee's rights under the lease, including its right to use the equipment, is a basic default remedy. As a part of this right a lessor usually has the ability to immediately enter the lessee's premises and take possession of the equipment. The reclaiming right is particularly useful when a lessee's creditors are trying to attach assets as security for their claims.

c. Redelivery of the Equipment

Having the right to require a lessee to redeliver the equipment is a common default remedy. It usually imposes a greater burden than if the lease normally ran its course. For example, the lessee may have to redeliver the equipment at its own expense and risk to *any* location which the lessor designates rather than the *nearest* general transportation pickup point. In an adversary proceeding, as a practical matter, the expanded right may not have much more meaning than helping to measure damages in a lawsuit because a great deal of cooperation cannot be expected.

d. Storage of the Equipment

In a default situation, a lessor is not likely to have a ready place for the equipment. Therefore, being able to obligate the lessee to store the equipment on its premises free of charge until it has been disposed of is a frequently listed default remedy. Whether or not it is actually advisable to let a lessee retain control over the equipment is a separate issue which would have to be addressed by the lessor when a default occurs. By doing so, for example, a lessor may run the risk that other creditors would seize the equipment. Even though the creditors did not have a valid claim, the possible renting time lost and equipment deterioration could endanger the lessor's investment.

RECOMMENDATIONS:

I. In order to avoid a prolonged obligation, a prospective lessee should place a time limit on any lessor storage right. If a time can not be negotiated, the lessor at least should be committed to diligently proceed to sell, lease, or otherwise dispose of the property.

II. Any lessor right to have equipment stored should be accompanied by a right to enter the storage area for any reasonable purpose, including inspection by a prospective purchaser or new lessee.

III. A lessee storage requirement may imply a responsibility for damage to the equipment. A prospective lessee, therefore, should specify that the risk of damage through third party acts during any forced storage period is on the lessor.

e. Sale of the Equipment

A prospective lessor should insist upon being able to sell or otherwise dispose of the leased equipment, free and clear of any of the lessee's rights and without any duty to account to the lessee, if the lessee defaults. This will provide a lessor with the freedom to act as it sees fit. If a lessee will be entitled to a credit for any proceeds received from the equipment disposition against, for example, any default damage amounts which may be due, it will, for obvious reasons, not be desirable to let the lessor have this much leeway.

RECOMMENDATIONS:

I. The more money a lessor gets through an equipment disposition, the less default damages a lessee may owe. To insure a maximum disposal effort a lessee should insist upon a disposition proceed accounting.

II. If a prospective lessor agrees to credit any sale or re-leasing proceeds received from third parties against any amounts which a defaulting lessee would owe, it should limit the credit obligation to the "net" proceeds actually received. The expenses which the lessor incurs, for example, to lease the equipment should be deducted from the amount which the lessee would be entitled to receive as a credit. In addition, until the money is in fact in the lessor's hands, it should not have to recognize any credit.

f. Right to Hold or Re-Lease the Equipment

A prospective lessor would be well advised to be in a position of being able to "hold, use, operate, lease to others, or keep idle" any equipment which it has reacquired as a result of a lease default. Ideally, then, a lessor could take what action it deems to be in its best interest. Of course, if a court finds that the lessor did not act in a manner to minimize the damages suffered, it may limit any recovery which a lessor may be able to get.

g. Liquidated Damages

A well-thought-out "liquidated damage" provision should always be included as an alternate default remedy. Under such a provision, the parties agree upon a method for determining what damages the lessor is entitled to if a default occurs. In general, courts will uphold a liquidated damage arrangement if it fairly anticipates the losses which may result from the lessee's nonperformance.

Although there are no industry standard formulas used to measure the damages which a lessor would suffer because of a lessee's default, there are two types frequently used. One provides for the lessee to pay an amount equal to the present worth of the aggregate remaining rentals which the lessor would have received but for the default, reduced by the equipment's fair market sales value or the present worth of the equipment's fair market rental value over the originally remaining lease term. The other calls for the payment of an amount equal to the equipment's stipulated loss value as of the date of default, reduced by the equipment's fair market sales value or the present worth of the equipment's fair market rental value over the originally remaining lease term. A prescribed per annum discount rate, such as the prime commercial lending rate in effect at the time of termination, is incorporated into the liquidated damage "formula" for present worth computation purposes.

OBSERVATION:

The discount rate agreed upon to compute the present worth of the remaining rental stream can have a significant impact on what will be owed. Too often parties agree to arbitrary rates without considering the consequences. The higher the rate, the less the offsetting credit and the greater the damage amount payable.

ILLUSTRATIVE EXAMPLE—LIQUIDATED
DAMAGE FORMULA COMPUTATION:

Company A leased a $1,000,000 aircraft to Company B for a 10 year term. As part of the agreement, the parties incorporated a liquidated damage formula which they considered to be a fair measure of the damages Company A would suffer if Company B defaulted. The formula provided that Company A would be entitled to an amount equal to the present worth of any remaining rents which would otherwise have been due but for the default, offset by the present worth of the aircraft's fair market rental value over the originally remaining lease term. The per annum discount rate to be used to compute the present worth was specified as 10%, the current prime lending rate at Company A's bank. At the end of the fifth year Company B defaulted. For simplicity we will assume that the rents are payable annually, in advance. The facts are:

Unexpired lease term	5 years
Annual rent	$120,000
Annual fair market rental value	$100,000

The present worth of the remaining rents under the lease, calculated using a 10% discount rate is $500,384. The present worth of the aggregate fair market rental value over a five year term is $416,986. The amount which the lessee owes is $83,398, the difference between the present worth of the unpaid rents and the fair market value rents.

If the parties had agreed upon a discount rate of 8% instead of 10% the lessee would owe $86,242, instead of $83,392. On the other hand, if the discount rate were 12% instead of 10%, the lessee would owe $80,747. As the reader can see the discount rate should not be treated lightly.

RECOMMENDATION:

Prospective lessors should keep in mind that any credit which must be applied in a liquidated damage computation based upon fair market sales or fair market rental value could be overstated. For example, if either value had been determined based upon an independent appraisal and, in fact, the actual amounts obtainable were much less, the lessor would not come out in as favorable a position as it might have if the appraisal had been closer. Of course, a lessee would have the reverse problem if the appraisals were too low. To solve this situation both parties might consider the possibility of allowing for a future adjustment if the actual amounts vary from the appraisal.

21. A Lessor May Want Certain Lease Assignment Rights

Prospective lessors frequently ask for the right to assign their interest in a lease and the equipment at any time during the term. A general assignment right sometimes makes prospective lessees uneasy. If properly negotiated, however, it should not cause concern. For example, a prospective lessee could insist that any assignment not adversely affect his lease rights.

a. Assignment to a Lender

In many cases a lessor's lenders will insist as part of their credit arrangement that the lessor incorporate in all future leases a right to assign them, including title to the equipment, to the lenders if certain loan restrictions are violated. Generally, the purpose is to enable a lender to take over the leases as security if there is a loan default. If such an assignment requirement exists in a lessor's loan agreement, it must be in each lease agreement and it is not a negotiable point between the parties.

RECOMMENDATION:

Any time a prospective lessee must agree to allow a lessor to be able to assign any or all of its interest in a lease to its lenders, it should require that any such transfer be subject, and subordinate, to the terms of the lease. In other words, if there is an assignment the lessee's rights, including the right to use the equipment, would not in any way be jeopardized. In addition, it should also be specified that any transfer will not relieve the lessor from any of its obligations under the lease. This will give a prospective lessee the assurance that it will always have what it originally bargained for.

b. Assignment to an Investor

A lessor's lease assignment rights may cover more than loan security transfers discussed in the previous section. It may, for example, allow him to "sell" the lease, including title to the equipment, to a third party. Under such an arrangement, the third party purchaser would become the equipment owner, would take subject to the terms and conditions of the lease agreement, and would, therefore, become the "lessor." The original lessor would no longer have any rights *or duties* under the lease.

A broad assignment right can expose a lessee to certain risks. A lease sold to a financially unstable lessor may, for example, endanger the lessee's right to the continued use of the equipment because of potential creditor actions. An assignment to a lessor who is difficult to deal with may also create problems. For example, some lessors are hard to work with if modifications become desirable.

RECOMMENDATIONS:

I. When a prospective lessor asks for a lease assignment right, it should be coupled with a right to require the lessee to execute any documents which are necessary to effect an assignment.

Without this, a lessee could intentionally or unintentionally, stand in the way of the assignment.

II. A prospective lessee should consider whether it would be wise to potentially allow a lease to be assigned to any of its banks or lending institutions because doing so may restrict its borrowing capability. Having the right to pass on any potential transferees or, if a prospective lessor is unwilling to grant such a right, by specifically defining the limits of who would be acceptable are two ways to control undesirable transfers.

22. A Lessee May Want Certain Equipment Sublease Rights

A lessee with the right to sublease equipment is in the best position to lessen or eliminate the impact of having to pay rent on assets which become unproductive because of changes in use needs during the lease term. If there are no restrictions, such as those which would limit transfers to affiliated companies only, a lessee will have the maximum flexibility.

RECOMMENDATIONS:

I. Prospective lessees desiring subleasing rights should avoid agreeing to any exercise conditions, such as having to obtain the lessor's prior written consent. Time wasted waiting for a consent, for example, could result in lost revenue.

II. Prospective lessors consenting to a subleasing right should insist that the lessee remain primarily liable under the lease agreement during the sublet period.

III. It may not be advisable for a prospective lessor to give a prospective lessee an unrestricted right to sublease the equipment to *any* party, *even though the original lessee will remain primarily liable under the lease.* Having the right to pass judgment on any proposed sublessee will prevent knowing transfers to parties, for example, who may misuse the equipment or who are financially unstable. Regardless of the original lessee's primary responsibility, misuse will result in diminished equipment value, and a sublessee's bankruptcy could interfere with the equipment's return.

23. A Lessor May Want Certain Options As a Part of The Deal

There are a few situations when prospective lessors will want certain rights which are not usually requested, such as a right to terminate the lease in a non-default situation, a right to force a sale of the equipment to the lessee, a right to force the lessee to renew a lease, or a right to abandon the equipment. These rights can create substantial tax problems or be otherwise undesirable from a lessee's viewpoint. Therefore, if proposed, their possible effect should be carefully reviewed.

a. The Right To Terminate The Lease

It is conceivable, although extremely unlikely, that a prospective lessor would want to be able to terminate a lease for *any reason it chooses* during its term without the lessee's consent. For example, if a prospective lessor feels the rental market will rise prior to the end of the negotiated lease term, it may want to have the ability to go after a better rate.

RECOMMENDATION:

For obvious reasons, a prospective lessee should not put itself in a position where a lease could be prematurely terminated by the lessor without its prior consent and without reason. Loss of the leased equipment's use could seriously interrupt its operations.

b. The Right to Force a Sale of The Equipment to the Lessee

In certain situations a prospective lessor, particularly when there is a good chance that the equipment may not be worth what it had assumed it would be in its rent analysis, will insist upon having the right, commonly referred to as a "put," to force a lessee to buy the equipment under lease at the end of the term. Generally, such a right is expressed as a fixed percentage of the original equipment's cost rather than a defined dollar amount. For example, a lessor may have the right to sell the equipment to the lessee for an amount equal to 10% of cost. In effect, a put eliminates any risk that a lessor will not realize his assumed residual value which, in turn, protects his anticipated profit. Certainly, if the equipment could be sold or re-leased under more favorable terms in the marketplace, the put would not be exercised. Transactions involving certain types of store fixtures or equipment which will be difficult or uneconomical to move, such as certain heavy storage tanks, sometimes incorporate a forced sale right.

RECOMMENDATIONS:

I. Although the use of a put may prohibit the issuance of a favorable Revenue Ruling, some experienced tax attorneys feel their usage will not endanger the tax nature of the transaction if properly structured. They should be used, however, only on the advice of tax counsel.

II. If a prospective lessor insists upon having a put, the prospective lessee should make sure it will not be liable for any loss of tax benefits a lessor may suffer if, because of its presence, the lease does not qualify as a true tax lease.

c. The Right to Abandon the Equipment

In the past, equipment abandonment rights have been used in leases of equipment which would be difficult and costly, if not totally impractical, to reclaim if the lessee decided not to purchase it at the end of the term. A good example of the type of leases which may involve abandonment rights are those relating to certain kinds of commercial storage tanks which are so large that the only way to move them is to cut them into pieces and then re-weld them at the new site. In these situations the expenses involved could be so great that the lessor could not reasonably recoup them through a re-leasing or a sale.

Lessors sometimes attempt to solve an equipment removal expense problem by requiring the equipment to be delivered to them at the end of the term at the lessee's expense. If the lessee refuses to do so, however, the lessor's only recourse, without a right of abandonment, would be to bring a lawsuit to force the lessee to live up to its agreement or, possibly, pay for any resulting damages. If the lessee is in financial trouble, a lawsuit may be of little use. Having an abandonment right would allow the lessor to drop the property in the lessee's lap and rid itself of any lingering responsibility or expense exposure.

From a tax standpoint, the right of abandonment has a cloud over it today. Under the current IRS lease guidelines set forth in Revenue Procedure 75-21 a favorable Revenue Ruling will not be issued on a transaction where a right of abandonment exists.

d. The Right to Require a Renewal of the Lease

In situations where a right of abandonment or a put might be considered, a lessor may instead use a forced lease renewal right. Under such a right, a lessor could make the lessee re-lease the equipment at a predetermined rental. Although not specifically mentioned in the IRS lease guidelines, many feel that using a forced renewal right would prohibit the issuance of a favorable Revenue Ruling.

24. A Lessee May Have Certain Options As a Part of the Deal

Invariably, a prospective lessee will ask for certain rights, referred to as "options," which will enable him to maintain some form of control over the equipment's use, such as an equipment purchase right, a lease renewal right, or a lease termination right. Generally, these types of options are willingly granted by prospective lessors.

a. The Right to Purchase the Equipment at Fair Market Value

A prospective lessee typically wants to be able to buy the leased equipment at the end of the lease. In many situations, this is done through a "fair market value purchase" option. Basically, the option gives him the right to purchase the equipment for whatever its fair market value is *at the time it is exercised.* As far as the IRS lease guidelines are concerned, and usually from the lessor's viewpoint, a fair market purchase option is fully acceptable.

Although the term "fair market value" appears self-explanatory, the parties should agree upon a method for its determination. In general, the "fair market value" of a piece of equipment is the amount which a willing buyer under no compulsion to purchase would pay a willing seller under no compulsion to sell in the open market. As a practical matter, however, how is the value actually determined between a lessor and a lessee? There are a number of ways. One common method is for the parties to designate in the lease an independent appraiser who will evaluate the equipment at the appropriate time. Another method is to provide for the parties to each select an independent appraiser to come in and make an assessment when necessary. If the two appraisers cannot agree upon a satisfactory value, then they must jointly select a third appraiser, whose opinion will be binding.

RECOMMENDATION:

A fair market value purchase option can be an expensive way for a lessee to acquire equipment with a typically strong re-sale value. A purchase price "cap" is sometimes negotiated to limit how much the lessee would have to pay. For example, the lessee would have the right to buy the equipment at fair market value or 30% of the equipment's original cost, whichever is less. Such an arrangement, however, may create certain tax problems.

b. The Right to Purchase the Equipment at a Fixed Price

When equipment has traditionally maintained a favorable re-sale value, many companies refuse to lease because it is likely they will eventually want to own the equipment and a fair market purchase option coupled with the lease rents could result in an economically unfavorable way of acquiring it. As a result, a fixed price purchase option is sometimes given in order to induce them to lease. Under a fixed price purchase option, commonly referred to as a "call," the lessee can buy the equipment at the end of the lease for a predetermined price. The price is usually expressed as a percentage of the equipment's original cost. For example, the lessee may have the right to purchase designated equipment for 35% of cost. In this way, the lessee knows the maximum amount of money he will have to spend if he wants to buy the equipment when the lease is over.

OBSERVATIONS:

I. Under the current IRS lease guidelines the Internal Revenue Service will not issue a favorable Revenue Ruling on transactions incorporating a fixed price purchase option. Although not specifically mentioned, this would also undoubtedly include situations where a lessee is given the right to purchase the equipment at the lesser of fair market value or a predetermined fixed price—an arrangement designed to protect a lessee from having to overpay in the event the fair market value actually turns out to be less than the agreed upon fixed price.

II. Whether a fixed price purchase option exercisable at a price which is not so low that a lessee would clearly buy the equipment will prevent the transaction from qualifying as a true tax lease seems to be an open question among many attorneys. Some feel that a properly structured call will still enable the transaction to qualify as a true tax lease. The mere fact that a favorable Revenue Ruling could not be obtained on a transaction does not mean it cannot so qualify. It does, however, add an element of risk.

c. The Right to Renew the Lease at Fair Rental Value

Providing a lessee with the right to renew a lease at the equipment's fair market rental value is acceptable, both from an IRS lease guideline standpoint and, generally, from a lessor's economic viewpoint. The fair rental determination can be made in a manner similar to that for the determination of the fair market purchase value, through independent appraisal at the time of the intended renewal.

RECOMMENDATION:

When equipment is vital to a prospective lessee's operations, it should make sure the lease renewal terms are adequate to cover any anticipated needs. For example, if a four-year renewal is desirable, an option which would allow a selection of two two-year periods, four one-year periods, one one-year period followed by a three-year period, or a four-year period would provide a great deal of flexibility as to *term* and as to *rental rate*. A structure such as this would give the lessee the ability to limit its renewal costs in a high rental market or to "lock in" for a longer period of time in a low rental market. From a lessor's viewpoint, of course, too much latitude on the lessee's side may lessen its chances of maximizing its renewal profits and, therefore, any such arrangement should be carefully thought out as to the possible future effects.

d. The Right to Renew the Lease At A Fixed Price

Prospective lessees sometimes request a fixed price renewal option. By knowing in advance the exact dollar amount of the renewal rents, they know where they would stand if they wanted to continue to use the equipment beyond the main lease term. This would, of course, not be possible with fair market renewal option. The current IRS lease guidelines limit fixed price renewal options. This does not necessarily mean that a transaction incorporating such a right cannot qualify as a true tax lease, only that the Service can refuse to issue a favorable Revenue Ruling on it.

OBSERVATION:

A properly structured fixed price renewal right will, in the opinion of some experienced attorneys, not prevent a transaction from qualifying as a "true" lease for tax purposes. The renewal rate and term must not, however, be so favorable that the lessee would undoubtedly take advantage of it simply because it costs so little. For example, if a lessee were given an option to renew a twenty-year lease on a $50,000,000 oil tanker for $1 a year for a thirty-year renewal period, the transaction could unquestionably be successfully attacked by the Internal Revenue Service as not being a true lease.

e. The Right to Terminate the Lease

It is not uncommon for a prospective lessee to want to have the ability to terminate a lease early, particularly when it feels the equipment could become technically obsolete or surplus to its needs before the lease would normally end. When this right is granted, the lessee frequently will be required to pay the lessor a predetermined amount of money, commonly referred to as the "termination value," upon exercise. Since most lessors do not like to grant termination rights, the termination amount is usually high.

f. The Right of First Refusal

A purchase "right of first refusal" is sometimes used as an alternative for a fair market value purchase option. Under such an option a lessee is given the right to purchase the leased equipment at the end of the lease term under the same terms and conditions as offered by an unaffiliated third party.

ILLUSTRATIVE LANGUAGE—
RIGHT OF FIRST REFUSAL:

Unless an Event of Default shall have occurred and be continuing at the end of the term of this lease, or any event or condition which, upon lapse of time or giving of notice, or both, would constitute such an Event of Default shall have occurred and be continuing at such time, the lessor shall not, at or following the end of the term of this lease, sell any item of equipment (including any sale prior to the end of such term for delivery of such equipment at or following the end of such term) unless:

(a) the lessor shall have received from a responsible purchaser a bona fide offer in writing to purchase such equipment;

(b) the lessor shall have given the lessee notice (i) setting forth in detail the identity of such purchaser, the proposed purchase price, the proposed date of purchase and all other material terms and conditions of such purchase, and (ii) offering to sell such equipment to the lessee upon the same terms and conditions as those set forth in such notice; and

(c) the lessee shall not have notified the lessor, within 20 days following receipt of such notice, of its election to purchase such equipment upon such terms and conditions.

If the lessee shall not have so elected to purchase such equipment, the lessor may at any time sell such equipment to any party at a price and upon other terms and conditions no less favorable to the lessor than those specified in such notice.

Upon payment of the purchase price of any such item of equipment, the lessor shall upon request of the lessee execute and deliver to the lessee, or to the lessee's assignee or nominee, a bill of sale (without warranties) for such equipment such as will transfer to the lessee such title to such equipment as the lessor derived from the vendor of the equipment, free and clear of all liens, security interests, and other encumbrances arising through the lessor.

It is generally felt that the advantage to using a purchase right of first refusal is that it allows a lessor to depreciate the leased equipment to a "zero" residual value over the lease term in situations where it could not otherwise do so. By doing so, a lessor can, in turn, offer a lower rental rate. The disadvantage to using it is that a lessee may run the risk that a competitor may bid for the equipment either to run the price up or to acquire it for its own operations.

25. A Defaulting Party Should Lose Certain Options.

In general, a well-drafted option section should cause the party holding the option to forfeit its exercise right if it is in default under the lease. For example, a lessee should lose its right to buy the equipment under a purchase option if the lease is terminated because of a default on its part.

26. It Is a Good Idea to Designate the Law Which Will Govern the Lease

It is always advisable for the parties to specify what jurisdiction's law shall apply to their rights and obligations under a lease agreement. For example, the parties may agree that all actions on lease issues will be decided in accordance with the laws of the State of New York, regardless of whether the proceedings are instituted in a New York court. By doing this the attorneys will be able to draft the documents in accordance with the law they feel will give the fairest known outcome.

RECOMMENDATION:

When a particular law is specified to govern the issues in a lease, it is considered good form to include a "severability" clause which in effect provides that any lease provision determined to be legally unenforceable will be "severed." The intent is to treat the agreement as if the offensive provision were never included for the purpose of any proceeding. It is an attempt at preventing the entire agreement from being held invalid in the event the controlling law says that agreements containing certain prohibited provisions will be totally unenforceable.

27. The Interest Penalty for Late Payments Should Be Agreed Upon

A lease agreement should prescribe the interest rate which will be charged on any overdue payments, such as delinquent rent payments. This will eliminate disputes over late charges and will assist in assessing damages if a lawsuit arises.

RECOMMENDATIONS:

I. When an overdue payment interest penalty is specified, the prospective lessor should also incorporate a qualification that the rate shall in no event be higher than the maximum enforceable legal rate in order to avoid any potential enforceability problems if the legal limit is inadvertently exceeded.

II. Prospective lessors should see to it that any interest on overdue obligations will run from the date the money is due to the date of payment. Prospective lessees, on the other hand, should attempt to get it to run from when the lessee receives written notice of the overdue obligation from the lessor. This will eliminate oversights.

28. The Lease Should Identify Where Any Required Notifications and Payments Must Be Sent

Lease agreements usually provide that all required notifications and payments, such as loss notifications and rent payments, must be promptly made, but they sometimes fail to identify exactly *where* they should be sent. As a result, payments or notifications could be misdirected and money or valuable time lost. The parties should, therefore, make sure appropriate mailing addresses are included.

In addition to specifying where payments and notifications must be sent, the parties should also state *how* they should be made. For example, it may be agreed that a notice shall be deemed given when it is deposited in a U.S. mail box or sent by prepaid telegraph.

29. The Lease Should Be Signed Correctly

All parties to a lease should make sure it is signed in the proper capacities. Leases to be signed by an individual representing himself generally do not present any problems. Leases to be signed by an individual representing a firm, such as a partnership, corporation, or trust, sometimes do. If, in the latter case, the signature is not made in the correct representative capacity the represented firm may not be bound. For example, if a vice president intends to sign on behalf of his corporation, the signature block should be set up as follows:

> XYZ Corporation
> by ──────────────────────
> Mr. R. Smith, Vice President

If the form of signature is not correct the signing individual may run the risk that he is *personally* bound to the contract. Certainly, a less-than-desirable outcome for all parties concerned.

D. A CHECKLIST FOR DRAFTING AND NEGOTIATING A LEASE AGREEMENT

A well-drafted lease agreement should cover all the important issues involved in a transaction. The following checklist is designed to pinpoint the issues frequently encountered.

1. What Form of Lease Is Appropriate?
   a. A Standard Lease.
   b. A Custom Lease.
2. Should a Master Lease Be Used?
3. Does the Lease Agreement Cover the Following Issues?
   a. Has a Page Index of All the Topic Headings Been Included?
   b. Have the Parties Been Properly Identified?
      (1) The Lessor.
      (2) The Lessee.
   c. Is the Lessee a Valid Legal Entity?
   d. Has a Factual Summary of the Circumstances Giving Rise to the Transaction Been Included?
   e. Has the Consideration for the Transaction Been Stated?
   f. Have the Key Terms Been Defined in a Definition Section? For Example:
      (1) Affiliate.
      (2) Business Day.
      (3) Buyer-Furnished Equipment.
      (4) Equipment Delivery Date.
      (5) Equipment Manufacturer.
      (6) Event of Default.
      (7) Event of Loss.
      (8) Fair Market Value.
      (9) Indenture.
      (10) Interim Rent.
      (11) Lease.
      (12) Lease Period.
      (13) Lease Supplement.
      (14) Lessor's Cost.
      (15) Lien.
      (16) Loan Certificates.
      (17) Loan Participant.
      (18) Overdue Interest Rate.
      (19) Primary Rent.
      (20) Tax Loss Date.

g. If Equipment Will Be Delivered after the Lease Is Signed, Has a Procedure for Adding It Been Established?
   (1) Can the Lessee Decide Not to Lease Future Delivered Equipment When It Arrives? If so, Will the Lessee Be Obligated to Pay:
       (a) A Non-Utilization Fee?
       (b) A Commitment Fee?
   (2) Can Future Delivered Equipment Be Accepted for Lease as It Arrives or Must the Lessee Aggregate a Minimum Dollar Amount.
   (3) Who Will Be Responsible for Any Tax Losses Resulting from Equipment Remaining Idle During an Equipment Grouping Period.
       (a) The Lessor.
       (b) The Lessee.

h. The Lease Period Should Be Defined.
   (1) Will There Be an Interim Lease Term? If so, When Will It Begin and End?
   (2) When Will the Primary Term Begin?
   (3) How Long Will the Primary Term Run?
   (4) Will the Lessee Be Permitted to Renew the Lease? If so, What Is the Renewal Period Arrangement?

i. The Rent Structure Must Be Defined.
   (1) Will a Percentage Rent Factor Be Used? If so, What May Be Included in the Equipment Cost Base?
       (a) Sales Tax.
       (b) Transportation Charges.
       (c) Installation Charges.
       (d) Other.
   (2) How Much Rent Must Be Paid?
   (3) When Will the Rent Be Due?
   (4) How Must the Rent Be Paid?
       (a) Check.
       (b) Immediately Available Funds.
       (c) Other.
   (5) Where Must the Rent Be Paid?
       (a) Has a Post Office Box or Other Address Been Specified?
   (6) Can or Must the Lessor Adjust the Rent Charge If There Is a Tax Law Change Affecting, Favorably or Unfavorably, the Lessor's Economic Return?
       (a) If a Rent Adjustment Is Provided for, Has The Exact Criterion for Making It Been Clearly Specified?
       (b) If the Tax Law Change Applies to Future Delivered Equipment and a Rent Adjustment Is Not

Acceptable, Can the Party Adversely Affected Elect to Exclude the Equipment?
(7) Will the Rent Obligation Be a Hell or High Water Obligation?
j. What Is the Lessor's Total Dollar Equipment Cost Commitment?
(1) Will a Percentage Variance Be Permitted?
k. Will The Lessee Be Required to Submit Reports? For Example:
(1) Financial Reports.
(a) Profit and Loss Statements.
(b) Balance Sheets.
(c) Other.
(2) Accident Reports.
(a) Has a Minimum Estimated Accident Dollar Amount Been Agreed Upon Below Which a Report Is Not Required?
(b) Will the Lessee Be Obligated to Immediately Telephone if a Serious Accident Occurs?
(3) Lease Conformity Reports.
(4) Equipment Location Reports.
(5) Third-Party Claim Reports.
l. Has a Time Been Established for When Lessee Reports Are Due?
m. Has a General Lessee Reporting Requirement Been Imposed as to Reports Which May Be Deemed Necessary by the Lessor in the Future?
n. Equipment Maintenance.
(1) Who Has the Responsibility for Insuring Proper Maintenance?
(a) The Lessor.
(b) The Lessee.
(c) A Third Party.
(2) Who Must Bear the Cost of the Maintenance?
(a) The Lessor.
(b) The Lessee.
(3) Will Maintenance Records Be Required?
(a) Will the Lessor Be Permitted Access to the Maintenance Records? If so, at What Times:
1. Normal Business Hours.
2. Any Time Requested.
o. Will Equipment Alterations Be Permitted? If so,
(1) Will the Lessor's Consent Be Required Prior to:
(a) An Addition Which May Impair the Equipment's Originally Intended Function or Which Cannot Be Removed Without so Impairing Such Function.
(b) Any Change.

    (2) Who Will Have Title to Any Addition or Other Alteration?

      (a) If It Can Be Easily Removed Without Equipment Damage?

      (b) If It Cannot Be Removed Without Function Impairment?

p. Will Certain Lessor Ownership Protection Filings Be Advisable or Necessary?

    (1) Federal Regulatory Agencies, Such as the Federal Aviation Administration.

    (2) Uniform Commercial Code.

    (3) Other.

q. If Lessor Ownership Protection Filings Will Be Made, Who Has the Responsibility for Making Them and Who Must Bear the Expense?

    (1) The Lessor.

    (2) The Lessee.

r. If the Lessee Must Make Required Filings for the Lessor, Will the Lessee Have to Confirm They Have Been Made?

s. Will the Equipment Be Marked with the Lessor's Name and Address? If so, Who Will Have the Marking Responsibility and Expense?

    (1) The Lessor.

    (2) The Lessee.

t. Has the Lessee Been Specifically Prohibited from Using, Operating, Storing, or Maintaining the Equipment Carelessly, Improperly, in Violation of the Law, or in a Manner Not Contemplated by the Manufacturer?

    (1) If the Lessee Must Use the Equipment for a Purpose Other Than Intended, an Exception Should Be Negotiated.

u. The Lessee Should Be Required to Provide Certain Key Representations.

    (1) That the Lessee Is Legally in Existence.

      (a) Proper Organization, Valid Existence, and Good Standing in Its State of Organization.

    (2) That It Has Proper Authorization to Do Business in the State Where the Equipment Will Be Located.

    (3) That the Lessee Has the Transactional Authority to Enter into the Lease.

      (a) That Necessary Board of Director Approvals Have Been Obtained Covering the Transaction *and* the Person Signing the Lease on Behalf of the Lessee.

      (b) That Any Other Required Approvals Have Been Obtained.

    (4) That There Are No Conflicting Agreements.

      (a) Bank Credit Agreements.

       (b) Other Loan Agreements.

       (c) Mortgages.

       (d) Other Leases.

    (5) That All Necessary Regulatory Approvals Have Been Obtained.

    (6) That There Are No Pending or Threatened Adverse Legal or Administrative Proceedings Which Would Affect the Lessee's Operations or Financial Condition.

    (7) That There Have Been No Adverse Changes as of the Lease Closing in the Lessee's Financial Condition Since the Latest Available Financial Statements.

v. The Lessor Should Be Required to Provide Certain Key Representations.

    (1) That The Lessor Has the Transactional Authority to Lease the Equipment.

       (a) That Any Necessary Board of Director Approval Has Been Obtained.

       (b) That Any Other Approvals Have Been Obtained or, if None Are Required, a Statement That None Are Required.

    (2) That the Lessor Will Pay for the Equipment in Full.

    (3) That the Lessor Will Not Interfere with the Lessee's Use of the Equipment.

       (a) Has an Exception When the Lessee Is in Default Been Negotiated by the Lessor?

w. The Lessee Should Require Product Warranties to Be Assigned if the Lessor Has No Equipment Defect Responsibility.

    (1) If the Warranties Are Not Assignable, The Lessor Should Be Required to Act on the Lessee's Behalf.

x. Who Has the Responsibility for Equipment Casualty Losses?

    (1) The Lessor.

    (2) The Lessee.

y. Do the Casualty Loss Values Give Adequate Financial Protection to the Lessor?

z. Are the Casualty Loss Values Competitive from the Lessee's Viewpoint?

aa. As of What Time Will a Casualty Loss Be Deemed to Have Occurred—Has a "Loss Date" Been Defined?

    (1) What Obligations Change or Come into Effect on the Loss Date?

bb. When Is the Casualty Loss Value Payable and When Does Interest on the Amount Payable Begin to Run?

cc. What Taxes Must Be Paid?

    (1) Sales Tax.

    (2) Property Taxes.

      (3) Rental Taxes.
      (4) Withholding Taxes.
      (5) Income Taxes.
      (6) Other.
  dd. Who Must Pay the Taxes?
      (1) The Lessor.
      (2) The Lessee.
  ee. For Any Taxes Which a Lessee Must Reinburse a Lessor for Payment, Does the Lessee Have the Right to Have the Taxes Contested?
      (1) What Happens if the Lessor Does Not Fully Pursue Its Contest Remedies?
  ff. Is Each Party Required to Immediately Notify the Other of Any Tax Imposition for Which They Will Be Responsible?
  gg. Do the Parties Intend a True Tax Lease? If so,
      (1) Inconsistent Actions and Filings Should Be Prohibited.
      (2) Will Tax Loss Indemnifications Be Required?
         (a) From the Lessor?
         (b) From the Lessee?
  hh. If the Lessee Is Claiming the Investment Tax Credit, Must the Lessor Make the Lessee Whole if the Lessor Causes a Loss?
  ii. Who Has the Economic Risk of a Change in Tax Law?
      (1) For Past Delivered Equipment.
      (2) For Future Delivered Equipment
         (a) Can either Party Elect Not to Lease if the Economics Are No Longer Favorabe?
  jj. Has a Formula Been Agreed Upon for Measuring the Amount of Any Tax Benefit Loss and the Amount of Any Required Reimbursement?
      (1) Does the Formula Make the Indemnified Party Whole?
      (2) Is the Formula Absolutely Clear?
  kk. Who Has the Expense Responsibility for the Equipment Return and Where Must It Be Returned To:
      (1) If the Lease Ends Normally?
      (2) If the Lease Ends Prematurely?
  ll. May Either Party Designate an Alternate Return Location? If so, What Is the Expense Responsibility?
  mm. The Lessor Should Be Able to Terminate the Lease Early or Take Other Protective Action in Certain Situations.
      (1) When the Rent Is Not Paid.
      (2) When the Lessee Makes an Unauthorized Transfer of the Equipment or Any of Its Rights Under the Lease.

    (3) When There Is a General Failure to Perform the Obligations under the Lease.

    (4) When the Lessor Discovers the Lessee Has Made a Material Misrepresentation.

    (5) When There Is a Bankruptcy or Similar Event Which Would Jeopardize the Lessor's Position.

nn. The Actions Which the Lessor May Take in the Event of Default Should Be Specified.

    (1) Court Action.

    (2) Terminate the Lease.

    (3) Cause a Redelivery of the Equipment.

    (4) Cause the Lessee to Store the Equipment.

    (5) Sell the Equipment under Its Own Terms.

    (6) Be Able to Hold or Re-Lease the Equipment.

    (7) Be Entitled to a Predetermined Amount of Money as Damages for a Lease Default.

oo. Certain Lessor Assignment Rights May Be Desirable.

    (1) To a Lender as Security.

    (2) To an Investor.

pp. Will the Lessee Be Able to Sublease the Equipment? If so,

    (1) Will the Lessee Remain Primarily Liable under the Lease During the Sublease Period?

    (2) Will the Lessor Have Any Control over Who the Sublessee Will Be?

qq. Have All the Lessor's Options Been Included? For Example:

    (1) Right to Terminate the Lease.

    (2) Right to Force a Sale to the Lessee.

    (3) Right to Abandon the Equipment.

    (4) Right to Force a Lease Renewal.

rr. Have All the Lessee's Options Been Included? For Example:

    (1) A Purchase Right.

        (a) Fair Market Purchase Value.

        (b) Fixed Purchase Price.

    (2) A Renewal Right.

        (a) Fair Market Rental Value.

        (b) Fixed Price Rental.

    (3) A Termination Right.

    (4) A Right of First Refusal.

ss. Will a Defaulting Party Retain Any of Its Option Rights under the Lease.

tt. Has the Law of a Jurisdiction Been Specified to Control Any Issues Which Arise under the Lease?

uu. Is There Any Penalty for Overdue Payments?
   (1) Interest.
   (2) Other.
vv. Has Each Side Specified How and Where Any Required Notifications and Payments Will Be Made?
   (1) The Address Where Notifications and Payments Must Be Sent.
   (2) The Manner in Which the Notifications and Payments Must Be Made.
      (a) U.S. Mail.
      (b) Other.
ww. Has the Signature Section Been Set Up Properly For:
   (1) An Individual.
   (2) A Corporation.
   (3) A Partnership.
   (4) A Trust.
   (5) Other.
xx. Has the Signature Been Made in the Proper Capacity?

4

REQUIRED SUPPLEMENTAL
LEASE DOCUMENTS

Certain Supplemental Documents Are a Must—for the Lessor—for the Lessee • Opinions of Counsel Have Their Limitations • Guarantees Are Useful and Sometimes Essential • Insurance Verification—Don't Forget It • The Risk of Disqualifying Use Can Be Handled Collaterally.

A. ARE SUPPLEMENTAL LEASE DOCUMENTS NECESSARY?

Although the lease agreement is the core document in any equipment lease financing, there are other documents which can also be important. The "collateral" documents range from those which essentially provide the parties with comfort on specified issues, such as opinions of counsel, to those which define critical supportive arrangements, such as guarantee agreements.

Drafting the various supplemental papers will be the responsibility of the transaction's lawyers and, therefore, will be carefully reviewed by them. The non-lawyer participants should, however, also review them for accuracy. In order to do this they must have a basic understanding of the fundamental concepts involved. A working appreciation is also useful from another viewpoint. It will enable the "business people" to intelligently negotiate compromises when the lawyers reach impasses.

Frequently, major equipment lease financings are structured as leveraged leases. Many think that leveraged lease transactions are radically different than standard lease transactions and, as a result, the documents bear no resemblance to each other. This is not the case. There will, however, be some *additional* documentation involved, such as a security and loan agreement, in order to incorporate the third-party loan, or leveraged, aspect. Special attention will be given to the basic additional documents called for in a leveraged lease in the latter part of this chapter.

The following discussion is intended to provide a working knowledge of the typical collateral lease documents. The reader should keep in mind that most transactions have their own unique aspects that must also be taken into account.

B. THE IMPORTANCE OF OBTAINING CERTAIN LEGAL OPINIONS

Legal opinions from the lessor's counsel, the lessee's counsel, and possibly certain other participants' counsel are important in providing comfort on the many legal assumptions vital to the viability of a lease financing. They are of particular use on issues which form the basics of a transaction's economics, such as wehether or not the lessor's tax assumptions are correct. In addition, they can also be used to give certain assurances on other areas which may adversely impact the financing.

Before discussing the various opinions which may be involved, the reader must understand the value of a legal opinion. Some think that a favorable attorney's opinion on a problematical legal issue can be relied on absolutely as to the issue's outcome. It can not. Although rendered by a legal expert, it is by no means a *guarantee* that the aspects covered will have the resolution stated. An opinion is nothing more than an *opinion*. For example, if a lawyer concludes that, in his opinion, a company is duly authorized to enter into a particular lease transaction, this does not mean that the company was in fact authorized to enter into the transaction. Why is this so? Because, as with any other expert's opinion, a legal opinion is only an educated statement on the issues addressed. It is based on the information which the attorney has *access* to and has reviewed. If some information were not disclosed or if it were incorrectly presented the opinion might be worthless. This possibility becomes apparent when reading well-drafted opinions. Attorneys typically "qualify" them by stating, in effect, they have relied on the information supplied to them and if it is incorrect or incomplete their opinion no longer stands. In addition, even if the opinion is based upon his own thorough and independent investigation, it is possible he may have overlooked or misunderstood an important fact. There, of course, is also the possibility that he may be incorrect as to the relevant law.

RECOMMENDATIONS:

I. Although legal opinions may make a party feel secure as to the issues addressed, there are times when it may be advisable to take further action. For example, if a prospective lessor is concerned about whether a certain type of equipment will qualify as "section 38 property" under the Internal Revenue Code, it may be worthwhile applying to the Internal Revenue Service for a ruling on the point. A favorable Revenue Ruling will put the parties in a much better position than if they were to rely solely on counsel's opinion.

II. The "expertness" of the attorney giving an opinion is a very important consideration, particularly when complex legal issues are involved. Even though a particular individual is authorized to practice law and, therefore, theoretically able to render opinions on all legal issues, he may not be as experienced as necessary to render the best available opinion. For example, a tax attorney without leasing experience may be less adept at offering an opinion on certain esoteric and complex tax aspects of a lease transaction than one with a strong background in the area. Therefore, it is always wise to investigate the qualifications of the attorney who will render an opinion in light of the area to be addressed.

1. From the Lessee's Counsel

A prospective lessee is frequently asked to have its counsel provide a favorable written opinion on certain issues which the prospective lessor considers important. Typically, the opinion covers areas which are directly related to the legal and financial viability of the prospective lessee and its ability to enter into the transaction. The financial side will not, however, address aspects normally handled by the accountants, but will instead deal with any potential legal issues which could adversely affect the lessee's financial condition. For example, the prospective lessee's counsel is commonly requested to state whether there are any lawsuits pending or threatened against the prospective lessee and, if there are any, the possible dollar outcome. The thrust of the inquiry, of course, is to determine whether there are any lawsuits which could jeopardize the prospective lessee's financial condition as of the closing or in the future.

The prospective lessee's counsel is also frequently asked to give its opinion on certain of the representations which the lessee must make in the lease document. For example, a corporate-type lessee may be asked to represent that it is duly organized, validly existing, and in good standing under the laws of the state of its incorporation. In this event, the prospective lessee's counsel will be required to verify this representation in his opinion.

A lessee's opinion of counsel typically addresses the following issues:

• The proper legal organization, valid existance, and good standing of the lessee.

• The authority of the lessee to enter into the lease agreement.

- The ability of the lessee to perform all of its obligations under the lease documents.

- The legally binding nature of all of the lessee's lease commitments.

- Whether any consents, such as those of the shareholders or lenders, are necessary and, if so, whether they have been obtained.

- Whether any regulatory approval, such as a state public utility commission, is necessary. If so, whether all the proper action has been taken.

- Whether there is any adverse pending or threatened court or administrative proceeding against the lessee and, if so, the probable outcome.

- Whether, by entering into the lease arrangement or complying with any of its terms, the lessee would violate any law, rule, or provision of any of its existing agreements.

2. From the Lessor's Counsel

It is always a good idea for a prospective *lessee* to ask the prospective *lessor* to have its attorney deliver a favorable written opinion relating to its ability to legally enter into and perform its side of the lease agreement. For example, in the case of a corporate-type lessor, it will be important to determine whether it is properly incorporated at the time it signed the lease. If it is not, the lessee may later have a problem defining the appropriate person or entity to sue if a conflict arises. It might also be important for a prospective lessee to insure that the prospective lessor is properly qualified to do business in the state where the equipment will be used. If it is not, there may be a risk that the equipment could be attached by the state authorities for the nonpayment of any taxes which the lessor may owe.

There are a number of core issues which a prospective lessee should request to be covered in the opinion from the lessor's attorney. For example, whether the lessor's obligations under the lease and related documents are valid and binding, whether the transaction has been duly authorized, whether the prospective lessor has the ability to perform its obligations, whether it will be in violation of any law, rule, or agreement by entering into the lease arrangement, and whether any shareholder's or lender's consent is necessary. It should be remembered that there is no guarantee that the points covered by the opinion will be true as stated. The opinion will, however, provide the kind of comfort on which a reasonable business decision can be made.

a. A Lender Should also Require an Opinion

A prospective lender should ask that the prospective lessor's counsel deliver a favorable written opinion on key issues which go to the essence of its loan arrangement with the lessor. The typical issues deal with the same areas as those covered in the opinion given by the lessee's counsel to the lessor. That is, for example, whether the lessor is duly organized, validly existing, and in good standing in its state of incorporation, whether all of the necessary authorizations have been secured, and whether the lessor's obligations under the loan documents are fully enforceable. Particularly when the loan will be made on a nonrecourse basis, the lender will also want to know that the lessor has good and marketable title to the equipment covered by the lease, that the equipment is free and clear of any liens or encumbrances other than those of which the lender is aware, that the lessor has not made any other assignments of the lease, and that it has a free and unencumbered right to receive all payments such as rent under the lease agreement.

RECOMMENDATION:

A prospective lessor should consider requiring an opinion from the prospective lender's counsel confirming that all the necessary action in connection with the authorization of the loan has been taken. Many prospective lessors are so "grateful" to get the loan commitment they sometimes neglect to determine whether it was properly authorized. Without proper authorization they may run the risk of its being withdrawn.

3. From the Guarantor's Counsel

In many situations a third party will guarantee the lessee's lease obligations. For example, the parent company of a prospective financially weak corporate lessee may have to provide a guarantee in order to induce the prospective lessor to enter into the transaction. In this event the strength and viability of the guarantor's commitment will be more important to a prospective lessor (and a prospective nonrecourse lender if the transaction is leveraged) than the strength and viability of the lessee's commitment. In order to help confirm the worth of the guarantee, a favorable opinion from the prospective guarantor's counsel on certain relevant aspects will be requested.

Generally speaking, the issues which will have to be addressed in a guarantor counsel's opinion are similar to those in the lessee counsel's opinion to the lessor. For example, the requesting party will be concerned whether the guarantor is duly organized, validly existing, and in good standing; whether there is anything which could adversely affect the quality of the guarantee, such as material litigation; whether the guarantee has been fully and properly authorized; and whether it is a legally enforceable obligation.

4. From the Vendor's Counsel

Usually the party selling the equipment to be put under lease, the "vendor," is not asked to provide any legal opinions because his obligation is to do essentially nothing more than deliver clear title to the equipment. An adequate bill of sale containing proper seller representations and warranties can typically give any necessary comfort. In certain situations, however, a prospective lessor will ask the vendor for its counsel's opinion corroborating, for example, the delivery of clear title and the due authorization of the sale, particularly if a substantial dollar amount of equipment is involved. These types of additional reassurances are always worthwhile.

C. HOW TO HEDGE AGAINST UNEXPECTED FINANCIAL PROBLEMS

The financial weakness of any party to a lease could endanger the transaction. Therefore, each participant should consider taking certain steps to properly assess the financial stability of the other parties. One method of doing this is to request and review the relevant financial statements, including profit and loss statements and balance sheets. In other words, conducting a credit investigation.

The thoroughness of a credit investigation, of course, depends on how much money will be involved. For example, a small transaction involving a few office typewriters will not warrant an extensive analysis because the dollar investment is low and the equipment can probably be reacquired with relative ease. On the other hand, leases involving millions of dollars worth of equipment would dictate a comprehensive evaluation.

1. Of the Lessor

All too often prospective lessees fail to check the prospective lessor's financial condition. They apparently operate under the impression that a lessor will always have the money for a committed purchase and that once the purchase is made there is nothing to worry about. This is not necessarily true. A financially weak lessor can quickly run out of funds. In addition, there is always a risk with this type of lessor that one of its creditors could seize the leased equipment as security for unpaid obligations. Therefore, a prospective lessee should ask for and review the prospective lessor's financial statements before making an award.

Whether adequate funds will be available for equipment purchases is of particular concern when a lease line of credit is involved—that is, when a lessor has agreed to purchase and lease equipment which will be delivered over a long period of time. In this type of situation there is always an increased risk that the cash may not be there to go through with the financing when the equipment arrives. If the equipment is needed for immediate use, the lack of financing could be a serious problem for a would-be lessee. Even if the user could let the equipment sit idle while alternate funding arrangements were made, there is a risk that any new equipment would be classified "used" for Federal income tax purposes, thereby precluding as favorable a lease rate from a new lessor.

2. Of the Lessee

A prospective lessee's financial condition is usually a critical element in a prospective lessor's decision of whether to enter into a particular financing. This is particularly true when a major long-term lease is involved and the prospective lessor wants to be sure there is little risk the lease will end prematurely. Toward this end, therefore, the prospective lessee's *current* and *past* financial statements should be reviewed.

3. Of a Controlling Corporation

If a prospective lessee is controlled by another corporation, such as in a wholly owned subsidiary-parent relation, many prospective lessors, regardless of how financially strong the potential lessee is, review the controlling corporation's relevant financial statements. This is true even though it will not guarantee the lessee's obligations, because the weaker its financial condition the greater the likelihood that it will drain a lessee's cash or other assets in order to solve its own problems. This, in turn, could increase a lessor's credit risk to unacceptable levels.

RECOMMENDATION:

When there is a risk that an uninvolved controlling corporation could drain a prospective lessee's assets, certain precautions should be taken. A prospective lessor, for example, may be well advised to consider imposing restrictions to limit the amount of dividends which may be declared and distributed to the controlling corporation by the prospective lessee.

4. Of a Guarantor

Any time a lease is to be guaranteed by a third-party entity, such as a parent corporation, the *guarantor's* financial statements must be reviewed. Typically, a guarantor only becomes involved when the prospective lessee's financial condition is felt to be inadequate. In this event, therefore, the financial strength of the guarantor becomes the critical credit issue, both for the prospective lessor and probably any prospective transaction lender.

D. CERTAIN FINANCIAL ASSURANCES SHOULD BE REQUIRED

Since complete financial statements are not generally prepared in the normal course of business more than four times a year, it is usually impractical to attempt to coincide a lease closing with any of the issuance dates. How then can a prospective lessor make sure there have been no adverse changes in the prospective lessee's financial condition as of a transaction closing date not falling on one of these dates? The simplest way is to require an appropriate financial officer to deliver a certificate at the closing which, in effect, brings the last published financial statements up to date. For example, if the most current financial statements reflect a company's condition as of May 15, 19XX and the transaction does not close until June 2, 19XX, the certificate should provide that as of the closing date, June 2, 19XX, there have been no materially adverse financial changes since the date of the latest financial statements, May 15, 19XX. Of course, it would be more comforting to get the company's independent accountants to issue the certificate, but this is generally not practical.

RECOMMENDATION:

The concept of requiring financial certificates should not be limited to the prospective lessee. They should be requested from any party whose financial condition may affect the viability of the transaction, such as a prospective guarantor.

E. HOW TO CONFIRM THAT NECESSARY CORPORATE ACTION HAS BEEN TAKEN

When a corporation is involved in a major lease transaction, the other party, or parties, should require a copy of the board of directors' resolutions authorizing the transaction. The resolutions should be certified by the corporate secretary or assistant secretary and delivered at the closing. A proper resolution from a prospective lessee's board of directors would in effect provide that the prospective lessee has been duly authorized to enter into the transaction for the specified dollar amount and that a certain person has been authorized to execute the documents on behalf of the corporation.

RECOMMENDATIONS:

I. Prospective lessors and lenders usually require prospective lessees to deliver appropriate board of directors' resolutions at a lease closing. Prospective lessees, however, frequently do not consider asking for authorizing resolutions from the other parties. They should make such a request, particularly from prospective corporate lessors not regularly in the leasing business and lenders not in the "regular" lending business.

II. If once a lease has been entered into it is discovered that any other party has failed to get necessary board of directors' approval, that party should be requested to deliver appropriate resolutions *approving, ratifying,* and *confirming* all the actions that have been taken.

III. While it is important to make board of directors' resolutions reasonably broad in scope, corporate directors should be careful not to grant more than is necessary. For example, if a lease transaction is to involve a vessel, its cost should be specified with leeway for reasonable changes. Without designating the cost, an individual representing the corporation may be able to bind it to a lease even if there were unexpected and significant cost increases.

F. IF GUARANTEES ARE NECESSARY, WHAT MUST THEY COVER?

Companies sometimes want to lease a dollar amount of equipment that is beyond their credit capability. In order, therefore, to get the desired lease financing, a financially strong third party may have to be brought in to guarantee the lease obligations. Depending on the situation, lease guarantees vary anywhere from a *full* guarantee of *all* the lease obligations to something significantly less.

In a typical full lessee guarantee, the guarantor would unconditionally obligate himself to insure the lessee's *full* and *prompt* performance of all the lease obligations, convenants, and conditions. In the event, for example, the lessee does not pay the rent, the lessor would have the right to go directly to the guarantor for payment. Generally, the guarantor would have the right to go against the lessee for reimbursement of any amounts paid.

A full and unconditional guarantee is to be distinguished from a partial guarantee in which the guarantor may, for example, only guarantee the repayment of 10% of the total lease payments. Partial guarantees frequently come about when the proposed transaction is very attractive to the prospective lessor and he is willing to make compromises.

G. PROOF OF INSURANCE IS THE BEST INSURANCE

Frequently lessees are required to take out personal injury and property damage insurance as to the leased equipment. In these situations the prospective lessor should make sure the insurance will be in effect when it accepts it for lease. One of the best ways to do this is to have the agreed-upon insurance company deliver a *certificate of insurance* stating that the necessary insurance has been purchased.

RECOMMENDATIONS:

I. A certificate of insurance should be carefully reviewed to verify that the coverage is proper and that it will be in effect when necessary. Any coverage limitations, such as restricted equipment usage, should be carefully considered.

II. A prospective lessor should make sure the required insurance coverage cannot be cancelled without prior written notice to him followed by an adequate grace period. In this way if the lessee does not keep the insurance in force, the lessor has the opportunity of taking over his obligations in order to prevent the insurance from lapsing.

H. SHOULD A PROSPECTIVE LESSOR ENTER INTO AN EQUIPMENT PURCHASE AGREEMENT?

Equipment purchase agreements are frequently entered into by prospective lessees well before they decide how the equipment is going to be financed, particularly when there is a long equipment delivery time. An equipment purchase agreement is simply a contract for the sale of specified equipment. Typically, it specifies the price, the type of equipment, the payment terms, and the obligations of the parties.

Before the lease agreement has been signed should a prospective lessor enter into a purchase agreement directly with a supplier for equipment which a prospective lessee needs? No, because if the "lessee," with or without justification, refuses to accept the equipment for lease, the "lessor" may still be legally obligated to buy the equipment. Therefore, if a purchase agreement must be executed early, the prospective lessor should insist that the prospective lessee be the signing party.

1. A Purchase Agreement Assignment—a Good Solution

As already discussed, if an equipment purchase agreement must be executed before a prospective lessee has fully committed to lease the equipment, the prospective lessor should not be talked into entering into it with the equipment supplier. When new equipment is involved, however, it is advisable for a prospective lessor to contractually take title to the equipment directly from the supplier to avoid any possible Internal Revenue Service contention that the equipment was not technically new equipment for tax purposes as to the prospective lessor when he became the owner. Therefore, when a purchase contract must be signed, how can a prospective lessor be in a position to be the direct contract transferee and at the same time not be obligated to purchase the equipment if the prospective lessee refuses to go through with the lease? The answer is by using a *purchase agreement assignment* in conjunction with the *purchase agreement*. Under such an arrangement the prospective lessee and the equipment supplier would enter into the necessary purchase agreement and then the prospective lessor and lessee would enter into an assignment of this agreement. Under the assignment the prospective lessor typically acquires the prospective lessee's contract purchase rights but not its obligations. The rights generally transferred not only include the right to purchase the designated equipment but also the rights to any service, training, or information which the prospective lessee would be entitled to as purchaser and any purchaser warranties or indemnities. The prospective lessor is then in a position of being able to walk away if the prospective lessee backs out at the last minute. In this situation, the prospective lessee remains ultimately liable to the supplier.

> RECOMMENDATION:
>
> If a prospective lessor enters into a purchase agreement assignment he should be careful not to assume any of the *duties* or *obligations* of the buyer under the purchase agreement. In this regard he should have it specified in the assignment that the prospective lessee will remain *liable* on the purchase contract as if the assignment had not been made.

a. It Is a Good Idea to Get the Equipment Supplier's Consent

When a prospective lessor enters into an equipment purchase agreement assignment with a prospective lessee it should, at the same time, get the supplier's written consent to the assignment. The consent should contain an acknowledgement of the assignment as well as a concession that any rights assigned, such as supplier warranties, will accrue to the benefit of the prospective lessor just as though it had been originally named as the buyer. In addition, the supplier should be asked to acknowledge that the prospective lessor will not be liable for any of the purchase contract duties or obligations.

I. AN EQUIPMENT BILL OF SALE IS IMPORTANT

A prospective lessor generally requires the seller to deliver a bill of sale when it pays for the equipment. The bill of sale is frequently a *warranty* bill of sale in which the seller not only transfers title to the subject equipment but also warrants that he has full legal and beneficial title to it, free and clear of any encumbrances, mortgages, or security interests. In addition, the seller generally represents that he has the lawful right and the appropriate authority to sell the equipment.

RECOMMENDATION:

A prospective lessor should require the seller to represent in an equipment bill of sale that he will defend the prospective lessor's title to the equipment against any person or entity claiming an interest in the equipment.

J. HOW TO AVOID PROBLEM CLAIMS FROM OWNERS OF LAND ON WHICH LEASED EQUIPMENT WILL BE LOCATED

Frequently the leased equipment will be located on property which is leased from a third party or which is subject to a mortgage. Statutory lien rights may exist which, for example, would permit a landlord to attach *any* equipment on his land, including leased equipment, if his rent were not paid. The holder of a mortgage on a lessee's building may, under a general mortgage claim right, be able to go after leased equipment located in the building. When such a situation exists, the prospective lessor should get a waiver from the landlord or mortgagee of any claim on the leased equipment.

K. ASSURANCE AGAINST PREMATURE EQUIPMENT USE CAN BE IMPORTANT

When new equipment is delivered prior to the execution of the lease, it is important for a prospective lessor to confirm that it will be the "first user" for Federal income tax purposes. In other words, that the equipment has not been "placed in service" prior to the lessor taking title to it.

A practical way to do this is to have a "certificate of non-use" delivered at the closing. In the certificate the lessee represents that the equipment has not been used by any person or entity in such a manner which precludes the "original use" from commencing with the lessor as of the date the equipment is acquired. A sample form of certificate of non-use has been included in the Appendix.

OBSERVATIONS:

I. Although a certificate of non-use will not guarantee that the lessor will be the "first user," most lessees will not execute such a statement unless they are sure there is no problem.

II. Even though a lessor is indemnified against any loss of tax benefits if the property does not qualify under the Internal Revenue Code as "new" property, most will not rely on the indemnification but rather will request confirmation in some form that the equipment will qualify as new.

L. HOW A LESSOR CAN GET EXTRA PROTECTION AGAINST THIRD-PARTY CLAIMS

When significant dollar amounts of equipment are involved, it is advisable for a lessor to consider filing appropriate Uniform Commercial Code financing statements. Filing such a statement in effect gives notice to the world of the lessor's interest in the equipment and will prevent successful claims against it by any of the lessee's creditors.

Uniform Commercial Code financing statements are generally filed in the state where the leased equipment will be located. If the statement is not correctly filed, the lessor's claim to the equipment will not be "perfected" as to third parties, such as general creditors of the lessee, and may not give the necessary protection. The statement is simple in form and basically requires nothing more than a description of the parties and the equipment. The procedures and expense of filing are nominal.

OBSERVATION:

Although, theoretically, many feel a *lessee's* creditors could not prevail against a lessor in a claim against the leased equipment even if a UCC financing statement had not been filed, the possibility always exists that a claim may succeed.

M. WHAT IS THE PURPOSE OF A PARTICIPATION AGREEMENT?

A participation agreement is frequently used in underwritten lease transactions, particularly leveraged transactions. Generally speaking, the parties to the agreement are the prospective lessee, the prospective debt participants, and the prospective equity participants. If a trust is established for either the debt or the equity participants, the representative trustee will also be a party.

The primary purpose of a participation agreement is to establish the general parameters of the financing. It prescribes the terms under which the debt participants must make their loans and the equity participants must make their equity investments. It also usually provides for a method for substituting any defaulting participants and, in addition, may set forth any prescribed tax indemnification provisions.

N. WHAT IS THE PURPOSE OF AN OWNER'S TRUST AGREEMENT?

A trust is often established for the equity participant side of a leveraged lease transaction, typically when more than one equity participant is involved. The trust arrangement provides the equity participants with corporate-like liability protection and partnership-like income tax treatment and therefore can be a desirable ownership vehicle for equity participants.

In order to set up a trust, the equity participants enter into a trust agreement with an entity, such as a bank, which will act as the trustee, commonly referred to as the "owner trustee." The trust agreement spells out in detail how and to what extent the trustee will act on behalf of the equity participants including establishing the trustee's duties.

Typically, the trustee will execute all relevant documents, including the lease, the participation agreement, the indenture, and the purchase agreement assignment, on behalf of each equity participant. The right, title and interest in the equipment, the lease, any purchase agreement, and any purchase agreement assignment is collectively referred to as the *trust estate* and legal title to it is held in the owner trustee's name. The owner trustee is, however, only a figurehead owner, the *beneficial interest* in the trust estate resting with the equity participants. The equity participant's interests are represented by certificates, commonly referred to as *owner certificates*, which are issued by the owner trustee.

O. WHAT IS THE PURPOSE OF A LENDER'S TRUST AGREEMENT?

Many lease underwriting transactions are structured as leveraged leases. In these cases the debt participants frequently act through a trust arrangement in order to receive favorable tax treatment and liability protection. The arrangement is typically set up through a *trust indenture and mortgage agreement* which is entered into between the equity side and debt side. A trust indenture and mortgage agreement defines the basic debt financing parameters and provides for the issuance of loan certificates that set out the debt repayment obligations. The agreement also grants a security interest to the lenders in the equipment and the lease while the loan is outstanding.

The debt participants are represented by a trustee, commonly referred to as the "loan trustee." The loan trustee stands in the same position to the debt participants as does the owner trustee to the equity participants. As the "watchdog" for the debt participants, the trustee is empowered to take any prescribed actions which may be necessary to protect the loan participants' interests, such as foreclosing on the lease in the event of a default.

P. AN ALTERNATE WAY FOR MULTIPLE EQUITY OR DEBT PARTICIPANTS TO ACT TOGETHER

If multiple equity or debt participants find it undesirable or impractical to act through a trust arrangement, they can use a partnership structure. In this case the "lessor" or "lender," as the case may be, is the partnership. Although not always absolutely necessary, it is advisable for a formal partnership agreement to be entered into which defines the rights and obligations of each partner.

Q. WHAT AN UNDERWRITER SHOULD DO TO PROTECT HIS FEE

The job of a lease underwriter is to bring together the equity participants, the lessee, and if the transaction is leveraged, sometimes the debt participants. These services are performed for a fee which varies with each transaction and each broker. The fee is typically payable by the equity participants. In order to protect himself and make sure there are no later "misunderstandings" as to the payment terms, the underwriter should require the equity participants to enter into a formal "fee agreement" in which the fee arrangement is clearly defined.

R. A SUPPLEMENTAL LEASE DOCUMENT CHECKLIST

Although the type of supplemental documents used in a lease transaction vary with each situation, the following checklist can be used as a general guide.

1. Have the Following Issues Been Addressed as to Required Legal Opinions?
   a. Is the Attorney Rendering a Critical Legal Opinion Thoroughly Experienced in the Area to Be Covered by the Opinion? For Example, if an Opinion Is Required on Esoteric Tax Issues, Is He Fully Knowledgeable on All the Relevant Aspects?

    b. Will the Legal Opinion Be Conditioned to Such an Extent That It Has Little Value? In Other Words, Has the Attorney Left Himself so Many Outs as to His Position That He Really Has Provided Little Comfort?

    c. If the Legal Opinion Is Based upon Facts Supplied to Counsel, Is There Any Great Likelihood That the Facts May Not Be Accurate?

2. Does the Opinion of the Prospective Lessee's Counsel, to Be Delivered to the Lessor, Address the Following Issues:

    a. Proper Organization, Valid Existence, and Good Standing of the Lessee.

    b. Full Authority of the Lessee to Enter into the Lease.

    c. Complete and Unrestricted Ability of the Lessee to Perform All Obligations.

    d. The Binding Nature as to the Lessee of All the Commitments.

    e. Whether Any Necessary Consents Have Been Obtained.

    f. Whether Any Necessary Regulatory Approvals Have Been Obtained.

    g. Whether There Are Any Pending or Threatened Adverse Court or Administrative Proceedings. If so, What the Potential Impact May Be.

    h. Whether Any Law, Rule, or Collateral Agreement Will Be Violated by the Lessee Entering the Lease Transaction.

3. Does the Opinion of the Lessor's Counsel, to Be Delivered to the Lessee, Address the Following Issues:

    a. Is the Lessor Properly Organized, Validly Existing, and in Good Standing?

    b. Is the Lessor Properly Authorized to Do Business in the Jurisdiction Where the Equipment Will Be Located?

    c. Has the Transaction Been Fully Authorized by the Lessor? For Example, Have All Necessary Committee and Board of Director Approvals Been Secured?

    d. Are All the Lessor's Commitments Binding?

    e. Will the Lessor's Ability to Perform Its Obligations Be Unrestricted?

    f. Are Any Shareholder, Lender, Etc., Consents Necessary? If so, Have They Been Obtained?

    g. Will the Transaction Violate Any Law, Rule, or Collateral Agreement as to the Lessor?

4. Does the Opinion of Lessor's Counsel, to Be Delivered to a Third-Party Lender, Address the Following Issues:

    a. Is the Lessor Properly Organized, Validly Existing, and in Good Standing?

    b. Have All Necessary Authorizations, Both as to the Lease Financing and the Loan Financing, Been Obtained?

    c. Are the Loan Obligations Fully Enforceable Against the Lessor?

    d. Does the Lessor Have Good and Marketable Title to the Leased Equipment?

    e. Will the Equipment Have Any Liens or Encumbrances on It?

    f. Are the Lessor's Rights under the Lease Unencumbered, Including Its Right to Receive the Rent Payments?

5. Does the Opinion of Guarantor's Counsel, to Be Delivered to the Lessor, Address the Following Issues:

    a. Whether the Guarantor Is Properly Organized, Validly Existing, and in Good Standing.

    b. Have All Necessary Authorizations, Both as to the Lease Financing and the Loan Financing, Been Obtained?

    c. Are Loan Obligations Fully Enforceable Against the Guarantor?

    d. Does the Guarantor Have Good and Marketable Title to the Leased Equipment?

    e. Whether the Equipment Has Any Liens or Encumbrances On It.

    f. Whether the Guarantor's Rights under the Lease Are Unencumbered, Including Its Right to Receive the Rent Payments.

6. Does the Opinion of Vendor's Counsel, to Be Delivered to the Lessor, Address the Following Issues:

    a. Will the Title to the Equipment Be Delivered Free and Clear to the Lessor?

    b. Have All Necessary Internal Authorizations Been Obtained?

7. Has the Lessor Obtained Adequate Lessee, Lessee Controlling Corporation, and Guarantor Financial Statements for the Last Five Years?

    a. Profit and Loss Statements.

    b. Balance Sheets.

    c. Other.

8. Has the Lessee Obtained Adequate Lessor Financial Statements for the Last Five Years?

    a. Profit and Loss Statements.

    b. Balance Sheets.

    c. Other.

9. Have All the Critical Financial Statements Been Certified by an Independent Certified Public Accounting Firm?

10. Has a Certified Copy of Any Relevant Corporate Board of Director Resolutions Been Delivered?
11. If the Lease Obligations Will Be Guaranteed by a Third Party, Will It Be a Full and Unconditional Guarantee? If Not, Is the Limited Extent of the Guarantee Understood?
12. If Personal Injury and/or Propery Damage Insurance Is Required, Does the Insurance Company's Certificate of Insurance Properly Represent the Required Insurance?
13. If the Prospective Lessor Must Enter into an Equipment Purchase Agreement Directly with the Vendor, Is It Prepared to Buy the Equipment if the Lessee Backs Away? If Not, Can a Purchase Agreement Assignment Be Used?
    a. Does Any Equipment Purchase Agreement Assignment Specifically Provide That Only the Rights, Not the Obligations, Will Be Transferred to the Prospective Lessor?
    b. Under an Equipment Purchase Agreement Assignment Will the Lessor Be Entitled to All Vendor Supplied Services, Training, Information, Warranties, and Indemnities?
    c. Has the Vendor's Consent Been Obtained as to the Purchase Agreement Assignment. If so, Does It
       (1) Acknowledge the Assignment?
       (2) Acknowledge That the Lessor Will Not Have to Buy the Equipment if the Lessee Backs Out Before the Lease Is Executed?
14. Has an Equipment Bill of Sale Been Included? If so,
    a. Is It a Warranty Bill of Sale?
    b. Does It Contain a Representation That the Seller Has the Lawful Right and Authority to Sell the Equipment?
15. If the Equipment Will Be Located on Leased or Mortgaged Property, has the Landowner or Mortgagee Supplied a Written Waiver of Any Present or Future Claim to the Leased Equipment?
16. If New Equipment Is Involved and It Has Been Delivered Before the Lease Execution, Has an Appropriate Certificate of Non-Use Been Requested?
17. Have Appropriate Uniform Commercial Code Financing Statements (UCC-1's) Been Prepared for Filing?
18. If the Transaction Is Underwritten:
    a. Has a Participation Agreement Been Prepared?
    b. Will the Lenders and the Equity Participants Each Act Through:
       (1) A Trust Arrangement?
       (2) A Partnership Arrangement?
19. Has a Fee Agreement Been Prepared to Formalize the Underwriter's Fee Arrangement?

5

INVESTMENT TAX CREDIT
UNDER THE CODE

**Exactly What Is The Investment Tax Credit? • How Is It Computed? •
There Are Many Eligibility Restrictions • A Lessee Can Cause A Lessor
To Lose It • Is There A Way For A Lessee To Claim It?**

A. INVESTMENT TAX CREDIT AND EQUIPMENT LEASING

Under Section 38 of the Internal Revenue Code, a taxpayer can claim a
credit against his Federal income tax liability based upon his investment in
certain types of depreciable property which have been *acquired* and *placed
in service* during a taxable year. The ability of a lessor to claim the investment tax credit available on equipment it leases is often a key ingredient in
the economic viability of its lease transactions. In these situations, the loss
or inability to claim the anticiptated credit in any particular transaction can
destroy his expected "economic" return. Because of this, it is absolutely essential for equipment lessors relying on investment tax credit availability,
and those representing them, to have a thorough understanding of all the
surrounding concepts and rules.

Prospective lessees, and their representatives, must have a solid appreciation of the investment credit rules for two basic reasons. First,
prospective lessees cannot properly evaluate whether it would be more
beneficial to purchase or lease an item of equipment unless they know how
to work with these rules. Secondly, prospective lessees are often asked to
provide lessors with certain indemnifications against the loss or inability to
claim the investment credit. In these instances, a prospective lessee cannot
adequately protect himself against undue indemnification risks unless he is
fully aware of what he is being asked to provide.

The investment tax credit rules prescribed in the Code and related
Treasury Regulations are complex. There are, however, five simple princi-

ples which generally sum up certain essential equipment lease related concepts that the reader should keep in mind. They are:

- The maximum investment tax credit allowed currently is equal to 10 percent of the cost of the equipment on which it is claimed.

- A taxpayer can only claim the maximum investment tax credit benefit if the equipment has a useful life of seven years or more.

- Equipment with a useful life of less than three years will not qualify for investment tax credit.

- Equipment will not be eligible for investment tax credit unless it is both tangible and personal property. Certain "other tangible property" is also eligible. This type of property is referred to under the Code as "section 38 property." Real property is generally excluded.

- Investment tax credit can only be *claimed* on section 38 property for the first taxable year in which it is placed into service.

B. ESSENTIALS IN COMPUTING INVESTMENT TAX CREDIT

The amount of investment tax credit which a taxpayer is allowed to claim for any taxable year is equal to a certain percentage of his "qualified investment" in section 38 property which *he* has acquired *and* placed in service during that year. A taxpayer's "qualified investment" in eligible property is in effect his *cost*. If the useful life of the property is less than seven years, only a portion of the qualified investment amount may be used in the investment credit computation.

NOTE:
If the useful life of otherwise eligible section 38 property is less than three years, no investment tax credit is allowed.

The actual percentage of a taxpayer's qualified investment which is to be used has varied widely over the years. Because the investment tax credit rate has been subject to continual governmental review in the past, the percentage at any point in time should always be verified with an appropriate tax advisor. The Revenue Act of 1978[1] and the Energy Tax Act of 1978[2], for example, made certain significant changes. At the time of this writing the percentage is generally equal to 10 percent[3].

1. There Are Special Restrictions

Can a taxpayer claim an unlimited amount of investment tax credit for a taxable year? No, the total amount of credit that a taxpayer may claim is limited to the sum of (i) an amount up to the first $25,000 of his Federal income tax liability and (ii) 60 to 90 percent, depending on when the taxable year ends, of his Federal income tax liability in excess of the first $25,000 of Federal income tax liability.[4] If his Federal income tax liability is less than $25,000 for a taxable year, the total credit which may be claimed for that year is restricted to his Federal income tax liability.

The amount of investment tax credit which may be claimed as to *used* property is further limited. A taxpayer may not claim, for a taxable year, investment credit on used property with an aggregate value in excess of $100,000.[5] If the aggregate cost of the property exceeds the specified limitation, a selection must be made as to which items of used property will be taken into account for the year. Special rules apply for corporate controlled groups, partnerships, and members of partnerships.

The Code makes a distinction between the amount of investment tax credit a taxpayer *earns* for a taxable year and the amount which may be *used* for the same year. The amount of credit a taxpayer earns is referred to as the "credit earned." The excess over that which may be used is referred to as the "unused credit." For Federal income tax purposes, a taxpayer currently may, in general, carry the unused credit back three years and forward seven years.

C. HOW IS A TAXPAYER'S "QUALIFIED INVESTMENT" COMPUTED?

The amount of investment credit that may be claimed by a taxpayer for a taxable year is calculated by multiplying the appropriate investment credit rate times his "qualified investment" in certain eligible property. Calculating a taxpayer's qualified investment takes a little work.

The basic determining rule, set forth in section 46(c)(1) of the Code, provides that a taxpayer's qualified investment for any taxable year is equal to the sum of:

- the *applicable percentage* of the *basis* of each item of new section 38 property which the taxpayer *places in service* during such taxable year, plus

- the *applicable percentage* of the *cost* of each item of used section 38 property which the taxpayer *places in service* during such taxable year.

Therefore, in order to make the computation, a taxpayer must ascertain the appropriate *basis or cost* and the *applicable percentage* for each item of eligible property which has been *placed in service* during the relevant tax year. Although the formula appears to be somewhat complex, everything will readily fall into place once the key ingredients are clearly understood.

1. "Basis" Defined

Is there anything unique about determining the "basis" of property for investment tax credit purposes? No, it is made in the same way as it is determined generally under the Code.[6] For example, if a taxpayer purchases new section 38 property, his basis in the property is his cost. In making the computation, he can include such items as freight, sales, and installation charges.

2. "Applicable Percentage" Defined

The "applicable percentage" to be applied by a taxpayer against his basis in new section 38 property and cost of used section 38 property is determined by reference to the property's useful life.[7] In the case of property with a useful life of at least three years, but less than five years, it is equal to 33⅓ percent. If the property has a useful life of at least five years, but less than seven years, it is equal to 66⅔ percent. For property with a useful life of at least seven years it is equal to 100 percent. Property with a useful life of less than three years is not eligible for investment tax credit and, therefore, there is no applicable percentage for such property.

OBSERVATION:

It is important to note that the useful life which a taxpayer selects in computing a property's depreciation allowance fixes the useful life which must be used in determining its "applicable percentage." In other words, if a taxpayer writes off an asset with a basis of $999 over a five year period, his qualified investment would be 66⅔ percent of $999, or $666. If the investment tax percentage were 10%, he would be entitled to claim a credit of $66 (10% x $666). If the asset had been depreciated over a seven year period instead (the useful life neces- sary for maximum investment credit benefit), the applicable percentage would be 100% of basis. The taxpayer would then be able to claim a credit of $99 (10% x 100% x $999). Therefore, a lessor intending to claim an investment tax credit must carefully analyze the economic benefits of depreciating an asset over a period shorter than seven years against not being able to claim the full available investment tax credit.

3. "Placed in Service" Defined

A taxpayer can claim investment tax credit only on eligible property which has been "placed in service" *by the taxpayer* during the relevant taxable year. For investment credit purposes, eligible property is deemed to have been placed in service in the *earlier* of the following taxable years:

- The year in which, under the taxpayer's depreciation practice, the taxpayer begins to depreciate the property.

- The year in which the property is in a *condition to be used*, whether in a trade or business, in the production of income, in a tax-exempt activity, or in a personal activity.

OBSERVATION:

As the reader can see, the second alternative will cause eligible property to be considered "placed in service" when it is first *available* for service, which may in fact be before its first *actual* use. This precludes a taxpayer from claiming investment tax credit on an eligible asset in a later taxable year merely by waiting until that year to begin depreciating it. Therefore, when it is in a condition to be used (i.e., under the Treasury Regulations in a condition or state of readiness and availability for a specifically assigned function), it will be considered "placed in service," regardless of when the taxpayer starts depreciating it.

Determining when property is in a condition for use is not always easy. The rules provide some assistance on this critical issue through sample situations. For example, parts which were acquired and set aside as replacement parts for a machine to avoid any loss of operation time in the event of a breakdown; operational equipment acquired for a specific function and which is put through a testing period to eliminate defects; and farm equipment which is operational and which was acquired for a specific function in the taxpayer's farming business, but was not put into use because it was not practicable to do so until a following taxable year are deemed to be in a condition for use when acquired. On the other hand, fruit-bearing trees and vines which have not reached an income-producing stage and materials and parts which were acquired to be used, but not yet used, to construct an item of equipment are not considered to be in a condition for use.

PITFALL:

Sometimes equipment ordered by a prospective lessee arrives before the lease agreement is executed. If the prospective lessor's rental rate determination is based on claiming the available investment tax credit, the early arrival could jeopardize its availability because of the placed in service criteria. That is, the equipment may be deemed placed in service before the lessor purchases it. If a lessor cannot, or does not, adjust the rent upward to reflect the unavailability, the transaction's anticipated yield could be materially reduced. When the investment credit is anticipated, therefore, lessors often put the risk of its loss on the lessee through *tax indemnification provisions*. These provisions typically not only cover a premature use, but also many other potential tax benefit loss possibilities.

Whether property *qualifies* as section 38 property is determined in the taxable year the property is placed in service by the taxpayer.[8] If the property is used during the first taxable year it is placed in service in such a manner that prevents it from qualifying as section 38 property, the investment tax credit is lost permanently even though it is used in later years in a non-disqualifying manner. If only a part of the property does not qualify as section 38 property when it is placed in service, the credit may still be claimed on the qualifying portion.

D. THE EQUIPMENT'S USEFUL LIFE IS A KEY FACTOR

In order for a taxpayer to compute his qualified investment in investment credit eligible property he must determine the appropriate *applicable percentage* to apply against its basis or cost, as the case may be. The applicable percentage depends on the property's *useful life*. Therefore, the property's useful life is an important factor. For example, if the property's useful life is at least seven years the applicable percentage is 100 percent.

How does a taxpayer actually determine the property's useful life for investment credit purposes? Generally speaking, it can be done, at the taxpayer's election, either under the "class life" method or under the "facts and circumstances" method, at the time the property is placed in service. Under the "class life" method, the useful life is determined in accordance with the rules in Section 4, Part II of Revenue Procedure 62-21. The rules prescribed establish certain lives for assets within specified categories. Under the "facts and circumstances" method, the taxpayer makes an estimate of the useful life based upon all of the facts and circumstances surrounding its use.

OBSERVATION:

A taxpayer's choice of useful life for depreciation computation purposes will "lock in" the useful life for the investment tax credit computation purposes. In other words, if a taxpayer depreciates an asset over a five year period useful life, the applicable percentage will be 66⅔ percent for qualified investment determination purposes.

E. INVESTMENT TAX CREDIT CAN BE LOST IN MANY WAYS

The fact that property would *appear* to qualify for investment tax credit at the time it is placed in service does not mean that it will actually qualify or continue to qualify. If section 38 property which is otherwise eligible for investment tax credit is disposed of by the taxpayer, or it ceases to be section 38 property, at any time during the first taxable year the property is placed in service, the taxpayer cannot initially claim the credit. In addition, if it were disposed of or ceases to be section 38 property in any subsequent tax year, a taxpayer might lose some or all of the credit initially claimed. In the latter case the taxpayer would be said to have suffered an investment credit "recapture."

If a taxpayer suffers an investment tax credit recapture, his Federal income tax liability will increase for the taxable year during which the disposition or cessation which caused the recapture took place. The increase in tax liability will be equal to the required decrease in investment tax credit initially claimed. In other words, the amount which must be recaptured will be equal to the difference between the total credit originally claimed and an investment tax credit computed on the basis of a useful life, computed from the time the property was placed in service by the taxpayer to the date of the disqualifying event. For example, if a taxpayer disposed of property four years after he purchased it (on which he had initially claimed an investment tax credit based on a useful life of nine years), his Federal income tax liability for the year of disposition would be *increased* by an amount equal to ⅔ of the credit initially claimed. As the reader will recall, this is due to the fact that the qualified investment applicable percentage for a four year useful life is 33⅓ percent, as opposed to 100 percent for a nine year useful life.

For the purpose of investment credit recapture calculations, the determining useful life is the shortest life within the useful life category used to establish the appropriate qualified investment applicable percentage. That is, if the taxpayer claimed a credit when the property was placed in service based upon a four year useful life, but the property was disposed of or ceased to be section 38 property in the third year, the property would not be deemed to have been disposed of prior to the end of its useful life.

1. Two Situations Which Look Like "Dispositions"—But Are Not

Section 38 property which is "disposed of" by a taxpayer is no longer eligible for investment tax credit. The term "disposition" is defined by the investment credit rules to include a sale in a sale-and-leaseback transaction, a transfer as a result of the foreclosure of a security interest, and a gift. However, the rules specifically provide that *a taxpayer-vendor* who disposes of section 38 property after he has placed it in service and, as part of the same transaction, leases it back, will not suffer a "disposition" for investment credit purposes. This is true *even though he must recognize a gain or loss as to the property and can no longer depreciate it.* In addition, the rules also provide that a "mere" transfer of title to a creditor upon the creation of a security interest in investment credit eligible property will not result in a "disposition."[9]

2. A Special Point About Leased Equipment

Generally speaking, a taxpayer is entitled to claim investment credit on section 38 property which he leases to a third party.[10] If, however, the leased property would not qualify as section 38 property in the hands of the lessee or any sub-lessee during the investment credit vesting period, it will cease to be section 38 property and the lessor will suffer a recapture.

a. The Recapture Risk for a Lessee Entitled To Claim the Credit

As will be explained in Section S of this chapter, a lessor of new section 38 property may elect, pursuant to Section 48(d) of the Code, to "pass through" to the lessee the available investment credit. Very simply this means that the lessee will be able to claim the available investment credit on the property which has been leased to him by the lessor. Once the election has been made, a subsequent disposition by the lessor of the property will not, in general, cause the lessee to lose the investment credit. If, however, it were disposed of during the credit vesting period to someone who would be unable to make a "pass through" election, the lessee would suffer a credit recapture. If the "election property" would not qualify in the hands of the lessor or any sublessee as section 38 property, it will not qualify as section 38 property with respect to the lessee.

RECOMMENDATION:

If a prospective lessor has agreed to "pass through" the available investment credit on the leased property to the prospective lessee, the prospective lessee must make sure that the lease prohibits the lessor from doing anything that would make the credit unavailable.

3. An Equipment Casualty Loss Can Be a Problem

In general, section 38 property will cease to be section 38 property if it is destroyed by fire, shipwreck, storm, or other such casualty. If, therefore, a taxpayer claimed the full investment credit on property that was completely destroyed by fire four years after it was acquired, the taxpayer would suffer a credit recapture of two-thirds of the credit claimed. It is interesting to note that under the tax rules a casualty loss would *not* have resulted in a "disposition" or "cessation" of section 38 status if the loss occurred after April 18, 1969, but before August 16, 1971.

4. A Change in Ownership Form Can Cause a Credit Loss

Generally, if a taxpayer changes the form of the trade or business in which section 38 property is used, a "disposition" or "cessation" for investment credit purposes is not deemed to have occurred.[11] For example, if the taxpayer were initially a partnership when it acquired investment credit eligible equipment, a change to a corporate form would not cause a loss of any credit which had been claimed and which had not yet vested. The rule however, is subject to the following conditions:

- The property must be retained as section 38 property in the same trade or business.

- The transferor of the property must retain a substantial interest in the trade or business.

- Substantially all of the assets of the trade or business necessary for its operation must be transferred to the transferee of the section 38 property.

Whether a transferor has retained a "substantial interest" in a trade or business is sometimes a difficult issue. The criterion is satisfied if, after the change in form, his interest is substantial in relation to the remaining interests or is at least equal to his prior interest.[12] For example, a taxpayer who formerly held a 5 percent interest in a partnership which was converted into a corporation and who, after the conversion, has a 5 percent interest in the corporation, is said to have retained a "substantial interest" in the trade or business.

F. WHETHER SECTION 38 PROPERTY HAS LOST ITS STATUS MUST BE REGULARLY REVIEWED

During the investment credit vesting period (the useful life period used to calculate the investment credit claimed) a taxpayer must, at the end of each taxable year following the year the investment tax credit was claimed, determine whether any section 38 property has ceased to be section 38 property. If any such property will no longer qualify as section 38 property, he must recompute the amount of credit to which he is entitled and make the appropriate adjustment to his Federal income tax liability.

OBSERVATION:

If property otherwise qualifies as section 38 property, the fact that it may no longer be *depreciated* under the taxpayer's depreciation practice will not cause it to lose section 38 status if the taxpayer continues to use the property in his trade or business or in the production of income.

G. SPECIAL CREDIT LOSS RULES ARE PRESCRIBED FOR USED SECTION 38 PROPERTY

If a taxpayer claims an investment tax credit on "*used* section 38 property" and if such property is disposed of or ceases to be section 38 property prior to the end of the credit vesting period, in certain cases the taxpayer may prevent a credit recapture by replacing the property. For example, the taxpayer can use as replacement property, used section 38 property which he had not elected to claim any credit on and which had been placed in service in the same year as the replaced property.[13] If the *replacement* property is disposed of or ceases to be section 38 property prior to the end of the investment credit vesting period for the originally selected property, then the general rule as to disposition and cessation shall apply to the replacement property unless a replacement reselection is made.

H. WHAT PROPERTY CHARACTERISTICS ARE NECESSARY FOR EQUIPMENT TO BE ELIGIBLE FOR INVESTMENT TAX CREDIT?

A taxpayer is not entitled to claim investment tax credit on property unless it qualifies as "section 38 property" under the Internal Revenue Code. In general, section 38 property is (i) *tangible personal property*, and

(ii) certain other *tangible property* (not including a building or its structural components) which:

- has an estimated useful life of at least three years on the date it is placed in service,

- may be depreciated (or amortized), and

- is not used by a person or in a manner prohibited by the Code.[14]

Therefore, intangible property such as patents, copyrights, and subscription lists do not qualify as section 38 property.

"Other tangible property" will not be entitled to section 38 status unless it meets certain additional criteria. It must also:

- be used as an integral part of a manufacturing, production, or extraction activity, or be an integral part of the furnishing of transportation, communication, electrical energy, gas, water, or sewage disposal services,

- constitute a research facility used in connection with any of the activities specified above, *or*

- constitute a facility used in connection with any of the activities specified above for the bulk storage of fungible commodities, including commodities in a liquid or gaseous state.

1. When Is Equipment "Depreciable"?

In order for equipment to qualify as section 38 property, it must be *depreciable* under Section 167 of the Code, or in lieu thereof, amortizable.[15] In general, property is not depreciable unless it is subject to exhaustion, wear and tear, or obsolescence and is owned and used in the taxpayer's trade or business or is held for the production of income. If the *start* of the depreciation period can be delayed through, for example, the use of an "averaging convention," the property can still qualify as section 38 property.

What happens if only a portion of the property qualifies for a depreciation deduction for a taxable year? In this case, only the qualifying portion may be used in computing the investment tax credit. For example, if new equipment is used 60 percent of the time for business purposes and 40 percent of the time for personal purposes, the basis of such property for the investment tax credit computation must be reduced by 40 percent.

2. Some Examples of Tangible Personal Property

Property which is *tangible* and *personal* can generally qualify as section 38 property. The term "tangible personal property" means any tangible personal property, except air conditioning and heating units.[16] Land and inherently permanent land improvements, such as swimming pools, paved parking areas, wharves, docks, bridges, and fences, will not qualify. Production machinery, printing presses, transportation and office equipment, refrigerators, grocery counters, testing equipment, display racks and shelves, neon and other signs, and other such property which is contained in or attached to buildings may qualify. In addition, property fixed to the ground, such as service station gas pumps, hydraulic car lifts, and automatic vending machines, often meet the tangible and personal criteria.

OBSERVATION:

It is worth pointing out that the determination of whether property is "tangible" or "personal" is not controlled by local property law. In other words, even though under the laws of the jurisdiction in which the property is located the property is considered to be real property, it may still be tangible personal property from the standpoint of the investment tax credit rules.

3. Some Points on the "Other Tangible Property" Rule

"Other tangible property" can qualify as section 38 property if it is not a building or a building structural component, if it is used as an integral part of certain activities, such as manufacturing, production, extraction, transportation, or communication activities, or if it is considered to constitute a specified research or storage facility.[17] The terms "manufacturing," "production," and "extraction" are defined to include the construction, reconstruction, or making of property (i) from scrap, salvage, junk material, new material, or raw material, either by processing, manipulating, refining, or changing the form of an article or (ii) by combining or assembling two or more articles. Therefore, property used as an integral part of the extracting, processing, or refining of metallic and nonmetallic minerals, including oil, gas, rock, marble, or slate; the construction of roads, bridges, or housing; the processing of meat, fish or other foodstuffs; the cultivation of orchards, gardens, or nurseries; the production of lumber, lumber products or other building materials; the fabrication or treatment of textiles, paper, leather goods, or glass; and the rebuilding of machinery may qualify.

Property used in connection with a "transportation" activity includes that used as an integral part of the business of a railroad, airline, bus company, shipping or trucking company, or oil pipeline company. The "communications" activity includes activities carried on by telephone or telegraph companies and radio or television broadcasting companies.

Research facilities, such as wind tunnels and test stands, and storage facilties, such as oil and gas storage tanks and grain storage bins, used in connection with a section 38 property qualifying activity may qualify as "other tangible property" *even though they are not an integral part of such activity.* Although a research or storage facility must be used *in connection with* a qualifying activity, the taxpayer-owner does not have to be engaged in such activity for the property to qualify as section 38 property.

Buildings are not section 38 property. The term "building" means, in general, any structure or edifice which encloses a space within its walls, usually covered by a roof, which is used, for example, to provide shelter or housing, or to provide working, office, parking, display, or sales space. Apartment houses, garages, barns, warehouses, factory and office buildings, railroad or bus stations, and stores are "buildings." Any structure which is basically an item of machinery or equipment, is not a "building" and may, therefore, qualify as section 38 property. Any structure which houses property used as an integral part of a qualifying activity and which is so related to the property that when the property is replaced it is likely the structure will have to be replaced is also not a "building." In addition, oil and gas storage tanks, grain storage bins, silos, fractionating towers, blast furnaces, basic oxygen furnaces, coke ovens, brick kilns, and coal tipples are not "buildings."

Building structural components are specifically excluded from the section 38 property category. They are basically components which relate to the operation or maintenance of a building and include walls, floors, ceilings, tiling, windows, doors, certain heating or air conditioning components, plumbing, electrical wiring, lighting fixtures, chimneys, stairs, sprinkler systems, and fire escapes. Machinery, however which is installed solely for the purpose of maintaining temperature or humidity requirements necessary for other machinery to be operated or for materials or foodstuffs to be processed will not be deemed to be a "structural component."

a. The Integral Part Rule

"Other tangible property" used as an *integral part* of certain specified activities can qualify as section 38 property.[18] The integral part criterion is satisfied if the property is used directly in, and is essential to the completeness of, the qualifying activity, regardless of whether the property is used by the owner or a lessee. For example, property such as docks, railroad tracks, and bridges may be considered to be an integral part of a manufacturing activity if it is used to acquire or transport raw materials or supplies to a point where processing is to begin. Property such as blast furnaces, oil and gas pipelines, railroad tracks and signals, telephone poles, broadcasting towers, oil derricks and livestock fences used in the processing of raw materials will also qualify. Generally, pavements, parking areas, inherently permanent advertising displays or outdoor lighting facilities, and swimming pools are considered incapable of being used as an integral part of any section 38 property qualifying activity even though used in a business operation.

I. BE CAREFUL OF EQUIPMENT COMPLETED ABROAD OR PREDOMINANTLY OF FOREIGN ORIGIN

At present, property which is built outside the United States and property whose basis is less than 50 percent attributable to value added within the United States *can* qualify as section 38 property. The Code does, however, provide that if its construction, reconstruction, or erection was begun after August 15, 1971, and on or before December 2, 1971, or if it was acquired after August 15, 1971 pursuant to an order placed by the taxpayer after August 15, 1971 and before December 20, 1971, it could not have qualified.[19] An "order" is essentially any written or oral request to purchase property at some future date. The order does not have to be a binding contract.

RECOMMENDATION:

The President of the United States has the power to reinstitute the foreign property restrictions by Executive Order in certain situations. Therefore, the current rule status should be investigated when such property is involved.

J. THERE IS A SPECIAL RULE FOR CERTAIN AMORTIZED PROPERTY

In general, property which a taxpayer has elected to apply certain allowable rapid amortizations under, for example, Code Section 167(k) (expenditures to rehabilitate low-income rental housing), Section 184 (certain railroad rolling stock), and Section 188 (certain expenditures for on-the-job training and child care facilities) will not qualify as section 38 property.[20]

K. SPECIAL RULE FOR RAILROAD TRACK

Railroad replacement track material, such as ties, rail, and ballast, may qualify as section 38 property if the railroad complies with the following two requirements. First, the railroad must use the retirement-replacement depreciation method of accounting for its railroad track. Secondly, the replacement must be (i) made pursuant to a scheduled track replacement program, (ii) necessary pursuant to observations by maintenance-of-way personnel, (iii) necessary pursuant to rail-test car detection, or (iv) made as a result of a casualty.[21] The term "railroad" includes railroad switching companies and railroad terminal companies.

L. EQUIPMENT MUST BE USED WITHIN THE UNITED STATES TO BE INVESTMENT TAX CREDIT ELIGIBLE

Property generally will not be entitled to section 38 property status if it is used *predominantly outside of the United States* during a taxable year. Property will be considered "predominantly" used outside of the United States if it is physically located for more than 50 percent of the taxable year outside of the United States.[22] In the event the property was placed in service during a taxable year, the 50 percent test shall be applied against the portion of the year beginning when it was so placed in service. If a lessor elects to "pass through" the investment tax credit to the lessee as permitted under Section 48(d) of the Code, the predominant use test will be based on the property's predominant use during the *lessee's* taxable year.

Property which is used predominantly outside the United States during the taxable year it was placed in service will not qualify as section 38 property even though, in a subsequent year, it is permanently returned to the United States. If the predominant use test is satisfied when the property was placed in service, but in a subsequent year it is not satisfied, the property will cease to be section 38 property regardless of who, in fact, used the property outside the United States during such year.

RECOMMENDATION:

If a lessee uses initially qualifying section 38 property predominantly outside of the United States before the end of the credit vesting period, the lessor will lose some or all of the investment credit claimed. It is important, therefore, for a lessor intending to claim investment tax credit on the leased equipment to incorporate a provision in the lease documentation which will provide him with compensating damages in the event the property is not used in a qualifying manner and he suffers an investment credit recapture.

M. THERE ARE CERTAIN EXCEPTIONS TO THE UNITED STATES USAGE REQUIREMENT

The Internal Revenue Code makes certain exceptions to the rule which prohibits property used predominantly outside the United States from qualifying as section 38 property.[23] As the reader will recall, unless property qualifies as section 38 property, it will not be eligible for investment tax credit treatment. These exceptions will now be discussed.

1. Aircraft

Any aircraft which is registered by the Administrator of the Federal Aviation Agency and which is operated, whether on a scheduled or non-scheduled basis, *to and from the United States* may qualify as section 38 property even though it is used predominantly outside the United States. The "to and from" test is met if the aircraft returns to the United States with some degree of frequency, even if during its use it travels from one point to another outside of the United States. Revenue Ruling 73-367 provides that any aircraft which is net leased to a foreign commercial airline and which is operated so that it returns to the United States approximately *once every two weeks* will meet the "to and from" test.

There is an interesting exception to the "to and from" criterion. *Any* Federal Aviation Agency registered aircraft operated *under contract* with the United States will qualify as section 38 property even though it is not operated to and from the United States if it meets one requirement. Its principal use, when operated outside the United States, must be pursuant to such contract.

2. Rolling Stock

Domestic railroad corporation rolling stock subject to Part 1 of the Interstate Commerce Act may qualify as section 38 property even though its predominant use is outside the United States. The term "rolling stock" means locomotives, freight and passenger train cars, floating equipment, and miscellaneous transportation equipment on wheels which are (or, in the case of leased property, would be) chargeable to equipment investment accounts established in accordance with the Interstate Commerce Commission's prescribed uniform system of accounts for railroad companies.

3. Vessels

Vessels documented under United States laws and operated in the foreign or domestic commerce of the United States may qualify as section 38 property although the predominant United States usage test is not satisfied. A vessel is documented under United States laws if it is registered, enrolled, or licensed under the laws of the United States by the United States Coast Guard Commandant. Vessels operated in the foreign or domestic commerce of the United States include those which will be used in foreign or coastwide trade, or fisheries.

4. Motor Vehicles

Any motor vehicle owned by a "United States person" and operated to and from the United States with some degree of frequency will qualify as section 38 property even though not used predominantly within the United States. A "United States person" is defined by the Code as a citizen or resident of the United States, a domestic partnership, a domestic corporation, and any estate or trust (other than certain foreign estates or trusts).

5. Containers

Any container owned by a United States person and used to transport property to and from the United States will qualify as section 38 property, even though predominantly used outside of the United States.

6. Exploratory and Development Equipment

Property, such as offshore drilling equipment, owned by a United States person and used to explore, develop, remove, or transport resources from the outer Continental Shelf (as defined by Section 2 of the Outer Continental Shelf Lands Act) may be used predominantly outside of the United States and still qualify as section 38 property. Vessels and aircraft are specifically excluded from this exception.

7. Property Used in a U.S. Possession

In general, property owned by a domestic corporation or by a citizen of the United States (other than a corporation or an individual entitled to special tax treatment because income is derived from certain United States possessions) which is used predominantly in a United States possession, either by the owner or by a corporation organized under the law of a U.S. possession, may qualify as section 38 property. The predominant use determination is made in accordance with the same principles used for United States predominant use determination explained in Subsection 1 of this section.

Under this exception, property owned by a domestic corporation not entitled to the aforementioned special tax treatment which is leased to a local U.S. possession corporation and which is used predominantly within a United States possession may qualify as section 38 property. However, if the leased property is owned by a corporation which cannot avail itself of such tax benefits, it will not qualify as section 38 property even if it is leased to a domestic corporation which would be able to qualify for such tax benefits.

8. Communications Satellites

Any communications satellite defined within Section 103(3) of the Communication Satellite Act of 1962, or any interest therein, of a United States person may qualify as section 38 property.

9. Communication Cable

In general, any cable (or interest therein) of a domestic corporation, or a wholly owned domestic subsidiary of such corporation, engaged in furnishing certain specified telephone services does not have to satisfy the United States predominant use test to achieve section 38 property status. The cable must, however, be a part of a submarine cable system which constitutes part of a communication link exclusively between the United States and one or more foreign countries.

10. Property Used in International or Territorial Waters

Property which is used in international or territorial waters within the northern portion of the Western Hemisphere to explore for, develop, remove, or transport resources or deposits from the ocean is excluded from the predominant United States usage rule and, therefore, will generally qualify as section 38 property. The property must be owned by a United States person. The exception does not, however, apply to aircraft or vessels.

N. CERTAIN LODGING RELATED PROPERTY WILL NOT QUALIFY FOR INVESTMENT TAX CREDIT

In general, property used predominantly to furnish, or in connection with the furnishing of, lodging will not qualify as section 38 property.[24] Property usually found in a lodging facility's living quarters, such as beds, furniture, refrigerators, and ranges, is considered to be used predominantly to furnish lodging. A "lodging facility" includes a facility, or any part of such a facility, where sleeping accommodations are rented. This would include, for example, an apartment house, a hotel, a motel, or a dormitory. Property which is used primarily as a means of transportation, such as aircraft, vessels or railroad cars, or facilities which are used primarily to provide medical or convalescent services do not come within the *lodging facility* category even though they have sleeping accommodations.

If property is used predominantly in the operation of a lodging facility or in serving tenants, it is considered to be used *in connection with* the furnishing of lodging. Lobby furniture, office equipment, and laundry and swimming pool facilities are examples of such property. Property used to furnish services, such as electricity, water, sewage disposal, gas, telephone or other similar services, either to the management of a lodging facility or its tenants, is not generally considered as property used in connection with the furnishing of lodging. This type of property would include, for example, gas and electric meters, telephone poles and lines, telephone station and switchboard equipment, and water and gas mains and other items of property furnished by public utilities.

Notwithstanding the general lodging rule, certain nonlodging commercial property, such as vending machines located in a lodging facility, which is equally available to persons who use the lodging facility as well as to those who do not, may qualify as section 38 property. In addition, property used by a motel, hotel, inn, or similar establishment in connection with its lodging trade or business does not come within the disqualifying rule if the predominant portion of the living quarters is used by transients during the taxable year. A facility has transient accommodations if the normal rental period is less than 30 days. The term "predominant portion" means greater than 50 percent of the living quarters.

O. EQUIPMENT USED BY TAX-EXEMPT ORGANIZATIONS IS NOT ELIGIBLE FOR INVESTMENT TAX CREDIT

In general, property used by Federal income tax-exempt organizations (other than certain farmers' cooperatives described in Section 521 of the Code) will not qualify as section 38 property. There is a limited exception to this rule for property used predominantly in an unrelated trade or business which produces taxable income.

Property owned by tax-exempt organizations, whether or not leased to another, and property leased to tax-exempt organizations is, for the purposes of this rule, "property used by a tax-exempt organization." Except in the case of the unrelated trade or business exception, property leased by a disqualifying organization to a tax-paying organization and property leased by a tax-paying organization to a disqualifying organization may not be the subject of an investment tax credit "pass through" election. Property, however, leased by a non-tax-exempt lessor on a casual or short-term basis to a tax-exempt organization can qualify for section 38 property status.

P. EQUIPMENT USED BY GOVERNMENTAL UNITS DOES NOT QUALIFY FOR INVESTMENT TAX CREDIT

Section 38 property status is denied for property used by the United States, any state (including the District of Columbia) or political subdivision, any international organization, or any agency or instrumentality of any of these.[25] An exception, however, is made for property used by the International Telecommunications Satellite Consortium or any successor organization. Property owned by a governmental unit, whether or not leased to another, and property leased to a governmental unit is "property used by the United States, etc." Therefore, property used in this manner will not qualify in the hands of the lessor or the lessee as section 38 property.

Q. WHAT IS "NEW" SECTION 38 PROPERTY?

"New" Section 38 property, in general, is section 38 property whose "original use" begins with a taxpayer at the time he acquires it.[26] Property is considered to have been "acquired by a taxpayer" at the time he first takes physical possession or control of the property.

1. The Issue of "Original Use"

Unless the property's "original use" begins with a taxpayer it cannot qualify as *new* section 38 property. "Original use" is considered to be the first use to which the property is put, regardless of whether the use corresponds to the use by the taxpayer.[27] Under this rule, therefore, the original use could not begin with a taxpayer if the property had been reconditioned or rebuilt before it was acquired. The fact that property has used parts, however, does not automatically disqualify it as new property unless there are so many used parts that it would fall within the rebuilt or reconditioned category.

> RECOMMENDATION:
>
> The "used parts" problem sometimes comes up when computer equipment is involved. "New" computer equipment often contains used parts. Therefore, if new section 38 property tax benefits are important, a purchaser should take certain precautions. An opinion of the equipment manufacturer's counsel to the effect that the equipment qualifies as new property at the time it is acquired may give some comfort. When the purchaser will be a lessor, the benefit unavailability risk can be shifted to the lessee through a lease tax indemnification provision. If the time and expense warrant it, the best course of action is to get a Revenue Ruling covering the new equipment issue.

R. WHAT IS "USED" SECTION 38 PROPERTY?

Determining whether section 38 property is "used" is easy. In general, it is used if it is not "new section 38 property" at the time it is acquired by the taxpayer.[28]

Property which initially qualifies as new section 38 property will not lose its status if the owner sells the property and simultaneously leases it back. The rationale is that the property continues to be used by the person who used it prior to its sale. If a lessee purchases equipment which was new section 38 property in the hands of the lessor at the time he leased it, it will remain new to the lessee because its use stays with the taxpayer who was the user at the time the property qualified as new section 38 property. In addition, if certain corporate, partner, or related taxpayer relationships exist between a seller and a purchaser, new section 38 property in the hands of the seller does not, upon transfer, become used section 38 property.

S. HOW A LESSEE CAN CLAIM INVESTMENT TAX CREDIT

In general, a lessor of new section 38 property may, under Section 48(d) of the Code, elect to treat the lessee as the purchaser of the property for investment tax credit purposes. In other words the lessor can "pass through" the credit to the lessee so that it can be claimed directly by the lessee.

The lessee's qualified investment in property on which a Section 48(d) election has been made is generally the fair market value of the property on the date of transfer. In the case of certain related corporation lease transactions, however, the lessee's qualified investment is instead equal to the basis of the property in the hands of the lessor on the date of transfer.

The determination of the property's "original use" as to a lessee is made within the same guidelines as if the lessee were the owner. In this regard, if the property had been used by the lessor, or any third party, prior to the lessee's use or if it had been reconstructed, rebuilt, or reconditioned property, the lessee would not be able to claim any investment credit because the property's original use would not commence with the lessee. The mere testing or storing of property by a lessor is not considered prior use as far as a lessee is concerned.

OBSERVATION:

A *lessee* may elect to "pass through" to a *sublessee* the investment tax credit which had been passed through to the lessee. The lessee's investment tax credit "pass through" is treated as if the original lessor had leased the property directly to the sublessee for the term of the sublease.

The "pass through" election may be made either (i) on an item-by-item basis or (ii) on a general basis as to all property which is leased by the electing lessor to the lessee. In either case, the lessor makes the election by filing an appropriate statement with the lessee, on or before the lessee's

Federal income tax return is due for the taxable year during which possession was transferred to the lessee. The election is irrevocable as of the time the statement is filed with the lessee.

1. How Is the Useful Life Determination Made?

When a lessor has "passed through" the investment tax credit to a lessee on leased property, what useful life must the lessee use in computing the allowable credit? The lessee must use the useful life which the *lessor* will use in computing the property's depreciation. No regard is to be given to the lease term.

T. NONCORPORATE LESSORS HAVE SUBSTANTIAL LIMITATIONS

In the case of noncorporate lessors, the availability of investment tax credit on equipment they lease to third parties is severely restricted. These lessors may claim the credit only in two situations. If the taxpayer-lessor has either manufactured or produced the property which is the subject of the lease, it may claim the credit. If the lease term (including all periods which the lessee or lessor has the right to renew) is less than one-half the useful life of the property and if the sum of the deductions allowed under Section 162 of the Code (trade or business expenses) during the initial 12-month period beginning on the date the property was transferred to the lessee exceeds 15 percent of the lease rental income, it may also claim the credit.

OBSERVATIONS:

I. A tax-option corporation (an electing small business corporation pursuant to the terms of Section 1371 of the Code) is not considered a corporation for purposes of the noncorporate lessor rule.

II. The noncorporate lessor rule does not apply to corporate lessor-partners. Therefore, each corporate partner is entitled to claim investment tax credit on its proportionate investment in section 38 property held by the partnership.

U. AN INVESTMENT TAX CREDIT CHECKLIST FOR LESSORS

The following checklist will provide an equipment lessor with a guide as to the key investment tax credit issues.

1. Has Investment Tax Credit Been Taken Into Account in Computing the Rental Rate?

2. Has the Equipment on Which Investment Tax Credit Will Be Taken:
   a. Been Acquired During the Taxable Year for Which It Will Be Claimed?
   b. Been Placed in Service During the Taxable Year for Which It Will Be Claimed?
3. If the Federal Income Tax Liability Is Not Less Than $25,000 for the Claiming Year, Has the Amount of Credit Claimed Been Limited to the Sum Of:
   a. An Amount Equal to $25,000 of Federal Income Tax Liability, and
   b. Sixty to Ninety Percent, As Appropriate, of Any Excess over the First $25,000 of Federal Income Tax Liability.
4. If the Federal Income Tax Liability Is Less Than $25,000 for the Claiming Year, Has the Amount of Credit to Be Claimed Been Limited to the Liability?
5. Has the Appropriate "Applicable Percentage" Been Determined to Apply Against the Basis of New Equipment and the Cost of Used Equipment to Be Included in the Credit Computation?
   a. For Equipment with a Useful Life of at Least Three Years, but Less Than Five Years, the Applicable Percentage Is 33⅓ Percent.
   b. For Equipment with a Useful Life of at Least Five Years, but Less Than Seven Years, the Applicable Percentage Is 66⅔ Percent.
   c. For Equipment with a Useful Life of at Least Seven Years, the Applicable Percentage Is 100 Percent.
6. If the Useful Life of the Equipment Is Less Than Three Years, Has It Been Excluded from the Investment Tax Credit Computation?
7. Has the Equipment's Placed-in-Service Date Been Determined as the Earlier of:
   a. The Year When the Equipment Depreciation Is Begun, or
   b. The Year When the Equipment Is In a Condition to Be Used?
8. Has the Equipment Included in the Investment Tax Credit Computation All Been "Placed in Service" by the Lessor During the Year for Which the Credit Is Claimed?
9. Has Anything Occurred During the Taxable Year for Which the Credit Will Be Claimed Which Would Cause the Equipment to Lose Section 38 Status?
   a. Has a "Disposition" Occurred?
   b. Has the Equipment Ceased to Be Section 38 Property?

10. Will Anything Occur During the Investment Tax Credit Vesting Period Which Would Cause a Loss of Section 38 Property Status?
    a. Which Would Cause a "Disposition"?
    b. Which Would Cause the Equipment to Cease to Be Section 38 Property?
11. Have Proper Economic Protections Been Incorporated into the Lease Documentation Against a Loss or Unavailability of Investment Tax Credit?
12. Will the Equipment Qualify as Section 38 Property in the Hands of the Lessee and Any Sublessee?
13. Will the Equipment Qualify as Section 38 Property?
    a. Is It Tangible Personal Property or "Other Tangible Property"?
    b. Does It Have a Useful Life of at Least Three Years?
    c. Is It Depreciable, or Amortizable in Lieu Thereof?
    d. Will It Be Used by a Person or in a Manner Permitted under the Credit Rules?
14. If the Equipment Will Be Considered "Other Tangible Property," Is It:
    a. Used as an Integral Part of a Manufacturing, Production, or Extraction Activity?
    b. Used as an Integral Part of the Furnishing of Transportation, Communication, Electrical Energy, Gas, Water, or Sewage Disposal Services?
    c. A Research Facility Used in Connection with Any Activity in Items a or b?
    d. A Fungible Commodity Bulk Storage Facility Used in Connection with Any Activity in Items a or b?
    If Not, It Will Not Qualify.
15. If the Equipment Is Considered "New" Section 38 Property, Will the Original Use Begin with the Lessor?
16. Will the Equipment Be Used Predominantly Within the United States? If Not, It Will Not Qualify as Section 38 Property Unless It Fits with Certain Exceptions:
    a. For Aircraft.
    b. For Rolling Stock.
    c. For Vessels.
    d. For Motor Vehicles.
    e. For Containers.
    f. For Exploratory and Development Equipment.
    g. For Property Used in a U.S. Possession.
    h. For Communications Satellites.
    i. For Communication Cable.
    j. For Property Used in Territorial or International Waters.

17. If Equipment Is Used in Connection with a Lodging Activity, It May Not Qualify as Section 38 Property.
18. If Equipment Is Used by Certain Tax-Exempt Organizations or Governmental Units It May Not Qualify as Section 38 Property.
19. If the Investment Tax Credit Will Be "Passed Through" to the Lessee, Have the Proper Steps Been Taken to Insure That Necessary Action Is Taken?
20. Have the Investment Tax Credit Restrictions Been Reviewed if the Lessor Is Not a Corporation?

FOOTNOTES

[1] Revenue Act of 1978 Enacted 11/6/78.

[2] Energy Tax Act of 1978 Enacted 11/9/78.

[3] I.R.C. Section 46(a)(2).

[4] I.R.C. Section 46(a)(3); Treas. Reg. Section 1.46-1(b)(1).

[5] I.R.C. Section 48(c)(2).

[6] Treas. Reg. Section 1.46-3(c)(1); I.R.C. Section 1012.

[7] I.R.C. Sections 46(c)(1) & (2).

[8] Treas. Reg. Section 1.46-3(d)(4)(i).

[9] Treas. Reg. Section 1.47-2(a)(1).

[10] Treas. Reg. Section 1.47-2(b)(1). For Representative Tax Discussions See *Lockhart Leasing Co.*, 71-1 USTC Para. 9470, 446 F.2d. 269; *O.W. Garner*, 71-1 USTC Para 9299; *Northwest Acceptance Corp.*, 74-2 USTC Para 9619, 500 F.2d 1222.

[11] Treas. Reg. Section 1.47-3(f)(1).

[12] Treas. Reg. Section 1.47-3(f)(2). For Representative Tax Discussion See *J. Soares* 50 TC 909, Dec. 29, 138; *Purvis*, D.C., 73-1 USTC Para 9157; *M. A. Aboussie*, 60 TC 549, Dec. 32, 046; *W. F. Blevins*, 61 TC 547, Dec 32, 433; *W. Flemning Engineering Co.*, 65 TC 847, Dec. 33, 634.

[13] Treas. Reg. Section 1.47-3(d).

[14] See Generally I.R.C. Section 48(a).

[15] I.R.C. Section 48(a)(1) For Representative Tax Discussions See Rev. Rul. 69-329, 1969-1 CB 30; Rev. Rul. 69-55, 1969-1 CB 26; *M. Bauer*, 32 TCM 887, Dec 32,108(M), TC Memo 1973-191; *Coca-Cola Bottling Co. of Baltimore*, 73-2 USTC Para. 9785, 487 F. 2d 528; *C. C. Everhart*, 61 TC 323, Dec 32,241; *R. S. Prickett*, 26 TCM 5, Dec 28,303(M), TC Memo 1967-2; Rev. Rul 75-491, 1975-2 CB 19.

[16] Treas. Reg. Section 1.48-1(c). For Representative Tax Discussions See Rev. Rul 67-417, 1967-2 CB 49; Rev. Rul. 67-433, 1967-2 CB 51; Rev. Rul. 67-359, 1967-2 CB 9; *Fort Walton Square, Inc.*, 54 TC 653; *Kramertown Co., Inc.*, 74-1 USTC Para. 9196, 488 F.2d 728; *W. K. Coors*, 60 TC 368, Dec 32,003; Rev. Rul. 75-77, 1975-1 CB 7; Rev. Rul. 71-377, 1971-2 CB 63; *B. R. Roberts*, 60 TC 861, Dec. 32,121; Rev. Rul 65-79, 1965-1 CB 26; Rev. Rul 68-62, 1968-1 CB 365; Rev. Rul. 68-209, 1968-1 CB 16; Rev. Rul. 68-50, 1968-1 CB 364; *R. E. Catron*, 50 TC 306, Dec 28,960; *Merchants Refrigerating Co. of California*, 60 TC 856, Dec. 32,120; Rev. Rul. 69-169; 1969-1 CB 27; Rev. Rul 68-530, 1968-2 CB 37; *Minot Federal Savings & Loan Assn.*, 71-1 USTC Para. 9131, 435 F. 2d.

1368; *King Radio Corp, Inc.*, 73-2 USTC Para. 9766, 486 F.2d. 1091; Rev. Rul 69-412, 1969-2 CB 2; Rev. Rul. 71-104, 1971-1 CB 5; *Ponderosa Mouldings, Inc.*, 53 TC 92, Dec 29,802; Rev. Rul. 70-160, 1970-1 CB 7: Rev. Rul. 75-78, 1975-1 CB 8; Rev. Rul. 73-281, 1973-2 CB 7; Rev. Rul. 70-103, 1970-1 CB 6; Rev. Rul. 69-614, 1969-2 CB 8; Walton Mill, Inc., 31 TCM 75, Dec. 31,236(M), TC Memo 1972-25; Rev. Rul. 74-2, 1974-1 CB 10; Rev. Rul. 74-392, 1974-2 CB 10; *Fancy Foods of Virginia, Inc.*, DC, 73-1 USTC Para 9372; *S. Morgan Est.*, 72-1 USTC Para. 9236, 448 F.2d. 1397; *J. Ward*, 71-2 USTC Para. 9506; Rev. Rul 72-398, 1972-2 CB 9; Rev. Rul. 66-156, 1966-1 CB 11; Rev. Rul. 67-23, 1967-1 CB 5; Rev. Rul. 71-555, 1971-2 CB 65; Rev. Rul. 72-397, 1972-2 CB 8; *Tejas Properties, Inc.*, 70-1 USTC Para 9240; *Hayden Island, Inc.*, DC, 74-2 USTC Para. 9604; Rev. Rul. 69-170, 1969-1 CB 28, Rev. Rul. 68-346, 1968-2 CB 32.

[17]I.R.C. Section 48(a)(1). For Representative Tax Discussions See Rev. Rul 66-215, 1966-2 CB 11; Rev. Rul. 66-299, 1966-2 CB 14; Rev. Rul. 72-223, 1972-1 CB 17; Rev. Rul. 68-345, 1968-2 CB 30; Rev. Rul. 69-273, 1969-1 CB 30; Rev. Rul. 67-51, 1967-1 CB 68; Rev. Rul. 68-347, 1968-2 CB 33; Rev. Rul. 69-169, 1969-1 CB 27; *F. J. Evans*, 69-2 USTC Para. 9522, 413 F. 2d. 1047; Rev. Rul. 69-13, 1969-1 CB 25; Rev. Rul. 69-329, 1969-1 CB 30; Rev. Rul 68-1, 1968-1 CB 8.

[18]I.R.C. Section 48(a)(1). For Representative Tax Discussions See Rev. Rul. 72-267, 1972-1 CB 18; Rev. Rul. 68-211, 1968-1 CB 17; *Northville Dock Corp.*, 52 TC 68, Dec. 29,524, Rev. Rul. 68-281, 1968-1 CB 22; Rev. Rul. 68-184, 1968-1 CB 7; Rev. Rul. 68-297, 1968-1 CB 27.

[19]I.R.C. Section 48(a)(7)(B); Treas. Reg. Section 1.48-1(o)(2)(ii)(b).

[20]I.R.C. Section 48(a)(8).

[21]I.R.C. Section 48(a)(9). For Representative Tax Discussion See Rev. Rul. 73-295, 1973-2 CB 5.

[22]Treas. Reg. Section 1.48-1(g); For Representative Tax Discussions See Rev. Rul 69-1, 1969-1 CB 24; Rev. Rul 71-178, 1971-1 CB 6.

[23]I.R.C. Section 48(a)(2)(B).

[24]I.R.C. Section 48(a)(3); For Representative Tax Discussions See *A. Liebl*, 72-2 USTC Para. 9581; *J. H. Moore*, 74-1 USTC Para. 9146, 489 F.2d 285; *S. Mandler*, 65TC586, Dec. 33,550.

[25]I.R.C. Section 48(a)(5); Treas. Reg. Section 1.48-1(k).

[26]I.R.C. Section 48(b).

[27]Treas. Reg. Section 1.48-2(b)(7); For Representative Tax Discussions See Rev. Rul. 67-247, 1967-2 CB 53; Rev. Rul. 69-272, 1969-1 CB 23.

[28]I.R.C. Section 48(c)(1).

6

DEPRECIATION ADVANTAGES IN
LEASE TRANSACTIONS

Depreciation Is an Essential Ingredient in Leasing Economics • A Lessor Cannot Be Competitive Unless He Knows All the Angles • A Prospective Lessee Must Understand the Rules to Make the Proper Decision • The ADR Method—a Real Advantage.

PART I: DEPRECIATION IN GENERAL

A. A SIMPLE PERSPECTIVE ON DEPRECIATION FOR LEASING

Generally speaking, the ability of a lessor to write off, or depreciate, the cost of the leased equipment is absolutely essential to the economic viability of a lease transaction. A prospective lessor, therefore, must have a thorough understanding of the depreciation rules established in the Internal Revenue Code and related Treasury Regulations. These rules are also important to a prospective lessee for several reasons. First, unless the benefits available are fully understood, an intelligent lease versus purchase analysis cannot be made. Secondly, if certain depreciation indemnities will be required by a prospective lessor, a proper assessment of the potential risks cannot be made without a clear appreciation of the technical intricacies.

The basic rule authorizing an equipment owner to charge off a portion of the equipment's cost each year is established in Section 167(a) of the Internal Revenue Code. The section provides that a taxpayer may, in computing his Federal income tax liability, deduct a "reasonable allowance" for exhaustion, wear and tear, or obsolescence of property owned and used in his trade or business or held for the production of income.[1] The actual amount, or depreciation allowance, which may be expensed each year depends on three basic elements: the equipment's *cost* (or more properly its *basis*), its *estimated useful life*, and its *estimated salvage value*. These factors will be discusssed in greater detail later on in the chapter.

The term "reasonable allowance" means that portion of the equipment's basis which can be written off for a particular year. The sum of all the allowances when added to the equipment's salvage value will, at the end of the property's estimated useful life, equal its original basis.[2]

In computing how much may be allocated for a particular year, a taxpayer will generally use one or a combination of certain "methods" of depreciation specifically authorized by the Code: the *straight line* method, the *declining balance* method, or the *sum-of-the-years-digits* method. The latter two techniques, commonly referred to as "accelerated" methods of depreciation, have certain use restrictions related to the equipment's useful life and its "original use." The choice of methods is not, however, limited to these three alternatives. The Code permits a taxpayer, within certain bounds, to use any other consistent method of depreciation.

OBSERVATIONS:

I. It is worthwhile keeping in mind that if equipment qualifies as "new section 38 property" for investment tax credit purposes all the use qualifications, which must be met for a taxpayer to have a full choice of accelerated depreciation methods, are also met.

II. Once depreciation is begun on an asset in accordance with a method of depreciation, the method may not be changed without the consent of the Commissioner of the Internal Revenue Service. There are, however, certain exceptions if an accelerated method of depreciation has been chosen.

When the various tax concepts are discussed in the Internal Revenue Code and related regulations, they are written in terms of their applicability to a "taxpayer." In the context of the discussion of depreciation in this chapter the term "taxpayer" will be used synonymously with "lessor."

B. WHAT IS AN ASSET'S "BASIS"?

The actual dollar amount which a lessor can write off each year for equipment he owns depends on his "basis" in the property. "Basis" for depreciation purposes is determined in the same manner as it is when determining the gain on the sale or other disposition of an asset. When a lessor purchases an item of equipment, therefore, his basis in the equipment is equal to the property's cost.[3]

C. WHY AN ASSET'S "USEFUL LIFE" IS IMPORTANT

The useful life of an asset determines the period of time over which it may be depreciated. Therefore, unless the asset's life is known, the amount which may be written off in a year cannot be determined. Consider, for example, a $10,000 truck with a useful life of 10 years and an anticipated salvage value of zero at the end of the 10 year period. If the straight line method of depreciation is used, the owner can write off $1000 per year:

$$\frac{\$10,000 - 0}{10 \text{ yrs.}} = \$1000/\text{year}.$$

In general, the "useful life" of an asset for depreciation purposes is that period which the owner *expects* it to be of use in the pursuit of *his* trade or business or the production of income.[4]

OBSERVATION:

The reader should be aware that the useful life as estimated by a taxpayer for the purpose of his depreciation calculations may, in fact, not be the same as the actual inherent physical life of the asset.

An asset's useful life can be established in one of two ways—under the "facts and circumstances" method, sometimes referred to as the "Non-ADR" method, or under the Class Life Asset Depreciation Range System method, commonly referred to as the "ADR" method.

Under the facts and circumstances method, a taxpayer determines an asset's useful life based upon his experience with similar property.[5] In making this determination he must take into account any current or anticipated future conditions that may affect his conclusion. For example, the taxpayer should consider wear and tear and decay or decline from natural causes; normal progress of the state of the art, economic changes, inventions, and current developments inside the taxpayer's industry and trade or business; climatic and other relevant local conditions that may affect the taxpayer's trade or business; and the taxpayer's repair, renewal, and replacement program. If he does not have enough experience with a particular asset in order to make a judgment, he can base his estimate on the general experience in his industry. Once the useful life determination has been made, it cannot be varied unless the anticipated conditions forming the basis for its determination change. If these conditions do change the useful life *must* be revised.

Under the ADR method, the useful life of an asset is determined by reference to specific guidelines set forth in Section 4, Part II of Revenue Procedure 62-21. This Revenue Procedure prescribes various useful lives for assets of specific types, such as trucks, and for assets used in specific activities, such as mining.

OBSERVATIONS:

I. As a general rule, a taxpayer will be entitled to depreciate an asset over a shorter period of time if he uses the ADR method. A shorter depreciation period translates into larger write-offs and, thus, greater early tax savings. For example, if a taxpayer under the straight line method could fully depreciate a $10,000 asset with a zero salvage value over a five year period instead of a ten year period he would have an annual depreciation allowance of $2000:

$$\frac{\$10,000}{5} = \$2000$$

as opposed to one of $1000:

$$\frac{\$10,000}{10} = \$1000$$

The sooner the tax savings are available, the more economically attractive a transaction can be to a lessor. This, in turn, can result in lower rents for a lessee.

II. It should be kept in mind that the determination of useful life for *depreciation* purposes fixes the useful life of the asset for *investment tax credit* purposes.

D. WHAT DOES SALVAGE VALUE HAVE TO DO WITH DEPRECIATION?

In calculating the amount an asset may be depreciated, a taxpayer must take into consideration the asset's "salvage value." Depending on the method chosen to depreciate an asset, i.e., declining balance, sum-of-the-years-digits, or straight line, the salvage value will either be deducted from the amount that is to be depreciated or will act as a depreciation cutoff. For example, unless an "ADR election" is made, salvage value must be deducted from the basis of an asset in depreciating it using the straight line method or sum-of-the-years-digits method. If the declining balance method is used, the asset's basis does not have to be reduced by its salvage value before computing the annual deductions. Under this method, however, the taxpayer may no longer depreciate the asset when it has been written down to its salvage value. If the Class Life Asset Depreciation Range System has been elected, the salvage value does not have to be deducted from an asset's basis prior to determining the depreciation allowance regardless of the way it is depreciated, i.e., whether the declining balance, sum-of-the-years-digits, or straight line method is used. The asset may not, however, be depreciated below its salvage value.

What is an asset's salvage value? It is that amount which a taxpayer estimates, when the asset is acquired, that it will bring when he retires it from service, whether through sale or other disposition.[6] This value is sometimes referred to as the asset's "gross salvage value." In computing the depreciation allowance, the asset's "net salvage value" may be used instead of its gross value provided the taxpayer's choice is consistent with his prior practice. The net value is nothing more than the gross value reduced by removal, disposition, or other similar costs.

OBSERVATION:

It is interesting to note that the salvage value of an asset may vary from owner to owner. That is, if a taxpayer typically disposes of an asset while it is still in good operating condition, the salvage value may be quite large. On the other hand, if the taxpayer typically uses the asset to a stage where it is no longer of use to anyone, the value may be no more than scrap value. From the standpoint of the Code, therefore, the use of the word "salvage" may be somewhat misleading inasmuch as it refers to the value of an asset at the end of the estimated useful life *to the taxpayer*, which may in fact be more than junk value if the practice is to dispose of assets while still in good operating condition.[7]

1. A Tip on Increasing the Depreciable Amount

In computing the depreciation allowance for personal property having a useful life of at least three years, a taxpayer may, in general, elect to reduce the property's expected salvage value by an additional amount up to 10% of its basis.[8] This, in effect, increases the amount which may be written off.

ILLUSTRATIVE EXAMPLE—
ADDITIONAL AVAILABLE DEPRECIATION:

If the expected salvage value of a $100 asset is $20, Section 167(f) of the Internal Revenue Code permits up to an additional $10 (10% of $100) to be added to the depreciation base. That is, $90 may be "written off," or depreciated, instead of only $80. The additional $10 would provide a Federal income tax saving of $5 for a taxpayer in the 50% tax bracket. This may, however, not be a net benefit. In other words, if the asset is sold at the end of its useful life at a price greater than the reduced salvage value, the reduction would result in an increased taxable gain. For example, if the asset is sold at the end of its useful life for $20, there would be no taxable gain upon disposition if the reduction had not been elected. There would be a $10 taxable gain if the maximum reduction was taken. By the same token if the asset is sold for less than the reduced salvage value, the taxable loss would be reduced over the loss if the additional amount had not been taken. Generally, lessors take the additional 10% to maximize the tax savings in the early years, thereby enabling them to price transactions more competitively.

E. HOW MUCH FLEXIBILITY DOES A LESSOR HAVE IN CALCULATING THE ANNUAL DEPRECIATION ALLOWANCE?

When depreciating equipment, is a lessor limited to using the straight line method, the sum-of-the-years-digits method, or the declining balance method? No, a lessor can basically use any *consistant method* he wants to use to compute his annual equipment depreciation allowance, *provided the sum of the annual allowance and all of his prior allowances does not exceed the total amount permitted during the first two-thirds of the asset's useful life if the declining balance method had been used.* The consistent method requirement is met if the treatment is consistent for a particular asset or group of assets. The requirement does not prevent other methods of depreciation to be chosen for *other* assets or groups of assets, or the same asset or group of assets acquired in a subsequent year.

Although there appears to be reasonable leeway in the choice of depreciation rate methods, lessors typically select one of three methods, or a combination thereof, specifically prescribed in Section 167(b) of the Internal Revenue Code. They are, as already mentioned, the *straight line* method, the *sum-of-the-years-digits* method, and the *declining balance* method. A basic understanding of each is a must.

1. The Straight Line Method Produces The Smallest Initial Deduction

The *straight line* method of computing an asset's *annual* depreciation allowance is mechanically simple. The basis of the asset, after subtracting its salvage value, is merely divided by its useful life. The resulting amount is how much can be charged off for each year of its useful life. As the reader will see when the other methods are explained, this method produces the smallest write-off in the early years of an asset's use. The straight line method can be elected whether the asset is *new* or *used*.

ILLUSTRATIVE EXAMPLE—
STRAIGHT LINE DEPRECIATION:

Consider an asset which has been purchased for $10,000 and which has a useful life of 10 years. If its anticipated salvage value is $2000, the *annual* depreciation would be $800. This is arrived at by subtracting $2000 from its $10,000 cost and dividing the result by 10 years:

$$\frac{\$10,000 - \$2000}{10 \text{ years}} = \$800.$$

The owner can elect to reduce the salvage value by an amount up to 10% of an asset's basis. If the election is made, an additional $1000 (10% of $10,000) may be depreciated. In other words, instead of subtracting a $2000 salvage value from the $10,000 cost, $1000 would be subtracted. The annual deduction would then be equal to $9000:

$$\frac{\$10,000 - \$1000}{10 \text{ years}} = \$900.$$

2. The Declining Balance Method Can Produce The Greatest Initial Deduction.

The *declining balance* method of determining the annual depreciation charge for an asset is more complex than the straight line method. The depreciation deduction for any year is calculated by multiplying the asset's basis (reduced by any prior years' depreciation deductions) by the declining balance rate. This method cannot be used unless the asset has a useful life of at least three years. This method can produce, for new assets, an initial deduction far greater than either of the other two methods.

Under the declining balance method, if the equipment is new, a lessor may claim an annual allowance of up to 200% of that permitted under the straight line method. If the equipment is considered used, a lessor may only claim up to 150% of that permitted under the straight line method. The 200% method is commonly referred to as the "double declining balance method." Whether a particular item of equipment is considered "new" or "used" is determined in the same manner as it is for investment tax credit purposes. In other words, the issue is whether the use to which the asset is first put begins with the taxpayer. If it does not, it is considered "used."

OBSERVATION:

The reader should keep in mind that an asset may be "used" for tax purposes even though it is not commonly understood as "used."

When the declining balance method is used, the asset's salvage value does not have to be deducted from its basis before calculating the annual depreciation allowance. The asset may not, however, be depreciated below its salvage value.

ILLUSTRATIVE EXAMPLE—
DECLINING BALANCE DEPRECIATION:

Company A purchased a "new" truck for $10,000. The useful life of the truck is 10 years and is considered to have a salvage value of $1,000 at the end of the 10 year period. Under the double, or 200%, declining balance method depreciation, how much can be written off each year?

The 200% declining balance rate is two times the straight line rate. The straight line rate, based on a 10 year life, is 10% per year. Therefore, the following deductions are available:

```
 1st year—$2,000   (2 x 10% x $10,000)
 2nd year—$1,600   (2 x 10% x $ 8,000)
 3rd year—$1,280   (2 x 10% x $ 6,400)
 4th year—$1,024   (2 x 10% x $ 5,120)
 5th year—$  819   (2 x 10% x $ 4,096)
 6th year—$  655   (2 x 10% x $ 3,277)
 7th year—$  524   (2 x 10% x $ 2,621)
 8th year—$  419   (2 x 10% x $ 2,097)
 9th year—$  336   (2 x 10% x $ 1,678)
10th year—$  268   (2 x 10% x $ 1,342)
```

The annual *straight line* deduction for the same period using a $1000 salvage value would be:

```
 1st year—$ 900
 2nd year—$ 900
 3rd year—$ 900
 4th year—$ 900
 5th year—$ 900
 6th year—$ 900
 7th year—$ 900
 8th year—$ 900
 9th year—$ 900
10th year—$ 900
```

The 200% declining balance method shows greater deductions up to the 5th year.

OBSERVATION:

As a way of maximizing the available depreciation deductions, lessors initially using the declining balance method sometimes switch to the straight line method when it will produce a greater annual allowance. When the change is made, the original depreciable amount, reduced by the sum of the previous deductions, is "straight lined" over the remaining useful life. For instance, in the preceding example, if the switch to straight line were made *after* the fifth year, the annual allowance would be computed on the remaining basis of $3,277 ($10,000 − $6,723). If an election had been made to reduce the salvage value by the permitted 10% of original basis and if the remaining basis were multiplied by the straight line rate, 20% over the remaining five years, the depreciation deduction for the 6th year would be equal to $655 (20% × $3,277). Since for the 7th through 10th year the amount would also be equal to $655, it is easy to see what the increase in benefit would be by switching to the straight line method.

3. The Sum-of-the-Years-Digits Method Is Somewhere in Between

The sum-of-the-years-digits method for calculating an item of equipment's yearly depreciation allowance is a commonly used method. Under this technique, the deduction for any year is determined by multiplying the basis of the asset (reduced by its salvage value) by a prescribed fraction which will vary for each year. The numerator of the fraction is the number of years remaining in its useful life as of the beginning of the computation year and the denominator is an amount equal to the sum of the number of years of the asset's useful life. This method may be used only for *new* assets with a useful life of at least three years.

ILLUSTRATIVE EXAMPLE—SUM-OF-THE-YEARS-DIGITS DEPRECIATION:

Company A purchased a new computerized drill press for $10,000. The useful life of the drill press was determined to be 10 years and its salvage value at the end of such period was estimated to be $1000. What will the depreciation allowances be for each of the 10 years using the sum-of-the-years-digits method?

The denominator of the multiplying fraction is the sum of 10 + 9 + 8 + 7 + 6 + 5 + 4 + 3 + 2 + 1 = 55. Therefore, for each of the 10 years the depreciation deductions are calculated as follows:

1st year—$1636 $\left[\dfrac{10}{55} \times (\$10,000 - \$1,000 = \$9,000) \right]$

2nd year—$1473 $\left(\dfrac{9}{55} \times \$9,000 \right)$

3rd year—$1309 $\left(\frac{8}{55} \times \$9,000\right)$

4th year—$1145 $\left(\frac{7}{55} \times \$9,000\right)$

5th year—$ 982 $\left(\frac{6}{55} \times \$9,000\right)$

6th year—$ 818 $\left(\frac{5}{55} \times \$9,000\right)$

7th year—$ 655 $\left(\frac{4}{55} \times \$9,000\right)$

8th year—$ 491 $\left(\frac{3}{55} \times \$9,000\right)$

9th year—$ 327 $\left(\frac{2}{55} \times \$9,000\right)$

10th year—$ 164 $\left(\frac{1}{55} \times \$9,000\right)$

A comparison with the 200% declining balance and the straight line depreciation allowance computation examples shows the sum-of-the-years-digits method to produce a compromise result.

F. THE MANNER OF ACCOUNTING FOR DEPRECIATION IS PRESCRIBED BY THE RULES

Equipment subject to depreciation is to be recorded in one of two ways by its owner. He may either account for each asset on an *item by item* basis or on a *group* basis. By using the group approach, the taxpayer would put two or more assets into a single depreciation account. This is referred to as *multiple asset accounting*.

Assets can be grouped into one account in a number of ways. One method is to group those used in a particular business into one account. Accounts such as this are referred to as *composite accounts* because no weight is given to the type of asset in the account or the useful life. Another way is to group them on the basis of similarity in kind and useful lives. These accounts are referred to as *group accounts*. Assets can also be grouped on the basis of similarity of use. Accounts formed in this manner are referred to as *classified accounts*. If the ADR method is elected, all ADR eligible assets must be put into "vintage" accounts. A vintage account is essentially a grouping of assets on the basis of the year the assets were first placed in service.

G. SOME IMPORTANT POINTS CONCERNING HOW AND WHEN EQUIPMENT SHOULD BE DEPRECIATED

If a taxpayer decides to depreciate an eligible asset, it must be written off on an annual basis, beginning with when *placed in service* and ending with *retired*.[9] Except for multiple asset accounts, if an asset was not placed in service on the first day of the first year only a percentage of a year's depreciation may be taken for the first year. The same is true for the last year if the asset is taken out of service before the end of the taxpayer's full reporting year. In these situations the percentage used is that percentage of the year the asset was held.[10]

For multiple asset accounts the treatment is different. The beginning and ending annual depreciation amounts are determined on the basis of certain "averaging conventions" which, in effect, create artificial beginning and ending depreciation dates. For example, a certain convention may call for all equipment additions and retirements in the first half of a tax year to be assumed to have taken place on the first day of such year and all those in the second half to have taken place on the first day of the following year. In this case *for the year the assets were placed in service*, a full year's depreciation allowance will be permitted on the "first half" assets and no allowance will be permitted on the "second half" assets. Under this convention, no depreciation could be claimed on assets retired in the first half of a reporting year *for that year*. However, assets retired during the second half of such retirement year would be entitled to a full year's depreciation deduction.

How is the depreciation calculation handled for assets which are not placed in service on the first day of a month or retired on the last day of a month? There are a number of methods commonly used. One provides that an asset placed in service after the first day of a month, but on or before the 15th of such month, will be entitled to a full initial month's depreciation. If it is placed in service after the 15th of the initial month, the taxpayer must exclude the initial month in computing the available depreciation. For example, an asset placed in service on June 14th will be entitled to a full seven months depreciation for a calendar year taxpayer. If the asset were placed in service on June 19th, only six months may be claimed. Under this method, asset retirements should be treated in a consistent manner. In other words, the full retirement month's depreciation would be claimed for assets retired after the 15th of such month. Another method often employed is for the initial month to be consistently excluded and the retirement month consistently included. The specific date of acquisition or retirement is ignored. Another alternative is for a taxpayer to claim the exact number of days an asset was held and, thereby, not lose or gain any depreciation for the acquiring or retiring year. Generally speaking, however, this technique may not be practical to use when many assets are involved.

H. CAN A LESSEE CLAIM DEPRECIATION ON EQUIPMENT IT LEASES?

A lessee cannot claim any depreciation on equipment it leases.[11] If, however, a lessee spends money for permanent improvements on the leased property, he may be permitted to recover these expenditures through depreciation or amortization allowances.[12] If the improvement's estimated useful life *to the lessee* is not greater than the remaining lease term, the general depreciation rules under Section 167 of the Code apply in determining the yearly recover allowance. That is, the capital expenditure may be written off over the useful life of the improvement without regard to how long the property is leased. If the improvement's life is greater than the remaining lease term, the annual recovery allowance must be computed by dividing the unrecovered cost of the expenditures by the number of years left in the lease term at the time the improvement was made.

Can a lessor derive any depreciation benefits from capital improvements made by a lessee on the leased equipment? No, the lessor may not depreciate the amount of such expenditures unless they are made by the lessee in the place of rent.[13] If an improvement is considered rent, the amount spent is gross income to the lessor and, therefore, the lessor can depreciate it over its useful life, without regard to how long the property on which it is made is leased.

What about when a lessor pays for a permanent improvement on property which it has on lease? In general, the expenditure can be recovered by the lessor through depreciation allowances over the estimated useful life of the *improvement*. No consideration is given to the remaining lease term.

PART II: DEPRECIATION UNDER ADR

I. WHAT IS THE ASSET DEPRECIATION RANGE SYSTEM CONCEPT?

Section 167(m) of the Code provides an alternate to the "facts and circumstances" approach to calculating an asset's depreciation allowances. This alternative is referred to as the *Class Life Asset Depreciation Range System*. Basically, the "ADR System" was promulgated by the Internal Revenue Service in an effort to reduce potential disagreements over the determination of an asset's useful life and salvage value as well as the treatment of asset repairs. An asset's useful life is determined by reference to a list of prescribed asset classes. Each such asset class has either a range of years ("asset depreciation range") from which a useful life may be chosen or a specified year life ("class life") which is to be used. The "reasonable allowance" for depreciation is computed by using the numbers of years selected as the useful life.

In the context of the ADR System, the "life" over which an asset may be depreciated is called the "asset depreciation period." This is done in order to make it clear that the ADR depreciation "life" may in fact be shorter than the asset's *actual* useful life, as determined under the facts and circumstances approach.

There are a number of important points which a taxpayer considering using the ADR method must know. To begin with, in order to use the ADR method, he must make an annual election to do so. In general, the election will apply to all assets added during an election year which are eligible for ADR treatment. The election for one year does not apply to asset additions in any other year. Once an ADR election has been made, it may not be revoked or modified after the last prescribed filing day. In addition, once it is made, one of two *first years conventions* (the "half year" or the "modified half-year" convention) must also be elected.

In general, asset grouping accounts, referred to as "vintage accounts," have to be established for all the assets covered by an ADR election. In addition, an ADR period must be selected which will be applicable for all the assets within each account. Once the period selection has been made, the taxpayer must then choose which method of depreciation, i.e. straight line, sum-of-the-years-digits, or declining balance, will be applied to compute the annual depreciation deductions for the asset account.

As a general rule, the gain or loss on an asset when it is "retired" from a vintage account will not be recognized unless it is considered to be an *extraordinary* retirement. An extraordinary retirement might occur, for example, through a casualty occurrence or the discontinuance of a substantial part of the taxpayer's trade or business. *Ordinary* retirements are accounted for merely by making an adjustment to the depreciation reserve account.

OBSERVATION:

A point to remember in making the asset depreciation period selection is that the period used will also determine the amount of investment tax credit which will be available. For example, if a five year depreciation period is chosen, only two thirds of the available credit may be claimed. Therefore, consideration must be given, when a depreciation period of less than seven years exists, as to whether a faster depreciation write-off will be more beneficial than any investment credit that would have to be relinquished. In most cases, it is not.

J. WHAT KIND OF PROPERTY IS ENTITLED TO ADR TREATMENT?

Only assets which are deemed to be "eligible property" under the tax rules can be depreciated using the ADR method. In general, "eligible property" is *depreciable, tangible* property which has been first placed in service by the taxpayer after 1970; which has during the election year an asset guideline class and asset guideline period in effect; and which either qualifies as (1) Code Section 1245 property (basically, depreciable personal property or certain other tangible property that is not a building or a structural component of a building), or as (2) Code Section 1250 property (basically, depreciable real property other than Section 1245 property).[14]

1. Certain Property Is Specifically Not Eligible for ADR Treatment

Property on which the taxpayer is permitted, and has elected, to take certain special depreciation or amortization deductions is not eligible for ADR treatment. This includes, for example, railroad rolling stock. If this type of property has not been specially depreciated or amortized during an ADR election year, it is eligible for ADR treatment. If, however, it is later so depreciated or amortized, any ADR election as to such property will be terminated as of the start of the year in which the special treatment is applied. In this event, the ADR treatment for the years before the special write-off is chosen will not be affected.

K. WHAT IS AN ASSET "VINTAGE ACCOUNT"?

If a taxpayer elects ADR treatment for a particular year, he must establish a "vintage account" for each eligible asset, or group of assets covered by a single asset guideline class. An asset vintage account is a closed-end depreciation account which contains ADR eligible assets, or groups of assets, which have first been placed in service during the election year. The taxable year during which the asset, or group of assets, was placed in service establishes the account's "vintage." If the account contains only one asset it is referred to as an *item* account. If it contains more than one asset it is referred to as a *multiple asset* account.

In setting up vintage accounts, a taxpayer must comply with many prescribed rules. For example, each account may only contain ADR eligible property which comes within a single asset guideline class. The number of vintage accounts that can be established, however, is unlimited, and different assets within the same asset guideline class may be placed in separate vintage accounts. A vintage account can only have one ADR depreciation period. In other words, all assets within a single account must have the same Federal income tax depreciation "life." The Code and related Treasury Regulations should be referred to for other restrictions and special rules.

A taxpayer must set aside a certain amount of money as a "depreciation reserve" for each vintage account and the reserve has to be included on each Federal income tax return. Essentially, an account's depreciation reserve is the total accumulated depreciation on the assets in the account, adjusted for certain required increases and decreases. The required adjustments call for increases in the event of ordinary asset retirements, salvage value reductions, and transfers to supplies or scrap. Decreases are prescribed for extraordinary and certain special retirements, when the reserve amount exceeds the account's unadjusted basis, and when property is removed from the account. The depreciation reserve can never be decreased below zero.

1. When Is an Asset Retired?

A vintage account asset is "retired" when it is permanently discontinued from use in the owner's trade or business or in the production of income. This can be due to a sale, exchange, or other act which causes a permanent disposition; a transfer to supplies or scrap; or a physical abandonment.

L. HOW THE DEPRECIATION PERIOD IS DETERMINED UNDER ADR

If a taxpayer elects ADR treatment, he must determine to which of the prescribed asset categories each eligible asset belongs. If an asset category (asset guideline class) does not exist for a particular asset, it must be depreciated under the general depreciation rules, as discussed in Part I of this chapter.

In order to determine the appropriate asset depreciation period under the Class Life Asset Depreciation Range System, certain terms, *asset guideline class*, *asset guideline period*, and *asset depreciation range*, which form the conceptual basis of the System, must be understood.

The term "asset guideline class" means essentially a specified category of assets for which a separate asset guideline period is provided. An "asset guideline period" is defined as the average class life which has been prescribed for a particular class of assets. Generally, the average class life, or "mid-range ADR depreciation life," is referred to simply as the "class life" of an asset. Typically, a particular class of assets has a range of years above and below their class life. This range is referred to as the "asset depreciation range" of the class of assets. The range lower limit is set at 80% of the asset guideline period and the upper limit is set at 120% of the asset guideline period. For example, the asset guideline period for assets includable within the asset category "mining" is currently 10 years. This asset category, at the time of this writing, has an asset depreciation range whose lower limit is 8 years and whose upper limit is 12 years. In making the range computation, fractional years are rounded off to the nearest half or whole year. If an asset depreciation range exists for a particular asset, a taxpayer may generally choose any number of years, plus a half year, within the established asset depreciation range. The period selected is the period over which the asset will be depreciated and is referred to as the "asset depreciation period." If an asset depreciation range is not in effect for an asset class, the asset depreciation period will be the prescribed asset guideline period. Assets used predominantly outside the United States, for example, do not currently have an asset depreciation range.

Generally speaking, the asset depreciation period is treated as the useful life of the asset for all Federal income tax purposes, including the available investment tax credit computation. It is not used, however, for the purpose of determining salvage value, whether a true tax lease exists, or whether an expenditure adds to an asset's useful life.

Asset guideline periods, as well as asset guideline classes and asset depreciation ranges, for classified assets are presently embodied in Revenue Procedure 77-10. Any changes or additions to these categories are usually published in the Internal Revenue Bulletin. In general, the periods, classes, and ranges in effect on the last day of an ADR election year are to be referred to for all vintage accounts established during an election year. A taxpayer cannot make changes in his selection to incorporate modifications effective following the last day of the election year.

1. The Selection of an Asset Guideline Class Is a Key Step

Ascertaining in which asset guideline class a particular asset belongs is a key step in the process of determining the appropriate asset depreciation period. In the event a "type" category exists, such as "trucks," the taxpayer will select the period to be used from the relevant type. If a "type" category does not exist, the taxpayer must refer to the appropriate "activity" category, such as "mining," to make the asset guideline class selection. The asset's *primary* use during the election year decides in which activity class an asset must be included. The fact that a taxpayer uses the asset in a different activity in a subsequent year will not affect the initial choice.

> OBSERVATION:
>
> It is interesting to note that the classification of an asset in an activity asset guideline class is strictly dependent on the asset's primary use during an election year, not the *taxpayer's* primary business activity during such year.

If an ADR electing taxpayer incorrectly characterized or classified an asset, his election will not be revoked. The mistake must, however, be corrected and all relevant adjustments must be made; including, for example, adjustments to basis, salvage value, and depreciation reserve. If the taxpayer forgot to establish a vintage account for any ADR eligible property, an account must be created and a depreciation period selected. If an incorrect asset depreciation period was chosen, a correct one must be selected.

M. WHAT METHODS OF DEPRECIATION ARE AVAILABLE UNDER ADR?

A taxpayer electing ADR treatment may, for new ADR eligible property, use the straight line method, the sum-of-the-years-digits method, or the double declining balance method of depreciation. If the property is used, however, he is limited to using the straight line method or the declining balance method at a rate not to exceed 150% of the straight line rate.

N. HOW TO FIGURE OUT HOW MUCH MAY BE WRITTEN OFF EACH YEAR

A taxpayer must depreciate all assets within a vintage account in accordance with the method of depreciation selected for the account. The actual amount of depreciation that may be claimed each year is calculated in the same basic way as it is under the facts and circumstances approach. An essential difference, however, is that the annual allowance is computed without deducting the salvage value from the property's basis, *regardless of whether the straight line, the sum-of-the-years-digits, or the declining balance method is selected.* The account's asset value cannot, however, be depreciated below its reasonable salvage value. No matter what method of depreciation is selected, the account's annual allowable deduction cannot be greater than the amount (determined as of the beginning of the taxable year) by which the *unadjusted* basis of the account exceeds the sum of the account's established depreciation reserve and salvage value.

OBSERVATIONS:

I. The reader should remember that "salvage value" is the amount expected to be realized from an asset at the end of the *Non-ADR* useful life, not the end of the chosen ADR depreciation period.

II. If ADR treatment is chosen the vintage account's asset salvage value does not have to be subtracted from the account's basis when the straight line method or the sum-of-the-years-digits method is used. This is not so when the facts and circumstances approach is used. If the declining balance method is selected, however, the basis does not have to be reduced by the salvage value before the annual allowance is determined in either case.

III. Under ADR, if a taxpayer elects to switch his method of depreciation from the declining balance method to, for example, the straight line method, no salvage value reduction has to be made in computing the remaining deductions. Under the Non-ADR method, such a switch requires that the depreciation base be reduced by the salvage value prior to computing the remaining annual allowances.

1. Using the Straight Line Method

If the straight line method of depreciation is selected, the annual depreciation allowance for a vintage account's assets is computed by dividing the account's *unadjusted* basis by the number of years in the selected asset depreciation period.[15] For example, if the unadjusted basis is equal to $100 and its asset depreciation period is 10 years, the annual depreciation would be $10:

$$\frac{\$100}{10} = \$10.$$

Under the ADR method, salvage value does not have to be deducted from the account's basis before making the allowance computation.

2. Using the Sum-of-the-Years-Digits Method

If a taxpayer chooses the sum-of-the-years-digits method, a vintage account's annual depreciation allowance is calculated by multiplying the *unadjusted* basis of the account by a prescribed fraction. The fraction's numerator is equal to the number of years that remain in the account's asset depreciation period, including the calculation year. The denominator is equal to the sum of all of the years' digits for the account's asset depreciation period.[16] For example, the first year's depreciation allowance for an account with an unadjusted basis equal to $100 and a selected depreciation period of 5 years is $33.33. This is obtained by multiplying the $100 basis by the fraction $\dfrac{5}{5+4+3+2+1}$.

Salvage value is not deducted from the account's basis before making the computation.

3. Using the Declining Balance Method

If the declining balance method of depreciation is elected, the yearly depreciation allowance is calculated by applying a uniform rate, not to exceed twice the straight line rate, to the excess of the vintage account's *unadjusted* basis over its established depreciation reserve.[17] For example, a vintage account containing a new asset costing $100 and having a depreciation period of 10 years would be entitled to a $20 deduction in the first year under the 200% declining balance method. This is calculated by multiplying the account's unadjusted basis ($100) by two times the straight line rate (2 x 10%). The depreciation reserve for the second year would be $20, the first year's allowance. Therefore, the second year's depreciation would equal $16 (2 x 10% x ($100-$20)).

O. CERTAIN DEPRECIATION METHOD CHANGES ARE PERMITTED

A taxpayer is permitted to make certain depreciation method changes during the asset depreciation period without securing the approval of the Commissioner of the Internal Revenue Service. For example, a taxpayer can switch form the declining balance method of depreciation to the sum-of-the-years-digits method when it is most beneficial. A change from the declining balance or the sum-of-the-years-digits method to the straight line method may also be made without the Commissioner's approval. With certain minor exceptions, no other changes are permitted without prior approval. Once a method change is made, *all* property in the vintage account affected must be depreciated under the new rate.

OBSERVATION:

An appropriately timed switch in depreciation methods can maximize the amount of "early" depreciation write-offs. This can increase a lessor's yield through earlier enhanced tax savings.

P. HOW ADR PERMITS "EXTRA" DEPRECIATION— FIRST YEAR CONVENTIONS

If a taxpayer elects to use ADR, one of two specified conventions must be applied—the *modified half-year* convention or the *half-year* convention. A taxpayer must apply the same convention to all vintage accounts established during an ADR electing year. He can, however, apply any convention which he deems the most beneficial for vintage accounts established *in any other year.*

1. The Modified Half-Year Convention

Under the *modified half-year* convention, the amount of first year depreciation for a vintage account is calculated by considering all the assets within the account placed in service during the first half of the taxable year as having been placed in service on the first day of such year. All assets placed in service during the second half are treated as having been placed in service on the first day of the following taxable year.[18] Under this convention, for example, a calendar year taxpayer may claim a full 12 months of depreciation on all property placed in service on or before June 30th of such year. He may not claim, for that year, any depreciation on property placed in service after June 30th. The taxpayer is eligible, however, to claim a full 12 months of depreciation on the "second half" property in the following year.

If the electing taxpayer entity was not in existence for a full 12 months during the taxable year the assets were placed in service, the initial "depreciation year" will only consist of the number of months of its existence. The first half of such year ends at the close of the last day of the calendar month closest to the middle of such period and the second half begins on the following day. If the taxable "year" consists of only one month, the first half is considered to end on the day nearest to the midpoint of the month and the second half is considered to begin on the following day. Therefore, for example, a calendar year taxpayer, using the modified half-year convention and coming into existence on May 1, will have an eight month taxable year for convention purposes. Assets placed in service in the first half of such "year" will be entitled to eight months depreciation. Assets placed in service after the second half will not be entitled to any depreciation for such year. They will, however, be eligible for a full 12 months in the following taxable year.

A taxpayer must follow certain specific rules for assets subject to the modified half-year convention which are extraordinarily retired. Those placed in service in the first half of a taxable year, and which must be extraordinarily retired during the first half of the retirement year, are deemed to have been retired on the first day of such year. Those retired in the second half are deemed to have been retired on the first day of the second half of such year. As to property first placed in service in the second half, extraordinary retirements during the first half of the retirement year are deemed to have occurred on the first day of the second half of the year and those in the second half are deemed to have occurred on the first day of the following year.

2. The Half-Year Convention

If the *half-year convention* is adopted, the allowance for depreciation for the first taxable year is computed by treating assets placed in service *anytime* during the taxable year as placed in service on the first day of the second half of the taxable year.[19] For example, for a calendar year taxpayer, an asset placed in service in January and an asset placed in service in November of the same year will each be entitled to one-half a year's depreciation. The "depreciation year" is determined in the same manner as it is for the modified half-year convention. Extraordinary retirements under this convention are treated as all having taken place on the first day of the second half of the retirement year.

Q. THERE ARE CERTAIN DEPRECIATION CHOICE LIMITATIONS

As explained earlier, a taxpayer must use the same depreciation method for all assets in a particular vintage account. For example, if he decides to use the straight line method for any asset in a vintage account, he must depreciate all assets in the account on this basis. If a vintage account consists entirely of new property (property whose "original use" began with the taxpayer) and if an asset depreciation period of at least three years has been selected, a taxpayer has the widest choice of depreciation methods. That is, he may choose the straight line, the sum-of-the-years-digits, or up to the 200% declining balance method. "Original use" is defined as the first use to which property is put, regardless of whether this use corresponds to the use the taxpayer first puts the property.[20] In general, if an asset depreciation period of less than three years has been chosen for a vintage account or if the account contains "used" property (property whose original use did not begin with the taxpayer), the straight line method of depreciation must be used. If, however, a vintage account contains used property and if the selected asset depreciation period is at least three years, the declining balance method using a rate not in excess of 150% of the straight line method may also be used.

R. UNADJUSTED BASIS AND ADJUSTED BASIS EXPLAINED

Unadjusted basis and *adjusted* basis are two important concepts that a taxpayer must understand in working with the ADR technique. The unadjusted basis of an asset is, in general, its undepreciated, or unamortized, cost. The excess of an asset's unadjusted basis over the allowable depreciation is called the adjusted basis of an asset. When reference is made to the unadjusted basis of a vintage account, it means the aggregate of the unadjusted basis (essentially cost) of all the assets in the account. The excess of a vintage account's unadjusted basis over its depreciation reserve is referred to as the account's adjusted basis.

S. HOW THE CONCEPT OF SALVAGE VALUE VARIES UNDER ADR

A taxpayer electing ADR treatment may not use the *net* salvage value concept in computing his annual depreciation allowances. He must use *gross* salvage value. The gross salvage value of an asset is basically the owner's estimate of how much the asset will be worth when it is sold or otherwise disposed of when it has no further use in the owner's trade or business or in the production of his income.[21] In determining this value, removal, dismantling, demolition, or similar costs may not be deducted. The "salvage value" of a vintage account is, therefore, the *gross* salvage value of the assets in the account.

The gross salvage value of a vintage account may, under Code Section 167(f), be reduced by an amount up to 10% of the account's unadjusted basis if the account contains depreciable personal property and if the taxpayer has chosen an asset depreciation period of three years or more. It may not, however, be reduced below zero. Therefore, if the salvage value is determined to be less than or equal to 10% of an asset's cost, an election to fix the value at zero may be made.

OBSERVATION:

It is important to emphasize that an asset's salvage value is the amount which the taxpayer anticipates he will realize at the end of the asset's useful life, as opposed to the end of the selected ADR depreciation period. In the case of leased property which the lessor contemplates selling at the end of the lease, salvage value is what the property is estimated to be worth at the end of the lease term. If the lessor anticipates re-leasing the asset, the value is estimated as of the end of the total period which the asset will be under lease.

A taxpayer electing ADR must, at the same time the ADR election is made, determine each vintage account's salvage value. The estimate must be based upon the facts and circumstances prevailing at the close of the taxable year in which the vintage account was established. The taxpayer must also specify the amount, if any, by which the gross salvage value was reduced under Code Section 167(f). Once a value has been established, a recalculation is not permitted based upon asset price changes or new facts and circumstances in later years.

The vintage account assets may not be depreciated below a "reasonable" salvage value, after taking into account the permitted Code Section 167(f) reduction. The value chosen will be considered "reasonable" unless it can be shown that the estimate is off by an amount greater than 10% of the account's unadjusted basis. If the difference exceeds 10%, or if the gross salvage value has been consistently underestimated to take advantage of the 10% leeway, an upward adjustment is required. The amount of the adjustment must be equal to the difference.

T. THE "PLACED IN SERVICE" CONCEPT UNDER ADR

When equipment is deemed to have been "placed in service" is an important consideration under the ADR method. An asset is first placed in service when it is first placed in service *by the taxpayer*, as opposed to the first time it is placed in service. It is clear that this point will occur when the taxpayer begins to actually use the property. It also, however, may occur prior to that time. This is due to the fact that the rules provide that property will be considered to have been first placed in service when it is in a *condition or state of readiness and availability for a specifically assigned function*, whether in a trade or business, in the production of income, in a tax-exempt activity, or in a personal activity.[22]

OBSERVATION:

The date on which an asset's depreciation is begun does not necessarily establish the "first placed in service" date. For example, an asset may be placed in service in November by an ADR electing calendar year taxpayer choosing the modified half-year convention, but pursuant to the convention rules it may not be depreciated until the following year.

U. LEASED PROPERTY HAS SPECIFIC RULES

An equipment lessor must be aware of certain rules when using the ADR approach. To begin with, the *asset depreciation range and the asset depreciation period* for leased equipment is determined without regard to the lease term. The *asset guideline class* which must generally be used is the class which the lessee would use if he had been the equipment owner, unless there is a class in effect for lessors covering the particular equipment.

V. HOW ARE EQUIPMENT REPAIRS TREATED?

In general, expenditures for equipment repairs, maintenance, rehabilitation, or improvements which substantially prolong its life, materially increase its value, or adapt it to a substantially different use are considered *capital* expenditures and, as such, are subject to an allowance for depreciation.[23] Expenditures which do not so qualify are expensed in the year paid or incurred. In many cases it is difficult to determine whether or not an expenditure is in the nature of a capital expenditure. Because of this, the ADR rules provide an easy procedure to determine whether expenditures on certain property will qualify as capital expenditures. The basis of the classification depends on whether the property qualifies as "repair allowance property."

"Repair Allowance Property" is, in general, property in asset guideline classes which has a prescribed *repair allowance percentage.* In effect, this includes all assets that will qualify for ADR depreciation. Basically, the "repair allowance" is the product of (i) the average of (a) the unadjusted basis of all repair allowance property in an asset guideline class at the start of the taxable year and (b) the unadjusted basis of all such property at the end of the taxable year and (ii) the prescribed asset guideline class repair allowance percentage. The prescribed repair allowance percentages are specified in Revenue Procedure 77-10.

If an election to use the repair allowance is made, the repair, maintenance, rehabilitation, or improvement expenditures that do not come within the prescribed set of guidelines for capital expenditures can, up to a certain amount, be expensed. The excess over the amount limitation is classified as a "property improvement" and is treated in the manner of a capital expenditure.

If an election to use the repair allowance is not made, or if the property in question will not qualify as repair allowance property, then the repair, maintenance, rehabilitation, or improvement expenditure is to be treated as a capital expenditure or as a deductible expense, in accordance with the general provisions of the Code and related Treasury Regulations.

W. AN ELECTION IS REQUIRED FOR ADR TREATMENT

In order for a taxpayer to use the ADR method for a particular tax year, he must elect to do so at the time when he files his Federal income tax return.[24] In general, once the election is made *all* ADR eligible property first placed in service during the electing year *must* be included within the election. Any related ADR elections, such as the choice of the preferred first year convention, must also be made at that time.

A taxpayer may, in general, not revoke or modify an ADR election after the last day that is prescribed for filing for the election. In addition, other modifications, such as changes in the vintage accounts, depreciation periods, or first year conventions, may generally not be made after this time unless required by the rules. An example of a required change would be when an incorrect asset guideline class has been selected.

X. A DEPRECIATION CHECKLIST FOR LESSORS

The following checklist will provide an equipment lessor with a guide as to key depreciation issues.

1. Will the Asset's Depreciation Be Calculated under the "Facts and Circumstances" Method or the "ADR" Method?
2. If the "Facts and Circumstances" Approach Will Be Used, Has the Asset's Useful Life Been Properly Computed by Reference to the Lessor's Experience with Similar Property.
   a. Have Current or Future Anticipated Conditions Which May Affect an Asset's Useful Life Been Considered?
      (1) From Wear and Tear and Decay or Decline from Natural Causes.
      (2) From the Normal Progress of the State of the Art, Economic Changes, Inventions and Current Developments.
      (3) From Climatic and Other Relevant Local Conditions.
      (4) From the Lessor's Repair, Renewal, and Replacement Program.
   b. If the Lessor's Experience with the Asset in Question Is Too Limited, Has the Useful Life Estimate Been Based on General Experience in His Industry?
3. Has the Asset's Salvage Value Been Computed?
   a. Has an Election Been Made to Take the 10% Reduction under Section 167(f) of the Code.

4. How Will the Annual Depreciation Allowance Be Calculated?
   a. Using the Straight Line Method.
   b. Using the Sum-Of-The-Years-Digits Method.
   c. Using the Declining Balance Method.
   d. Another Consistent Method.
5. If the Straight Line Method Will Be Used:
   a. Under the Non-ADR Approach, Has the Salvage Value Been Subtracted from the Basis of the Equipment Before Calculating the Annual Deduction?
   b. Under the ADR Approach, Has the Asset's Depreciation Allowance Been Computed Without Subtracting Salvage Value from the Basis of the Equipment?
6. If the Declining Balance Method Will Be Used Under Either the ADR or Non-ADR Approach, Has the Asset's Depreciation Allowance Been Calculated Without Subtracting Salvage Value from the Basis of the Equipment?
7. If the Sum-of-the-Years-Digits Method Will Be Used:
   a. Under the Non-ADR Approach, Has the Salvage Value Been Subtracted from the Basis of the Equipment Before Calculating the Annual Deduction?
   b. Under the ADR Approach, Has the Asset's Depreciation Allowance Been Computed Without Subtracting Salvage Value from the Basis of the Equipment?
8. Has the Appropriate Asset "Placed in Service" Date Been Determined?
   a. If an Asset Has Only Been in Service for a Percentage of a Tax Year, Has This Been Taken into Account in Determining the Depreciation Allowance?
9. Has the Depreciation Been Properly Claimed as to Capital Improvements:
   a. If Made by the Lessee?
   b. If Made by the Lessor?
10. If the ADR Method Will Be Used:
    a. Has the Proper Asset Guideline Class Been Selected?
       (1) From the "Type" Categroy.
       (2) From the "Activity" Category.
    b. Has the Proper Asset Depreciation Period Been Selected?
    c. Has the Most Beneficial First Year Convention Been Chosen?
       (1) The Half-Year Convention.
       (2) The Modified Half-Year Convention.
    d. Has the Equipment Qualified as "Eligible Property"?
       (1) Is It Depreciable?
       (2) Is It Tangible?

    (3) Does It Have an Asset Guideline Class Period in Effect?

    (4) Will It Qualify as Code Section 1245 Property?

  e. Has the Lessor, as to Any Equipment That Is Eligible for a Special Depreciation or Amortization Deduction, Elected to Take Such Approach? If so, the Equipment Is Not Eligible for ADR Treatment.

  f. Have Appropriate Vintage Accounts Been Established as to Equipment Placed in Service During the Election Year?

    (1) Will Proper Depreciation Reserves Be Set Up?

  g. Has the Lessor Been in Existence for 12 Months of the ADR Election Year? If Not, Will the ADR Election "Year" Be Accordingly Reduced?

  h. Have the Proper Procedures Been Established to Make the ADR Election When the Federal Income Tax Return Is Filed?

FOOTNOTES

[1]For Representative Tax Discussions See *Gladding Dry Goods Co.,* 2 BTA 336, Dec. 642; and *L. Ocrant,* 65 TC 1156, Dec. 33, 726.

[2]Treas. Reg. Sec. 1.167(a)-1(a).

[3]I.R.C. Section 1012.

[4]Treas. Reg. Sec. 1.167(a)-1(b); For Representative Tax Discussions See *Hertz Corp.,* 60-2 USTC Para. 9555, 364 U.S. 122; *J. W. Roddy,* 20 TCM 1129, Dec. 24, 978 (M), TC Memo. 1961-228.

[5]Treas. Reg. Sec. 1.167(a)-1(b); For Representative Tax Discussions See Letter of Commissioner of Internal Revenue, Jan. 21, 1960; *M. Z. Bryan Est.,* 66-2 USTC Para. 9601, 364 F.2d. 751; Special Ruling, May 18, 1955; *American M.A.R.C. Inc.* 67-1 USTC Para 9277; and *New England Tank Industries of N.H., Inc.,* 69-2 USTC Para 9504.

[6]Treas. Reg. Sec. 1.167(a)-1(c).

[7]For Representative Tax Discussions See *Massey Motore, Inc.* 60-2 USTC Para. 9554, 364 U.S. 92; *R. H. Evans,* 60-2 USTC Para. 9554, 365 U.S. 92; *Hertz Corp.,* 60-2 USTC Para. 9555, 364 U.S. 122; Special Ruling, May 18, 1955, 1954 Code Tr. Binder Para 37,233; *W. H. Williams Co., Inc.* 56-2 USTC Para 9839.

[8]I.R.C. Section 167(f).

[9]Treas. Reg. 1.167(a)-10(b); For Representative Tax Discussions See *Hillcone Steamship Co.,* 22 TCM 1096, Dec. 26, 365 (M), TC Memo 1963-220; *R. A. Biggs,* 71-1 USTC Para. 9306, 440 F.2d.1; *Rev. Rul.* 76-238, 1976-1CB 55; *Sears Oil Co., Inc.* 66-1 USTC Para. 9384, 359 F.2d. 191; *F. D. Cooper,* 76-2 USTC Para. 9723, 542 F.2d 599.

[10]For Representative Tax Discussions See *Kern Co.,* 1 TC 249, Dec. 12,906; *National Map Co.* 17BTA 1098, Dec. 5543; *W. R. Collins,* 53-1 USTC Para. 9377, 203 F.2d 565; *Shagan* 11 TCM 730, Dec. 19,099 (M); *W. E. Clairmont,* 64 TC 1130, Dec. 33,443; and *E. M. Schroder,* 34 TCM 1572, Dec. 33,562 (M) TC Memo. 1975-364.

[11]For Representative Tax Discussions See *Ostheimer*, 1 BTA 18, Dec. 13; *Terminal R.R. Association* of St. Louis, 17 BTA 1135, Dec. 5557; *Michigan Central R.R. Co.*, 28 BTA 437, Dec. 8120; *Union National Bank of Youngstown vs. Moore*, 39-2 USTC Para. 9613; *Belt Railway Co.*, 36 F.2d 541 (Cert. Denied 281 U.S. 742)

[12]For Representative Tax Discussions See *Reisinger*, 44-2 USTC Para. 9443, 144 F.2d 475; *Halleran*, BTA Memo, Dec. 12,813-B; and *Revere Land Co.*, 48-1 USTC Para 9313, 169 F.2d. 469 (Cert. Denied, 335 U.S. 853).

[13]For Representative Tax Discussions See *P. Wilson*, 20 TCM 676, Dec. 24,833 (M), TC Memo 1961-135; *O. L. Bardes*, 37 TC 1134, Dec. 25,416.

[14]Treas. Reg. Sec. 1.167(a)-11(b)(2).

[15]Treas. Reg. Sec. 1.167(a)-11(c)(1)(i)(b).

[16]Treas. Reg. Sec. 1.167(a)-11(c)(1)(i)(c).

[17]Treas. Reg. Sec. 1.167(a)-11(c)(1)(i)(d).

[18]Treas. Reg. Sec. 1.167(a)-11(c)(2)(ii).

[19]Treas. Reg. Sec. 1.167(a)-11(c)(2)(iii).

[20]Treas. Reg. Sec. 1.167(a)-11(c)(1)(iv)(c).

[21]Treas. Reg. Sec. 1.167(a)-11(d)(1)(i).

[22]Treas. Reg. Sec. 1.167(a)-11(e)(1)(i).

[23]Treas. Reg. Sec. 1.167(a)-11(d)(2)(i)(a).

[24]Treas. Reg. Sec. 1.167(a)-11(f)(1)(i).

7

HOW TO WORK WITH THE NEW TAX RULES

Unless Your Lease Is a "True" Lease You're in Trouble • What Must You Do to Be Safe • The IRS Now Has Definite Demands • You Must Know What They Are and How to Work with Them to Avoid Economic Disaster.

A. HOW CAN YOU BE SURE YOU HAVE A "TRUE" LEASE?

Does it matter whether a lease-type transaction actually qualifies as a lease *for Federal Income Tax purposes?* In virtually all situations it does. In fact, the failure to qualify as a "true" lease can ruin the anticipated economics. The "lessor" would not be able to claim the equipment ownership tax benefits, such as depreciation and investment tax credit, and the "lessee" would not be able to treat the rental payments as a deductible expense. Simply, the reasons that made the arrangement attractive at the beginning would no longer be present.

Is there any way the parties can make sure they have a true tax lease? Yes, by getting the Internal Revenue Service to issue a finding that they will receive the anticipated tax treatment. This is the safest route; however, it is not always practical because the time involved in getting a "Revenue Ruling" can typically range anywhere from six to twelve months and the legal fees can be prohibitive. In addition, if an unfavorable ruling is issued after the transaction has been closed, there is a risk that this will draw attention to an issue that may eventually cause a problem. On the other hand, if the ruling is favorable the parties can assume there will be no future IRS problems because the Service will not generally reverse its position.

Another course of action is to try to get tax counsel to give a favorable written opinion as to the tax treatment. This can also be costly and may not mean much if the IRS decides to challenge it. Further, there is always the possibility that counsel could be wrong.

Fortunately, there is another good alternative. The transaction can be structured in accordance with a new and comprehensive set of tax guidelines set forth in Revenue Procedure 75-21. The "Guidelines" were promulgated by the Service for advance ruling purposes and, therefore, if the parties conform to the stated criteria they can feel comfortable that the lease will in fact qualify as a true tax lease, even though they did not go for a Revenue Ruling.

The reader should be aware that the Guidelines do not establish as a matter of law whether a transaction is a true lease; therefore, there is the possibility that even if it does not follow the rules it may still qualify. In fact, the Guidelines themselves indicate that the Service may consider giving a favorable Revenue Ruling on a nonconforming transaction if warranted by the particular facts. Those experienced in the tax ruling area, however, know that it is extremely difficult to get the Service to issue a favorable ruling when there are substantive variances from general tax guidelines.

The Guidelines appear to apply only to *leveraged* lease situations. This could imply that a non-leveraged lease may not have to fit within the restrictive relevant criteria in order to be a true lease. However, it seems to make more sense that this will not be the case and to the extent the tests fit it would be prudent to keep the Guidelines in mind regardless of whether or not the transaction is leveraged.

When a Revenue Ruling will not be involved, the Guideline rules are sometimes stretched in order to keep all the parties satisfied. For example, a company may not be willing to lease equipment unless they have a low fixed-price purchase option. Although prohibited under the new rules, a prospective lessor may grant such a right just to win the transaction.

> OBSERVATION:
>
> Syndicators should be careful when deviating from the Guidelines in structuring a lease financing even though each party initially states a Revenue Ruling will not be required. Invariably, once the parties, particularly the equity investors, hear all about the theoretical risks from their lawyers, they get nervous and frequently ask for a favorable opinion from tax counsel as to the true lease nature. In many situations counsel is reluctant to give such an opinion when there is a Guideline variance because of the uncertainty as to the effect. Coming at the last minute, this can lead to a serious roadblock to the completion of the deal.

B. WHAT MAKES A DEAL QUALIFY AS A LEASE UNDER THE NEW TAX GUIDELINES?

There is no doubt that a transaction will qualify as a lease for Federal income tax purposes if the rules in the new IRS lease guidelines are followed. As already mentioned the rules seem to be aimed at only *leveraged* leases; however, they should be considered when dealing with other types of leases. Now to examine the major aspects of these complex rules:

1. There Must Be a Minimum Investment

Under the Guidelines the lessor must initially make an unconditional equity investment in the equipment equal to at least 20% of its cost. This can be done in a number of ways: with cash, with other consideration, or by personally assuming the obligation to purchase the equipment. Typically, the lessor makes a cash payment from its own funds. The 20% equity investment is referred to as the "minimum investment."

The uncondtional nature of the initial investment was established in order to prevent the lessor from arranging to receive, either from the lessee or certain lessee-related parties, all or any part of his equity back once the equipment is put into service. This is consistent with the Service's feeling that *if a lessor wants to be treated as an equipment owner for tax purposes and therefore be entitled to claim the tax benefits, there must be an ownership risk.*

If the personal liability assumption alternative is used to meet the minimum equity test, the assumption must in fact be meaningful. There must be a real dollar exposure. For example, if the lessor's net worth is not sufficient to stand behind the assumed obligation, the test won't be met.

The lessor must also maintain a 20% "minimum investment" in the equipment during the lease term. *The test for determining whether the minimum investment rule has been met during the term is complicated; follow it carefully.* The test will be met if the amount by which the cumulative payments which the lessee is obligated to pay exceeds the cumulative disbursements which the lessor is obligated to pay as a result of the equipment ownership is never greater than the sum of any excess of the initial equity investment over 20% of the equipment cost and the cumulative pro rata portion of the transaction's projected profit, not considering tax benefits. Simply, this means that the excess of the amounts coming in over the amounts going out must never be more than the sum of any equity investment amount greater than 20% of equipment cost and the pro rata portion of the anticipated profit. The tax benefits accruing from ownership cannot be considered as "profit" in the computation.

In addition to the two previously mentioned investment requirements, the lessor must also satisfy a minimum investment criterion as of the end of the lease term. It consists of two basic parts. First, the lessor must be able to show that the estimated fair market residual value of the leased equipment is equal to at least 20% of its original cost. Second, the lessor must be able to show that a reasonable estimate of the equipment's useful life at the end of the lease term is the *longer* of 1 year or 20% of the equipment's originally estimated useful life.

ILLUSTRATIVE EXAMPLE— AT-RISK RESIDUAL TEST:

Company A wants to lease a $10,000 steel shipping container from Company B for an 11 year lease term. The container has an estimated useful life of 12 years and an estimated fair market value at the end of 11 years of $2,300. Will the end-of-the-lease-term "at risk" investment test be met?

The estimated fair market residual value test *has* been met. That is, the $2,300 residual meets the first test (20% of $10,000 = $2,000, the minimum).

The useful life test has *not* been met. Twenty percent of 12 years is 2.4 years. When the lease term is over there will only be 1 year of useful life left and the second test says the remaining useful life must be the *longer* of 1 year or, in our example, 2.4 years.

In making the fair market residual value determination, no weight can be given to any inflationary increases or deflationary decreases during the lease term. In other words, the determination must be made as to future value based upon "today" dollars. In addition, the estimated residual amount must be reduced by any anticipated costs that may be incurred in removing and delivering the property to the lessor at the end of the lease term.

The calculations cannot be made without first figuring out what the "lease term" will be for a particular transaction. It is not necessarily the "primary term" designated by the lease document. By definition, the "term" must include all renewal and extension periods *other* than those which are at fair market rental value *and* are at the lessee's option. For example, the lessor would have to include any period for which it could *require* the lessee to continue to lease the equipment *even though it would be at fair market rental value.* This rule prevents a lessor from avoiding his "residual risk" through a forced renewal of the lease which would in effect run until the lessor had no residual value risk. This again reinforces the Guideline intent that if *an equipment owner wants to be a "lessor" he must incur real ownership risks.*

OBSERVATIONS:

I. In the past some equipment lessors adopted a practice of anticipating an inflationary increase in the residual value in calculating their projected profit transaction. Under the Guidelines the elimination of inflationary "upside" in the residual value in effect would require such a lessor to charge higher rents on similar transactions because inflation gain must be ignored.

II. In the past many leveraged lease transaction lessors typically assumed a 15% equipment residual value. The effect of the 20% residual floor is the elimination in such situations of some of the available depreciation which in turn causes a relative increase in rents.

ILLUSTRATIVE EXAMPLE—
WRITE-OFF LIMITATIONS:

Company A wants to lease from Company B a $10,000 truck on a finance leveraged lease basis over a period of 10 years.

Assume the lessor, Company B, computes its depreciation benefits using the facts and circumstances method of depreciation under the following facts:

Lease term	10 years
Initial cost	$10,000
Residual value (20% of $10,000)	$ 2,000
Depreciation base ($10,000 − $2,000)	$ 8,000

If Company B depreciated the truck over 10 years on the double-declining basis it could claim a maximum depreciation in the first year of $1600 (2 x 10% x $8000). For a 50% taxpayer this would mean a first-year tax savings, based upon the available depreciation, of $800 (50% X 1600).

Suppose instead the lessor had been able to write off 90% of the cost over the 10 year period. The assumptions would be as follows:

Lease term	10 years
Initial cost	$10,000
Residual value (10% of $10,000)	$ 1,000
Depreciation base ($10,000 − $1,000)	$ 9,000

Under this Company B would have a tax saving of $900 in the first year through depreciation (50% x 2 x 10% x $9000).

As can be seen, the Guidelines reduce the available depreciation write-off, thereby causing less of a "tax" profit to the lessor. The result: *the lessee must pay more rent in order for the lessor to make the same time value return in a given situation.*

2. The Transaction Must Produce a Profit

The Guidelines provide that the lessor must make a *profit* on the transaction. At first this statement seems ridiculous. What businessman would be involved in a situation in which he didn't make a profit! None, so what is the IRS getting at? Simply, that the lessor must make money on the deal *aside* from the return generated by the tax benefits, such as depreciation and interest deductions, investment credits, or other allowances. In other words, the lessor must be able to show that the lease transaction makes economic sense without considering the tax benefits. The Service wants to make sure that lease deals are not merely tax avoidance devices.

How does a lessor know whether he has met the profit requirement? By meeting the following Guideline test: the total rent which the lessee is obligated to pay over the lease term when added to the equipment's estimated residual value has to be greater than the amount of money which the lessor is obligated to pay out with respect to the equipment, such as debt service, and his equity investment, including any related direct equity financing costs. Simply, the lessor must anticipate having money left over, when adding in the estimated residual value, at the end of the lease term after repaying any transaction debt, the money it took out of its own pocket to acquire the equipment, and any other direct equity investment financing costs.

ILLUSTRATIVE EXAMPLE—
THE PROFIT TEST:

Company B has leased a new $100,000 barge to Company A under the following facts:

Lease term	10 years
Barge residual value	$20,000
Equity investment	$20,000
Debt principal	$80,000
Debt interest rate	10%
Loan term	10 years
Investment tax credit rate	10%
Total aggregate rentals	$125,000
Legal fees	$5,000
Miscellaneous fees	$1,000

For simplicity, assume that the debt repayment is based upon an average outstanding principal of $40,000 over the 10 year period. Based on the above, the deal evolves as follows:

ITC available	$10,000
Depreciation available	$80,000

Debt interest due	$40,000
Principal repayment	$80,000
Fees	$ 6,000
Total	$126,000

Does the lessor pass the IRS profit test? The formula is:

Aggregate rentals + residual value must exceed cash out.

Aggregate rentals + residual =
$125,000 + $20,000 = $145,000
Equity investment + debt service + fees = cash out =
$20,000, + $80,000 + $40,000 + $6,000 = $146,000

The lessor fails the test.

The net result: the rents must be increased to pass the test.

The IRS did not stop with the profit requirement. The lessor must also demonstrate that the transaction will produce a *positive cash flow* which is "reasonable" in amount. That is, the aggregate rents must comfortably exceed the aggregate outflows, basically the debt service and the direct equity financing costs.

OBSERVATIONS:

I. The positive cash flow determination must be made without giving any consideration to the residual value of the equipment. This seems to be unusual in light of the profit test requirement where the residual value is considered.

II. The Guidelines do not define what is deemed a "reasonable" spread with respect to the positive cash flow requirement. The IRS will undoubtedly make a case-by-case determination and, with time, a rule of thumb should develop.

3. The Lessee Cannot Be an Owner

In general, a lessee or certain lessee-related parties cannot contribute any part of the funds necessary to buy, add to, or improve the equipment. Additions or improvements which can be easily removed without causing material damage are excepted from this rule, provided the lessor does not have a right to buy them at a below-market price.

Ordinary maintenance and repairs which the lessee must make at its expense are not deemed "additions or improvements" and are therefore excluded from the rule. The problem with this exception is that the Guidelines do not set up any parameters for determining what is considered "ordinary maintenance and repairs." If the IRS successfully challenges any expenditures as not "ordinary," there may be a risk that the true lease nature will be lost.

RECOMMENDATION:

It will be a matter of time before the legal community will have a good perspective on the issue of "ordinary maintenance and repairs." If there is any concern, tax counsel should be consulted.

Under the same basic concept, the lessee is prohibited from paying for any equipment cost overruns. Usually the only time this could become a problem is when equipment with a long construction period is involved. In many of these situations the purchase contracts have price escalation clauses. Some prospective lessors committing to lease such equipment before completion limit their cost exposure by specifying they will not pay for any excess over a certain amount. If a lessor had this type of "cap," he could refuse to pay for any excess, with the possible result that the prospective lessee would run the risk of having to negotiate a new lease deal at the last minute or purchase the equipment.

4. The Lessee Cannot Be a Lender

In the past some lessees and parties related to them have loaned money to the lessor to be used toward the purchase of the equipment. For example, a prospective lessee may want to lease equipment manufactured by its parent company. The parent company would offer to sell the equipment to the lessor on a favorable installment basis. The payment delay would "pump up" a lessor's time value yield over a non-delayed payment and at least part of the benefit would be reflected in a more attractive rental rate.

Under the new tax rules, the lessee and members of the lessee group are specifically prohibited from lending funds to the lessor to assist in the equipment financing. Therefore, direct loans and other credit-extending techniques similar to that described in the previous paragraph will prevent the issuance of a favorable Revenue Ruling on the transaction.

5. Certain Guarantees Cannot Be Used

The lessee and certain lessee-associated parties, such as its parent company or sister subsidiary, may not guarantee any equipment debt. For example, a lessee's parent company cannot guarantee the repayment of a leveraged lease third-party loan. In most cases this will not be a great loss; however, it was a handy technique for lessors to use when, for example, third-party, nonrecourse lenders wanted added security.

The Guidelines *do* permit lessee related parties to guarantee certain *conventional* obligations found in a net lease, such as rent, maintenance, or insurance premium obligations. This takes some of the sting out of the debt guarantee prohibition.

6. Only Fair Market Value Purchase Rights Are Allowed

Arrangements that give a lessee or lessee-related party the right to buy the leased equipment at a price below its fair market value are forbidden under the Guidelines. If a purchase right exists, it must be exercisable for no less than the equipment's fair market value *at the time of purchase.*

The above rule eliminates below-market fixed-priced purchase rights, including so-called nominal purchase options. A typical nominal purchase right is one in which the lessee can buy the equipment at the end of the lease term for $1.00. In the past some lessors have used such an option to induce a prospective lessee to take their deal. Lessees had the best of both worlds: a rental deduction during the lease term and, in effect, an equipment purchase credit for the rent paid.

Low fixed-price purchase options are also in trouble. They were particularly attractive to companies who were aware certain equipment would have a "high residual" at the end of the term. With a fair market value purchase option they would run the risk that their cost to buy would be substantial in relation to the original price. This would, in turn, relatively increase their effective leasing cost. Therefore, the lower the exercise price of the option, the less the overall cost.

ILLUSTRATIVE EXAMPLE—
THE PURCHASE COST IS CRITICAL:

Company A wants to lease a barge from Company B. The facts are as follows:

Original barge cost	$100,000
Estimated residual value	$ 20,000

If the lessee, Company A, had an option to purchase the barge at the end of the lease term for $20,000 its cost for leasing could be easily determined in advance. The rents are known and the purchase price is known. Assume instead that the lessee was only granted a fair market value purchase option in accordance with the Guidelines. If, at the end of the lease term the barge was actually worth $50,000 because of inflation and the current demand, the lessee would have to pay out an additional $30,000—thus increasing the overall cost.

The above example is not unrealistic. There are many cases where items, such as barges, have a market value after years of use *equal to or greater than the original cost.* Leasing such equipment, therefore, can be expensive if the lessee wants to purchase it at the end of the term and must pay the fair market value.

7. The Lessor Must Have a Market Risk

A lessor is specifically prohibited from having any *initial* right to require "any party" to buy the leased equipment for any reason whatsoever except when there are nonconformities with written supply, construction, or manufacture specifications. The lessor's investment in the equipment would, therefore, be said to be subject to the "risks of the market."

Under the above rule a lessor can not have the right to force a sale of the equipment at a predetermined price at the end of the lease term to, for example, the lessee, a manufacturer, or a dealer. This type of right is commonly referred to as a "put." What does this mean for a lessor concerned about whether certain equipment will have any residual value? Simply, that a zero residual value may have to be assumed in calculating the rent to insure the return will be maintained. If "puts" had not been eliminated, a lessor could base his investment return analysis upon a residual value equal to the "put." The lessee would receive a relatively better rental rate on potentially poor residual equipment than if a zero value had been chosen.

The right of a lessor to abandon the property is considered to be a right to require a purchase and, therefore, is also prohibited.

There may be some leeway under this rule. The Guidelines provide that *after the equipment goes on lease* the Service *may*, depending on the particular facts and circumstances, permit an arrangement in which the lessor could require someone to buy the equipment.

A WORD OF CAUTION:

Parties may be tempted to try to go around the aforementioned rule by entering into a "side" agreement before the lease is closed giving the lessor a sale right. After the equipment is placed in service, the "side" agreement is to be submitted to the IRS for approval as a *proposed* arrangement, without mention that it had been agreed to during the prohibited period. This is dangerous and clearly not recommended. Revenue Rulings are granted strictly on the basis of the facts submitted in the ruling request and if they actually vary from that as presented, the Service may very well not adhere to the tax treatment stated.

8. Uneven Rent Programs Must Meet Certain Tests

"Step rentals," such as "low-high" or "high-low" rent structures, have been a valuable lessor marketing tool. Low-to-high rent structures, for example, have been used in situations where the lessee was interested in showing higher reported profits or having increased cash flow in the early years of the equipment use. The Guidelines, however, have significantly restricted these types of rent arrangements. The net effect is to reduce the attractiveness of this technique to the lessee.

Two limited uneven rent structures are permitted. The first allows an uneven rent program in which the rent for each year does not vary more than 10% above or below the *average* rent payable over the lease term. The average rent is computed by dividing the aggregate rent payable for the entire lease term by the number of years in the term. As a practical matter, this does not permit a lessor to offer anything significant, when compared to some of the pre-guideline uneven rent programs.

ILLUSTRATIVE EXAMPLE—
UNEVEN RENT TEST:

Company A wants to lease a fuel truck for ten years for a start-up operation, but anticipates that its cash flow will only allow a $1000 annual rent expense for the first three years. The following rent program is proposed by Company B, the prospective lessor:

Lease term:	10 years
Annual rent for years 1-3	$1000
Annual rent for years 4-10	$2000

Company A finds the rent to be within its cash flow projections. Can they get a Revenue Ruling?

Let's examine the numbers. The rule says the rent for *each* year cannot be above *or* below 10% of the average rent. The average rent is computed by dividing the total of the 10 year rents (3 x $1000 + 7 x $2000 = $17,000) by the number of years in the lease.

Annual average rent = $17,000/10 = $1,700

Since 10% of $1700 is $170, the rent per year can not be above $1870 ($1700 + $170) or below $1530 ($1700 − $170). Therefore, this rent program does not qualify.

The second permitted rent structure allows an uneven program if, during at least the initial two-thirds of the lease term, the yearly rent is not more than 10% higher or lower than the average rent for such selected initial portion and the remaining individual yearly rent is not greater than the highest annual rent payable during the initial portion and not less than one-half of the initial term average yearly rent. There is somewhat more flexibility in using this alternative, but it is still limited.

ILLUSTRATIVE EXAMPLE—
ALTERNATIVE UNEVEN RENT TEST:

Assume the following rent program:

Lease term	9 years
Annual rent for years 1-3	$1000
Annual rent for years 4-6	$1200
Annual rent for years 7-9	$ 600

Will this rent structure pass the IRS alternative test?

First the average rent must be computed for the initial two-thirds of the lease term as follows:

$$\text{Average rent} = \frac{(3 \times \$1000 + 3 \times \$1200)}{6 \text{ years}} = \$1100$$

The yearly rent cannot be greater than $1210 ($1100 + 10% x $1100) or less than $990 ($1100 − 10% x $1100). The test is met for the initial two-thirds of the lease.

What about years 7 through 9? The annual rent ($600) cannot be greater than the highest rent payable during the initial two-thirds of the lease term ($1200) and less than one-half of the initial term average annual rent (1/2 x $1100 = $550). This program just meets the test so the IRS would not object to the "steps" as presented.

9. Special Purpose Property—Are There Changes?

The issue of special purpose property, basically property that has a use only to the lessee, is mentioned in the new leasing rules. The Guidelines, however, specifically withhold a position.

Following the release of the Guidelines, however, the Internal Revenue Service did issue Revenue Procedure 76-30 dealing directly with the special purpose property question for advance ruling purposes. It essentially reinforces the general rules which have previously been followed by tax counsel in tackling the issue. Basically, special purpose property cannot be the subject of a true tax lease.

C. CAN A GUIDELINE DEVIATION SURVIVE A TAX AUDIT?

The Guidelines specifically state that they are to be used to assist in the preparation of requests for Revenue Rulings and in the issuance by the

Service of ruling letters. They were not intended to be used for Internal Revenue Service audit purposes. Therefore, a transaction that deviates from the rules may still, for audit purposes, be treated as a true tax lease.

OBSERVATION:

As a practical matter, the Guideline rules will most likely creep into the audit process. Therefore, to protect against possible audit challenges, variances should be cleared with tax counsel.

D. THE REQUEST-FOR-RULING HAS CERTAIN SUBMISSION REQUIREMENTS

The basic information and representations that must be submitted in connection with a request for a leveraged lease Revenue Ruling are extensive. They are stated in Internal Revenue Service Revenue Procedure 75-28. The information and representations are directly related to the areas discussed in Revenue Procedure 75-21.

In general, all the parties to the transaction, including the lessor and the lessee, must join in the ruling request. The request must contain a summary of the surrounding facts and must be accompanied by certain relevant documents, such as the lease, or in the case of a brokered transaction, any economic analysis, prospectus, or other document used to induce the lessor to invest.

Detailed information must be provided covering, for example, the type and quality of the leased equipment; all parties to the transaction and their relationship; and the status of the equipment—that is, whether it is new, reconstructed, used, or rebuilt; when, how, and where it will be, or was, first placed in service or use; and whether it will be permanently or temporarily attached to land, buildings, or other property. In addition, the flow of funds between the parties must be described.

The lease term and any renewals or extensions must be disclosed along with any purchase and sale options. This includes any right the lessor has to force a purchase or abandon the equipment. If there is any intention to give such a right in the future, this must be specified.

If the lessee or any related party must pay for any cost overruns or will invest in the equipment, by, for example, contributing to its cost or paying for an improvement, modification, or addition, this must be disclosed. Also, any unrelated parties who will provide funds must be identified.

Information covering any lessee related guarantees, whether the profit and positive cash flow tests have been satisfied, any uneven rent structure, and any special purpose nature must be presented. An economic analysis showing that the minimum "at risk" investment rules will be satisfied has to be submitted. A detailed description of the debt and the repayment terms; any lease provisions relating to indemnities, termination, obsolescence, casualty, or insurance; and the party who is to claim the investment credit must be set forth. The parties must submit an expert's opinion on the equipment's residual value. The opinion must set out the manner in which the conclusion was determined, any removal or delivery costs at the end of the lease term, and the useful life of the equipment remaining at the end of the term.

E. A QUICK "TRUE" LEASE CHECKLIST

The following checklist can be used as a guide to determine whether the basic features of a lease transaction comply with the requirements for the issuance of a favorable Revenue Ruling. If any answer is "No," there may be a problem.

Questions:	Yes	No
1. Has the Lessor made an initial equity investment equal to at least 20% of equipment cost?		
2. Is the initial equity investment unconditional in nature?		
3. Will the lessor's minimum investment remain equal at least to 20% of equipment cost during the lease term?		
4. Is the estimated residual value of the equipment at least equal to 20% of equipment's original cost?		
5. Will the useful life of the equipment remaining at the end of the lease term be equal to the longer of one year or 20% of the originally estimated useful life?		
6. If there is a lessee purchase option, is it at fair market value as of the time of exercise?		
7. Is the lessor without any rights to force a sale of the equipment to any party?		
8. Is the lessor without any specific right to abandon the equipment?		
9. Has the lessor furnished all of the equipment cost other than any third-party debt?		
10. Will the lessor have to bear the cost of any permanent equipment improvement or addition?		
11. Can the lessor purchase at a price other than fair market value any improvement or addition which is readily removable and whose cost was paid by the lessee or related party?		
12. Will the lessor pay for any equipment cost overruns?		
13. Are all the equipment loans from lenders unrelated to the lessee?		

Questions: (Cont'd)

	Yes	No

14. Is the transaction devoid of any indebtedness guarantees by the lessee or related parties?
15. Will the lessor make a profit on the lease without considering the tax benefits?
16. Will the transaction generate a positive cash flow for the lessor?
17. Are any uneven rent structures within the IRS Guideline tests?
18. Will the equipment have a use at the end of the lease term to someone other than to the lessee?
19. Has the required backup information and material been submitted with the request for ruling?

8

THE ADVANTAGES AND RISKS
OF LEVERAGED LEASING DECISIONS

How Different Is Leveraged Leasing from "Straight" Leasing? • The Fundamental Structure Is Easy—It Has Many Advantages, but also Some Substantial Risks • Understanding Each Is Critical.

A. WHAT IS THE CONCEPT OF LEVERAGED LEASING?

The *leveraged* lease can be one of the most complex and sophisticated vehicles for financing capital equipment in today's financial market place. The individuals and firms in the leveraged leasing industry are aggressive and creative. As a result, the environment is one of innovation and intense competition.

Is the concept of a leveraged lease complex? Not really. It is simply a lease transaction in which the lessor puts in only a portion, usually 20% to 40%, of the funds necessary to purchase the equipment and a third-party lender supplies the remainder. Since the benefits available to the lessor are generally based upon the entire equipment cost, the lessor's investment is said to be "leveraged" with third-party debt.

Generally speaking, the third-party loan is on a *nonrecourse-to-the-lessor basis* and ranges from 60% to 80% of the equipment's cost. The nonrecourse nature means the lender can only look to the lessee, the stream of rental payments that have been assigned to it, and the equipment for repayment. The lessor has no repayment responsibility *even if the lessee defaults and the loan becomes uncollectible.*

The fact that a nonrecourse lender cannot look to the lessor for the loan repayment if there is a problem is not as bad as it seems for two reasons. First, a lender will not make a nonrecourse loan unless the lessee is considered creditworthy and, second, the lender's rights to any proceeds coming from a sale or re-lease of the equipment comes ahead of any of the lessor's rights in the equipment and lease. The lessor's *equity investment* is said to be *subordinated* to the loan repayment obligation. If a lender only contributed, for example, 70% of the funds necessary, the subordination arrangement would put him in an over-collateralized loan position which, in turn, would decrease his lending risk.

Although the third-party loan is usually made on a nonrecourse basis, this is not always the case. If the lessee's financial condition is weak, a lender may only be willing to make a *recourse* loan. Under this type of loan the lender may look to, or has recourse against, the lessor for repayment if it cannot be satisfied through the lessee or the equipment. The lessor still, however, has the economic advantage of a leveraged investment.

Although the *concept* of leveraging a lease investment is simple, the *mechanics* of putting the concept together is often extremely complex. Leveraged lease transactions, particularly ones involving major dollar commitments, frequently involve many parties brought together through intricate arrangements. The "lessor" is typically a group of investors joined together by a partnership or trust structure. The partnership or trust is in fact the legal owner, or "titleholder," of the equipment. The "lender" is often a group of lenders usually acting through a trust arrangement. This is further complicated by the fact that each participant will be represented by counsel with varying views. As a result, the job of organizing, drafting, and negotiating the myriad of necessary documents is generally very difficult.

OBSERVATION:

Because the expenses involved in documenting a leveraged lease can be substantial, transactions involving less than $2,000,000 worth of equipment can be economically difficult to structure as a leveraged lease. If, however, documentation fees such as counsel fees can be kept within reason, smaller equipment amounts can be financed in this manner. In many cases a prospective lessor or underwriter has an in-house legal staff with the ability to originate and negotiate the required documents. If so, this will help keep the costs down.

In general, leveraged lease financings are arranged for prospective lessees by companies or individuals who specialize in structuring and negotiating these types of leases. These individuals and firms are commonly referred to as *lease underwriters*. Essentially their function is to structure the lease economics, find the lessor-investors, and provide the necessary expertise to insure the transaction will get done. In a limited number of situations, they also find the debt participants. They do not generally participate as an investor in the equipment. Since the vast majority of leveraged leases are brought about with the assistance of lease underwriters, lease underwriting has become synonymous with leveraged leasing.

The premise on which lease underwriting services are provided by an underwriter, i.e., on a "best efforts" or "firm" basis, varies significantly. It is, therefore, worthwhile at this stage to explore the two types of underwriter offers.

1. A "Best Efforts" Underwriting Arrangement Can Be Risky

Lease underwriting transactions are frequently bid on a "best efforts" basis. This type of bid is simply an offer by the underwriter to do the best he can to put a transaction together in accordance with the terms set forth in his proposal letter. There are no guarantees of performance and, as a result, a prospective lessee accepting such an offer may not know for some time whether he has the financing or not.

In practice a best efforts underwriting is not as risky as it appears. Most reputable underwriters have a good feel for the market when bidding on this basis and usually can deliver what they propose. In other words, there is a good chance they will be able to get "firm commitments" from one or more prospective lessor-investors to participate on the basis offered.

RECOMMENDATIONS:

I. A prospective lessee should always keep in mind that a best efforts underwriting proposal gives no guarantee the transaction can be completed in accordance with the terms proposed. Therefore, he should give careful consideration to the experience and reputation of an underwriter proposing on this basis before awarding a transaction to him. An inability to perform as presented can result in the loss of valuable time.

II. When there is adequate equipment delivery lead time, a prospective lessee may be inclined to award a transaction to an unknown underwriter who has submitted an unusually low bid. There is, however, a risk which must be considered. If the transaction is so underpriced that it cannot be sold in the "equity" market, it may meet resistance when it is re-offered on more attractive investor terms merely because it has been seen, or "shopped," too much. It is an unfortunate fact that when an investor is presented with a transaction which he knows has been shopped, even if the terms are favorable, he may refuse to consider it merely because it has been around for a long time. A prospective lessee, therefore, should not be too eager to accept a "low ball" best efforts bid unless he has taken a hard look at the underwriter's ability to perform.

III. Best efforts underwriters sometimes submit proposals which are substantially below the market. At times this happens by mistake. For example, transactions may have been priced in good faith based upon acceptable investor market yields but by the time the award is made the market has moved upward. At other times an underwriter may intentionally underprice a transaction in order to make sure he wins it. If it cannot be placed as proposed, he will go back and attempt to get the prospective lessee to agree to a higher rental rate. With his competitors no longer involved, he may be in a good position to do this. A prospective lessee with near-term deliveries must be particularly careful in recognizing this possibility, otherwise he may have little choice but to be pushed into a less favorable deal.

IV. A prospective lessee can control the risk of nonperformance under a best efforts proposal by putting a time limit on the award. For example, requiring the underwriter to come up with, or "circle," interested parties within one week following the award and securing formal commitments by the second week.

V. It is not unheard of for a prospective lessee to make a time limit award to an unusually low bidding, or unknown, underwriter without telling the remaining bidders. The purpose is to try to keep them around just in case the underwriter cannot perform. Obviously, this can be extremely unfair to an underwriter who, in good faith, is continuing to spend time and money on the transaction in the hope of winning it. Doing this can also hurt a prospective lessee in the long run because it is likely that the other underwriters will find out that this happened. Once the word gets around that a company does business in this manner, reputable underwriters may refuse to participate in future biddings. Even if they do participate, they may quote rates which have not been as finely tuned as possible because they will not spend the time or money necessary in situations in which they may not be treated fairly. This tactic, therefore, is not recommended because a prospective lessee may, as a result, not see the best possible market rates.

2. A "Firm Commitment" Underwriting Arrangement Is Often The Best

From a prospective lessee's viewpoint, a "firm commitment" underwriting proposal is generally the preferred type of offer. When an underwriter has "come in firm" he is *guaranteeing* to put the proposed lease financing together. Typically, before an underwriter submits such a proposal, he has solid commitments from lessor-investors, usually referred to as "equity participants," to enter into the transaction on the terms presented. This, however, is not always the case, and his firm bid may only represent his willingness to be the lessor if he cannot find a third-party lessor.

RECOMMENDATIONS:

I. If an underwriter proposing on a firm basis does not have "committed equity" at the time his proposal is submitted, a prospective lessee may be subject to certain risks. Unless he is in a strong financial position, his commitment may be worthless if a third-party lessor cannot be found. Therefore, a prospective lessee should always investigate whether such an underwriter has lined up the necessary lessor-investors. If not, the underwriter's financial condition should be reviewed to determine, prior to making the award, whether he has the financial wherewithal to stand behind it.

II. Underwriters sometimes state they have firm "equity" even though they have nothing more than a verbal *indication* from a prospective lessor-investor's contact man that he will recommend the transaction to his approving committee. Therefore, it is advisable for a prospective lessee to ask to be put in touch with each lessor-investor to confirm his position. Doing this will also insure that there are no misunderstandings as to the terms of the transaction.

B. LEVERAGED LEASE PARTICIPANTS HAVE CERTAIN UNIQUE CHARACTERISTICS

Generally speaking, a leveraged lease transaction will involve more parties than a non-leveraged one. At a minimum, the participants will include an equity participant (lessor-investor), a debt participant, a lessee, and an equipment supplier. In the event the equity or debt participant acts through a trust arrangement, a trustee will also be a party. Very often these participants have certain unique characteristics, which will be discussed in the following material.

1. The Equity Participants

An investor in a leveraged lease is commonly referred to as an "equity participant". Generally, more than one investor is involved on the "equity side" of a leveraged lease. These equity participants, or owners, often act together through a trust arrangement. A trust provides partnership-like tax treatment, while at the same time giving corporate-like liability protection. The equity participants are deemed the *beneficial* owners of the equipment, legal title being held by the representative (the trustee) of the trust.

It is not uncommon for more than one lessor-investor to act through a partnership arrangement, rather than a trust. In this case, the partnership is the lessor. Legal title to the equipment is held in the partnership name.

RECOMMENDATION:

The actual form of equipment owning entity, i.e., trust, partnership, etc., will depend on the particular needs of each transaction and the participants. Counsel should be used to select the best form for a particular situation.

The typical leveraged lease equity participant is an "institutional investor." Banks, for example, come within this category. Because, however, a leveraged lease can be an attractive investment, many "regular" corporations and, in a limited number of situations, wealthy individuals are also potential lessor-investor candidates.

Some prospective leveraged lease investors have their own leasing companies actively looking for lease investment opportunities, but many do not. Those that do not, often referred to as "passive" investors, usually rely exclusively on the lease underwriting community to locate leveraged lease investments for them. Typically, the passive type investor also depends heavily on underwriters for advice on the structure and documentation of these investments.

OBSERVATION:

Frequently, the prospective non-leveraged lease lessor is a company whose *primary* business is the leasing of equipment. Those typically in the leveraged market are firms whose focus is on leasing as a way to provide tax shelter for income generated by their other activities, rather than leasing as a basic business.

2. The Lessee

A leveraged lease transaction, as with any lease transaction, does not begin to come into existence until an equipment user, the prospective lessee, decides to consider leasing as a way to finance the acquisition of equipment it needs. Therefore, the lessee is the key participant in any lease financing.

Because documenting a leveraged lease transaction tends to be expensive, this type of lease usually only makes economic sense for financings involving a significant dollar amount of equipment. As a result, the type of potential lessee is usually a large equipment user who has the financial strength to support the obligations involved.

3. The Debt Participants

A lender in a leveraged lease transaction is generally referred to as a "debt participant." It is not uncommon for there to be more than one debt participant involved in a particular lease. When this is the case they frequently form a trust, referred to as an indenture of trust, through which they will act. The amount of money each debt participant intends to loan is transferred to the trust, which in turn lends it to the lessor. The loan made to the lessor is generally nonrecourse in nature and is represented by a note or series of notes payable over the lease term from the rent proceeds received by the lessor.

If properly organized, the lender's trust will receive partnership-like income tax treatment and corporate-like liability protection. In other words, each participant as a *beneficial* owner of the trust estate will be treated for income tax purposes as though he had made his loan directly to the lessor and will not have a direct exposure to any third-party claim.

Leveraged lease third-party debt is often supplied by banks or insurance companies. However, since a leveraged lease loan is no different than any other loan secured by personal property, generally any lender able and willing to make a secured loan is a potential loan source. There is, however, one limiting factor—*the prospective lender's ability to offer competitive market interest rates*. The debt interest rate is a critical factor in the rent computation. A leveraged lease rent quotation is usually premised on an assumed debt interest rate. Therefore, the lower the interest rate the more profit a lessor makes and vice versa; unless, of course, the prospective lessee gets the benefit or bears the risk of interest rate variations. In the latter case the underwriter's proposal will provide that if the debt interest rate comes in other than assumed, the rent will be adjusted upward or downward to appropriately reflect the variance. As a result only the most rate aggressive lenders such as banks and insurance companies are usually able to compete, particularly in the better credit transactions.

4. The Underwriter

The lease underwriting business has a relatively low capital entrance requirement and because of this there is an overabundance of "packagers" offering lease underwriting services. These packagers run the gamut from individuals operating essentially out of telephone booths to investment bankers to specialized lease underwriting firms. Some are well versed in leveraged leasing economics and documentation and others know little more than the very preliminary basics. The choice of an underwriter, therefore, can be critical to the success of a transaction. Those who have a solid understanding of the business and who are continually active in the underwriting market are more likely to be able to better structure and insure the success of a leveraged lease financing.

RECOMMENDATION:

Prospective lessees entertaining leveraged lease proposals should make sure before awarding a transaction that the intended underwriter has the qualifications to do the job necessary, both from an experience and a technical standpoint.

5. The Equipment Manufacturer

The equipment manufacturer or distributor involved in a leveraged lease transaction usually does nothing more than sell the agreed-upon equipment to the lessor at the negotiated price. Once the full price has been paid, his only obligation is to stand behind his product for any warranty period.

In some situations the vendor's role is not limited to the mere sale of the equipment to the lessor. He sometimes provides various inducements to a lessor to assist in the sale of his equipment. For example, he may be willing to guarantee some or all of the lessee's lease obligations in situations when the lessee's financial condition is weak.

6. The Investor's Representative—The Owner's Trustee

In the event equity participants act through a trust, a trustee will be appointed to be the trust's representative. The trustee is sometimes referred to as the *owner's trustee* and is usually a commercial bank or trust company.

The owner's trustee is considered the mechanical arm of the trust because his responsibilities are specifically defined by the trust arrangement. For example, one of his prescribed duties will be to divide up and disburse the lease funds among the various equity participants in accordance with a predetermined formula. As the equity participants' representative, he makes sure their investment is protected by monitoring their rights under the lease.

7. The Lender's Representative—The Indenture Trustee

When a trust arrangement is established for the debt participants, a trustee, commonly referred to as the *indenture trustee,* is employed to represent the trust. The duties of the indenture trustee are clearly defined in the trust agreement. For example, the indenture trustee collects the money to be loaned from the debt participants and then turns it over to the lessor. As a part of the loan transaction, the indenture trustee takes an assignment of the lease and a security interest in the equipment as security for the loan repayment. Typically, a commercial bank or trust company is selected to act as the indenture trustee.

C. HOW DIFFERENT IS THE LEVERAGED LEASE DOCUMENT?

The format of a typical leveraged lease document is essentially the same as that of any other finance lease. The terms and provisions are usually somewhat more detailed, however, because the major dollar commitments involved usually dictate that greater attention be paid to each aspect.

What about the supplemental documents? As the reader might suspect there are typically a greater number involved in a leveraged lease transaction than in a "straight" lease transaction. For example, in addition to those found in non-leveraged lease situation, such as the lease, opinions of counsel, and board of director resolutions, the leveraged transaction documentation will at a minimum usually include trust agreements, a participation agreement, one or more promissory notes, and a security and loan agreement.

D. THREE ADVANTAGES TO THE LESSEE IN A LEVERAGED LEASE

A leveraged lease transaction offers many benefits for a prospective lessee in certain situations. Generally speaking, for example, the rent charges will be lower than a comparable non-leveraged lease. The most significant advantages will now be discussed.

1. The Rent Can Be More Attractive

As a broad rule of thumb a competitively bid leveraged lease transaction will provide a lower cost to a lessee than a comparable term non-leveraged lease. Logically, if a company can borrow at a more favorable interest rate than a lessor, it stands to reason that if the lessor pays part of the equipment's cost with a loan based upon the lessee's credit he can charge lower rents without sacrificing his economic return. There are, of course, exceptions to this rule and each situation must be examined on its own. For example, if the dollar amount of equipment financed is small, the documentation expenses involved can offset the economic benefits gained through leveraging.

2. There Is a Better Market for Large Transactions

Major dollar equipment lease financings can generally be arranged more readily by using a leveraged lease structure for two basic reasons. First, a lessor-investor has a substantially lower investment requirement. Typically, he only has to invest 20% to 40% of the equipment's cost. Second, by leveraging his investment with third-party debt, his economic return can be enhanced.

Because many investors and lenders are unwilling to make a major dollar investment in one transaction, a number of lessor-investors and lenders must frequently be brought together. By forming investor and lender syndicates, the dollar exposure for each can be kept within desired limits.

Bringing together more than one investor and lender can be beneficial for a lessee. When the investment risk is spread among several participants, there is a greater likelihood that a large dollar lease financing can be done at more reasonable rates. No one party has such a great exposure that he feels he must charge a premium for the risk. The disadvantage is the added paperwork. Because of the additional parties it can be extremely complex. However, a competent and experienced underwriter will be able to successfully usher everyone through the documentation tangle—a reason why the choice of the underwriter is a critical factor.

OBSERVATION:

There are a small number of prospective lessor-investors willing to act as the sole equity participant in major equipment lease financings. The advantage to using such an investor is that the necessary approvals and potential complications will be kept to a minimum. Generally, however, this type of investor realizes not many others are willing to take an entire major transaction and their rent charge will usually be high. Whether the extra rate is worth the reduced risks of a simpler transaction is a matter of judgment. An experienced underwriter should be of great assistance in evaluating the trade-off.

3. The Lessors Can Be More Competitive

The type of lessor interested in pursuing a leveraged lease investment is often most concerned over the available equipment ownership tax benefits. As a result, such a lessor may be more willing to be more aggressive on all aspects of a lease transaction.

OBSERVATION:

An *underwritten* leveraged lease transaction is likely to produce more favorable rental rates for a prospective lessee than a non-underwritten one. An underwriter must find the most aggressive equity participant in order to win. This, in turn, results in a more competitive rent quotation.

E. INVESTMENT PITFALLS AND RECOMMENDATIONS FOR PROSPECTIVE LESSORS

A prospective lessor must consider many factors before deciding whether to enter into a particular lease transaction, leveraged or not. These considerations, however, are particularly crucial for the passive type investors participating in leveraged transactions, because their experience with lease investments is often limited. Many institutional investors, for example, rarely participate in more than one or two lease transactions each year. As a result, they often do not have the broad exposure necessary to realistically assess the possible problems.

OBSERVATION:

The fewer the number of transactions in which a prospective equity participant invests a specific amount of money, the greater the relative impact of a bad investment decision. In other words, investing $500,000 in each of two leases, other things being equal, will be relatively safer than investing $1,000,000 in one lease.

In order for a prospective lessor-investor to evaluate the risks involved, he must know what they are. The following discussion will alert the reader to the fundamental points which must be considered by every lease investor.

1. Equipment Delivery Delays Can Destroy Profits

The date when the equipment delivers determines when the ownership tax benefits will be available to a lessor. When these benefits are available is a critical factor in a prospective lessor's analysis of his anticipated economic return, and an unexpected delivery delay can have a serious negative impact. Consider, for example, a transaction entered into by a calendar year taxpayer-investor based upon the assumption that the equipment will deliver no later than June of the following year. If the investor's return had been calculated using the modified half-year depreciation convention, a July delivery would jeopardize his contemplated return, because he could not start claiming depreciation on the asset until the year following the delivery. Under this convention all assets delivering in the first half of a tax year are entitled to a full 12 months of depreciation and those assets delivering in the second half of the year are not entitled to any depreciation for that year. The effect would be that the investor would have less tax savings and therefore less available cash to put to work in the first year. If the transaction had been priced in a competitive market, such a slippage could easily make the transaction's economics completely unacceptable to the investor.

RECOMMENDATIONS:

I. A prospective lessor-investor can protect himself against a potential yield deterioration because of equipment delivery delays in two ways. The first is by establishing a commitment cutoff date. That is, setting a point in time after which he will no longer be obligated to purchase and lease delivering equipment. A second way is to provide for a rent adjustment which preserves the transaction's economics if the outside delivery date is passed.

II. From a lessee's viewpoint, either of the lessor delivery delay solutions discussed in Recommendation I can create problems. The first solution, however, is generally considered the more dangerous. When a delivery cutoff date is imposed, a prospective lessee could end up without a lease financing source for the late equipment. When a rental adjustment is permitted, a lessee may be confronted with an undesirably high rent. In the latter situation, however, he at least knows that lease financing will be available regardless of the delay.

III. A prospective lessor should be careful when establishing the rental adjustment criterion to apply to late delivering equipment. For example, if the rental analysis is based upon certain yield and after-tax cash flow standards, he should make sure the adjustment provision will permit him to maintain both criteria because they will not run parallel. In other words, maintaining yield will not necessarily maintain after-tax cash flows and vice versa.

2. The Lessee's Financial Condition Is Crucial

The financial strength of a prospective lessee is an important lessor consideration in any lease transaction. It should be of prime concern to a passive type lessor-investor with limited equipment knowledge and remarketing capability. A lease default could easily endanger his invested capital and anticipated economic return. It is of utmost importance, therefore, for the prospective lessee's financial standing to be thoroughly reviewed.

3. Changes in Tax Law Can Eliminate Profits

If the tax benefits anticipated by investing in an equipment lease are eliminated or reduced because of a change in tax law, a lessor-investor could be confronted with an extremely unfavorable investment. The possibility of a tax law change is difficult, if not impossible, to predict. It is not, however, generally considered an unreasonable risk to assume in certain situations.

In major leveraged leases, lessees are sometimes "forced" to indemnify the lessor against any adverse change in the tax law that causes a tax benefit loss. The tax indemnification provisions are usually incorporated directly in the lease agreement. If a lessor, for example, lost his right to claim the investment tax credit, the lessee would be required to pay the lessor an additional sum of money that would enable him to maintain his economic return.

OBSERVATIONS:

I. Prospective lessees have become increasingly successful in placing the tax benefit loss risks from changes in law on the lessor. It usually depends, as the reader might suspect, on who has the most negotiating strength. A favorite lessee argument is that the burden properly belongs on the lessor because he is better able to assess them through his experience. The argument has some validity as to "regular" leasing companies. It may not be true, however, as far as the typical leveraged lease investor is concerned. In his passive role he may not have the type of exposure necessary to make the appropriate evaluation. Unfortunately for these investors, what becomes standard in the "straight" leasing market usually runs over into the leveraged market, and they must often assume the change-in-law risk in order to have access to this type of investment opportunity.

II. A prospective lessor-investor can hedge against the change-in-tax-law risk by having the right to appropriately adjust the rental rate or to exclude equipment which will be affected and which has not yet been delivered. The danger to a prospective lessee with these lessor solutions is that, respectively, he may have to pay too high a lease rate or may be without financing at the last minute.

4. Income Variations Can Be Dangerous

A typical leveraged lease transaction may not be economically viable for a lessor-investor unless he can use all of the available equipment ownership tax benefits. For example, consider a corporate taxpayer who is in the 50% income tax bracket. If he is entitled to claim a 10% investment tax credit he can save $100,000 in Federal income taxes for each $1,000,000 worth of new equipment he puts on lease. This type of tax saving is considered a part of a transaction's "profit." If the investor had, for example, a net loss for the year the equipment was placed in service, he would have no taxable income against which to apply the tax credit. Although the tax credit can be carried forward and backward, the inability to use it when anticipated would reduce the transaction's expected *time value* return. The time value concept says $1 received today is worth more than $1 received a year from today because of its earning capability. A lease investment, therefore, must be looked at by a prospective lessor-investor in light of a careful and realistic appraisal of his present and future earning situation. Without earnings, the available tax shelter loses its attractiveness.

5. Tax Rate Variations—Consider The Possibility

How valuable the tax benefits which are available from owning equipment are to a lessor-investor depends to a large extent on his overall effective income tax rate. The greater his effective tax rate the more tax savings he will realize from the tax benefits. Any decrease in his tax rate will reduce the favorable impact of the available write-offs. Therefore, a prospective lessor-investor should consider any potential income tax rate change in light of the future tax benefits coming from a lease investment.

ILLUSTRATIVE EXAMPLE—
TAX RATE HAS AN EFFECT:

The effective income tax rate which an investor is subject to will determine how valuable the available tax savings are. Consider, for example, the following lease income (loss) situation from a hypothetical lease investment:

Year	Lease Income (Loss)	After-Tax Annual Benefit (70% Tax Bracket)	After-Tax Annual Benefit (50% Tax Bracket)
19X1	$ (90,000)	$63,000	$45,000
19X2	(120,000)	84,000	60,000
19X3	(50,000)	35,000	25,000
19X4	(20,000)	14,000	10,000

As the reader can see, the higher the income tax bracket the greater the tax savings from the same tax loss.

OBSERVATION:

It was not uncommon for an underwriter to compute a "best efforts" lease proposal rent quotation on the basis of a 48% tax bracket corporate investor. In many cases, however, lessor-investors were in a higher overall *effective* income tax bracket when state and local taxes were considered. A transaction priced for a "48% taxpayer" would look more attractive to a "52% taxpayer" and, therefore, more easily sold to him. On the other hand, a lease investment could be more aggressively priced if a 52% tax bracket was assumed. The problem, of course, for a best efforts underwriter in assuming a higher tax bracket is that there will be a greater risk that he will not be able to find an investor in this bracket. Whether a more aggressive tax rate should be used by a proposing underwriter, therefore, comes down to a matter of judgment.

Can a prospective lessor-investor protect himself against an adverse tax rate change? Yes, by getting a prospective lessee to agree to indemnify him in the event it occurs. In today's market, however, it is unlikely that *any* prospective lessee would agree to provide this type of indemnity.

6. Incorrect Residual Value Assessment— An Easy Trap

In general, the value of the equipment at the end of a lease, commonly referred to as its "residual value," can have a dramatic impact on the profitability of the transaction. If a prospective lessor's residual value estimate is too high when he analyzes a lease investment, his return will be adversely affected. For example, if a prospective investor makes his investment analysis assuming a certain return based upon selling the equipment at the end of the lease for 20% of its original cost, the transaction's profitability would be reduced if the equipment only sold for 5% of its original cost. The overall effect of the diminished value, of course, depends on its importance in the investor's analysis. Very often it is a significant factor.

RECOMMENDATIONS:

I. There is no sure method of determining what equipment will in fact be worth at the end of a lease term. A detrimental variance from that assumed will always be a risk. The risk can be reduced, however, if a prospective lease investor makes sure a realistic evaluation is made of the estimated residual value of the equipment.

II. It is advisable for a prospective lessor-investor to consult an equipment appraiser for assistance in making a reasonable residual value estimate. It should be remembered, however, that an appraiser's opinion as to future value is nothing more than a professional guess. It does not assure the investor of the equipment's future worth. It does, of course, provide a degree of comfort which would otherwise not exist.

The general state of price inflation has brought to the surface an interesting side of the equipment residual value issue. If a very conservative estimate of the residual value was made in a lessor's original economic analysis, there is a reasonable likelihood the lessor will receive a windfall profit. It is not unheard of, for example, for items to bring in 20% to 60% more than had been anticipated. These profits are certainly not undue such investors, since in many cases they had assumed a substantial residual value risk when the lease was entered into.

7. An Early Lease Termination Must Be Considered

A prospective lessor-investor must make sure that an early lease termination will have little, if any, impact on his lease investment economics. This is particularly true when finance, or full payout, leases are involved. Consider, for example, a twenty-year full payout lease that is terminated at the end of two years. To begin with, the investor's future lease profits will be cut off. Depending on how the rents have been reported for income purposes, an early termination may cause a "book" loss. For example, if the rent income was reported faster than actually received the early termination might make it necessary to report as a loss the difference between what was reported on the income statement and what has actually been taken in.

If the equipment cannot be favorably re-leased in a timely manner, the lessor may be forced to sell the equipment immediately. An unplanned sale situation can make it difficult for a lessor to realize the best price, particularly if large amounts of equipment scattered all over the country are involved. Having adequate and inexpensive storage space can ease the problem, because the lessor may be better able to afford to wait the market out. In this regard, lessors sometimes negotiate the right to store it on the lessee's premises free of charge; however, this may not be a good solution if the parties are in an adversary situation.

Having to sell equipment early may also create another problem—a recapture of tax benefits claimed. If the tax benefits are an important part of the lessor's yield, a recapture can further destroy the already faltering lease economics.

Incorporating a "termination value" concept into the lease can solve the early termination economic risk. Essentially a termination value is an amount a lessee would be obligated to pay to the lessor to help protect his anticipated return.

8. Casualty Loss—Are There Protections?

The type of problems confronting a lessor if there is an equipment casualty loss are similar to those that must be addressed if a lease termination occurs, i.e., future profits will end, tax benefit recapture may result, and a "book" loss may have to be reported. There is, however, an important difference—the equipment will have little, if any, value. When a casualty loss occurs, therefore, the lessor is left without its collateral protection and must look to the lessee and any insurance proceeds for loss repayment. This is a good reason why prospective lessor-investors must make sure that the lessee is a creditworthy entity and, in addition, that adequate insurance will be secured and maintained.

RECOMMENDATION:

If a prospective lessee will be obligated to insure the leased equipment, the prospective lessor should require evidence at the time of the lease closing that the appropriate insurance coverage has been secured. In addition, arrangements should be made for the insurance company to notify the lessor in the event the lessee does anything, such as neglecting to pay the premiums, which could cause the policy to lapse. In this way, the lessor will have the opportunity of taking over any lapsed obligations to assure continued coverage.

Even though the lessee is required to maintain casualty loss insurance, prospective lessors should also incorporate a "casualty loss value" concept. Casualty values, sometimes referred to as "stipulated loss values," are calculated in much the same manner as termination values and their purpose is to protect the lessor's investment position in the event of a casualty loss. Under this concept the lessee in effect guarantees the lessor that he will receive a certain amount of money if there is an equipment casualty. The amount usually decreases after each rent payment is made, to reflect an appropriate recognition of the lessor's decreased investment exposure and is usually at all times sufficient to repay the lessor's outstanding investment and profit at least to the date of the loss. Typically, the lessee is given a credit for any insurance money received as a result of the loss against the amount owed. In effect, the lessee becomes an *insurer* of the lessor's investment *and* profit.

9. The Economic Analysis—A Critical Aspect

When a lease underwriter presents a lease investment to a prospective lessor-investor, he generally submits an economic analysis showing the return the investor can expect. If the method of analysis is incorrect, a prospective investor may end up with a disastrous investment. It is not uncommon, for example, for an underwriter to incorporate a sinking fund arrangement in his analysis calculations. The sinking fund simply improves the investor's economics by assuming that cash available over the lease term will earn a certain amount of interest. If for some reason the interest rate assumption is too high, the return analysis will be misleading. Therefore, a prospective investor must always verify any economic presentation on which it intends to base its investment decision.

RECOMMENDATION:

If a prospective lessor-investor cannot independently analyze the resulting economics of investing in a lease submitted by an underwriter, he should bring in an independent expert to review the presentation.

10. Long Term Commitments Can Present Problems

Frequently, an equipment lease agreement is entered into well before the equipment actually delivers. This is done for a number of reasons. From a lessor's viewpoint, the faster he gets the lease "signed up," the less risk there will be that the prospective lessee will change his mind. Prospective lessees on the other hand, are often interested in proceeding as quickly as possible in order to avoid last minute documentation problems. If the transaction calls for the lessor to hold a substantial amount of money available over a long delivery period, an unexpected decision by the lessee not to lease the equipment when it arrives will result in an alternate investment opportunity loss for the lessor during the commitment period. To avoid this type of problem, lessors frequently require lessees to agree to pay commitment fees or non-utilization fees. In effect, these fees guarantee that they will be compensated for holding their funds available.

11. Documentation Expenses Can Ruin A Lease Investment

The expenses, such as legal fees, involved in documenting most underwritten leveraged lease transactions are substantial. Depending on the transaction's complexity, it is not unheard of for the expenses to run into the hundreds of thousands of dollars. A $30,000 expense for a $3,000,000 lease investment may be acceptable, a $500,000 expense will probably not be. If an investor must pay these expenses, a substantial bill could ruin his investment economics. Therefore, it is essential for a prospective leveraged lease investor to know who is responsible for the various charges and what the estimated amounts will be. Of particular concern will be who is responsible for the expenses if the transaction falls apart before the lease is signed.

RECOMMENDATIONS:

I. The responsibility for the various documentation expenses is frequently outlined in an underwriter's proposal letter. In many cases the underwriter will offer to pay most of the expenses. It is, however, an area of negotiation between the parties and a prospective investor should make sure he has not inadvertantly assumed any expense responsibility that has not been considered. The more the expense burden can be shifted to someone else, the less the risk the economic integrity of the investment will be endangered.

II. Frequently, an underwriter will place the burden for expenses incurred in a collapsed lease transaction on the prospective lessee. It is recommended, however, that a prospective lessee at least require a sharing of the expenses with any other party contributing to the failure.

F. A CHECKLIST FOR THE LEVERAGED LEASE INVESTOR

Before making a commitment to invest in a leveraged lease, a prospective lessor-investor must consider the following points:

1. If the Equipment Will Not Be Put On Lease at the Time the Lease Commitment Is Signed, Does It Matter When the Equipment Actually Delivers? If so:
   a. Does the Lease Agreement Provide for a Cutoff Date Beyond Which the Lessor Will Not Be Obligated to Purchase and Lease the Equipment?
   b. If There Is Not an Equipment Delivery Cutoff Date, Does the Lease Permit the Lessor to Appropriately Adjust the Rents if His Economics Are Affected?
   c. Can the Lessee Substitute Equipment in the Event Equipment Delivers Late or Never Arrives? If so, Are There Controls on the Type Which Will Be Acceptable?
2. Has the Prospective Lessee's Financial Condition Been Thoroughly Reviewed?
3. If Any Credit Support for the Lessee's Lease Obligations Will Be Provided, Has the Financial Condition of the Supporting Party Been Carefully Reviewed?
4. Has Tax Counsel Been Consulted as to Any Near-Term Possibility of the Tax Laws Changing so as to Affect the Anticipated Equipment Ownership Tax Benefits?
5. In the Event There Is a Tax Law Change Affecting the Equipment Ownership Tax Benefits, Will the Lessee Have to Indemnify the Lessor for Any Resulting Adverse Effect?
6. Can the Entire Future Tax Shelter Generated by a Lease Investment Be Used? That Is, Will the Lessor's Unrelated Taxable Income Be Sufficient to Cover the Available Write-Offs and Any Investment Tax Credit?
7. Has Tax Counsel Been Consulted as to Any Future Federal Income Tax Rate Changes? If There Is a Change Adversely Affecting the Leased Equipment, Who Must Bear the Burden?

8. Is the Residual Value of the Equipment an Important Factor in the Lessor's Economic Analysis? If so, Has It Been Properly Assessed?
    a. Has a Qualified Equipment Appraiser Been Consulted?
9. Will the Lessor's Economics Be Protected if There Is an Early Lease Termination?
    a. If It Results from a Lease Default?
    b. If It Results from a Permitted Termination?
10. If a Termination Value Concept Has Been Incorporated to Protect a Lessor's Investment Position, Have the Values Been Verified?
11. Will the Lessor's Investment Position Be Protected If There Is an Equipment Casualty Loss?
12. If a Stipulated Loss Value (Also Referred to as Casualty Loss Value) Concept Has Been Incorporated in the Lease, Has Each Value Been Verified?
13. Will an Underwriter's Economic Analysis of a Proposed Lease Investment Be Relied on? If so, Has It Been Independently Checked?
    a. Are All the Investment Criteria Assumptions, Such as Sinking Fund Interest Rate, Realistic from the Prospective Lessor's Standpoint?
14. Will the Prospective Lessor Be Required to Make a Long-Term Commitment to Purchase and Lease Equipment? If so:
    a. Will the Lessee Be Able to Decide at the Last Minute Not to Lease the Equipment Without a Penalty? If Not, Has a Proper Commitment Fee or Non-Utilization Fee Been Incorporated?
15. Have the Expenses for Documenting the Lease and the Responsibility for Payment Been Clearly Defined:
    a. If the Transaction Actually Goes Through?
    b. If the Transaction Collapses Before the Lease Documents Are Signed?

9

FINANCIAL ANALYSIS OF THE LEASE

What Analysis Approach Should a Prospective Lessee Use? • How Does a Prospective Lessor-Investor Analyze an Investment Presentation?

A. THE FINANCIAL ANALYSIS OF A LEASE IS CRITICAL

Whether a prospective lessee or a prospective lessor should enter into a particular long-term equipment lease transaction depends heavily on the resulting financial effect. A prospective lessee, therefore, should not choose the leasing alternative before making a financial comparison with the other available methods of financing the equipment's acquisition. The extent of the analysis will, of course, depend on how significant the commitment will be. By the same token, a prospective lessor should not commit to a lease until he has reviewed it for investment soundness.

The material in this chapter will discuss the financial concepts involved in the analysis of a finance lease, both from a prospective lessee's and a prospective lessor's viewpoint. The discussion will not exhaustively explore *every* possible method of financial lease analysis, but will provide the reader with a concise foundation in lessor and lessee financial lease analysis.

B. WHAT IS IMPORTANT IN A LESSEE'S ANALYSIS?

Once a company has decided it needs certain equipment, it must determine which method is best for financing its acquisition. For example, should the prospective user take out a specific loan to buy the equipment, should he draw upon his general funds to make the purchase, or should he lease the equipment? In order to make a finance lease versus a purchase decision, he must understand the concepts basic to a proper evaluation. These will now be discussed.

1. Is the Interest Rate the Key?

In evaluating whether it would be less expensive to lease certain equipment or take out a loan to purchase it, would it be accurate for a company to merely compare the relative interest rates charged? No, a comparison of the interest rates does not take into account the varying *cash flows* for each alternative. In other words, taking out a loan to buy an asset will result in different cash outflows and inflows than if it were leased. For example, if a company took out a loan to purchase necessary equipment, as the owner it would be entitled to the ownership tax benefits. These tax benefits, depreciation and possibly investment tax credit, would reduce the amount of income taxes a company would have to pay. Tax savings can be viewed as cash inflows. If the equipment were leased, typically the only tax benefits which would be available would be the rent expense deductions. Because money has a time value, i.e. $1.00 received today is worth more than $1.00 received a year from today, the alternative providing a greater amount of early cash inflows could be less expensive, *even though its interest charge is higher.*

ILLUSTRATION OF THE
TIME VALUE CONCEPT:

Consider, for example, a seven-year lease with an annual rent of $990. If the rent were payable *in advance,* this alternative would, from a payment time value point of view, usually be more costly than a seven-year loan with an annual debt service of $1000, payable *in arrears.* By choosing the lease alternative, the company would have to pay the $990 out one year earlier than the $1000 loan payment. If, for instance, the company could earn 6% per annum after taxes on its available funds, giving up the $990 in advance would result in a "loss" of $59.40 (6% x $990 = $59.40) the first year. In other words, it could have earned $59.40 on the $990 if the rent had been payable annually in arrears. In this case, the advance payment could be said to cost $1049.40 ($990 + $59.40 = $1049.40). Other considerations aside, therefore, the $1000 loan payment would have been less expensive.

If the company were only able to earn 1% per annum after taxes, paying the $990 yearly in advance rather than in arrears would only result in a $9.90 "loss" (1% x $990 = $9.90). That is, the effective cost of payment in advance would have been $999.90, instead of $1049.40.

2. A Basic Approach—The Present Value Method
Of Analysis

In determining whether equipment should be leased, bought outright with internal funds, or purchased using third-party debt, equipment users use a variety of analysis techniques. One method compares the *present value* of the *after-tax cash flows* provided by each financing alternative. This method is sometimes referred to as the *discounted cash flow method*. By using this approach, the cash flow amounts and the cash flow timing differences are in effect taken into account so that a meaningful comparison can be made. Very simply, the present value approach reduces the relevant cash flows to a comparable frame of reference—*their present worth*. The reader must keep in mind that this is one of many methods which have been used and may not provide the absolute answer for a particular situation. It is interesting to note, however, that some feel *no* approach will provide a simple and conclusive solution.

In order to compute the present value of a series of future cash flows the interest rate to be used to discount them back to their present worth must be decided upon. This rate is commonly referred to as the *discount rate*.

The most effective way to explain the concepts involved in present value analysis is to work through a hypothetical example. Three basic financing possibilities will be explored: an outright cash purchase, a loan financing, and a long-term lease. Let us assume that White Industries wants to acquire a new corporate aircraft and is able to use all the available tax benefits.

Let us also assume the following additional facts:

Aircraft Cost	$1,000,000
Depreciable Life	10 years
Residual Value	$0
Investment Tax Credit	0%
White Industries' Income Tax Rate	50%
White Industries' Tax Year	Jan. 1 to Dec. 31
Tax Payment Basis	Cash/Current
Delivery Date	1/1/19X0
Depreciation Method	Sum-of-the-years-digits
Proposed Financial Lease	
Lease Term	10 years
Rental Payments	$147,950, payable in 10 annual payments in arrears.
Lease Simple Interest Rate	7.839% per annum
Proposed Bank Loan	
Loan Amount	$1,000,000, repayable in 10 equal annual payments of $162,745 in arrears.
Loan Term	10 years
Loan Interest Rate	10% per annum

The facts have been assumed arbitrarily for ease of illustration without regard to whether any applicable accounting or tax rules will be satisfied. In addition, all amounts are rounded to the nearest dollar.

In order for White Industries to compare the attractiveness of leasing to an outright cash purchase or bank loan financing, the after-tax cash flows for each alternative must be computed. For leasing the cash flows are:

Year	Rental Payments	Tax Savings From Rent Deductions	Net After-Tax Cost	Cumulative Net After-Tax Cost
1	$147,950	$73,975	$73,975	$ 73,975
2	147,950	73,975	73,975	147,950
3	147,950	73,975	73,975	221,925
4	147,950	73,975	73,975	295,900
5	147,950	73,975	73,975	369,875
6	147,950	73,975	73,975	443,850
7	147,950	73,975	73,975	517,825
8	147,950	73,975	73,975	591,800
9	147,950	73,975	73,975	665,775
10	147,950	73,975	73,975	739,750
Tot.	$1,479,500	$739,750	$739,750	$739,750

It is worthwhile at this point to go over how each column is computed. The RENTAL PAYMENTS column should be self-explanatory. The rent is payable annually in the amount of $147,950. The next column, TAX SAVINGS FROM RENT DEDUCTIONS, represents the annual income tax savings White Industries will realize from the rent expense deduction. Since White Industries is in the 50% income tax bracket, the savings are easy to calculate. The $73,975 annual amount is arrived at by multiplying 50% times the rent expense (50% x $147,950 = $73,975). The NET AFTER-TAX COST column represents how much cash White Industries is actually out-of-pocket each year. In other words, it is the difference between the rent payment of $147,950 and the rent expense tax savings of $73,975. The CUMULATIVE NET AFTER-TAX COST column represents the total after-tax cost as of the end of each year. Over the term of the lease this adds up to a total net cash outlay of $739,750.

If White Industries paid for the aircraft entirely with its own internal funds, the following cash flows would result:

Year	Annual Depreciation Expense	Tax Savings	Net After-Tax Cost	Cumulative After-Tax Cost
0			$1,000,000	$1,000,000
1	$181,818	$90,908	(90,909)	909,091
2	163,636	81,818	(81,818)	827,273
3	145,455	72,728	(72,728)	754,545
4	127,273	63,636	(63,636)	690,909
5	109,091	54,546	(54,546)	636,363
6	90,909	45,454	(45,454)	590,909
7	72,727	36,364	(36,364)	554,545
8	54,546	27,273	(27,273)	527,272
9	36,364	18,182	(18,182)	509,090
10	18,182	9,091	(9,091)	499,999
Tot.*	$1,000,000	$500,000	$500,000	$500,000

*Rounded off

At this point it is not possible to make any valid comparisons. The total CUMULATIVE NET AFTER-TAX COST to White Industries would be $739,750 if the aircraft were leased and $500,000 if the aircraft were purchased outright. But we cannot say, based on this, that it would be more expensive to lease the aircraft than to purchase it. We must first compare the yearly CUMULATIVE NET AFTER-TAX COST cash flows.

Year	Lease Cumulative Net After-Tax Cost	Outright Purchase Cumulative Net After-Tax Cost	Lease Cash Advantage
0		$1,000,000	$1,000,000
1	$ 73,975	909,091	835,116
2	147,950	827,273	679,323
3	221,925	754,545	532,620
4	295,900	690,909	395,009
5	369,875	636,363	266,488
6	443,850	590,909	147,059
7	517,825	554,545	36,720
8	591,800	527,272	(64,528)
9	665,775	509,090	(156,685)
10	739,750	499,999	(239,751)

It is easy to see that leasing will conserve money in the early years. If these available funds are put to work, the resulting earnings will go toward offsetting the cumulative cost disparity. Therefore, we cannot say that leasing is more expensive until the *present value* of the cash flows shown in each alternative NET AFTER-TAX COST column is compared.

If White Industries chooses a discount rate (after-tax opportunity rate of return on available cash flows) equal to 10% per annum, the present values of the NET AFTER-TAX COST cash flows in Years 1 through 10 are as follows:

Year	LEASE CASH FLOW Net After-Tax Cost	Present Value	Purchase Cash Flow Net After-Tax Cost	Present Value
0			$1,000,000	$1,000,000
1	$73,975	$67,250	(90,909)	(82,644)
2	73,975	61,136	(81,818)	(67,618)
3	73,975	55,578	(72,728)	(54,642)
4	73,975	50,526	(63,636)	(43,464)
5	73,975	45,933	(54,546)	(33,869)
6	73,975	41,757	(45,454)	(25,658)
7	73,975	37,961	(36,364)	(18,660)
8	73,975	34,510	(27,273)	(12,723)
9	73,975	31,373	(18,182)	(7,711)
10	73,975	28,521	(9,091)	(3,505)
Total		$454,545		$350,494

As the reader can see the present worth of the leasing after-tax cash flows is $454,545. The net present value of the purchase cost after-tax cash flows is $649,506. Since in the purchase situation White Industries paid out $1,000,000 in Year "0", the present value of the tax savings must be subtracted from $1,000,000 to get the *net* present value cost of purchasing ($1,000,000 - $350,494 = $649,506). Based on this analysis, *leasing* the aircraft would be *more* favorable than *purchasing* with internal funds.

If White Industries decided to borrow the money to pay for the aircraft, the cash flow picture would look as in the following chart.

Year	Debt Payments	Principal Balance Outstanding	10% Interest On Principal	Tax Savings On Interest	Tax Savings (Dep. & Interest)	Net After-Tax Cost	Present Value
0	—	$1,000,000	—	—	—	—	—
1	$162,745	937,255	$100,000	$50,000	$140,909	$21,836	$19,851
2	162,745	868,236	93,726	46,863	128,681	34,064	28,152
3	162,745	792,314	86,824	43,412	116,140	46,605	35,015
4	162,745	708,800	79,231	39,616	103,252	59,493	40,634
5	162,745	616,936	70,880	35,440	89,986	72,759	45,178
6	162,745	515,884	61,694	30,847	76,301	86,444	48,795
7	162,745	404,727	51,588	25,794	62,158	100,587	51,617
8	162,745	282,455	40,473	20,236	47,509	115,236	53,758
9	162,745	147,956	28,246	14,123	32,305	130,440	55,319
10	162,745	0	14,796	7,398	16,489	146,256	56,388
Total	$1,627,450	—	$627,458	$313,729	$813,730	$813,720	$434,707

The present value of the NET AFTER-TAX COST is $434,707. In the lease cash flow analysis, this value turned out to be $454,545, and in the case of the outright purchase it was $649,506. Based on our analysis method, therefore, purchasing the aircraft using 100% bank borrowings would be the most attractive alternative at a 10% discount rate.

C. WHAT ARE THE KEY CONCEPTS IN A LESSOR'S LEASE INVESTMENT ANALYSIS?

A prospective lessor should not consider entering into a lease without thoroughly reviewing the financial implications of making such an investment. In order to do this properly he must understand certain analytical and conceptual fundamentals. The material in this section is designed to provide the necessary background.

Two types of lease investments will be considered, the *non-leveraged* financial lease and the *leveraged* financial lease. The difference between the two is that in a leveraged lease investment the lessor borrows a portion of the cost of the equipment from a third-party lender. In a non-leveraged lease, the lessor supplies the entire purchase cost from his own internal funds. The non-leveraged lease will be considered first since it forms the basis of the leveraged lease discussion.

1. A Non-Leveraged Lease Investment Analysis

As explained earlier, a non-leveraged lease is one in which the investor (lessor) supplies *all* the money necessary to purchase the equipment from his own funds. Whether an investment in this type of lease will make economic sense depends on how profitable the transaction will be to the lessor. Therefore, the determination of the profit (commonly referred to as the *rate of return*) is a threshold issue in any financial lease investment evaluation.

Traditionally, an investor's *rate of return* has been defined as the interest rate (sometimes referred to as the *discount rate*) which will discount a lease's after-tax cash flows back to a value equal to his initial cash outlay. Looking at it another way, it is that rate which, when applied to the original cash investment, will produce the future cash flow amounts generated by the lease.

The best way to explain the investor rate of return analysis approach is to work through a hypothetical *non-leveraged* lease example. We will assume the following facts:

EQUIPMENT DATA

Equipment Cost	$1,000,000
Depreciable Life	10 years
Residual Value	$0
Delivery Date	1/1/19X0
Description	15 rail tank cars

LEASE INVESTMENT DATA

Lease Term	10 years
Rental Payments	10 annual payments in arrears each equal to $140,000
Investment Tax Credit	Passed through to lessee
Investor Income Tax Rate	50%
Depreciation Method (Facts and Circumstances)	Sum-of-the-years-digits

Based on the above information, the resulting cash flows are as follows:

YEAR	RENT INCOME	ANNUAL DEPRECIATION	PRE-TAX INCOME (LOSS)	TAXES DUE (SAVED)	AFTER-TAX CASH FLOW
0	—	—	—	—	$(1,000,000)
1	$140,000	$181,818	$(41,818)	$(20,909)	160,909
2	140,000	163,636	(23,636)	(11,818)	151,818
3	140,000	145,455	(5,455)	(2,728)	142,728
4	140,000	127,273	12,727	6,364	133,636
5	140,000	109,091	30,909	15,455	124,545
6	140,000	90,909	49,091	24,546	115,454
7	140,000	72,727	67,273	33,637	106,363
8	140,000	54,546	85,454	42,737	97,273
9	140,000	36,364	103,636	51,818	88,182
10	140,000	18,182	121,818	60,909	79,091

The RENT INCOME column is straightforward. It represents the yearly rent payments due. The ANNUAL DEPRECIATION column lists the annual depreciation deductions, calculated using the sum-of-the-years-digits method of depreciation.

The next column, PRE-TAX INCOME (LOSS), is arrived at by subtracting the ANNUAL DEPRECIATION expense from the RENT INCOME. As the reader can see, the depreciation expense exceeds the rent income in the early years and a tax loss results. This loss produces a *tax savings* equal to 50% (the income tax rate) of the loss amount. When the rent income exceeds the depreciation expense in the later years, the lessor must pay taxes on the income generated.

With the foregoing information, the AFTER-TAX CASH FLOW column is easy to compute. When the equipment is delivered, Year "0", there is an *outflow* of $1,000,000, the cost of the tank cars. In Year "1" the After-Tax Cash Flow is a *positive* $160,909. This is determined by *adding* the rent income to the taxes saved ($140,000 + $20,909 = $160,909). The after-tax cash flows for years "2" and "3" are determined in the same manner. For Year "4" and following, the lease produces taxable income because the rental income is greater than the depreciation deductions. For these years, the after-tax cash flow is calculated by *subtracting* the taxes due from the rent income.

Once the after-tax cash flows have been calculated, the rate of return is found by trial and error. In this example the interest rate which will discount these cash flows back to $1,000,000 is equal to 3.9341%. For an investor in the 50% tax bracket, this is equivalent to a *pre-tax* return rate of 7.8682%.

2. How to Analyze a Leveraged Lease Investment Presentation

A *leveraged* lease investment analysis is complex. As in the case of a non-leveraged lease, there are many approaches used to evaluate this type of lease investment. The most sophisticated of these analyses are done by computer because it is too time consuming to factor in the multitude of varying inputs "by hand." In such a situation, the prospective lease investor will typically be presented with a "computer run" showing the results of the analysis. In order to make sure he is making a good investment, a prospective lessor must know how to properly read an investment presentation.

A computer run investment presentation often begins by summarizing certain key information. This information will enable the reviewer to quickly assess the important facts, including lease terms, tax benefits, and yield. The reader is referred to Table 9-1 and Table 9-2 for a typical summary format.

As the reader can see from reviewing the INVESTMENT DATA section of Table 9-1, the equipment involved is a new item of mining equipment (a drag line). The total cost is $1,112,780 (TOTAL COST). The funds necessary to buy the equipment will come from an equity investment (EQUITY) of $222,556.88, representing 20% of the total cost, and a third-party loan (DEBT) of $890,223.13, representing 80% of the total cost. The equity investment must be paid in one lump sum on October 1, 1980 (EQUITY DISBURSEMENTS), the assumed equipment delivery date (DELIVERY DATE).

The INVESTOR ASSUMPTIONS section outlines certain basic tax and tax-related assumptions used in the program analysis. In this example the prospective investor was assumed to be in the 50% Federal income tax bracket (TAX RATE). Since no state taxes are payable, his overall effective tax rate (OVERALL) is also 50%. The overall rate is sometimes referred to as the "composite" rate.

TABLE 9-1

- ANALYSIS SUMMARY -

PROPOSED LEASE INVESTMENT ANALYSIS

BASIC LEASE DATA

PRIMARY LEASE TERM: 8 Years 0 Months
COMMENCEMENT DATE: Oct. 1, 1980
COST TO LESSEE (Primary Lease Term): 4.38148%
RENT PAYMENTS: Quarterly In Advance
PAYMENT STRUCTURE: 32 Payments of
$40,963.70 (3.6812%)

INVESTMENT RESULTS

	Nominal	Effective
PRE-TAX YIELD:	31.7902%	34.2115%
AFTER-TAX YIELD:	15.8951%	17.1058
AFTER-TAX CASH FLOW:	$72,061.47 (6.4758%)	
PRE-TAX CASH FLOW:	$144.125.06 (12.9518%)	

SINKING FUND RATE: 4.38% - After-Tax
SINKING FUND EARNINGS: $1,927.69 (0.1732%) After-Tax
METHOD OF ANALYSIS: Multiple Investment Method

INVESTMENT DATA

LESSEE: White Industries
EQUIPMENT: One (1) New Drag Line
EQUIPMENT USE: Mining
DELIVERY DATE: Oct. 1, 1980
TOTAL COST: $1,112,780.00 (100%)
DEBT: $890,223.13 (80%)
EQUITY: $222,556.88 (20%)
EQUITY DISBURSEMENTS: $222,556.88 - Oct. 1, 1980

INVESTOR ASSUMPTIONS

TAX RATE: Fed: 50% State: 0% Overall: 50
FIRST TAX IMPACT MONTH: Dec. 1980
FIRST TAX YEAR: Jan. 1, 1980 to Dec. 30, 1980
BASIS OF TAX PAYMENT: Cash/100% Current
MONTHS TAX ESTIMATES PAID: Apr, Jun, Sep, Dec.
RESIDUAL VALUE: $278,195.00 (25%)
TOTAL ITC: $0
FEE: $0

The FIRST TAX IMPACT MONTH subcategory shows the first month the investor will realize a tax savings from the tax benefits. In our case, the investor was assumed to pay taxes on an estimated basis in April, June, September, and December (MONTHS TAX ESTIMATES PAID). Since the equipment is to be delivered in October, the next tax payment date will be December. The analysis also assumes that the investor is a calendar year taxpayer (FIRST TAX YEAR: Jan. 1, 1980 to Dec. 30, 1980) and that he pays his taxes on a cash/current basis (BASIS OF TAX PAYMENT).

The equipment's residual value was assumed to be $278,195 for analysis purposes (RESIDUAL VALUE), or 25% of the equipment's original cost. The investment tax credit is to be "passed through" to the lessee (TOTAL ITC: $0) and, in this situation, the prospective investor will not be charged a brokerage fee (FEE: $0).

The BASIC LEASE DATA section sets out the fundamental lease structure. As the reader can see, the main lease term is 8 years (PRIMARY LEASE TERM), beginning on October 1, 1980 (COMMENCEMENT DATE). The rent is due quarterly in advance (RENT PAYMENTS) and is payable in 32 payments of $40,963.70 each (PAYMENT STRUCTURE). The quarterly *percentage* rent is also listed in the PAYMENT STRUCTURE section. The actual dollar amount of rent due each quarter can be arrived at by multiplying the quarterly percentage rent (3.6812%) times the total equipment cost ($1,112,780). The COST TO LESSEE (4.38148% in our example) is the implicit lease interest rate.

The INVESTMENT RESULTS section is self-explanatory. The projected yield to the investor, both on a pre-tax and an after-tax basis, is listed. In addition, the summary shows the total cash flow on an after-tax and a pre-tax basis, the interest rate assumed for the sinking fund, the total earnings generated by the sinking fund, and the method of lease analysis (in our example the Multiple Investment Method).

The summary grouping on Table 9-2 lists the fundamental depreciation and debt assumptions. The DEPRECIATION ASSUMPTIONS section shows that the equipment will begin to be depreciated on July 1, 1980 (DEPRECIATION START DATE) and that it will be depreciated over a period of 8 years (DEPRECIATION PERIOD) down to a salvage value of 15% of original cost (SALVAGE VALUE). The reviewer can also see that the Class Life Asset Depreciation Range System has been selected (CONVENTION) and that the yearly depreciation was determined using the double-declining method with a switch to the sum-of-the-years-digits method (METHOD OF DEPRECIATION).

The DEBT ASSUMPTIONS category lists the third-party loan parameters which were assumed in the analysis. In our example, the principal amount of the loan ($890,223.13) is stated as well as the annual inter-

TABLE 9-2

- ANALYSIS SUMMARY -

DEPRECIATION ASSUMPTIONS

DEPRECIATION START DATE:	July 1, 1980
DEPRECIATION PERIOD:	8 Years
SALVAGE VALUE:	15%
METHOD OF DEPRECIATION:	DDB/SYD
CONVENTION:	Half-Year (ADR)

DEBT ASSUMPTIONS

PRINCIPAL AMOUNT IN DOLLARS:	$890,223.13
AS A % OF COST:	80%
INTEREST RATE:	8.45%
FUNDING DATE:	Oct. 1, 1980
FINAL PMT DATE:	July 1, 1988
NO. OF PMTS:	31
NO. OF I/O PMTS:	0
BALLOON PMT:	$0
PAYMENT PERCENTAGE:	3.543443%
PAYMENT STRUCTURE:	Quarterly In Arrears

est rate (8.45%). The analysis further anticipates that the loan will be taken out on October 1, 1980 (FUNDING DATE) and that it will be repaid in 31 payments (NO. OF PMTS). In addition, there are no interest-only payments (NO. OF I/O PMT.) and there is no balloon payment (BALLOON PMT.). The final payment will be due on July 1, 1988 (FINAL PMT. DATE). The amount of each debt service payment, expressed as a percent of original equipment cost, is 3.543443% (PAYMENT PERCENTAGE).

An AMORTIZATION SCHEDULE, as shown in Table 9-3, is often included in the investment presentation. For each debt service payment due, the schedule shows the beginning loan principal outstanding (BEGINNING PRINCIPAL), the total payment amount (DEBT SERVICE), the interest component of each payment (INTEREST), the principal component of each payment (PRINCIPAL), and the principal amount outstanding after each payment (REMAINING BALANCE).

The Federal tax consequences of a lease investment is a critical consideration. A complete lease investment presentation will, therefore, incorporate a tax analysis similar to that included in Table 9-4. It is not difficult to understand the tax statement once the derivation for each component listed is known. To begin with, the investor will receive, as of the end of the first *tax* year, a total lease income (LEASE REVENUE) of $40,963.70.

AMORTIZATION SCHEDULE

LOAN AMOUNT: 890223.13
DEBT RATE: 8.450001 %
NO. PERIODS PER YEAR: 4
TOTAL NO. OF PAYMENTS: 31

PAY NO.	DATE	BEGINNING PRINCIPAL	DEBT SERVICE	INTEREST	PRINCIPAL	REMAINING BALANCE
1	1/ 1/81	890223.25	39430.73	18805.97	20624.76	869598.38
2	4/ 1/81	869598.38	39430.73	18370.27	21060.46	848537.88
3	7/ 1/81	848537.88	39430.73	17925.37	21505.36	827032.63
4	10/ 1/81	827032.63	39430.73	17471.07	21959.66	805073.00
5	1/ 1/82	805073.00	39430.73	17007.17	22423.56	782649.50
6	4/ 1/82	782649.50	39430.73	16533.47	22897.26	759752.13
7	7/ 1/82	759752.13	39430.73	16049.76	23380.97	736371.25
8	10/ 1/82	736371.25	39430.73	15555.84	23874.89	712496.38
9	1/ 1/83	712496.38	39430.73	15051.48	24379.25	688117.00
10	4/ 1/83	688117.00	39430.73	14536.47	24894.26	663222.75
11	7/ 1/83	663222.75	39430.73	14010.58	25420.15	637802.63
12	10/ 1/83	637802.63	39430.73	13473.58	25957.15	611845.50
13	1/ 1/84	611845.50	39430.73	12925.24	26505.49	585340.00
14	4/ 1/84	585340.00	39430.73	12365.31	27065.42	558274.50
15	7/ 1/84	558274.50	39430.73	11793.55	27637.18	530637.38
16	10/ 1/84	530637.38	39430.73	11209.71	28221.02	502416.38
17	1/ 1/85	502416.38	39430.73	10613.54	28817.19	473599.19
18	4/ 1/85	473599.19	39430.73	10004.78	29425.95	444173.19
19	7/ 1/85	444173.19	39430.73	9383.15	30047.58	414125.69
20	10/ 1/85	414125.69	39430.73	8748.40	30682.33	383443.25
21	1/ 1/86	383443.25	39430.73	8100.23	31330.50	352112.81
22	4/ 1/86	352112.81	39430.73	7438.38	31992.35	320120.50
23	7/ 1/86	320120.50	39430.73	6762.54	32668.19	287452.25
24	10/ 1/86	287452.25	39430.73	6072.42	33358.31	254093.97
25	1/ 1/87	254093.97	39430.73	5367.73	34063.00	220030.97
26	4/ 1/87	220030.97	39430.73	4648.15	34782.58	185248.41
27	7/ 1/87	185248.41	39430.73	3913.36	35517.37	149731.03
28	10/ 1/87	149731.03	39430.73	3163.06	36267.67	113463.34
29	1/ 1/88	113463.34	39430.73	2396.91	37033.82	76429.52
30	4/ 1/88	76429.52	39430.73	1614.56	37816.17	38613.35
31	7/ 1/88	38613.35	39430.73	815.70	38615.03	-1.68
32	10/ 1/88	-1.68	-1.68	.00	-1.68	.00

| TOTALS | | | 1222351.00 | 332127.75 | 890223.25 | |

AVERAGE LIFE FROM 10/ 1/1980   4 YEARS 4 MONTHS 29.47 DAYS

TABLE 9-3

FEDERAL TAX RATE: 50.000%   **** F E D E R A L   T A X   S T A T E M E N T ****   (CASH METHOD)

PD	TAX YEAR	LEASE REVENUE	INTEREST	DEPRECIATION	FEES(DEF. EXPENSES)	OTHER EXPENSES	NET STATE TAXES PAID	TAXABLE INCOME	TAX CREDITS	NET FEDERAL TAX LIABILITY	TOTAL TAXES PAID
1	12/80	40963.70	.00	139097.50	.00	.00	.00	-98133.80	.00	-49066.90	-49066.90
2	12/81	163854.81	72572.67	243420.66	.00	.00	.00	-152138.50	.00	-76069.25	-76069.25
3	12/82	163854.81	65146.25	193743.09	.00	.00	.00	-95034.55	.00	-47517.27	-47517.27
4	12/83	163854.81	57072.11	163936.50	.00	.00	.00	-57153.80	.00	-28576.90	-28576.90
5	12/84	163854.81	48293.80	134129.84	.00	.00	.00	-18568.84	.00	-9284.42	-9284.42
6	12/85	163854.81	38749.88	71536.06	.00	.00	.00	53568.89	.00	26784.45	26784.45
7	12/86	163854.81	28373.57	.00	.00	.00	.00	135481.25	.00	67740.63	67740.63
8	12/87	163854.81	17092.30	.00	.00	.00	.00	146762.53	.00	73381.27	73381.27
9	12/88	401086.13	4827.17	166917.00	.00	.00	.00	229341.97	.00	114670.98	114670.98
TOTALS		1589034.25	332127.75	1112781.00	.00	.00	.00	144125.06	.00	72062.53	72062.70

TABLE 9-4

Since the loan is repayable quarterly *in arrears*, the first debt service payment is not due until January 1, 1981 (see Table 9-3). Therefore, there is no interest deduction for this year (see INTEREST column). There is, however, a depreciation expense item of $139,097.50 (see DEPRECIATION column). Inasmuch as there are no other expense items for the first year, the year's TAXABLE INCOME is computed by subtracting the depreciation expense from the lease revenue. In this example the taxable income is −$98,133.80 ($40,963.70 − $139,097.50 = $98,133.80). The negative sign indicates a tax *loss*.

The *tax savings* (NET FEDERAL TAX LIABILITY) resulting from a $98,133.80 tax *loss* is $49,066.90. In other words, a 50% tax bracket investor would pay $49,066.90 less in Federal income taxes the first year than if he had not made the investment. After the first tax year, the interest payable on the third party loan is factored in. In those years, therefore, the interest expense must be added to the depreciation amount and the total subtracted from the lease revenue. The flow analysis, otherwise, for the second through the last year follows that for the first year.

It is interesting to note that in the tax year ending in December of 1985 the investment "crosses over." That is, the lease is no longer providing a tax loss. This is because the lease revenue for this year and the remaining years exceed the offsetting expenses. The investment is said to have turned "tax positive" and is generating taxable income.

In years 1986 and 1987, the depreciation expense is "0" because the asset has, through 1985, been depreciated down to its 15% tax salvage value. In 1988, the analysis assumes the asset is sold for 25% of its original cost ($278,195). The lease revenue for this year consists of the nine months rent due plus the proceeds from the sale (lease revenue = $122,891.13 + $278,195 = $401,086.13). Only nine months of revenue are payable in 1988 because the lease ends October 1 of that year, 8 years from October 1, 1980. The revenue in this year is "offset" by the loan interest expense of $4,827.17 and the asset's remaining basis of $166,917 (15% salvage value x $1,112,780 original cost = $166,917).

Another frequently included part of an investor presentation is a detailed cash flow analysis similar to that shown in Table 9-5. This particular report presents the cash flows on a monthly basis. As the reader can see, the $222,557 equity investment must be paid in when the equipment is delivered, October 1980 (see EQUITY, DEFERRED & OTHER EXPENSES column). At this time, the investor will receive his first rent payment of $40,946 (see LEASE REVENUE column). Since the loan is repayable quarterly in arrears, there is no debt expense until January 1981 (see DEBT SERVICE) column. Therefore as of October 1980, the investor has "free cash" of $40,964 (see UNASSIGNED REVENUE column). Since

CASH FLOWS AND SINKING FUND ANALYSIS

PD	MONTH & YEAR	EQUITY, DEFERRED & OTHER EXPENSES	LEASE REVENUE	DEBT SERVICE	UN-ASSIGNED REVENUE	TAXES PAID	AFTER TAX CASH FLOW	SINKING FUND FOR TAX RESERVE	CASHFLOW AFTER SINKING FUND	CASHFLOW RETURN @ 15.90% ON INVEST. BALANCE	CHANGE IN INVEST. BALANCE	INVEST. BALANCE	SINKING FUND INTEREST @ 4.380%	SINKING FUND BALANCE
1	10/80	222557	40964	0	40964	0	-181593	0	-181593	0	-181593	-181593	0	0
2	11/80	0	0	0	0	-49067	49067	0	49067	2405	-2405	-183999	0	0
3	12/80	0	0	0	0	-49067	49067	0	49067	2437	46630	-137369	0	0
4	1/81	0	40964	39431	1533	0	1533	0	1533	1820	-287	-137656	0	0
5	2/81	0	0	0	0	0	0	0	0	1823	-1823	-139479	0	0
6	3/81	0	0	0	0	0	0	0	0	1848	-1848	-141326	0	0
7	4/81	0	40964	39431	1533	-19017	20550	0	20550	1872	18678	-122648	0	0
8	5/81	0	0	0	0	0	0	0	0	1625	-1625	-124273	0	0
9	6/81	0	0	0	0	-19017	19017	0	19017	1646	17371	-106901	0	0
10	7/81	0	40964	39431	1533	0	1533	0	1533	1416	117	-106785	0	0
11	8/81	0	0	0	0	0	0	0	0	1414	-1414	-108199	0	0
12	9/81	0	0	0	0	-19017	19017	0	19017	1433	17584	-90615	0	0
13	10/81	0	40964	39431	1533	0	1533	0	1533	1200	333	-90282	0	0
14	11/81	0	0	0	0	0	0	0	0	1196	-1196	-91478	0	0
15	12/81	0	0	0	0	-19017	19017	0	19017	1212	17806	-73672	0	0
16	1/82	0	40964	39431	1533	0	1533	0	1533	976	557	-73115	0	0
17	2/82	0	0	0	0	0	0	0	0	968	-968	-74084	0	0
18	3/82	0	0	0	0	0	0	0	0	981	-981	-75065	0	0
19	4/82	0	40964	39431	1533	-11879	13412	0	13452	994	12418	-62647	0	0
20	5/82	0	0	0	0	0	0	0	0	830	-830	-63477	0	0
21	6/82	0	0	0	0	-11879	11879	0	11879	841	11039	-52438	0	0
22	7/82	0	40964	39431	1533	0	1533	0	1533	695	838	-51600	0	0
23	8/82	0	0	0	0	0	0	0	0	683	-683	-52284	0	0
24	9/82	0	0	0	0	-11879	11879	0	11879	693	11187	-41097	0	0
25	10/82	0	40964	39431	1533	0	1533	0	1533	544	989	-40108	0	0
26	11/82	0	0	0	0	0	0	0	0	531	-531	-40639	0	0
27	12/82	0	0	0	0	-11879	11879	0	11879	538	11341	-29298	0	0
28	1/83	0	40964	39431	1533	0	1533	0	1533	388	1145	-28154	0	0
29	2/83	0	0	0	0	0	0	0	0	373	-373	-28526	0	0
30	3/83	0	0	0	0	0	0	0	0	378	-378	-28904	0	0
31	4/83	0	40964	39431	1533	-7144	8677	0	8677	383	8294	-20610	0	0
32	5/83	0	0	0	0	0	0	0	0	273	-273	-20883	0	0
33	6/83	0	0	0	0	-7144	7144	0	7144	277	6868	-14015	0	0
34	7/83	0	40964	39431	1533	0	1533	0	1533	186	1347	-12668	0	0
35	8/83	0	0	0	0	0	0	0	0	168	-168	-12836	0	0
36	9/83	0	0	0	0	-7144	7144	0	7144	170	6974	-5862	0	0
37	10/83	0	40964	39431	1533	0	1533	0	1533	78	1455	-4406	0	0
38	11/83	0	0	0	0	0	0	0	0	58	-58	-4465	0	0
39	12/83	0	0	0	0	-7144	7144	2621	4524	59	4465	0	0	2621

TABLE 9-5

CASH FLOWS AND SINKING FUND ANALYSIS

PD	MONTH & YEAR	EQUITY, DEFERRED & OTHER EXPENSES	LEASE REVENUE	DEBT SERVICE	UN-ASSIGNED REVENUE	TAXES PAID	AFTER TAX CASH FLOW	SINKING FUND FOR TAX RESERVE	CASHFLOW AFTER SINKING FUND	CASHFLOW RETURN @ 15.90% ON INVEST. BALANCE	CHANGE IN INVEST. BALANCE	INVEST. BALANCE	SINKING FUND INTEREST @ 4.380%	SINKING FUND BALANCE
40	1/84	0	40964	39431	1533	0	1533	1533	0	0	0	0	10	4163
41	2/84	0	0	0	0	0	0	0	0	0	0	0	15	4178
42	3/84	0	0	0	0	0	0	0	0	0	0	0	15	4194
43	4/84	0	40964	39431	1533	-2321	3854	3854	0	0	0	0	15	8063
44	5/84	0	0	0	0	0	0	0	0	0	0	0	29	8092
45	6/84	0	0	0	0	-2321	2321	2321	0	0	0	0	30	10443
46	7/84	0	40964	39431	1533	0	1533	1533	0	0	0	0	38	12014
47	8/84	0	0	0	0	0	0	0	0	0	0	0	44	12058
48	9/84	0	0	0	0	-2321	2321	2321	0	0	0	0	44	14423
49	10/84	0	40964	39431	1533	0	1533	1533	0	0	0	0	53	16009
50	11/84	0	0	0	0	0	0	0	0	0	0	0	58	16067
51	12/84	0	0	0	0	-2321	2321	2321	0	0	0	0	59	18447
52	1/85	0	40964	39431	1533	0	1533	1533	0	0	0	0	67	20047
53	2/85	0	0	0	0	0	0	0	0	0	0	0	73	20120
54	3/85	0	0	0	0	0	0	0	0	0	0	0	73	20194
55	4/85	0	40964	39431	1533	6696	-5163	-5163	0	0	0	0	74	15104
56	5/85	0	0	0	0	0	0	0	0	0	0	0	55	15159
57	6/85	0	0	0	0	6696	-6696	-6696	0	0	0	0	55	8519
58	7/85	0	40964	39431	1533	0	1533	1533	0	0	0	0	31	10083
59	8/85	0	0	0	0	0	0	0	0	0	0	0	37	10120
60	9/85	0	0	0	0	6696	-6696	-6696	0	0	0	0	37	3460
61	10/85	0	40964	39431	1533	0	1533	1533	0	0	0	0	13	5006
62	11/85	0	0	0	0	0	0	0	0	0	0	0	18	5024
63	12/85	0	0	0	0	6696	-6696	-5043	-1654	0	-1654	-1654	18	0
64	1/86	0	40964	39431	1533	0	1533	1533	1533	22	1511	-142	0	0
65	2/86	0	0	0	0	0	0	0	0	2	-2	-144	0	0
66	3/86	0	0	0	0	0	0	0	0	2	-2	-146	0	0
67	4/86	0	40964	39431	1533	16935	-15402	-15402	-15402	2	-15404	-15550	0	0
68	5/86	0	0	0	0	0	0	0	0	206	-206	-15756	0	0
69	6/86	0	0	0	0	16935	-16935	-16935	-16935	209	-17144	-32900	0	0
70	7/86	0	40964	39431	1533	0	1533	1533	1533	436	1097	-31803	0	0
71	8/86	0	0	0	0	0	0	0	0	421	-421	-32224	0	0
72	9/86	0	0	0	0	16935	-16935	-16935	-16935	427	-17362	-49586	0	0
73	10/86	0	40964	39431	1533	0	1533	1533	1533	657	876	-48710	0	0
74	11/86	0	0	0	0	0	0	0	0	645	-645	-49355	0	0
75	12/86	0	0	0	0	16935	-16935	-16935	-16935	654	-17589	-66944	0	0
76	1/87	0	40964	39431	1533	0	1533	1533	1533	887	646	-66298	0	0
77	2/87	0	0	0	0	0	0	0	0	878	-878	-67176	0	0
78	3/87	0	0	0	0	0	0	0	0	890	-890	-68066	0	0

TABLE 9-5 (continued)

CASH FLOWS AND SINKING FUND ANALYSIS

FD	MONTH & YEAR	EQUITY, DEFERRED & OTHER EXPENSES	LEASE REVENUE	DEBT SERVICE	UN-ASSIGNED REVENUE	TAXES, AID	AFTER TAX CASH FLOW	SINKING FUND FOR TAX RESERVE	CASHFLOW AFTER SINKING FUND	RETURN @ 15.90% ON INVEST. BALANCE	CHANGE IN INVEST. BALANCE	INVEST. BALANCE	SINKING FUND INTEREST @ 4.380%	SINKING FUND BALANCE
79	4/87	0	40964	39431	1533	18345	-16812	0	-16812	902	-17714	-85780	0	0
80	5/87	0	0	0	0	0	0	0	0	1136	-1136	-86916	0	0
81	6/87	0	0	0	0	18345	-18345	0	-18345	1151	-19497	-106413	0	0
82	7/87	0	40964	39431	1533	0	1533	0	1533	1410	123	-106289	0	0
83	8/87	0	0	0	0	0	0	0	0	1408	-1408	-107697	0	0
84	9/87	0	0	0	0	18345	-18345	0	-18345	1427	-19772	-127469	0	0
85	10/87	0	40964	39431	1533	0	1533	0	1533	1688	-155	-127625	0	0
86	11/87	0	0	0	0	0	0	0	0	1691	-1691	-129315	0	0
87	12/87	0	0	0	0	18345	-18345	0	-18345	1713	-20058	-149373	0	0
88	1/88	0	40964	39431	1533	0	1533	0	1533	1979	-446	-149819	0	0
89	2/88	0	0	0	0	0	0	0	0	1984	-1984	-151803	0	0
90	3/88	0	0	0	0	0	0	0	0	2011	-2011	-153814	0	0
91	4/88	0	40964	39431	1533	-6107	7640	0	7640	2037	5602	-148212	0	0
92	5/88	0	0	0	0	0	0	0	0	1963	-1963	-150175	0	0
93	6/88	0	0	0	0	-6107	6107	0	6107	1989	4117	-146058	0	0
94	7/88	0	40964	39431	1533	0	1533	0	1533	1935	-402	-146459	0	0
95	8/88	0	0	0	0	0	0	0	0	1940	-1940	-148399	0	0
96	9/88	0	0	0	0	-6107	6107	0	6107	1966	4141	-144259	0	0
97	10/88	0	278195	0	278195	0	278195	132026	146169	1911	144258	0	0	132026
98	11/88	0	0	0	0	0	0	0	0	0	0	0	482	132508
99	12/88	0	0	0	0	132991	-132991	-132991	0	0	0	0	484	0
TOTALS		222257	1589034	1222353	366681	72063	72061	-1928	73989	73989	0	0	1928	0

TABLE 9-5 (continued)

the investor does not pay income taxes until the month of December (See Table 9-1, INVESTOR ASSUMPTIONS), the TAXES PAID column reflects a "0" tax amount due for October 1980. The AFTER TAX CASH FLOW for the October 1980 period is $181,593. This is calculated by subtracting the cash inflows from the outflows. As of this month there is outflow of $222,557, the equity investment, and a lease revenue inflow of $40,964 (+$40,964 − $222,557 = −$181,593). The negative sign indicates a net cash *outflow* for October 1980.

In our example analysis, a "sinking fund" was established out of which deferred taxes are to be paid (see SINKING FUND FOR TAX RESERVE column). Since the analysis method anticipates the investor will get all of his investment back first, along with the projected profit, no cash will be allocated to the fund until December 1983. At that time an amount equal to $2621 is "transferred" to the fund. The CASH FLOW-AFTER SINKING FUND for October of 1980 is, therefore, the same as the AFTER-TAX CASH FLOW amount ($181,593).

The RETURN AT 15.90% ON INVEST. BALANCE column represents how much money must be earned to maintain the anticipated after-tax yield. Since the return is computed on a monthly basis, the return is "0" for the first month (October 1980). In November 1980, however, a 15.90% return on the $181,593 investment balance, earned during *October*, is $2405.

The presentation includes a column (CHANGE IN INVEST. BALANCE) showing how the lessor's investment in the lease changes as a result of the various cash flows. For example, in December 1980 the prior month's investment is increased by a cash inflow of $49,067 (see CASH FLOW AFTER SINKING FUND column) and decreased by $2437, the return that must be earned on the invested capital to maintain the 15.90% yield.

The INVEST. BALANCE column shows, at any point in time, how much money is invested in the lease. In October 1980, the investor has a net investment equal to $181,593. The negative sign means that the investor has money in the transaction.

The SINKING FUND INTEREST AT 4.380% column represents how much the sinking fund has earned *after taxes* at a 4.380% per annum interest rate. Until money is allocated to the fund, this amount will be equal to "0". The SINKING FUND BALANCE column also shows a "0" balance until a sinking fund cash allocation is made. When it is, this column will indicate the total amount of money transferred to the fund from the lease cash flow and the interest which these funds have earned.

It might be helpful to make a few general observations about the sinking fund. In December 1983 the SINKING FUND FOR TAX RESERVE column shows that funds are being put into the fund ($2621). In April 1985 the transaction turns "tax positive" (see TAXES PAID column). When this happens money will be drawn out of the sinking fund to pay the taxes due. The amount drawn out is shown as $5163. As of January of 1986, the fund is depleted. The investor, therefore, must begin to pay the taxes due out of his own pocket. Because of this he is said to be making a further investment in the lease. This "investment" continues through the end of the lease (October 1988), at which time the expected proceeds from the sale of equipment will repay this further investment.

10

COMPLIANCE WITH THE NEW
LEASE ACCOUNTING RULES: FASB-13

There Are New Accounting Standards • The Impact Is Significant—
Both for the Lessee and the Lessor • The Reporting Rules Must Be
Reviewed Before a Lease Commitment Is Made—The Treatment Can Be
Unsatisfactory.

A. BACKGROUND

For many years the accounting profession has devoted a considerable
amount of time and effort discussing how leases should be accounted for,
both from the standpoint of the lessor and the lessee. Unfortunately, there
have been many inconsistencies and substantive disagreements. Finally, in
1973, the subject of accounting for leases was addressed by the accounting
profession's standard setting body, The Financial Accounting Standards
Board, with the firm intent of resolving the many problems. After issuing
several exposure drafts and considering a multitude of letters of comments,
position papers, and oral presentations from interested parties, they
adopted, in November 1976, the "Statement of Financial Accounting
Standards No. 13—Accounting for Leases." "FASB No. 13" established the
standards which must be followed by lessors and lessees in accounting for
and reporting lease transactions.

The new lease accounting guidelines apply to lease transactions and
certain lease revisions which are entered into on or after January 1, 1977. If
a written commitment, which at least outlines the principal terms of the
transaction, has been entered into before January 1, 1977, the new rules do
not apply to the transaction covered. In other words, even if the lease is
consummated on or after January 1, 1977, the old accounting rules govern.
For reporting years beginning after December 31, 1980, however, the new
rules must be *retroactively* applied to *all leases* reported.

OBSERVATION:

It is helpful for the reader to keep in mind that FASB No. 13 is saying
that a lease which transfers substantially all of an asset's ownership

benefits and risks to the lessee should be treated by him in the same way as a purchased asset is treated, and that the lessor should account for such a lease as a sale or a financing. All other types of leases should be treated as operating leases.

Because of the scope and detail of the new lease accounting rules and because the intent of this chapter is to provide the reader with an awareness of the most relevant concepts, every aspect of the rules will not be discussed. The material will, however, point out and generally explain the fundamental issues which have an impact on the everyday decisions involved in the leasing of equipment.

B. LEASE CLASSIFICATIONS FOR A LESSEE VARY SIGNIFICANTLY—A CAREFUL ANALYSIS IS ESSENTIAL

Under the Statement of Financial Accounting Standards No. 13, a lessee is required to account for and report a lease in its financial statements as either a "capital" lease or an "operating" lease, depending on how the transaction is structured. The way the two types of leases are to be treated varies significantly. In many cases it may not be advisable for a company to lease equipment because of the accounting treatment impact.

The criteria for determining whether a lease *from the lessee's viewpoint* must be classified as *capital* lease or an *operating* lease have been well defined in FASB No. 13. A lease must be treated as a capital lease if, at its inception, it meets *one or more* of the following criteria:

- The lease arrangement provides for a transfer of the property's ownership to the lessee by the end of the lease term.

- There is a *bargain purchase* option in the lease. A bargain purchase option is basically one in which the lessee has a right to purchase the property for a price which is so far below its anticipated fair market value, at the time it can be exercised, that it is likely the lessee will elect to buy the property.

- The term of the lease is for a period of at least 75 percent of the property's *estimated* economic useful life.

- The present value of the "minimum lease payments" at the inception of the lease (excluding any executory costs included in the payments such as insurance, maintenance, and taxes which the lessor will pay and any profits on such costs) is equal to or greater than 90 percent of the fair market value of the leased property (reduced by any investment tax credit claimed and expected to be realized by the lessor) determined at the beginning of the lease. The present value computation is calculated by discounting the payments at the lower of the lessor's implicit lease interest rate or the interest rate the lessee would have to pay for a loan running the length of the lease term (the lessee's "incremental borrowing rate"). If the lessee is unable to determine the lessor's implicit lease rate of interest, the lessee must use its borrowing rate to make the present value computation. FASB No. 13 defines "minimum lease payments" as those payments which the lessee is obligated to make or can be required to make. This includes minimum rent payments, residual value guarantees, and penalty payments for failure to renew or extend the lease.

If the lease does not meet any of the above criteria, it will be classified as an *operating* lease.

ILLUSTRATIVE EXAMPLE—
THE PRESENT VALUE TEST:

Company A is considering leasing a new truck from Company B. Will the present value test for capital lease classification be met? The facts are as follows:

Noncancelable Lease Term	5 Years
Monthly Rent (in arrears)	$180
Fair Market Value at Lease Inception	$10,000
Truck's Estimated Useful Life	6 Years
Executory Costs	To Be Paid by Company A
Investment Tax Credit	Passed Through to Lessee
Company A's Borrowing Rate	10%
Company B's Implicit Lease Rate	Unknown to Company A

In this example the minimum lease payments are the rental payments. The present value of the monthly rental payments computed by discounting the future rent payment stream by 10% per annum is equal to $8472. Ninety percent of the truck's fair market value at the beginning of the lease is $9000. Since the present value of the rental stream is less than $9000, the present value test for capital lease classification is not met.

C. THE ACCOUNTING REQUIREMENTS HAVE AN IMPACT ON A LESSEE

The way a lessee must account for a lease in its financial statements depends on its classification, i.e., whether it falls within the capital or operating lease category. If a lease is classified as a capital lease, the lessee must record it both as an asset and an obligation at an amount equal to the present value of the minimum lease payments. Executory costs included in the payments, such as insurance, maintenance, and taxes which the lessor must pay, and any profit on these costs must be excluded before making the present value computation. If, however, the minimum lease payment present value amount turns out to be greater than the property's "fair value" (essentially the property's purchase cost) determined at the beginning of the lease, then the fair value is to be recorded.

The lease payment present value calculation is to be made in the same manner as it is when determining whether a lease meets the present value criteria for capital lease classification. In other words the payment stream is to be discounted at the lower of the lessee's incremental borrowing rate for a loan of a similar term or the lessor's implicit lease interest rate. If the lessee does not know the lessor's implicit interest rate, the incremental borrowing rate is to be used.

A lessee must write off (amortize) a capital lease according to certain specific rules. Which rule must be followed depends on which of the four capital lease classification criteria is met. For example, if the lease meets the first or second criterion, i.e., if the ownership of the property is transferred to the lessee at the end of the lease term or the lessee has a bargain purchase option, the lessee must write it off in a manner consistent with its usual depreciation practice for assets it owns. If the lease does not meet either of these two criteria, the lessee must amortize the property, over a period equal to the lease term, in a manner consistent with its normal depreciation practice down to a value it expects the property to be worth at the end of the lease.

A lease categorized as an *operating* lease must be accounted for in a much different manner by a lessee than one which is classified as a capital lease. Generally, the rental payments will be charged to expense as they become due on a straight line basis, whether or not they are in fact payable on a straight line basis. There is, however, an exception to the straight line reporting rule. If another systematic and rational method for reflecting the property's use benefit exists, that method may be used in reporting the rent expense.

RECOMMENDATION:

The difference in reporting impact between a capital lease and an operating lease is significant. If a prospective lessee does not want a lease obligation to appear as a long-term liability, he must make sure that it will be classified as an operating lease. If it cannot be so treated, and there are no other compelling reasons to lease, the possibility of purchasing the asset should be carefully considered in view of the effect on its financial picture.

D. THE LEASE CLASSIFICATION CATEGORIES FOR A LESSOR ARE EXTENSIVE.

From the standpoint of *lessor* accounting, FASB No. 13 provides that all leases must be categorized as either *sales-type* leases, *direct financing* leases, *leveraged* leases, or *operating* leases. Each category has certain specific attributes which must be carefully taken into account by a lessor when making the classification determination.

OBSERVATION:

It is interesting to note that whether or not a lease is considered to be a leveraged lease under FASB No. 13 has no impact from a lessee's standpoint. That is, as far as a lessee is concerned even though a lease is leveraged with third-party debt it must be classified and accounted for, depending on the criteria satisfied, as either a capital lease or an operating lease.

A lease will be classified as a *sales-type* lease if all of the following tests are met:

- The lease gives rise to a dealer's or manufacturer's profit, *or loss.*

- One or more of the lessee criteria for capital lease classification are met.

- The minimum lease payment collectibility is reasonably predictable.

- There are no important uncertainties as to the unreimbursable costs which the lessor has not yet incurred.

A dealer's or manufacturer's profit, or loss, will exist if the fair market value of the leased equipment at the beginning of the lease is greater, or less as the case may be, than the lessor's cost, or carrying amount if different than the cost. The profit test is usually met when an equipment manufacturer or dealer leases, instead of sells, his equipment to a lessee. In this case the fair market value of the equipment will typically be greater than his cost or carrying amount.

OBSERVATION:

There are situations under FASB No. 13 when a lessor could accrue a dealer's or manufacturer's type of profit, or loss, without actually being a dealer or manufacturer. The lease accounting rules provide that a sales-type lease can exist if the equipment's fair market value at the lease inception is greater, or less, than the lessor's cost or carrying amount if this amount is different than the cost. Such a situation could conceivably exist for any lessor.

The criteria for determining whether a lease will be classified as a *direct financing* lease is easy to understand once the governing rules for a sales-type lease have been mastered. Very simply, a lease will be a direct financing lease if, at its inception, *all* of the following five tests are satisfied:

- One or more of the criteria for *lessee* capital lease classification has been met.

- The lease does not fall within the category of leveraged lease.

- The lease does not give rise to a dealer's or manufacturer's profit or loss.

- The collectibility of the rent payments are reasonably predictable.

- There are no important uncertainties as to the amount of unreimbursable costs which the lessor will incur under the lease.

Ascertaining whether a lease will be categorized as a *leveraged* lease is somewhat more complex than determining whether it is a sales-type lease or a direct financing lease. Basically, if a lease meets all of the following criteria it will be considered a leveraged lease.

- The criteria for classification as a direct financing lease is met.

- No less than three participants, a lessee, a lessor, and a long-term lender, are involved.

- The long term debt is nonrecourse as to the general credit of the lessor.

- The principal amount of the long term debt will substantially leverage the lessor's investment.

- The lessor's net investment goes down in the early lease years after it has been fully committed and goes up in the later lease years before it is entirely eliminated.

The definition of an *operating* lease is straightforward. It is simply a lease that does not qualify as a direct financing lease, a sales-type lease, or a leveraged lease.

E. THE LESSOR'S ACCOUNTING REQUIREMENTS ARE COMPLEX

FASB No. 13 carefully details how lessors must account for sales-type, direct financing, leveraged, and operating leases. The rules are complex and a lessor must make sure they are clearly understood before committing to a lease transaction, in order to avoid an undesirable accounting treatment.

1. For a Sales-Type Lease

If a lease fits within the sales-type lease category, a lessor must record his *gross investment* in the lease. The lessor's gross investment is essentially the sum of the lease rents and other minimum lease payments and the equipment's unguaranteed residual value. The minimum lease payment sum must be computed net of any executory costs included in the payments, such as insurance, maintenance, and taxes, which the lessor must pay and any profit on such costs.

The lessor must also record the lease's *unearned income*. Unearned income is defined as the difference between the lessor's gross investment and the sum of the present values of the minimum lease payments, adjusted for certain executory costs and the equipment's unguaranteed residual value. The present value computations are to be made using the implicit lease interest rate as the discount rate. In general, the lease's unearned income must be amortized to income over the lease term in such a manner so as to produce a constant periodic rate of return on the lessor's *net investment* in the lease. Net investment is the difference between the gross investment and the unearned income.

The accounting rules require that the lessor's net investment in a lease be treated in the same way as other current or noncurrent assets in a classified balance sheet. The rules also require that any *contingent rents* be credited to income at such time as they become receivable.

The equipment's *sales price*, defined as the present value of the minimum lease payments, net of certain executory costs and any profits on such costs, must also be recorded. The equipment's cost (or carrying amount if different), increased by any initial negotiation and cosummation expenses such as legal fees and reduced by the present value of the lessor's unguaranteed residual value, must be charged against income. The present value computation is to be made using a discount rate equal to the implicit lease interest rate.

The leased equipment's *residual value* is given special attention. The rules require a lessor to review the estimated value used in the required computations on an annual basis. If the value experiences a permanent decline, the reporting criteria must be adjusted accordingly. If, on the other hand, there has been an increase in the expected residual value no adjustments are permitted.

2. For a Direct Financing Lease

A lessor must account for a direct financing lease in somewhat the same manner as a sales-type lease. As with a sales-type lease, he must record his *gross investment* in the lease. Gross investment is defined in the same way as it is for a sales-type lease. *Unearned income,* defined for a direct financing lease as simply the difference between the lessor's gross investment and the equipment's cost, must also be recorded. In the event the carrying amount of the equipment is different than its cost, the carrying amount must instead be used in making this computation.

The lessor's *net investment* in the lease, defined as the gross investment minus unearned income, is to be classified under the same considerations as other current or noncurrent assets in a classified balance sheet. Any *contingent rents* must be credited to income when they become due.

The rules make special mention of the *initial direct costs* of putting a lease transaction together, such as commissions or legal fees. These costs must be expensed against income when they are incurred. The lessor must also recognize, as income for that period against any such charge, an amount of unearned income equal to the initial direct costs. The amount of unearned income remaining must be treated in the same manner as unearned income is in a sales-type lease situation, i.e., generally amortized "to income" over the remaining term in such a way as to show a constant periodic return rate on the lessor's net investment.

The equipment's estimated *residual value* must be annually reviewed. If a permanent decrease in the value estimate has occurred, the computations incorporating the value must be adjusted accordingly. No adjustments are allowed to reflect an increase in the value estimate.

3. For an Operating Lease

If a lease is deemed to be an operating lease, the accounting treatment is somewhat simpler for a lessor than if the lease is a sales-type or direct financing lease. Equipment subject to such a lease must be recorded on the lessor's balance sheet in or near the "property, plant, and equipment" category. In addition, the equipment must be depreciated in accordance with the lessor's usual depreciation policy, and the investment in the equipment is to be shown reduced by the accumulated depreciation.

The rent received under an operating lease is handled in a straightforward manner. It is reported as income when and as due and is taken in on a straight line basis, regardless of how the rent is actually received. There is, however, an exception to this requirement. If any other systematic method for reporting the rent income would more accurately reflect the reduction in the property's use benefit, then that method may be used.

Any *initial direct costs* incurred by the lessor in connection with putting the transaction together cannot, in general, be treated as they are in a direct financing lease situation. They must be written off over the term of the lease in proportion to how the rent income is recognized. They may, however, be expensed when incurred if the effect would not be materially different than it would be under the deferred treatment.

4. For a Leveraged Lease

The lessor's *investment* in a leveraged lease must be stated net of the transaction's *nonrecourse* debt. The lessor's investment at any point in time is computed by adding together (a) the rents receivable, minus the portion going to pay the debt service on the nonrecourse debt; (b) a receivable for any investment tax credit amount to be realized; (c) the equipment's estimated residual value; and (d) the transaction's *unearned and deferred income.* The unearned and deferred income at any point is defined as the sum of the lease's estimated remaining and unallocated pre-tax income or loss, adjusted by subtracting any initial direct costs, and any investment tax credit that has not yet been allocated to income over the lease term.

The lessor is also required to determine the *rate of return* on his *net investment* during the years it is positive. The rate of return is defined as that rate which when applied to the net investment during the years it is positive will distribute the net income to these years. The lessor's *net investment* in a leveraged lease is simply the lessor's investment reduced by the deferred taxes arising because of the difference between the lessor's pretax accounting income and its taxable income.

As with a sales-type lease and a direct financing lease, the lessor must review the estimated residual value of the equipment each year and adjust it downward if it appears to have undergone a permanent reduction over that originally estimated. If an adjustment is necessary, certain other recalculations are necessary using the new residual assumption. No upward adjustment is permitted if there has been an estimated increase in the residual value.

F. ACCOUNTING RULES GOVERNING SALE-LEASEBACK SITUATIONS

Because many leases arise though sale-leaseback transactions, it is worthwhile mentioning the governing lease accounting rules. A "sale-leaseback" is defined as a transaction in which an owner sells equipment to a third party and leases it back. The purchaser will then be the lessor and the original owner will become the lessee.

From the lessee's viewpoint the lease accounting rules are the same as in any lease situation. That is, if the lease would otherwise have to be classified as a capital lease, it will still be considered as a capital lease. If it qualifies as an operating lease, it will still be accounted for as an operating lease. The reporting of the *profit* or *loss* from the equipment's sale, however, is specially treated. If the lease is a capital lease, the seller-lessee must defer any profit or loss resulting from the sale to the lessor-purchaser and amortize it in proportion to the amortization of the leased equipment. If the lease is classified as an operating lease, any profit or loss must be amortized in proportion to the rents over the period the equipment is expected to be used. There is, however, an exception to both situations. If the property's fair market value is less than the equipment's undepreciated cost when the sale-leaseback occurs, the difference must immediately be taken as a loss.

From the lessor's standpoint, if the lease meets the criteria for a sales-type lease or a direct financing lease it must be treated as a purchase and a direct financing lease. If it does not, it must be accounted for as a purchase and an operating lease.

G. WILL THE NEW RULES AFFECT THE DESIRABILITY OF LEASING FOR A LESSEE?

Because of the many factors to be considered in a lease decision it is hard to estimate the impact the new accounting rules will have on an equipment user. It is fairly safe to assume, however, that the new rules will not increase the attractiveness of leasing from a prospective lessee's viewpoint. Equipment under leases which are classified as capital leases must be treated in a manner similar to owned equipment. Therefore, from a financial reporting standpoint the question arises in each such situation whether an asset should really be purchased rather than leased.

H. A LEASE CLASSIFICATION CHECKLIST FOR LESSEES

The following checklist may be used by a lessee as a general guide in classifying its leases for accounting and reporting purposes.

1. If a Lease Meets One or More of the Following Criteria, Has It Been Classified as a Capital Lease?

    a. Does the Lease Transfer the Equipment's Ownership to the Lessee by the End of the Lease?

    b. Does the Lessee Have the Right to Purchase the Leased Equipment at a Price Well Below Its Value at the Time the Right Can Be Exercised?

    c. Does the Lease Run for a Term Which Is Equal to or Greater Than 75 Percent of the Equipment's Estimated Economic Useful Life? (This Rule Does Not Apply if at the Time the Lease Is Signed the Equipment Only Has a Remaining Useful Life of 25 Percent or Less of Its Original Life.)

    d. Is the Present Value of the Rent and Other Minimum Lease Payments, Net of Certain Executory Costs and Profits on Such Costs, Equal to or Greater Than 90 Percent of the Equipment's Fair Market Value as of the Lease Inception, Minus Any Investment Tax Credit to be Retained by the Lessor?

2. If the Lessee Knows the Implicit Lease Rate Computed by the Lessor and It Is Lower Than the Lessee's Incremental Borrowing Rate, Has the Present Value Test in Item 1d Been Computed Using This Rate.

    a. If It Is Not Lower, Has the Value Been Calculated Using the Lessee's Incremental Borrowing Rate?

3. If a Lease Does Not Meet *Any* of the Tests in Item 1, Has It Been Classified as an Operating Lease?

I. A LEASE CLASSIFICATION CHECKLIST FOR LESSORS

The following checklist may be used by a lessor as a general guide in classifying its leases for accounting and reporting purposes.

1. A Lease Must Be Classified as a Sales-Type Lease if It Meets All of the Following:

    a. The Lessor Incurs a Manufacturer's or Dealer's Type of Profit or Loss.

    b. The Lease Meets at Least One of the Following Criteria:

        (1) The Lease Transfers the Equipment's Onwership to the Lessee by the End of the Lease.

        (2) The Lessee Has the Right to Purchase the Leased Equipment at a Price Well Below Its Expected Fair Market Value at the Time the Right Can Be Exercised.

        (3) The Lease Runs for a Term Which Is Equal to or Greater Than 75 Percent of the Equipment's Estimated Economic Useful Life. (This Rule Does Not Apply if at the Time the Lease Is Signed the Equipment Only Has a Remaining Useful Life of 25 Percent or Less of Its Original Life.)

        (4) The Present Value of the Rent and Other Minimum Lease Payments, Net of Certain Executory Costs and Profits on

Such Costs, Is Equal to or Greater Than 90 Percent of the Equipment's Fair Market Value as of the Lease Inception, Minus Any Investment Tax Credit to Be Retained by the Lessor.

c. The Collectibility of the Rent and Other Minimum Lease Payments Are Reasonably Predictable.

d. There Are No Important Uncertainties Concerning the Lessor's Yet to Be Incurred Unreimbursable Costs.

2. A Lease (Other Than a Leveraged Lease) Must Be Classified as a Direct Financing Lease if It Meets All of the Following:

a. The Lessor Does Not Incur a Manufacturer's or Dealer's Type of Profit or Loss.

b. The Lease Meets at Least One of the Following Criteria:

(1) The Lease Transfers the Equipment's Ownership to the Lessee by the End of the Lease.

(2) The Lessee Has the Right to Purchase the Leased Equipment at a Price Well Below Its Expected Fair Market Value at the Time the Right Can Be Exercised.

(3) The Lease Runs for a Term Which Is Equal to or Greater Than 75 Percent of the Equipment's Estimated Economic Useful Life. (This Rule Does Not Apply if at the Time the Lease Is Signed the Equipment Only Has a Remaining Useful Life of 25 Percent or Less of Its Original Life.)

(4) The Present Value of the Rent and Other Minimum Lease Payments, Net of Certain Executory Costs and Profits on Such Costs, Is Equal to or Greater Than 90 Percent of the Equipment's Fair Market Value as of the Lease Inception, Minus Any Investment Tax Credit to Be Retained by the Lessor.

c. The Collectibility of the Rent and Other Minimum Lease Payments Are Reasonably Predictable.

d. There Are No Important Uncertainties Concerning the Lessor's Yet to Be Incurred Unreimbursable Costs.

3. A Lease Must Be Classified as a Leveraged Lease if All of the Following Criteria Are Met:

a. The Lease Qualifies as a Direct Financing Lease.

b. The Lease Involves at Least Three Parties—a Lessee, a Long Term Lender, and a Lessor.

c. The Long Term Debt Financing Is on a Nonrecourse-to-Lessor Basis.

d. The Amount of Long-Term Debt Will Substantially Leverage the Lessor's Invested Funds.

e. The Lessor's "Net Investment" Goes Down in the Early Lease Years Once Made and Rises During the Later Lease Years Before Eliminated.

f. Any Investment Tax Credit Will Not Be Accounted for Using the "Flow Through" Method.
4. If the Lease Does Not Qualify as a Sales-Type Lease, a Direct Financing Lease, or a Leveraged Lease, It Must Be Classified as an Operating Lease.
5. If the Lease Arises Out of a Sales-Leaseback Transaction, Have the Governing Rules Been Checked?

11

EQUIPMENT LEASE TERMINOLOGY—

THE DEFINITIONS

The Leasing Industry Has Its Own "Language" • Knowing What The Terms Mean Is Essential To Intelligent Negotiation.

The following terms have been explained according to their common usage in the leasing industry:

ACCEPTANCE SUPPLEMENT. A document in which a lessee acknowledges that certain specified equipment is acceptable for lease. It is generally used in transactions where the lease document is entered into well in advance of the equipment delivery. It serves to notify the lessor that the equipment has been delivered, inspected, and accepted for lease as of a specified date. The typical form requires the lessee to list certain pertinent information, including the equipment manufacturer, purchase price, serial number, and location.

ASSET DEPRECIATION RANGE SYSTEM (ADR). ADR is a method prescribed by Section 167(m) of the Internal Revenue Code of 1954, as amended, which may be used in computing depreciation deductions for certain assets. A range of useful lives is given for specified assets from which a taxpayer may select a depreciation period. The lives listed are generally shorter than the period over which an asset may be depreciated under the "facts and circumstances" method of depreciation.

ADRINDEMNITY. A form of tax indemnification given by the lessee to the lessor covering equipment depreciated in accordance with the ADR method. The lessee, in effect, guarantees the lessor against loss of, or inability to claim, anticipated ADR tax benefits. This type of indemnification is frequently found in a finance lease.

ADVANCE RENTAL. The term refers to any payment in the form of rent made prior to the start of the lease term. It is also sometimes used to describe a rental payment program in which the lessee pays all rentals, on a per period basis, at the start of each rental payment period. For example, a quarterly, in advance, rental program requires the lessee to pay one-fourth of the annual rental at the start of each consecutive three month period during the lease term.

BALLOON PAYMENT. Balloon payments are commonly found in mortgage financings and refer to a final payment that is larger than the periodic term payments. Usually it results because the debt has not been fully amortized during the repayment period. For example, a one year financing arrangement providing for interest-only monthly payments during the year, with the principal plus the last interest payment due on the final payment date, is said to have a "balloon payment" or simply a "balloon" due at the end of the term.

BAREBOAT CHARTER PARTY. A form of net financial lease relating to vessels. Also sometimes referred to simply as a "bareboat charter."

BENEFICIAL INTEREST HOLDER. Refers to a beneficial, as opposed to legal (title), owner. For example, when a trust has been created by the equity participants to act as the lessor, the equity participants are deemed the holders of beneficial interest. They hold interests in the trust which owns the equipment.

BOND. An instrument which represents a long-term debt obligation. The debt instruments, sometimes referred to as loan certificates, issued in a leveraged lease transaction are referred to as bonds or notes.

BOOK REPORTING. The reporting of income or loss for financial, as opposed to tax, purposes on the "books" of the corporation or other reporting entity.

BOOK RESIDUAL VALUE. The amount of equipment residual value which a lessor uses, or "books", at the end of the lease term for the purposes of calculating his return on a lease transaction.

BROKER. In the leasing industry a broker is a person or entity who, for compensation, arranges lease transactions for another's account. A broker is also referred to as a "syndicator" or "underwriter."

CALL. A fixed price purchase option. It describes the right a lessee may have to buy specified leased equipment for a predetermined fixed price. The price is usually expressed as a percentage of original cost. Commonly, if given, such an option does not become exercisable until the end of the lease term, and it lapses if the lessee fails to give the lessor timely notice of its intention to exercise it. For example, a lessee may have a right to buy equipment at the end of the lease term for 30% of original cost, notice of intention to exercise the option to be given not less than ninety days prior to the end of the lease term.

CASH FLOW. In a lease transaction this usually refers to the amount of actual cash a lease generates for a lessor.

CASUALTY VALUE. A predetermined amount of money that a lessee guarantees the lessor will receive in the event of an equipment casualty loss during the lease term. The value varies depending on the period during the lease term in which the loss occurs. It is generally expressed as a percentage of original cost. It is also referred to as a "stipulated loss value."

CHARTER PARTY. A document which provides for the lease (charter) of a vessel or vessels. The format is basically the same as any other lease. There are certain additions and modifications in order to reflect the requirements dictated by a vessel transaction.

CHARTERER. In the case of vessels, the lessee.

CHATTEL MORTGAGE. A mortgage relating to personal property. A mortgage on equipment would be considered a chattel mortgage.

COLLATERAL. In general, the term refers to assets used as security for the repayment of a debt obligation. The term is also used to describe equipment which is the subject of a lease.

COMMISSION AGREEMENT. An agreement entered into between a lease broker and a prospective equity participant providing for the payment of a fee to the broker for services in arranging a lease transaction.

CONDITIONAL SALES AGREEMENT. A contract that provides for the time financing of asset purchases. The seller retains title to the assets until all the conditions, such as installment payments, have been fulfilled. At that time title is automatically vested in the purchaser. Also referred to simply as a "CSA."

COMMITMENT FEE. Compensation paid to a lender in return for an agreeement to make a future loan. It also refers to a flat fee paid to a lessor for its commitment to lease equipment to a company in the future.

COST OF MONEY. Commonly, the cost which a lessor incurs to borrow money under, for example, its bank lines of credit. This includes the interest rate and any additional costs related to such borrowing, such as fees or compensating balances. In pricing a lease transaction, a lessor factors this cost into the computation.

COST-TO-CUSTOMER. The simple interest rate on a lease transaction.

DDB/SYD/TAN. A technique of switching methods of depreciation to maximize early depreciation write-offs. Depreciation deductions are initially computed using the double-declining balance method with an appropriately timed change to the sum-of-the-years-digits method followed by another appropriately timed change to the straight line method.

DEBT SERVICE. The aggregate annual repayment amount, including principal and interest, due on a loan.

DEBT PARTICIPANT. A long-term lender in a leveraged lease transaction. Frequently a leveraged lease transaction has more than one "debt participant."

DEFAULT. In a lease transaction it is a breach of a designated lease obligation.

DELIVERY AND ACCEPTANCE CERTIFICATE. The same as an Acceptance Supplement.

DEPRECIATION INDEMNITY. A tax indemnification given by a lessee against the lessor's loss of anticipated depreciation tax benefits on leased equipment. It is frequently found in a finance lease.

DEFICIENCY GUARANTEE. A guarantee given to a lessor by a third party, such as an equipment vendor or manufacturer, to induce a lessor to enter into a lease which it would not otherwise enter into. The prospective lessee may be a poor credit risk or the future value of equipment may be highly speculative. For example, a deficiency guarantor may agree to pay the lessor for any shortfall below a designated amount, say 20% of original cost, incurred when the equipment is sold at the end of the lease.

DISCOUNTED CASH FLOW ANALYSIS. The process of determining the present value of future cash flows.

EQUIPMENT CERTIFICATE OF ACCEPTANCE. The same as an Acceptance Supplement.

EQUITY PARTICIPANT. The equity investor in a leveraged lease. Frequently, a leveraged lease transaction has more than one equity participant. An equity participant is also sometimes referred to as an "owner participant."

FACTS AND CIRCUMSTANCES DEPRECIATION. A method of determining the depreciable life of an asset. Under the facts and circumstances method, the useful life determination is based upon the experience with similar property giving due consideration to current and anticipated future conditions, such as wear and tear; normal progress of the art; economic changes, inventions, and current developments within the industry and the taxpayer's trade or business; climatic and other relevant local conditions which may affect the taxpayer's repair, renewal, and replacement program.

FAIR MARKET PURCHASE VALUE. The value of an asset as determined in the open market in an arm's length transaction under normal selling conditions. It is also referred to simply as the "fair market value."

FAIR MARKET RENTAL VALUE. The rental rate which an asset would command in the open market in an arm's length transaction under normal renting conditions. It is also referred to simply as the "fair rental value."

FINANCE LEASE. The same as a Full Payout Lease.

FINANCING AGREEMENT. An agreement commonly entered into by the principal parties to a leveraged lease prior to equipment delivery. The agreement identifies each party's obligation to the transaction and any conditions that must be satisfied before the obligations are fixed. Typically, it will involve the debt and equity participants, their representatives, and the lessee. It is also referred to as a "participation agreement."

FLOATING RENTAL RATE. A form of periodic rental payments which change or "float" upward and downward over the term of the lease with changes in a specified interest rate. Frequently, a designated bank's prime rate is the measuring interest rate.

FULL PAYOUT LEASE. A form of lease which will provide the lessor with a cash flow generally sufficient to return his equipment investment; pay the principal, interest and other financing costs on related debt; cover his related sales and administration expenses; and generate a profit. The cash flow is determined from the rental payments, the ownership tax benefits, and the equipment residual value. The lessee typically has the right to the use of the leased asset for most of its actual useful life.

GROSS INCOME TAX. A tax imposed by a taxing authority on gross income generated from sources within its jurisdiction. The tax is deductible by the taxpayer for Federal income tax purposes.

"GROSSING UP." A lessee obligated to reimburse a lessor for any monetary loss incurred, as a result, for example, of a tax indemnification provision, will frequently have to "gross up" any such payment by paying the lessor sufficient additional monies so that the after-tax amount will equal the lessor's loss. The lessor is said to be made "whole" for his loss since the amount paid must take into account any taxes he will have to pay as a result of the receipt of the monies from the lessee. The concept is commonly found in finance leases.

GUARANTEED RESIDUAL VALUE. The term describes an arrangement in which, for example, a broker or equipment manufacturer guarantees that a lessor will receive not less than a certain amount for specified equipment when it is disposed of at the end of the lease term. It is also sometimes referred to simply as a "guaranteed residual."

HELL OR HIGH WATER CLAUSE. A lease provision which commits a lessee to absolutely and unconditionally pay the rent. The lessee waives any right which exists or may arise to withhold any rent from the lessor or any assignee of the lessor for any reason whatsoever, including any set-off, counterclaim, recoupment, or defense. Finance lease agreements commonly contain this type of clause.

HIGH-LOW RENTAL. A rental structure in which the rent payments are "stepped" from a higher rate to a lower rate at a prescribed point in the lease term.

INDEMNITY AGREEMENT. A contract in which one party commits to insure another party against anticipated and specified losses.

INDENTURE TRUSTEE. Lenders in a leveraged lease transaction frequently lend through a trust arrangement and, in such event, a representative is appointed, the indenture trustee, to carry out the terms of the trust. As the lenders' representative the indenture trustee may, for example, have to effect and maintain a security interest in the equipment, receive rentals from the lessee, pay out the proper amounts to the lenders and the lessor, and take certain action to protect the outstanding loan in the event of a loan default.

INSTITUTIONAL INVESTORS. Institutions which invest in lease transactions are sometimes referred to as "institutional investors." They can be, for example, insurance companies, pension funds, banks, and trusts.

INSURED VALUE. The same as Casualty Value.

ITC INDEMNITY. A type of indemnification in which the lessee commits to reimburse the lessor for any financial loss incurred through the loss of, or inability to claim, any or all of the anticipated equipment investment tax credit. If the lessor has "passed through" the ITC to the lessee, the lessor may have to give the indemnity. The indemnity is frequently found in finance leases.

ITC "PASS-THROUGH." An election made by the lessor to treat, for the purpose of the investment tax credit available under Section 38 of the Internal Revenue Code, the lessee as the purchaser of the equipment subject to lease. Under such an election, a lessee can claim the investment tax credit on the equipment covered by the election.

INVESTMENT TAX CREDIT (ITC). A credit allowed against Federal income tax liability, pursuant to Section 38 of the Internal Revenue Code. It can be claimed by a taxpayer for certain "section 38 property" acquired and placed in service by a taxpayer during a taxable year.

LAY OFF. A term that commonly refers to the sale by a lessor of his interest in the lease agreement, including the onwership of the leased equipment and the right to receive the rent payments.

LEASE AGREEMENT. A contractual arrangement in which an owner of equipment, the lessor, transfers its use subject to the specified terms and conditions to another, the lessee, for a prescribed period of time and rental rate.

LEASE LINE. A present commitment by a lessor to lease specified equipment to be delivered in the future. A "lease line" can cover a variety of types of equipment, at varying rental rates and lease terms. It is also referred to as a "lease line of credit."

LEASE UNDERWRITING. The process in which a lease broker arranges, or "puts together" a lease transaction for the account of third parties—a prospective lessor and a prospective lessee. This can be on a "best efforts" basis or on a "firm commitment" basis. In a "best efforts" underwriting the broker only offers to diligently attempt to arrange the financing on certain proposed terms. In a "firm commitment" underwriting the broker in effect guarantees to arrange the financing as proposed.

LESSEE. The user of equipment which is the subject of a lease agreement.

LESSOR. The owner of equipment which is the subject of a lease agreement.

LEVEL PAYMENTS. The term refers to payments which are equal for each payment period during the payment term. Frequently, rent and debt service payments will be paid in level payments over the payment period.

LEVERAGED LEASE. A lease in which a portion, generally 60% to 80%, of the acquisition cost of the equipment is borrowed from a bank or other lending institution with the remainder coming from the lessor. The debt is commonly on a nonrecourse basis and the rental payments are usually sufficient to cover the loan debt service.

LOW-HIGH RENTAL. The reverse of a high-low rental.

LOAN CERTIFICATE. A certificate which evidences a debt obligation.

LOAN PARTICIPANT. A debt participant.

MANAGEMENT AGREEMENT. A contract in which one party agrees to manage a lease transaction during its term, including, for example, rental payment processing and equipment disposal.

MANAGEMENT FEE. A fee which a lease transaction manager receives for services performed under a management agreement.

MASTER LEASE AGREEMENT. The term is commonly used to describe a lease agreement which easily permits future equipment not contemplated when the lease is executed to be added. The document is set up in two parts. The main body contains the general, or "boiler plate" provisions, such as the maintenance and indemnification provisions. An annex, or "schedule," contains the type of items which usually vary with a transaction, such as rental rates and options.

MORTAGE. A mortgage is an arrangement whereby a lender (mortgagee) acquires a lien on property owned by a taxpayer (mortgagor) as security for the repayment of the loan. Once the debt obligation has been fully satisfied, the mortgage lien is terminated.

NEGATIVE SPREAD. The amount by which a value is below a certain prescribed amount. Generally "negative spread" in a leveraged lease is the amount by which the transaction's simple interest rate is below the leveraged debt interest rate.

NET LEASE. A lease arrangement in which the lessor's rental payments are "net." That is, all costs, such as maintenance, certain taxes, and insurance, related to the use of the leased equipment are to be paid directly by the lessee. They are not included as part of the rental payments. Typically, finance leases are net leases.

NONPAYOUT LEASE. A lease arrangement which does not, over the primary term of the lease, generate enough cash flow to return all or substantially all of the lessor's investment, debt financing costs, and sales and administration expenses.

NONRECOURSE DEBT FINANCING. Many transactions are leveraged through the use of outside debt. In most cases, the debt is supplied on a nonrecourse basis. This means the lender has agreed to look solely to the lessee and the equipment for repayment of the loan. As security for the loan repayment, the lender receives an assignment of the lessor's rights under the lease agreement and a grant of a first lien on the equipment. Although the lessor has no obligation to repay the debt in the event of a lessee default, his equity investment in the equipment is usually subordinated to the rights of the lender.

NON-UTILIZATION FEE. A fee which a lessor may impose in return for its present commitment to purchase and lease specified equipment in the future. The fee is generally expressed as a percentage of the aggregate unused portion of the initial dollar commitment. For example, 1% of the unused balance of a $1,000,000 lease line of credit. Therefore, if all the commitment is used, no fee is payable.

OPERATING LEASE. In the non-accounting sense, it is a form of lease arrangement in which the lessor generally commits to provide certain additional equipment related services, other than the straight financing, such as maintenance, repairs, or technical advice. In general, operating leases are nonpayout in nature.

OPTION. A right. The party holding an option in his favor may exercise the option pursuant to the granting terms. For example, a fair market value purchase option in a lease is the right to purchase the equipment covered by it for its fair market value.

PACKAGER. A syndicator. A person or entity who arranges a lease transaction for third parties. Also referred to as an underwriter or sometimes a broker.

PARTICIPATION AGREEMENT. The same as a Financing Agreement.

PORTFOLIO LEASE. The term commonly refers to a lease which is entered into by a "professional" lessor for his own account and investment.

PRESENT VALUE. The term refers to the present worth of a future stream of payments calculated by discounting the future payments at a desired interest rate.

PROGRESS PAYMENTS. The term refers to payments which may be required by an equipment manufacturer or builder during the construction period toward the purchase price. These payments are frequently required for costly equipment with a long construction period. They are designed to lessen the manufacturer's or builder's need to tie up his own funds during construction.

PURCHASE OPTION. A right to purchase. In a lease transaction it represents the right to purchase agreed-upon equipment at the times and for the amounts specified. Frequently, such options are only exercisable at the end of the primary lease term, although they sometimes may be exercised during the primary lease term or at the end of any renewal term.

PUT. In lease arrangements, if present, it describes a right which a lessor may have to sell specified leased equipment to the lessee at a fixed price at the end of the initial lease term. It is usually imposed to protect the lessor's residual value assumption.

RECOURSE DEBT FINANCING. If a lease is leveraged with recourse debt, the lender may look to the lessor in addition to the lessee and the equipment for repayment of any outstanding loan obligation. The lender is said to have "recourse" against the lessor.

RENEWAL OPTION. An option frequently given to a lessee to renew the lease term for a specified rental and time period.

RESIDUAL SHARING. A compensation technique sometimes used by syndicators for arranging a lease transaction. Under this, the equity participants must pay a predetermined percentage of what the equipment is sold for at the end of the lease. For example, a syndicator may get 50% of any amount realized in excess of 20% of the equipment's original cost upon sale.

RESIDUAL VALUE. The value of leased equipment at the end of the lease term.

REVENUE RULING. A written opinion issued by the Internal Revenue Service setting forth its position on the tax treatment of a proposed transaction. The parties to an underwritten leveraged lease transaction frequently seek a Revenue Ruling.

RIGHT OF FIRST REFUSAL. In a lease transaction it is the right of the lessee to purchase the leased equipment, or renew the lease, at the end of the lease term for an amount equal to that offered by an unaffiliated third party.

SLV. Stipulated loss value.

SALE-LEASEBACK. An arrangement in which an equipment purchaser buys equipment for the purpose of leasing it back to the seller.

SALES TAX. A tax imposed on the sale of equipment.

SALVAGE VALUE. The amount, estimated for Federal income tax purposes, which an asset is expected to be worth at the end of its useful life.

SECTION 38 PROPERTY. Tangible personal property, as defined by Section 38 of the Internal Revenue Code, which is depreciable (or amortizable), has a useful life of not less than three years, and is not used in certain prohibited ways.

SECURITY AGREEMENT. In a leveraged lease transaction, it is an agreement which evidences an assignment by the lessor to the lender, as security for the loan, of the lessor's rights under the lease agreement and a granting of a security interest in the equipment.

SIMPLE INTEREST. The amount by which the annual lease rent exceeds the amortization of the cost of the equipment.

SINKING FUND. A fund frequently established in leveraged lease transactions by the lessor to accumulate funds to pay for future taxes. A reserve fund.

SINKING FUND RATE. The interest rate that a sinking fund is deemed to earn on accumulated funds.

SPECIAL PURPOSE EQUIPMENT. Equipment which has a substantive economic use only to the user because, for example, of its immobility or unique nature.

SPREAD. The difference between two values. In a lease transaction the term is generally used to describe the difference between the lease simple interest rate and the interest rate on the debt.

STIPULATED LOSS VALUE. The same as Casualty Value.

SUBLEASE. The re-lease by a lessee of equipment which is on lease to the lessee.

TAKE OR PAY CONTRACT. Generally refers to an agreement in which one party commits to purchase an agreed-upon quantity of goods or material from another at a predetermined price. If the goods or material are not so purchased, the party making the purchase commitment must pay the party an amount of money equal to the cost of goods or materials it had committed to purchase. For example, a public utility may agree to purchase 100 tons of coal annually from a mining company, and if it does not purchase this amount in any year it will pay an amount of money equal to its sale price.

TERMINATION OPTION. An option entitling a lessee to terminate the lease during the lease term for a predetermined value, termination value, if the equipment becomes obsolete or surplus to the lessee's needs. The lessor usually requires the lessee to sell the equipment to an unaffiliated third party and the lessee is obligated to pay the lessor any amount by which the sale proceeds are less than the termination value. Typically, any excess sale proceeds go to the lessor.

TERMINATION VALUE. In the event a lessee is given a termination option, a value is established as of each rental payment period which the lessee must insure that the lessor receives for the terminated equipment. Termination values are generally expressed as a percentage of equipment cost. For example, the lessee may be permitted to terminate the lease at the end of the third year of a seven year lease for an amount equal to 60% of cost.

TIME SALE. An installment sale.

TOTAL EARNINGS. In a lease transaction this generally represents the amount by which the aggregate rentals due the lessor over the entire lease term exceed the total equipment costs, including equity investment and debt financing costs. This concept does not consider the time value of money.

TRUE LEASE. The term is generally used to describe an arrangement which qualifies for lease treatment for Federal income tax purposes. Under a "true" lease, the lessee may expense the rental payments and the lessor may claim the tax benefits accruing to an equipment owner.

TRUST CERTIFICATE. A trust document issued by a trust to evidence the beneficial ownership in the trust estate.

TRUST. An arrangement in which property is held by one party for the benefit of another. It is frequently used in leveraged lease transactions.

TRUSTEE. The person or entity who has been appointed, or designated, to carry out the terms of a trust. In leveraged lease transactions the trustee is generally a bank or trust company.

TRUSTOR. A person or entity who causes the creation of a trust and for whose benefit it is established.

TRUSTEE FEES. Fees payable to a trustee as compensation for services performed.

UNLEVERAGED LEASE. A lease in which the lessor puts up 100% of the equipment's acquisition cost.

USE TAX. A tax imposed upon the use, storage, or consumption of tangible personal property within a taxing jurisdiction.

USEFUL LIFE. Commonly, the economic usable life of an asset.

VENDOR. A seller of property. Commonly, the manufacturer or distributor of equipment.

VENDOR PROGRAM. In the leasing industry it typically describes a program in which an equipment lessor provides a lease financing service to customers of an equipment manufacturer.

Appendices: Sample Documents

The following sample equipment lease documents have been included in this Appendix:

A—Request For Lease Quotation.
B—Non-Underwriting Proposal Letter.
C—Underwriting Proposal Letter.
D—Net Finance Lease.
E—Certificate Of Non-Use.

The documents are offered merely as a reference guide. They should not be used without expert guidance.

The Request For Lease Quotation follows the form of an actual situation. It was chosen because of its concise format. The Non-Underwriting Proposal Letter follows a typical form actually in use by some leasing companies. The Underwriting Proposal Letter is typical of a format currently in use by some major lease underwriters. The Net Finance Lease was selected because of its comprehensive and fully negotiated nature. The sample Certificate Of Non-Use was included because it is a hard form to find.

Appendix A

THE MIDEASTERN RAILWAY CORPORATION

Lessee:	The Mideastern Railway Corporation.
Equipment:	6 SD-40-2 3,000 h.p. diesel locomotives (est. unit cost—$525,000).
Estimated Total Cost:	$3,150,000.
Equipment Delivery:	February, 19X9—Two units. March, 19X9—Two units. April, 19X9—Two units.
Equity Contribution:	Not less than 20% of cost. The equity investor(s) must agree to purchase equipment with a maximum equipment cost up to $3,500,000.
Interest Rate Assumption:	8 3/4%, 9%, 9 1/4%.
Agent for Debt Placement:	Samon & Smith Co.
Counsel for Long Term Lenders:	Carr, Swift & Moore, subject to agreement of the long term lenders.
Structuring of the Transaction:	15 year net finance leveraged lease with semi-annual, in arrears, level payments. Any other proposal format will be considered provided a bid as requested has been submitted.
	The lessee must have three two-year fair market rental renewal options. A fair market purchase option at the end of the initial term and each renewal term should also be provided. The lessor will give a letter stating that, in its opinion, the locomotives will have a useful life in excess of 18 years and a residual value equal to 20% of the original cost at the end of 15 years.
Delivery Cutoff Date:	The cutoff date for the equipment deliveries will be July 1, 19X9. All equipment not delivered prior to this

date will be excluded from the transaction unless the lessor and the lessee agree to extend such date.

Investment Tax Credit:

The 10% investment tax credit is to be retained by the lessor.

Expenses:

All expenses of the transaction, including rating fees and the investment banking fees, will be borne by the lessor.

Security:

The lessee's lease obligations will be unconditionally guaranteed by The Eastern Railway Company. The Mideastern Railway Company is a wholly owned subsidiary of The Eastern Railway Company.

The long term debt will be secured by an assignment of the lease. An agent bank will be selected by The Eastern Railway Company and Samon & Smith Co. after the long term debt is placed. The long term debt will be non-callable except for casualty occurrences.

Indemnification:

The lessee will certify that the equipment is Section 38 property under the Internal Revenue Code. Preference will be given to bids with minimum indemnification and not requiring a Revenue Ruling. If the equity investor(s) desire a ruling, receipt of such ruling should not be considered a prerequisite to executing the lease documents. *All indemnification requirements must be precisely stated in the proposal.*

Interim Rentals:

All quotations must assume not more than three equity closing dates and provide interim rents from such dates to July 1, 19X9, the commencement of the primary lease term. Interim rentals will be equal to the daily equivalent of the long term debt interest rate.

Casualty Values:

All bidders must provide a schedule of casualty values, expressed as a percentage of original cost, both for the primary lease term and any extensions thereafter. The method of calculating the casualty values must also be supplied.

Insurance: The equipment will be self-insured.

Please mail us your proposal in writing postmarked no later than April 15, 19X8. Your proposal must be on a "firm" basis and at the time of submission you must be prepared to identify the investor source(s) so that they may be contacted immediately by telephone for verification in the event you are the successful bidder.

Appendix B

NON-UNDERWRITING PROPOSAL LETTER

December 5, 19X8

Secour Mining Corporation
800 Second Avenue
New York, New York 10017

Attention: Mr. R. Babcox
           President

Gentlemen:

Able Leasing Corporation ("ALC") offers to purchase and lease to Secour Mining Corporation ("Secour") an item of newly manufactured underground mining machinery upon the following terms and conditions:

1. Equipment Description:	The equipment will consist of one (1) new continuous miner, model no. EA-1, manufactured by Dod Manufacturing Co.
2. Equipment Cost:	Approximately $1,000,000
3. Delivery and Payment:	Delivery of the Equipment is anticipated on January 1, 19X9, but in no event shall be later than March 1, 19X9. ALC shall pay for the Equipment upon delivery and acceptance.
4. Lease Term:	Eight (8) years, commencing upon delivery and acceptance of the Equipment.
5. Rental Program:	Secour shall remit thirty-two (32) consecutive, level, quarterly payments, in advance, each equal to 4.4000% of Equipment Cost.
6. Options:	At the conclusion of the Lease Term, Secour may (with at least one hundred twenty (120) days' prior written notice):

A. Purchase the Equipment for an amount equal to its then fair market value.

B. Renew the lease with respect to the Equipment for its then fair rental value.

7. Investment Tax Credit:

ALC shall elect to treat Secour as the purchaser of "new Section 38 property" pursuant to Section 48(d) of the Internal Revenue Code of 1954, as amended, for the purpose of passing through the available investment tax credit.

8. Depreciation:

ALC shall use one of the accelerated methods of depreciation pursuant to Section 167(b) of the Internal Revenue Code, elect the Asset Depreciation Range System ("ADR") pursuant to Section 167 (m) of the Code and Section 1.167(a)-11 of the Treasury Regulations, include the Equipment in Asset Guideline Class 10.0 ("Mining"), and select the ADR lower limit of eight (8) years. Secour shall indemnify ALC for any loss of such depreciation deductions.

9. Fixed Expenses:

This is a net financial lease proposal and all fixed expenses such as insurance, maintenance, and personal property taxes shall be for the account of Secour.

10. Conditions Precedent:

A. ALC will require a satisfactory written appraisal substantiating the lease term to which the Equipment will be committed.

B. This offer is subject to the approval of the Board of Directors of ALC and to the execution of lease documentation mutually acceptable to Secour and ALC.

If the foregoing is satisfactory to you, please indicate your acceptance of this offer by signing the duplicate copy of this letter in the space provided therefor and returning it directly to the undersigned.

This offer expires as of the close of business on December 19, 19X8.

Very truly yours,

ABLE LEASING CORPORATION

By _____
Vice President

Accepted and Agreed to on this
____ day of _____, 19X8.

SECOUR MINING CORPORATION

By _____

Its_____

Appendix C

UNDERWRITING PROPOSAL LETTER

October 8, 19X7

The White Corporation
200 Park Avenue
New York, New York 10017

Attention: E. Ross
           Assistant Treasurer

Gentlemen:

Able Leasing Corporation ("ALC"), on behalf of its nominees, proposes to use its best efforts to arrange a lease for one new DC-10 aircraft for use by The White Corporation according to the following terms and conditions:

Lessee:	The Lessee shall be The White Corporation.
Lessor:	The Lessor will be a commercial bank or trust company acting as owner trustee ("Owner Trustee") pursuant to one or more owners' trusts (the "Trust") for the benefit of one or more commercial banks or other corporate investors (herein referred to singularly or collectively as "Trustor"). The Trust shall acquire the Aircraft and lease it to the Lessee.
Aircraft:	One new McDonnell Douglas DC-10.
Cost:	For purposes of this proposal, a total cost of $28,000,000, plus or minus 5%, has been assumed. Any transportation charges, sales taxes, or other charges, to the extent that they are investment tax credit and depreciation eligible, can be included.
Delivery Date:	Delivery of the Aircraft is anticipated as of November 1, 19X8, however, shall be no later than December 30, 19X8.

301

Interim Lease Term:

The interim lease term shall extend from the Delivery Date until the Commencement Date. For the purposes of this proposal the Commencement Date is assumed to be January 1, 19X9.

Interim Rent:

The Lessee shall pay interim rent equal to interest-only on the total cost of the Aircraft at an interest rate equal to the Long Term Debt Interest Rate.

Primary Lease Term:

The primary lease term shall be 20 years from the Commencement Date.

Primary Rent:

From the Commencement Date, the Lessee shall make forty (40) consecutive, level, semi-annual payments, in arrears, each equal to 4.400% of Cost.

Debt Financing:

An investment banker acceptable to ALC and the Lessee shall arrange for the private placement of secured notes or similar instruments ("Indebtedness") to be issued by the Lessor for a principal amount equal to eighty percent (80%) of total Aircraft cost to certain institutional investors ("Lenders") who may be represented by an indenture trustee or agent bank ("Agent"). This proposal assumes that the Indebtedness shall be amortized in semi-annual payments of principal and interest at an 8% per annum interest rate ("Long Term Debt Interest Rate"), payable in arrears over the term of the lease. In the event that the Long Term Debt Interest Rate varies from that assumed, the rent shall be adjusted, upward or downward, so that the Lessor's yield and after-tax cash flows will be maintained. The Indebtedness shall be secured by an assignment of the lease and a security interest in the Aircraft but otherwise shall be without recourse to the Lessor.

Insurance:

The Lessee may self-insure the Aircraft.

Purchase & Renewal Options:

At the end of the Primary Lease Term, the Lessee may (with one hundred eighty (180) days' written notice prior to the end of the term):

A. Renew the lease on the Aircraft for its then fair rental value for one five-year period.

B. Purchase the Aircraft for an equivalent price and under similar conditions as rendered by a third party approached by the Lessor and agreed to by the Lessor prior to sale to that third party.

If the Lessee does not elect to exercise any of the above options, the Lessee shall return the Aircraft to the Lessor at the end of the term at a mutually agreeable location.

Termination Option:

At any time during the Primary Lease Term, on or after ten (10) years from the Commencement Date, the Lessee may (with one hundred eighty (180) days' prior written notice) terminate the lease in the event the Aircraft becomes obsolete or surplus to its needs, upon payment of a mutually agreed upon termination value.

Fixed Expenses:

This is a net financial lease proposal with all fixed expenses, such as maintenance, insurance, taxes (other than net income taxes) for the account of the Lessee.

Expenses of Transaction:

ALC shall pay the following reasonable expenses as may be appropriate:

1. Fees and disbursements of special counsel for the Agent and the Lenders.

2. Acceptance and annual fees and expenses of the Agent.

3. Fees and disbursements of special counsel for the Owner Trustee and the Trustor.

4. Acceptance and annual fees and expenses of the Owner Trustee.

5. Fees and disbursements in connection with obtaining a ruling from the Internal Revenue Service.

6. Expenses of documentation, including printing and reproduction.

7. Fees and disbursements in connection with the private placement of the Indebtedness.

If the transaction is not consummated for any reason, the Lessee shall pay all of the above fees and expenses.

Non-Utilization Fee:

Once ALC has obtained equity investor commitments satisfactory to the Lessee, the Lessee shall be liable to ALC for a non-utilization fee equal to 4/8 of 1% of the Aircraft's cost in the event it does not lease the Aircraft in accordance with intent of this proposal.

Commitment Fee:

A commitment fee of 1/2 of 1% per annum shall be paid by the Lessee to the equity investors on the outstanding equity investor commitment. The fee shall accrue as of the date investor commitments satisfactory to The White Corporation have been obtained, shall run up to the Commencement Date, and shall be payable quarterly, in arrears.

Tax Assumptions:

A. In respect of this transaction, we have made the following tax assumptions:

1. The organization created by the Trust will be treated as a partnership for Federal income tax purposes.

2. The Trust so created shall be considered the original user, owner, and lessor of the Aircraft.

3. The Trust shall be entitled to use the most accelerated method of depreciation available pursuant to Section 167(b) of the Code.

4. The Trust shall elect to use the Asset Depreciation Range System ("ADR") pursuant to Section 167(m) of the Code and Section 1.167(a)-11 of the Treasury Regulations, shall include the Aircraft in Asset Guideline Class 00.21, and shall select the ADR lower limit of five (5) years.

5. The Trust shall be entitled to a minimum of six (6) months depreciation for the calendar year 19X8 under the half-year convention.

6. The Trust shall be entitled to depreciate the Aircraft to a salvage value of 0%.

7. The Trust shall be entitled to deduct interest on the Indebtedness pursuant to Section 163 of the Code.

B. The Lessee shall provide necessary representation relating to the estimated economic life and residual value of the Aircraft.

Tax Ruling: The Lessor plans to obtain a Internal Revenue Service ruling with respect to the tax assumptions stated above. The Lessee shall agree to indemnify for the tax assumptions above. Such indemnity shall remain in effect until a favorable ruling has been obtained.

Investment Tax   The Lessor shall elect to treat the Lessee
Credit: as the purchaser of the Aircraft pur-
                             suant to Section 48(d) of the Internal
                             Revenue Code of 1954, as amended, for
                             the purpose of passing through the
                             available investment tax credit.

If the foregoing proposal is satisfactory to you, please indicate your acceptance by signing the duplicate copy of this letter in the space
provided therefor, and returning it directly to the undersigned.

This offer expires at the close of business on October 28, 19X7 and is
subject to the approval of the Trustor's Board of Directors and mutually satisfactory lease documentation.

Very truly yours,

ABLE LEASING CORPORATION

By _____
   Vice President

Accepted and Agreed to on this
____ day of _____, 19X7.

THE WHITE CORPORATION

By _____

Its _____

Appendix D

NET FINANCE LEASE

EQUIPMENT LEASE

dated as of September 1, 19XX

between

AMERICAN BANK AND TRUST COMPANY

Lessor

and

THE MANHATTAN COMPANY

Lessee

EQUIPMENT LEASE

CONTENTS

NOTICE: THIS LEASE OF EQUIPMENT AND CERTAIN OTHER SUMS DUE AND TO BECOME DUE HEREUNDER ARE SUBJECT TO A SECURITY INTEREST IN FAVOR OF ARLINGTON NATIONAL BANK AND TRUST COMPANY AND THE MILFORD BANK, AS LENDERS, UNDER THE SECURITY AND LOAN AGREEMENT REFERRED TO HEREIN.

EQUIPMENT LEASE

Lease Agreement (the "Lease") dated as of September 1, 19XX by and between American Bank and Trust Company, an Illinois banking corporation with its office at 100 South Plaza Drive, Chicago, Illinois 60606 (the "Lessor), and The Manhattan Company, a Delaware corporation with its principal office at 100 East 40th Street, New York, New York 10017 (the "Lessee").

WITNESSETH:

In consideration of the premises and of the rentals to be paid and the covenants hereinafter mentioned to be kept and performed by Lessee, Lessor hereby agrees to lease the Equipment to Lessee, and Lessee hereby agrees to lease the Equipment from Lessor, upon the following terms and conditions:

Section 1. Definitions.

The following terms shall have the respective meanings set forth below for all purposes of this Lease:

"Agent" shall mean The Milford Bank.

"Basic Rent" shall mean the rent payable throughout the term of this Lease pursuant to Section 3(a) hereof.

"Basic Rent Dates" shall mean the dates specified in Schedule 2 to this Lease.

"Basic Lease Rate Factor" shall mean, with respect to the Equipment subject to this Lease, the percentage set forth in Attachment A to Schedule 2 to this Lease.

"Business Day" shall mean a day which is not a Saturday, Sunday or a bank holiday under the laws of the United States or the State of Illinois.

"Casualty Occurrence" shall have the meaning set forth in Section 12(a) of this Lease.

"Casualty Value of the Equipment" shall be the amount, determined as of the date provided in this Lease, calculated in accordance with the provisions of Attachment B to Schedule 2 to this Lease.

"Closing Date" with respect to the Equipment shall mean September 1, 19XX or such other date as may be agreed upon by Lessor, Lessee and the Lenders.

"Code" shall mean the Internal Revenue Code of 1954, as amended from time to time.

"Cut-Off Date" shall mean the date specified in Schedule 2 to this Lease.

"Equipment" shall mean the machines and features constituting the computer equipment described in Schedule 1 to this Lease and any equipment features, field-installable modifications or standard system units which are leased by Lessor to Lessee pursuant to Section 2(g) of this Lease.

"Event of Default" shall mean any event specified in Section 17 of this Lease.

"Financing Statement" shall mean a financing statement contemplated by the Uniform Commercial Code as enacted by the applicable jurisdiction.

"First Basic Rent Date" shall mean the date specified in Schedule 2 to this Lease.

"Indemnitee" shall mean Lessor or either of the Lenders (two or more of such parties being collectively referred to as the "Indemnitees").

"Invoice Purchase Price" shall mean the aggregate amount payable by Lessor to Manufacturer in respect of the Equipment described in an invoice or invoices covering such Equipment.

"Lenders" shall mean Arlington National Bank and Trust Company and The Milford Bank.

"Lender's Interest Rate" shall mean the Lender's Interest Rate described in Schedule 2 to this Lease.

"Lessor's Cost" shall mean, with respect to the Equipment subject to this Lease, the Invoice Purchase Price therefor.

"Loan" shall mean the Loan referred to in the Security Agreement.

"Manufacturer" shall mean International Computer Manufacturer Corporation ("ICM").

"Operative Agreements" shall mean this Lease, the Security Agreement and the Purchase Documents.

"Overdue Rate" shall mean the Overdue Rate described in Schedule 2 to this Lease.

"Person" shall mean an individual, corporation, partnership, joint venture, association, joint-stock company, trust, unincorporated organization or a government or agency or political subdivision thereof.

"Purchase Documents" shall mean the Assignment of on order ICM Machines, the Agreement for Purchase of ICM Machines and the Supplement to Agreement for Purchase of ICM Machines, each duly executed by the appropriate parties, pursuant to which the Manufacturer sells and the Lessor purchases the Equipment described therein.

"Rent" shall mean Basic Rent and Supplemental Rent.

"Security Agreement" shall mean the Security and Loan Agreement dated as of September 1, 19XX between Lessor and Lenders.

"Supplemental Rent" shall mean the payments Lessee agrees to pay pursuant to Section 3(b) of this Lease.

"Termination Value of the Equipment" shall be the amount, determined as of the date the Termination Value is payable as provided in this Lease, calculated in accordance with the provisions of Attachment C to Schedule 2 to this Lease.

"Unit(s)" shall mean one (or more) of the machines or features constituting the computer equipment described in Schedule 1 to this Lease and for which a separate invoice price is specified in Schedule 1.

The words "herein," "hereof," "hereunder" and other words of similar import used herein refer to this Lease as a whole and not to any particular Section or other subdivision thereof.

Section 2. Acquisition, Delivery and Acceptance
of Equipment; Location of Equipment; Term of Lease.

(a) Lessor will, subject to the terms of this Lease (including the conditions precedent hereinafter set forth) and the terms of the Purchase Documents, purchase the Equipment from the Manufacturer thereof under the Purchase Documents and lease such Equipment to Lessee hereunder, provided that the Equipment shall be delivered and installed by the Manufacturer in good working order, and accepted on behalf of Lessor as set forth in Section 2(d) below, on or before the Closing Date but no later than the Cut-Off Date.

(b)   The Equipment shall be installed at the address set forth in Schedule 2 hereof. Lessee shall not move the Equipment from such address without first giving Lessor and the Lenders 30 days' written notice of any such proposed change of location and receiving Lessor's and the Lenders' written consent thereto, during which time Lessor or the Lenders shall, should either of them deem it necessary, make all appropriate filings or recordings necessary to fully protect Lessor's title to or the Lenders' security interest in the Equipment and the sums due under this Lease; provided, however, that no such consent shall be required if Lessee moves the Equipment to a subsidiary, affiliate or parent of Lessee and further provided that in no event shall the Equipment be moved to a location (i) outside of the United States of America, (ii) within any jurisdiction within the United States of America which has not adopted the Uniform Commercial Code or (iii) within any jurisdiction where it would be unlawful for the Lessor to own the Equipment.

(c)   Lessee agrees to provide and maintain, or cause to be provided and maintained, a suitable installation environment for the Equipment with all utilities, wiring and other facilities prescribed by the appropriate Manufacturer's installation and operating manuals and to furnish, or cause to be furnished, all labor required for unpacking and placing the Equipment at the location for such Equipment.

(d)   Lessor hereby authorizes one or more employees of Lessee, designated by Lessee, as the authorized representative(s) of Lessor, to accept delivery of the Equipment pursuant to the Purchase Documents. Upon the delivery and installation of the Equipment, Lessee will cause such representative(s) to inspect the same, and, if such Equipment is in good working order, to accept delivery of such Equipment. Lessee shall execute and deliver to Lessor a Certificate with respect to such acceptance in the form of Annex A hereto. Lessee hereby agrees that such acceptance of delivery by such representative(s) on behalf of Lessor shall, without further act, irrevocably constitute acceptance by Lessee and Lessor of such Equipment for all purposes of this Lease. Lessor does not assume any liability to Lessee for any matter relating to the ordering, manufacture, shipment, delivery, installation, rigging, setting up, testing, adjusting or servicing of the Equipment (including, without limitation, taking such acts as may be necessary to keep the Manufacturer's warranty with respect to the Equipment in full force and effect), for any failure or delay in obtaining or delivering the Equipment or in placing the same in good working order, or for delivery of wrong equipment, or for defects in manufacture, construction or operation of or for damage to the Equipment.

(e)   Lessor shall and hereby does retain full title to the Equipment notwithstanding the delivery of the Equipment to and the possession and use thereof by Lessee as herein provided, subject only to the rights of the Lenders under the Security Agreement. Lessee hereby consents to the granting of the security interest provided for in the Security Agreement and acknowledges that this Lease and all payments due or to become due hereunder have been or will be assigned by Lessor to the Lenders.

(f)   The primary term of this Lease shall begin on the Closing Date and shall end on the seventh anniversary of such date, unless earlier terminated pursuant to the terms of Sections 12, 18 or 21 hereof.

(g)   Upon 60 days written notice from Lessee, Lessor may agree, in its sole and absolute discretion, to purchase or otherwise obtain from the Manufacturer, or other sources acceptable to Lessor, and to lease to Lessee pursuant to this Lease, such equipment features, field-installable modifications or standard system units which are available for such purchase or other acquisition from such Manufacturer or other source, and which Lessee may desire to add to or interface and connect with the other Units covered by this Lease and which have an aggregate purchase price of not less than $50,000 for a single closing nor an aggregate purchase price of more than $750,000 for all closings. Lessor agrees to lease such features, modifications and units to Lessee until September 1, 19XX or as this Lease may be extended or renewed as provided herein, upon the same terms and conditions as are herin specified at a rate to be negotiated between Lessor and Lessee; provided, however, that Lessor's obligations under this paragraph are subject to the prior mutual agreement of Lessor and Lessee upon such rate, and are subject to there being no material adverse change in the business or financial condition of Lessee since the date of this Lease.

Section 3. Rent.

(a)   Lessee hereby agrees to pay to Lessor Basic Rent as set forth in Schedule 2 hereof.

There shall be no limit on the number of hours for which the Equipment may be used and there shall be no hourly extra use charge. If any of the Basic Rent Dates referred to in Schedule 2 hereof shall not be a Business Day, the payment otherwise due thereon shall be payable on the next succeeding Business Day.

(b)   Lessee hereby agrees to pay Lessor (or to whomsoever shall be entitled thereto as expressly provided in this Lease) on written demand as Supplemental Rent:

(i)   All amounts, liabilities and obligations which Lessee agrees to pay to Lessor or others under this Lease, except Basic Rent;

(ii)   with respect to any part of any installment of Basic Rent which is not paid on the date when due, interest at the Overdue Rate, to the extent not prohibited by applicable law, for any period for which part of any installment of Basic Rent shall be overdue, such interest to begin accruing on the day after such Basic Rent is due; and

(iii)   on any other payment due under this Lease and not paid within thirty (30) days after demand by Lessor, for the period until the same shall be paid, interest at the Overdue Rate, to the extent not prohibited by applicable law, such interest to begin accruing on the day after demand therefor by Lessor.

Interest payable by Lessee hereunder shall be computed on the basis of a 365 day year (or 366 day year, when applicable) for actual days elapsed.

(c)   Lessee hereby agrees to pay promptly all costs, expenses and obligations of every kind and nature incurred in connection with its use of the Equipment including, without limitation, all parts, service and other items required to operate and maintain the Equipment.

(d)   All payments provided for in this Lease (other than indemnity payments for the benefit of an Indemnitee pursuant to Sections 8, 9 and 13 hereof, which shall be made to the Indemnitee) shall be made to the Agent at the address of the Agent set forth in Schedule 2 hereof or at such other address as may be furnished to Lessee by notice in writing from the Agent, except that the rent payable on the first Basic Rent Date shall be paid to Lessor.

(e)   This Lease is a net lease and Lessee acknowledges and agrees that Lessee's obligation to pay all Rent payable hereunder, and the rights of Lessor in and to such Rent, shall be absolute and unconditional and shall not be subject to any abatement, reduction, setoff, defense, counterclaim or recoupment whatsoever, including, without limitation, abatements, reductions, setoffs, defenses, counterclaims or recoupments due or alleged to be due to, or by any reason of, any past, present or future claims which Lessee may have against Lessor, the Manufacturer, the Lenders or against any person for any reason whatsoever; nor, except as otherwise expressly provided herein, shall this Lease terminate, or the respective obligations of Lessor or Lessee be otherwise affected, by reason of any defect in the Equipment, the condition, design, operation or fitness for use thereof, or any damage to, or any loss or destruction of, or any liens, encumbrances, security interests or rights of others with respect to the Equipment, any prohibition or interruption of or other restriction against Lessee's use, operation or possession of the Equipment for any reason whatsoever, the interference with such use, operation or possession by any private person or entity, or by reason of any other indebtedness or liability, howsoever and whenever arising, of Lessor, Lessee or the Lenders to any other person, firm or corporation or to any governmental authority, or by reason of any insolvency, bankruptcy or similar proceedings by or against Lessor or Lessee, or for any other cause whether similar or dissimilar to the foregoing, any present law to the contrary notwithstanding, it being the intention of the parties hereto that the Rent payable by Lessee hereunder shall continue to be payable in all events and in the manner and at the times herein provided unless the obligation to pay the same shall be terminated pursuant to the express provisions of this Lease.

(f)   Notwithstanding anything to the contrary contained herein, all rights and obligations under this Lease and in and to the Equipment, upon the occurrence of any Event of Default hereunder, are subject to the rights of the Lenders under the Security Agreement. If an "event of default" as defined in Section 9 of the Security Agreement and as defined in Section 17 of this Lease should occur, the Lenders or Lessor may terminate this Lease unless the Agent continues to receive the Rent as provided in Section 3(d) hereof.

Section 4. Conditions Precedent.

(I)   Lessor's obligation to execute and deliver the Purchase Documents and to lease the Equipment to Lessee hereunder shall be subject to satisfaction of the following conditions precedent on or before the Closing Date:

(a)   Lessor and the Lenders shall have received the following, in each case in form and substance satisfactory to Lessor and the Lenders:

(1)   a copy of the Articles of Incorporation of Lessee certified as of a recent date by the Secretary of State of the State of Lessee's incorporation, or a copy thereof, and a copy of the By-Laws of Lessee certified by the Secretary or an Assistant Secretary of Lessee;

(2)   an incumbency certificate as to the person or persons who execute and deliver this Lease, the Purchase Documents and any instruments or documents incidental thereto or hereto on behalf of Lessee in substantially the form annexed hereto as Annex B hereof;

(3)   an opinion of counsel for Lessee, dated the date of execution of this Lease and addressed to Lessor and the Lenders in substantially the form annexed hereto as Annex C hereof; and

(4)   the Purchase Documents to be executed by Lessee with respect to the Equipment.

(II) Lessor's obligation to make payment for the Equipment on the Closing Date shall be subject to satisfaction of the following conditions precedent on or before the Closing Date:

(a) Lessor and the Lenders shall have received the following, in each case in form and substance satisfactory to Lessor and the Lenders:

(1) a Manufacturer's invoice applicable to the Equipment, accompanied by a certification, dated such Closing Date, by the Lessee as to the correctness of the prices of such Equipment, such certification to be in the form annexed hereto as Annex D hereof;

(2) a bill of sale from the Manufacturer to Lessor, dated such Closing Date, warranting to Lessor and Lessee that, at the time of sale of such Equipment under the Purchase Documents, the Manufacturer was the lawful owner of such Equipment, and had good and lawful right to sell the same and that title to the same was free from any charge or encumbrance whatsoever and covenanting that the Manufacturer will defend said title;

(3) a Certificate of Lessee, in the form annexed hereto as Annex A hereof, dated the Closing Date for such Equipment;

(4) copies of the Purchase Documents applicable to the Equipment, fully executed by the appropriate parties thereto and effective as of or prior to the date of installation of the Equipment by the Manufacturer;

(5) a certificate of insurance, or copy thereof, with respect to each of the insurance policies required by Section 11(f) hereof, provided that if any such certificate is unavailable on the Closing Date, Lessor and the Lenders shall accept a telegram, or copy thereof, from Lessee's insurance broker or other representative with respect to the effectiveness of such insurance, and Lessee shall deliver the required certificate to Lessor within 60 days after the Closing Date; and

(6) such other documents as may be reasonably requested by Lessor.

(b) All of the conditions precedent to the making of the Loan pursuant to the Security Agreement required to be fulfilled on or before the Closing Date shall have been fulfilled, and copies of all documents and opinions required by the Security Agreement shall have been furnished to the Lessor and the Lenders.

(III) In the event that on the Closing Date the foregoing conditions precedent have not been fully satisfied, then on the Closing

Date, or in the event the Closing Date shall not have been fixed, or shall not be on or before the Cut-Off Date, then on the Cut-Off Date, as the case may be, Lessee shall purchase or otherwise arrange for the acquisition or disposition of the Equipment, Lessor shall be relieved of any obligation to purchase the Equipment from the Manufacturer and to lease the Equipment to Lessee under this Lease, Lessee will assume all obligations under the Purchase Documents, and Lessee will indemnify, protect, save and keep harmless the Lessor and the Lenders from any and all liabilities that Lessor or Lenders may have or incur to the Manufacturer under the Purchase Documents with respect to the Equipment in the manner set forth in Section 13 hereof.

In the event that on the Closing Date Lessee shall have notified Lessor of a Casualty Occurrence pursuant to Section 12 hereof with respect to the Equipment, Lessee shall purchase or otherwise arrange for the acquisition or disposition of any such Equipment, Lessor shall be relieved of any obligation to purchase the Equipment from the Manufacturer and to lease such Equipment to Lessee under this Lease, Lessee will assume all obligations under the Purchase Documents; and Lessee will indemnify, protect, save and keep harmless Lessor and the Lenders from any and all liabilities that Lessor or Lenders may have or incur to the Manufacturer under the Purchase Documents with respect to the Equipment in the manner set forth in Section 13 hereof.

Section 5. Lessee's Representations and Warranties.

Lessee represents and warrants for the benefit of Lessor and the Lenders (all such representations and warranties, except for those set forth in paragraphs (e) and (f) below, being continuing) that:

(a) Lessee is a corporation duly organized, validly existing and in good standing under the laws of the jurisdiction of its incorporation, with adequate corporate power to enter into this Lease and the Purchase Documents and is duly qualified to do business and in good standing in the jurisdiction where the Equipment will be located;

(b) this Lease and the Purchase Documents have been duly authorized, executed and delivered by Lessee and constitute valid, legal and binding agreements, enforceable in accordance with their terms;

(c) no approval, consent or withholding of objection is required from any governmental authority or any other party with respect to the entering into or performance by Lessee of this Lease or the Purchase Documents, of if any such approval is required, it has been obtained;

(d)   the entering into and performance of this Lease and the Purchase Documents by Lessee will not violate any judgment, order, law or regulation applicable to Lessee or any provision of Lessee's articles of incorporation or by-laws or result in any breach of, or constitute a default under, or result in the creation of any lien, charge, security interest or other encumbrance upon any assets of Lessee or on the Equipment pursuant to, any indenture, mortgage, deed of trust, bank loan or credit agreement or other instrument or agreement to which Lessee is a party or by which it or its assets may be bound, other than the rights of Lessee under this Lease and the rights of the Lenders under the Security Agreement;

(e)   there are no suits or proceedings pending or, to the knowledge of Lessee, threatened in any court or before any regulatory commission, board or other governmental authority against or affecting Lessee, which may have a material adverse effect on the ability of Lessee to fulfill its obligations under this Lease;

(f)   Lessee is not in default in the payment of the principal of or interest on any indebtedness for borrowed money or in default under any instrument or instruments or agreements under and subject to which any indebtedness for borrowed money has been issued; and no event has occurred and is continuing under the provisions of any such instrument or agreement which with the lapse of time or the giving of notice, or both, would constitute an event of default thereunder;

(g)   the consolidated balance sheet of Lessee and its consolidated subsidiaries as of December 31, 19XX, and the statements of operations and changes in financial position for the fiscal year ended December 31, 19XX accompanied by a report thereon containing an opinion unqualified as to scope and otherwise without qualification by Waterbarrel & Co., contained in the Annual Report of Lessee for such year, copies of which have been delivered to Lenders, have been prepared in accordance with generally accepted accounting principles consistently applied, and present fairly the financial position of Lessee and its consolidated subsidiaries as of such date and the results of their operations and changes in their financial position for such period. These consolidated financial statements include the accounts of all consolidated subsidiaries of Lessee for the respective periods during which a subsidiary relationship has existed. Since December 31, 19XX and until the Closing Date, there has been no change in the condition, financial or otherwise, of Lessee and its consolidated subsidiaries as shown on the consolidated balance sheet as of such date except changes in the ordinary course of business, none of which individually or in the aggregate has been materially adverse;

(h)   the financial statements referred to in paragraph (g) above do not, nor does any written statement furnished by Lessee to Lessor or the Lenders in connection with the negotiation of the transactions contemplated by the Operative Agreements, contain any untrue statement of a material fact or omit a material fact necessary to make the statements contained therein or herein not misleading. There is no fact which Lessee has not disclosed in writing which materially affects adversely the properties, business, profits or condition (financial or otherwise) of Lessee and its subsidiaries or the ability of Lessee to perform under the Operative Agreements;

(i)   neither Lessee nor Able Leasing Corporation (the only persons authorized or employed by Lessee as agents, brokers, dealers or otherwise in connection with the placement of the beneficial interest in the Equipment or any similar security of Lessee) has offered any of the beneficial interests or any similar security of Lessee for sale to, or solicited offers to buy any thereof from, or otherwise approached or negotiated with respect thereto with, any prospective purchaser, other than Lessor and not more than eight other institutional investors, each of which was offered the beneficial interests at private sale for investment;

(j)   neither Lessee nor Able Leasing Corporation (the only person authorized or employed by Lessee as agents, brokers, dealers or otherwise in connection with the placement of the Notes (as defined in the Security Agreement)) has offered the Notes for sale to, or solicited offers to buy the Notes from, or otherwise approached or negotiated with respect thereto with, any prospective purchaser, other than the Lenders and not more than ten other institutional investors, each of which was offered the Notes at private sale for investment;

(k)   the Equipment is new and no part of such Equipment has been put into use or operation prior to the execution and delivery of this Lease or prior to the date of installation of such Equipment by the Manufacturer, other than usual testing by the Manufacturer of such Equipment;

(l)   the estimated remaining useful life of the Equipment at the end of the primary term of this Lease is at least two years; and

(m)   the estimated fair market value of the Equipment at the end of the primary term of this Lease (determined (i) without including in such value any increase or decrease for inflation or deflation during such term, and (ii) after subtracting from such value any cost to Lessor for removal and delivery of possession of the Equipment as provided in Section 6 hereof to Lessor at the end of such term) is at least 20% of Lessor's Cost of the Equipment;

It is understood and agreed that the representations and warranties set forth in paragraphs (l) and (m) of this Section 5 are estimates of useful life and market value, respectively, and that such estimates do not guarantee a residual value or payment to the Lenders of the amounts due under the Notes.

Section 6. Return of Equipment.

Upon the expiration of the term of this Lease or any earlier termination thereof with respect to the Equipment, Lessee will, at its own cost and expense, at the request of Lessor, dismantle and deliver possession of the Equipment to Lessor, in the condition required for it to be maintained by Lessee hereunder, at the location of the Equipment on the final day of the term of this Lease. In that it is the intent of Lessor to retain the Equipment for re-lease upon the expiration of the term of this Lease or any earlier termination thereof, the dismantling and delivery of the Equipment as hereinbefore provided are of the essence of this Lease, and, upon application to any court of equity having jurisdiction in the premises, Lessor shall be entitled to a decree against Lessee requiring specific performance of the covenants of Lessee so to dismantle and deliver the Equipment.

Section 7. Identification Marks.

Lessee will keep and maintain, plainly, distinctly, permanently and conspicuously marked on the Equipment leased hereunder, (i) the name of Lessor followed by the legend "Lessor" and (ii) the names of the Lenders followed by the words "Security Owners" or other appropriate words designated in writing by Lessor or the Lenders, with appropriate changes thereof and additions thereto as may from time to time be required by law or are, in the judgment of Lessor or the Lenders, necessary in order to protect the title of Lessor to the Equipment, the rights of Lessor under this Lease, the rights of the Lenders under the Security Agreement and the rights of any assignee thereof. Except as provided above, Lessee will not allow the name of any person, association or corporation other than Lessor or the Lenders to be placed on the Equipment as a designation that might be interpreted as a claim of ownership; provided, however, that Lessee may allow the Equipment to be lettered with the names or initials or other insignia customarily used by Lessee on equipment of the same or similar type for convenience of identification.

Section 8. Fees and Taxes.

(a)   Lessee agrees to pay and to indemnify and hold the Indemnitees harmless from all license and registration fees and all taxes, including, without limitation, income, franchise, sales, use, personal property, stamp or other taxes, levies, imposts, duties, charges or withholdings of any nature, together with any penalties, fines or interest thereon, imposed upon any Indemnitee or the Equipment by any Federal, state or local government or taxing authority with respect to the Equipment, or the purchase, ownership, delivery, leasing, possession, use, operation, return or other disposition thereof, or upon or with respect to the income or other proceeds received with respect to the Equipment while, and to the extent only that the Equipment has been delivered to Lessor in accordance with Section 6 hereof, or upon or with respect to this Lease excluding, however, (i) taxes, fees or other charges included in Lessor's Cost, (ii) any taxes, fees or other charges on, or measured by, the net income of the Lessor or the Lenders, (iii) any taxes based on gross income or gross receipts of the Lessor or the Lenders which may hereafter be imposed in any jurisdiction as a substitute for and not in addition to taxes based on net income or (iv) franchise taxes imposed by the jurisdiction in which the Indemnitee is incorporated or the jurisdiction in which the principal office of the Indemnitee is located (hereinafter collectively referred to as "impositions").

(b)   Lessee agrees to comply with all state and local laws requiring the filing of ad valorem tax returns on the Equipment. Any statements for impositions or for ad valorem taxes received by Lessor or the Lenders shall be promptly forwarded to Lessee by Lessor or the Lenders.

(c)   Lessee shall not be responsible for any governmental fines or penalties which are imposed as a result of (i) the willful misconduct of Lessor or the Lenders or (ii) a knowing failure by Lessor or the Lenders to take reasonable action or to furnish reasonable cooperation to Lessee which prevents Lessee from diligently fulfilling its obligations under this Section 8.

(d)   If a claim is made against any Indemnitee for any imposition which Lessee is obligated to pay hereunder, the party receiving notice of such claim shall promptly notify in writing Lessee and the other Indemnitees. In the event any reports with respect to impositions are required to be made, Lessee will either make such reports in such manner as to show the interests of Lessor and the Lenders or notify Lessor of such requirement and make such reports in such manner as shall be satisfactory to Lessor.

(e)   Lessee shall be under no obligation to pay any imposition of any kind so long as (i) Lessee is contesting such imposition in good faith and by appropriate legal proceedings, (ii) the nonpayment thereof or such contest does not, in the opinion of any Indemnitee, adversely affect the title, property or rights of such Indemnitee or subject such Indemnitee to criminal liabilities or penalties and (iii) Lessee shall have agreed to indemnify such Indemnitee in a manner reasonably satisfactory to such Indemnitee including, without limitation, a surety bond in the event that Lessee's net worth as determined in accordance with generally accepted accounting principles falls below $100,000,000 at any time during the term of this Lease, for any liability or cost which such Indemnitee may incur as a result of such action by Lessee. Lessor and the Lenders shall cooperate in any such contest by Lessee to the extent necessary to enable Lessee to make such contest.

(f) If any imposition shall have been charged or levied against any Indemnitee directly and paid by such Indemnitee, Lessee shall reimburse the Indemnitee on presentation of evidence of payment therefor if (i) Lessee shall have approved the payment thereof or (ii) prior to such payment (A) the Indemnitee shall have determined that the failure to make such payment would adversely affect the title, property or rights of such Indemnitee or subject such Indemnitee to criminal liabilities or penalties or (B) Lessee shall not have agreed to contest such imposition in good faith and in appropriate legal proceedings at its sole cost and expense and agreed to indemnify the Indemnitee in a manner reasonably satisfactory to such Indemnitee, including, without limitation, a surety bond in the event that Lessee's net worth as determined in accordance with generally accepted accounting principles falls below $100,000,000 at any time during the term of this Lease, for any liability or cost which the Indemnitee may incur as a result of Lessee's action. Notwithstanding the preceding sentence, if, as a result of the contest described in the preceding sentence, it is finally determined that the imposition paid by the Indemnitee was properly charged or levied, Lessee shall reimburse such Indemnitee for amounts originally paid, plus interest and penalties paid, plus interest at the Lender's Interest Rate.

(g) If Lessee has reimbursed an Indemnitee for any imposition pursuant to this Section 8 (or if Lessee has made a payment to the appropriate taxing authority for an imposition which it is required to pay hereunder), Lessee may, at its sole cost and expense, take such steps (in the name of Lessee or in the name of such Indemnitee) as are reasonably necessary or appropriate to seek such a refund of such imposition, and the Indemnitee shall cooperate with Lessee in seeking such a refund. Notwithstanding the preceding sentence, Lessee shall not take any action in the name of any Indemnitee unless it shall have first agreed to indemnify such Indemnitee in a manner reasonably satisfactory to such Indemnitee for any liability or loss which the Indemnitee may incur as a result of Lessee's action. In the event that an Indemnitee receives a refund of any tax paid by it relating to this Lease for which it has received a payment from the Lessee pursuant to this Lease, the Indemnitee shall pay the amount of such refund to Lessee immediately.

(h)   Lessee agrees to pay all stamp or documentary taxes and recording or filing fees or taxes, Federal, state, county, city, municipal or otherwise, levied or assessed or otherwise payable on, or with respect to, the filing at any time while this Lease remains in effect, of financing statements with respect to this Lease, the Security Agreement or the filing or recording of any other document whatsoever to which Lessee is a party which creates or transfers an interest in the Equipment.

(i)   In the event that, during the continuance of this Lease, an event occurs which gives rise to a liability of Lessee for any payment or reimbursement of any imposition pursuant to this Section 8 or for the payment by an Indemnitee to Lessee, such liability shall continue, notwithstanding the expiration or termination of this Lease, until all such payments or reimbursements are made by Lessee or the Indemnitee, as the case may be.

(j)   All indemnities provided for in this Section 8 are expressly made for the benefit of, and shall be enforceable by, the Indemnitees.

Section 9. Income Tax Indemnities.

(a)   *General.* For United States Corporation income tax purposes (and to the extent allowable for state and local tax purposes), Lessor (or the consolidated Federal taxpayer group of which Lessor is a part) intends:

(i)   to take the investment tax credit under Section 38 of the Code with respect to the Equipment for new tangible personal property in an amount equal to ten percent (10%) of the Lessor's Cost of Equipment and further that for purposes of said investment tax credit the Equipment will be treated as having been placed in service not later than December 31, 19XX;

(ii)   to deduct accelerated depreciation based on the system prescribed in Section 1.167(a)-11 of the regulations promulgated under the Code, over a depreciation period of seven (7) years, computed under the double-declining balance method provided in Section 167(b)(2) of the Code and switching to the sum-of-the-years-digits method provided in Section 167(b)(3) of the Code, using an original basis equal to the Lessor's Cost of the Equipment and a 0% salvage value (after applying Section 167(f)(1) of the Code) and further, that for purposes of computing such depreciation, the Lessor will be entitled to adopt the half-year convention for 19XX as described in Treas. Reg. §1.167(a)-11(c)(2);

(iii)　not to "recapture" any investment tax credit by reason of any replacement, alterations, modifications and/or additions to the Equipment made by Lessee or any of its subsidiaries or affiliates pursuant to this Lease or otherwise ("Lessee Expenditures"); and

(iv)　to deduct the interest paid or accrued on the Notes on a current basis.

(b)　*Loss of Investment Credit.* If for any reason there shall be a disallowance, elimination, reduction or disqualification ("Loss of Investment Credit"), in whole or in part, with respect to Lessor, of the Federal investment tax credit for the Equipment referred to in paragraph (a)(i) of this Section 9, Lessee shall pay to Lessor an amount equal to the sum of (i) an amount which, after deduction of all taxes required to be paid by Lessor for the year of receipt and any year prior or subsequent thereto attributable to the receipt of such amount under the laws of any Federal, state or local government or taxing authority, shall be equal to the sum of the amount of investment credit lost and the amount of any interest and Additions to Tax payable by Lessor as a result of such Loss of Investment Credit which do not reduce Lessor's Federal, state and local income tax payments in the year paid or accrued, plus (ii) the amount of any interest and any Additions to Tax payable by Lessor as a result of such Loss of Investment Credit which reduce Lessor's Federal, state and local income tax payments in the year paid or accrued. (For purposes of this Lease, "Additions to Tax" shall mean those penalties imposed under Federal, state and local income tax laws and those payments described in Sections 6651(a)(3), 6653 and 6655 of the Code and corresponding provisions of the state and local income tax laws, but only if such penalties are imposed or such payments, other than payments under Section 6655, are required, as the result of an act or failure to act of Lessee.) Recapture of investment credit shall not be considered a Loss of Investment Credit.

(c)　*Loss of Depreciation Deduction.* If for any reason there shall be a disallowance, elimination, reduction or disqualification ("Loss of Depreciation Deduction"), in whole or in part, with respect to Lessor, of any Federal, state or local income tax deduction of amortization or depreciation referred to in paragraph (a)(ii) of this Section 9, including, without limitation, accelerated depreciation, Lessee shall pay to Lessor the Additional Income Tax Liability thereby incurred. (For purposes of this Section 9, "Additional Income Tax Liability" shall not include any taxes imposed under Sections 531 and 541 of the Code.)

For purposes of definition and explanation, such amount payable in relation to any such Loss of Depreciation Deduction shall be equal to: (i) for the period prior to the payment by Lessor of additional

Federal, state and local tax(es) as a result of such Loss of Depreciation Deduction, a sum equal to (A) an amount which, after deduction of all taxes required to be paid by Lessor for the year of receipt and any year prior or subsequent thereto attributable to the receipt of such amount under the laws of any Federal, state or local government or taxing authority, shall be equal to the amount of any additional tax liability plus any interest and Additions to Tax payable by Lessor as a result of such Loss of Depreciation Deduction which do not reduce Lessor's Federal, state and local income tax payments in the year paid or accrued, plus (B) the amount of any interest and Additions to Tax payable by Lessor as a result of such Loss of Depreciation Deduction which reduce Lessor's Federal, state and local income tax payments in the year paid or accrued, and (ii) for the period after such payment by Lessor, an amount, computed and paid separately for each taxable year of Lessor, which, after deduction of all taxes required to be paid by Lessor in respect of receipt of such amount under the laws of any Federal, state or local government or taxing authority, shall be equal to the amount of additional tax(es) payable by Lessor as a result of such Loss of Depreciation Deduction for the taxable year of Lessor for which this computation is made.

(d) *Recapture.* If for any reason arising from the conduct of Lessee, Lessor shall be required to recapture any investment tax credit ("Recapture") at any time during the term of this Lease other than as a result of events which require the payment of Casualty Value or Termination Value under Section 12 or Section 21 hereof, Lessee shall pay to Lessor an amount sufficient, after deducting any taxes payable thereon or with respect thereto, to compensate Lessor for the Additional Income Tax Liability thereby incurred.

For purposes of definition and explanation, such amount payable by reason of Recapture shall be equal to the sum of (i) an amount which, after deduction of all taxes required to be paid by Lessor for the year of receipt and any year prior or subsequent thereto attributable to the receipt of such amount under the laws of any Federal, state or local government or taxing authority, shall be equal to the amount of any additional tax liability plus any interest and Additions to Tax payable by Lessor as a result of such Recapture which do not reduce Lessor's Federal, state and local income tax payments in the year paid or accrued, plus (ii) the amount of any interest and Additions to Tax payable by Lessor as a result of such Recapture which reduce Lessor's Federal, state and local income tax payments in the year paid or accrued.

(e) *Loss of Interest Deduction.* If for any reason not arising from the conduct of Lessor, there shall be a disallowance, elimination, reduction or disqualification of the applicable interest expense paid or payable under the Notes ("Loss of Interest Deduction") as a deductible expense, by Lessor, for Federal, state and local income tax purposes, Lessee shall compensate Lessor for the Additional Income Tax Liability thereby incurred.

For purposes of definition and explanation, such amount payable by reason of the Loss of Interest Deduction shall be equal to the sum of (i) an amount which, after deduction of all taxes required to be paid by Lessor for the year of receipt and any year prior or subsequent thereto attributable to the receipt of such amount under the laws of any Federal, state or local government or taxing authority, shall be equal to the amount of any additional tax liability plus any interest and Additions to Tax payable by Lessor as a result of such Loss of Interest Deduction which do not reduce Lessor's Federal, state and local income tax payments in the year paid or accrued, plus (ii) the amount of any interest and Additions to Tax payable by Lessor as a result of such Loss of Interest Deduction which reduce Lessor's Federal, state and local income tax payments in the year paid or accrued.

(f)   *Payments: Notice.* Any Indemnitee who claims payment under this Section 9 on account of any Loss of Investment Credit, Loss of Depreciation Deduction, Loss of Interest Deduction or Recapture (collectively referred to as "Loss of Tax Benefits") shall provide Lessee with a written notice of such claim, which notice shall be accompanied by a statement describing in detail the Loss of Tax Benefits and setting forth the computation of the amount(s) so payable. The amount(s) payable to any Indemnitee shall be made on or prior to the later of (i) the date that the Indemnitee (or the consolidated Federal taxpayer group of which said Indemnitee is a party) shall pay the tax increase resulting from such Loss of Tax Benefits (or suffers a reduction in the amount of any refund which the Indemnitee would have been entitled to receive but for the Loss of Tax Benefits) or (ii) 30 days after the date of the notice described in this Section 9.

(g)   *Offsetting Benefits.* If the event which results in a Loss of Tax Benefits for which an amount has been paid pursuant to this Section 9 has the effect of reducing Lessor's tax liability, including, without limitation, a reduction in the tax liability of Lessor which results from a disposition of any interest in the Equipment, Lessor shall pay to Lessee immediately after Lessor has filed its income tax return for the year in which its tax payments have been reduced the sum of (i) the amount by which Lessor's tax liability has been reduced as a result of such Loss of Tax Benefits and (ii) the reduction in tax payments attributable to the deduction of the amount described in clause (i) of this sentence.

(h)   *Exception.* An Indemnitee shall not be entitled to a payment under this Section 9 on account of any Loss of Tax Benefits which would not have occurred but for one or more of the following events: (i) a disposition of the Equipment or this Lease by Lessor, in each such case other than pursuant to its rights under Section 18 hereof, or (ii) a failure of Lessor to claim investment tax credit or depreciation for the Equipment in its tax return in a timely or proper manner (or the consolidated Federal taxpayer group of which Lessor is a part), or (iii) a disqualifying change in the nature of the business of Lessor or the liquidation thereof, or (iv) a foreclosure by any person holding through any Indemnitee a lien on the Equipment (other than pursuant to Section 18 hereof) which foreclosure results from an act of such Indemnitee, or (v) in the case of Lessor or the Lenders, any event which by the terms of this Lease requires payment by Lessee of the Casualty Value or Termination Value, if such Casualty Value or Termination Value is thereafter actually paid by Lessee, (vi) the failure of Lessor to have sufficient liability for Federal income tax against which to credit the investment tax credit or sufficient income to benefit from the depreciation, amortization or interest deductions which constitute the Loss of Tax Benefits or (vii) a breach of Lessor's warranty and covenant set forth in Section 10(c) hereof. Unless the Lease is terminated pursuant to Section 18 hereof, an Indemnitee shall not be entitled to a payment under this Section 9 on account of any Loss of Tax Benefits which (i) occurs after the termination of this Lease and (ii) does not relate to any period of time prior to the termination of the Lease.

(i)   *Procedure.* Upon receipt by any Indemnitee of a written notification from a Federal, state or local taxing authority of a proposed disallowance or adjustment of any credit or deduction (or a proposed inclusion in income) for which an amount may be payable by Lessee in accordance with this Lease (hereafter called a "Disallowance"), said Indemnitee shall promptly notify Lessee of said Disallowance after receipt of such written notification from the applicable taxing authority (which notice to Lessee shall include all relevant information relating to such Disallowance which may be particularly within the knowledge of the Indemnitee).

The Indemnitee shall vigorously contest such Disallowance, if Lessee so requests, until a final administrative adjudication of the issues raised by the Disallowance is made. Lessee, in its discretion, may contest such Disallowance until a final judicial decision of the issues raised by the Disallowance is made. Lessee shall be responsible for and pay all reasonable fees, costs and expenses incurred by it and the Indemnitee in connection with any such administrative or judicial contest. The Indemnitee shall cooperate in any such contest by Lessee to the extent necessary to enable Lessee to make such contest.

In the event that an Indemnitee receives a refund of any tax paid by it relating to this Lease for which it has received a payment from Lessee pursuant to this Section 9, the Indemnitee shall pay to Lessee the sum of (i) such refund (and any interest thereon paid by the United States Government or state or local taxing authority) and (ii) an amount equal to the reduction in the tax payments of the Indemnitee attributable to the deduction of the amount described in clause (i) of this sentence. The payment described in clause (i) of the preceding sentence shall be made immediately after receipt of such refund, and the payment described in clause (ii) of the preceding sentence shall be made immediately after the Indemnitee has filed its income tax return for the year in which its income tax payments have been reduced.

In the event that an Indemnitee elects to pay the tax resulting from a Disallowance for which it has not received a payment from Lessee pursuant to this Lease and to seek a refund thereof, Lessee shall pay to the Indemnitee an amount equal to interest at the Lender's Rate, computed from the date of payment of such tax to the date of a final determination of such Indemnitee's claim for refund, such amounts to be payable on Rent Payment Dates during such period. Upon receipt by an Indemnitee of a refund of any tax paid by it in respect of which Lessee has paid interest thereon while such tax payable was contested by such Indemnitee, any interest on such refund paid to such Indemnitee by the United States Government or state or local taxing authority shall be paid to Lessee immediately after receipt of such interest.

Notwithstanding the preceding paragraphs of this Section 9(i), each Indemnitee reserves the right at all times prior to final administrative and judicial adjudication of the issues raised by the Disallowance to direct tax counsel not to take or to cease taking all legal or other appropriate action deemed reasonable by such counsel in order to sustain all or any part of any bona fide Disallowance herein, whereby such action by Indemnitee will relieve Lessee of its obligation to said Indemnitee under this Lease in respect to the Disallowance.

(j) *Benefit.* All of the Indemnitees' rights and privileges arising from the indemnities contained in this Section 9 shall survive the expiration or other termination of this Lease and said indemnities are expressly made for the benefit of, and shall be enforceable by, the Indemnitees and their respective successors and assigns.

(k) *Tax Rates.* In computing the amounts payable under subparagraphs (b), (c), (d) and (e) for any Loss of Tax Benefits, the "taxes required to be paid" by the Indemnitee shall be computed at the respective marginal federal, state and local income tax rates with respect to the amounts received by the Indemnitee for (i) the year of receipt and (ii) any year prior or subsequent thereto affected by the receipt.

(l)   *Change in Law.* The indemnities set forth in this Lease specifically do not include any Loss of Tax Benefits arising from any change in statutes or regulations arising after the date this Lease is executed.

Section 10. Disclaimer of Warranties.

(a) LESSOR MAKES NO WARRANTY OR REPRESENTATION, EITHER EXPRESSED OR IMPLIED, AS TO THE DESIGN, OPERATION OR CONDITION OF, OR AS TO THE QUALITY OF THE MATERIAL, EQUIPMENT OR WORKMANSHIP IN, OR TITLE TO, THE EQUIPMENT DELIVERED TO LESSEE HEREUNDER, AND LESSOR MAKES NO WARRANTY OF MERCHANTABILITY OR FITNESS OF THE EQUIPMENT FOR ANY PARTICULAR PURPOSE OR ANY OTHER REPRESENTATION OR WARRANTY WHATSOEVER, IT BEING AGREED THAT ALL SUCH RISKS, AS BETWEEN LESSOR AND LESSEE, ARE TO BE BORNE BY LESSEE AND THE BENEFITS OF ANY AND ALL IMPLIED WARRANTIES OF LESSOR ARE HEREBY WAIVED BY LESSEE. LESSOR SHALL NOT BE RESPONSIBLE FOR INCIDENTAL OR CONSEQUENTIAL DAMAGES.

(b)   Lessor hereby irrevocably appoints and constitutes Lessee its agent and attorney-in-fact during the term of this Lease, so long as Lessee shall not be in default hereunder, to assert from time to time, in the name of and for account of Lessor, but for the benefit of Lessee, whatever claims and rights including warranties of the Equipment which Lessor may have against the Manufacturer, any sub-contractors of the Manufacturer or any vendors. Lessee will not assert any claim of any nature whatsoever against Lessor based on any of the foregoing matters unless Lessor shall refuse to cooperate to the extent necessary to enable Lessee to assert such claims against the Manufacturer, its subcontractors and vendors. To the extent that any claims or rights of Lessor with respect to the Equipment may not be assigned or otherwise made available to Lessee, Lessor will use its best efforts, at Lessee's cost, to enforce such claims or rights.

(c)   Lessor warrants that at the inception of the term of this Lease, its investment in the Equipment is at least $800,000 and that throughout the term of this Lease it will not reduce such investment other than as contemplated by the terms and provisions of this Lease.

Section 11. Use, Operation, Maintenance, Insurance.

(a)   Throughout the term of this Lease, the possession, use, operation and maintenance of the Equipment shall be at the sole risk and expense of Lessee. Lessee shall use the Equipment only in the manner for which it was designed and intended and so as to subject it only to ordinary wear and tear. Any parts or accessories provided by Lessee in the course of repairing or maintaining the Equipment shall be considered accessions to such Equipment and title thereto shall be immediately vested in Lessor, without cost or expense to Lessor, but the replaced parts shall no longer be the property of Lessor.

(b)   Notwithstanding the foregoing, Lessee shall be entitled, from time to time during the term of this Lease, to acquire and install, at Lessee's expense (and Lessor hereby irrevocably appoints and constitutes Lessee its agent and attorney-in-fact so long as no Event of Default shall have occurred and be continuing hereunder, for such purpose), such additional features or options as may be available at such time, so long as such features or options are readily removable. Such additional features or options shall be removed by Lessee before the Equipment is returned to Lessor and Lessee shall repair all damage to the Equipment resulting from such installation and removal so as to restore the Equipment to the condition in which it existed prior to the installation of such additional features or options.

(c)   Lessee shall, upon expiration of any Manufacturer's warranty period applicable to the Equipment, enter into and maintain in force a maintenance agreement with such Manufacturer or with another qualified party (the "Maintenance Agreement") covering at least prime shift maintenance of the Equipment. Lessee will cause the person providing maintenance service under the Maintenance Agreement to keep the Equipment in good working order in accordance with the provisions of the Maintenance Agreement and to make all necessary adjustments and repairs to the Equipment. Lessee shall allow such person access to the Equipment for such purposes. Such person is hereby authorized to accept the directions of Lessee with respect to such maintenance, adjustments and repairs.

(d)   Charges under the Maintenance Agreement and all other maintenance and service charges, including installation and dismantling charges, shall be borne by Lessee, and Lessee agrees promptly to reimburse Lessor for any amount thereof paid by Lessor during the term of this Lease.

(e)   Lessee agrees to comply with all governmental laws, regulations, requirements and rules and with all requirements of the

Manufacturer (including any requirements included in the Manufacturer's current manual of operation, or supplements thereto, with respect to which any failure in compliance would limit or excuse the obligations of the Manufacturer contained in the Purchase Documents) or the Maintenance Agreement with respect to the use, maintenance and operation of the Equipment. In case any additional or other equipment, appliance or alteration is required to be made or installed on the Equipment in order to comply with such laws, regulations, requirements and rules, Lessee agrees to make or install such equipment, appliance or alteration at its own cost and expense, and any such equipment, appliance or alteration shall, without any further act of Lessor or Lessee, become the property of Lessor and be considered Equipment for all purposes of this Lease. Any such equipment, appliance or alteration may be leased by Lessor to Lessee as contemplated by Section 2(g) hereof if Lessor and Lessee so agree in accordance with the provisions of such Section 2(g).

(f)   Lessee will, at all times while this Lease is in effect, at its own expense, cause to be carried and maintained insurance in respect of the Equipment at the time subject hereto, and public liability insurance, in amounts and against risks customarily insured against by Lessee on similar equipment, and in any event in amounts and against risks comparable to those insured against by Lessee on equipment owned by it. Lessor and the Lenders shall not be named insureds or loss payees with respect to any such insurance; provided, however, that in the event Lessee's net worth as determined in accordance with generally accepted accounting principles falls below $100,000,000 at any time during the term of this Lease, then Lessor and the Lenders shall have the right to be named as insureds with respect to such insurance. On each annual anniversary of the Closing Date during the term of this Lease, Lessee shall furnish Lessor and any assignee pursuant to Section 19 hereof a copy of a certificate of insurance with respect to each of the insurance policies described above.

The excess of any insurance proceeds paid or payable in respect of any loss of or damage to the Equipment, including a Casualty Occurrence, as hereinafter defined, with respect to the Equipment over the amount required to repair, restore or replace the Equipment, or in the event of such a Casualty Occurrence, over the Casualty Value, shall be paid to the Lessor by Lessee and shall be applied in accordance with Section 12 hereof.

Section 12. Payment for Casualty Occurrence;
Requisition.

(a)   In the event that any Unit shall be or become destroyed, lost or stolen, or title thereto shall be taken by any governmental authority under power of eminent domain or otherwise or any Unit is returned to the Manufacturer pursuant to the patent indemnity provisions of the Purchase Documents, or in the event of any damage or wearing out under circumstances in which the Lessee does not determine within 30 days after the date of occurrence of such damage or wearing out that such Unit can be repaired or replaced, such Unit shall be deemed to have suffered a "Casualty Occurrence" on the date of the occurrence of the destruction, loss, theft, taking of title, return, damage or wearing out and such fact shall be promptly reported by Lessee to Lessor and the Lenders.

(b)   In the event any Unit shall be or become damaged or worn out, and Lessee determines, within 30 days after the date of occurrence of any such damage or wearing out, that such Unit can be repaired or replaced, Lessee shall cause the Unit to be repaired or replaced within 90 days after the occurrence of such damage or wearing out. Any replacement by Lessee in accordance with the provisions of this Section 12(b) shall be in as good operating condition as, and shall have a value and utility at least equal to, the Unit replaced, assuming the replaced Unit was in the condition and repair required to be maintained by the terms hereof, and such replacement shall, without further act of Lessor or Lessee, be considered a Unit for all purposes of this Lease. In the event that Lessee shall, within said 90-day period, have commenced the repair or replacement of the Unit and be diligently pursuing such repair or replacement but is prevented from completing the repair or replacement within said 90-day period due to causes beyond Lessee's control, then the time for repair or replacement shall be extended by the number of days necessary to complete such repair or replacement up to a maximum of 90 additional days, and further provided, that if Lessee fails to repair or replace the Unit within the above-described repair or replacement period, the Unit will be deemed to have suffered a Casualty Occurrence on the date of the occurrence of such damage or wearing out.

(c)   In the event of a Casualty Occurrence, Lessee shall pay to Lessor an amount equal to (i) the sum of (A) the Casualty Value of the Unit determined as of the Basic Rent Date next succeeding the date of the Casualty Occurrence and (B) interest on such Casualty Value at the Lender's Interest Rate from the Basic Rent Date next succeeding the date of the Casualty Occurrence to the date of payment of such Casualty Value, less (ii) the sum of (A) all Basic Rent applicable to such Unit due and paid after the Basic Rent Date as of which such Casualty Value was determined and (B) interest on such payment of Basic Rent at the Lender's Interest Rate from the date(s) of payment of Basic Rent to the date of payment of such Casualty Value. Such amount, together with the Basic Rent and all Supplemental Rent then due, shall be paid on a Basic Rent Payment Date which occurs not more than 210 days after the date of the Casualty Occurrence (or, in the event Lessee fails to repair or replace the Unit within the above-described repair or replacement period, on the Basic Rent Date next following the end of such repair or replacement period). Upon making such payment in respect of the Unit, the Rent for such Unit shall cease to accrue as of the date of such Casualty Value payment, the term of this Lease as to such Unit shall terminate and (except in the case of such loss, theft, destruction, taking of title or return to the Manufacturer) Lessor shall be entitled to recover possession of such Unit. In the case of the taking of title to any Unit by governmental authority under power of eminent domain or otherwise, any payments received from such governmental authority as compensation for such taking of title shall, if Lessee has theretofore paid the Casualty Value, be paid over to or retained by Lessee until the aggregate of all such payments so made or retained shall equal the Casualty Value paid by Lessee for such Unit and any balance shall be paid over to or retained by Lessor. Lessor shall be under no duty to Lessee to pursue any claim against any governmental authority but Lessee may at its own cost and expense pursue the same on behalf of Lessor, and Lessor shall cooperate to the extent necessary to enable Lessee to pursue such claim.

(d) Following payment of the Casualty Value of a Unit in accordance with the provisions of Section 12(c), Lessee shall, as agent for Lessor, dispose of such Unit as soon as it is able to do so for the best price obtainable. Any such disposition shall be on an "as is," "where is" basis without representation or warranty, express or implied. As to each separate Unit so disposed of, Lessee may, after paying Lessor the amounts specified in Section 12(c), retain all proceeds from such disposition plus any payments for damages to the Equipment received by Lessee by reason of such Casualty Occurrence up to an amount equal to the Casualty Value and Lessee's reasonable costs and expenses of disposition attributable thereto, and shall remit the excess, if any, to Lessor; provided, however, that Lessee shall not be required to remit any payments for damages received by it for injuries to it by third parties arising out of such Casualty Occurrence. As to each Unit returned to the Manufacturer in the manner described in Section 12(a) and not replaced or modified by the Manufacturer pursuant to the patent indemnity provisions of the Purchase Documents, Lessee shall be entitled to receive and retain all amounts payable to Lessor by the Manufacturer for the return of such Unit, up to the Casualty Value paid by Lessee hereunder, and any excess shall be paid over to or retained by Lessor. As to each Unit replaced or modified by the Manufacturer pursuant to the patent indemnity provisions of the Purchase Documents, such replacement or modified Unit shall be delivered to Lessee and shall, without any further act of Lessor or Lessee, be considered a Unit for all purposes of this Lease.

(e)   Except as hereinabove in this Section 12 provided, Lessee shall bear the risk of loss and shall not be released from its obligations hereunder in the event of any damage or Casualty Occurrence to any Unit after delivery to and acceptance by Lessee hereunder.

(f)   In the event that during the term of this Lease the use of any Unit is requisitioned or taken by any governmental authority without the taking of title thereto, such requisition or taking shall not terminate this Lease and each and every obligation of Lessee with respect thereto shall remain in full force and effect. So long as no Event of Default shall have occurred and be continuing hereunder, Lessor shall pay to Lessee all sums received by Lessor by reason of said requisition or taking, up to the Rent paid by Lessee during the period of said requisition or taking.

Section 13. Indemnification.

The provisions of this Section 13 are in addition to, and not in limitation of, the provisions of Sections 8 and 9 hereof. In the event of a conflict between any provision of this Section 13 and a provision or provisions of Section 8 or Section 9, such provision or provisions of Section 8 or Section 9 shall control.

(a)   Lessee hereby agrees to assume liability for, and does hereby agree to indemnify, protect, save and keep harmless each Indemnitee and their respective successors, assigns, legal representatives, agents and servants from and against, any and all liabilities, obligations, losses, damages, penalties, claims, actions, suits, costs, expenses or disbursements arising out of Lessee's actions of any kind and nature whatsoever which may be imposed on, incurred by or asserted against the Indemnitee or any of their respective successors, assigns, legal representatives, agents and servants (whether or not also indemnified against by the Manufacturer or any other person) in any way relating to or arising out of this Lease or any document contemplated hereby, or the performance or enforcement of any of the terms hereof, or in any way relating to or arising out of the manufacture, purchase, acceptance, rejection, return, lease, ownership, possession, use, condition, operation, sale or other disposition of the Equipment or any accident in connection therewith (including, without limitation, latent and other defects, whether or not discoverable); provided, however, that Lessee shall not be required to indemnify any Indemnitee or its successors, assigns, legal representatives, agents and servants for loss or liability in respect of the Equipment arising from acts or events which occur after possession of such Equipment has been delivered to Lessor or the Lenders or loss or liability resulting from the willful misconduct of the party otherwise to be indemnified hereunder. Lessee agrees that no Indemnitee shall be liable to Lessee for any liability, claim, loss, damage or expense of any kind or nature caused directly or indirectly by the inadequacy of the Equipment for any purpose or any deficiency or defect therein or the use or maintenance thereof or any delay in providing, or failure to provide, any thereof or any interruption or loss of service or use thereof or any loss of business.

(b)   All amounts payable to an Indemnitee under Section 13(a) shall be (i) computed on an "after-tax" basis so that such payments shall be in an amount which, when reduced by the increase in the income tax liability or liabilities of the recipient as a result of such payment by Lessee, shall equal the after-tax cost of the damage, injury, claim, demand or expense and (ii) payable, to the extent not theretofore paid, on written demand of such Indemnitee. The provisions of Section 9(k) shall apply in computing the "after-tax" liability of Lessee under this Section 13(b).

(c)   All of the Indemnitees' rights and privileges arising from the indemnities contained in Section 13(a) shall survive the expiration or other termination of this Lease and said indemnities are expressly made for the benefit of, and shall be enforceable by, the Indemnitees and their respective successors and assigns; provided, however that no claims relating to such indemnities may be asserted against Lessee more than five years after the occurrence of the event which is the basis for making such claim or five years after the expiration or other termination of this Lease, whichever is earlier.

(d)   It is understood and agreed that the indemnities and assumptions of liabilities set forth in Section 13(a) do not guarantee a residual value.

Section 14. Title of Lessor; Equipment to Be
and Remain Personal Property.

(a)   Except as otherwise provided herein, title to the Equipment as between Lessor and Lessee shall at all times remain in Lessor. Lessee will at all times protect and defend, at its own cost and expense, the title of Lessor from and against all claims, liens and legal processes of creditors of Lessee and keep the Equipment free and clear from all other claims, liens and processes and other encumbrances, except:

(i)   the respective rights of Lessor and Lessee as herein provided and the rights of the Lenders under the Security Agreement;

(ii)   liens or encumbrances which result from acts of Lessor, the Lenders or their respective agents, successors or assigns; and

(iii)   inchoate materialmen's, mechanics', workmen's, repairmen's, employees' or other like liens arising in the ordinary course of business and not delinquent.

Lessee will promptly at its own expense take such action as may be necessary duly to discharge any such claim, lien, process or other encumbrance not excepted above if the same shall arise at any time.

(b)   It is the intention and understanding of both Lessor and Lessee that the Equipment shall be and at all times remain separately identifiable personal property. Lessee shall not permit the Equipment to be installed in, maintained with, stored or used in such manner or under such circumstances that such Equipment might be or become an accession to or confused with such other personal property; provided, however, that the use or maintenance in accordance with normal operating procedures of Lessee of the Equipment with any other computer equipment owned by or leased to Lessee shall not be a violation of the foregoing provisions of this sentence. Lessee shall not permit the Equipment to be installed in, maintained, stored or used with any real property in such a manner or under such circumstances that any person might acquire any rights in such Equipment paramount to the rights of Lessor or the Lenders by reason of such Equipment being deemed to be real property or a fixture thereon.

Section 15. Performance of Obligations of Lessee by Lessor.

If an Event of Default should occur hereunder, Lessor may thereafter make the payment or perform or comply with the agreement, the nonpayment, nonperformance or noncompliance which caused such Event of Default, and the amount of such payment and the amount of the reasonable expenses of Lessor incurred in connection with such payment or the performance of or compliance with such agreement, as the case may be (all on an after-tax basis computed in accordance with Section 9(k)), together with interest at the Overdue Rate, shall be payable by Lessee upon demand.

Section 16. Right of Inspection.

Lessor and the Lenders and their respective agents, designees and assigns shall have the right from time to time, upon written notification and during reasonable business hours, to enter upon the premises where the Equipment may be located for the purposes of confirming the existence, condition and proper maintenance of the Equipment. The foregoing rights of entry are subject to any applicable governmental security laws, regulations and rules and reasonable security regulations and procedures of Lessee.

Section 17. Events of Default.

The following events shall constitute Events of Default:

(a)   Lessee fails to pay when due any installment of Rent and such failure shall continue uncured for a period of 10 Business Days after notice thereof to Lessee by Lessor or the Lenders; or

(b)   Lessee shall fail to perform any of the other covenants herein and such failure shall continue uncured for 30 days after written notice thereof to Lessee by Lessor or the Lenders; or

(c)   Lessee ceases doing business as a going concern, makes an assignment for the benefit of creditors, admits in writing the inability to pay its debts as they become due, files a voluntary petition in bankruptcy, is adjudicated a bankrupt or an insolvent, files a petition seeking for itself any reorganization, arrangement, composition, readjustment, liquidation, dissolution or similar arrangement under any present or future statute, law or regulation or files an answer admitting the material allegations of a petition filed against it in any such proceeding or consents to or acquiesces in the appointment of a trustee, receiver or liquidator of it or of all or any substantial part of its assets or properties, or if it shall take any action looking to its dissolution or liquidation; or

(d)   within 60 days after the commencement of any proceedings against Lessee seeking reorganization, arrangement, readjustment, liquidation, dissolution or similar relief under any present or future statute, law or regulation, such proceedings shall not have been dismissed, or if within 60 days after the appointment without Lessee's consent or acquiescence of any trustee, receiver or liquidator of it or of all or any substantial part of its assets or properties, such appointment shall not be vacated; or

(e)   Lessee attempts to remove, sell, transfer, encumber, part with possession or assign or sublet (except as expressly permitted by the provisions hereof or with the prior written consent of Lessor and the Lenders) the Equipment or any part thereof; or

(f)   any representation or warranty made by Lessee herein or in any document or certificate furnished Lessor or the Lenders in connection herewith or pursuant hereto or in connection with the Purchase Documents or pursuant thereto shall at any time prove to be incorrect at the time made in any material respect, and Lessee shall be unable to correct such incorrect statement within thirty (30) days after notice thereof to Lessee from Lessor or the Lenders.

Section 18. Remedies.

Upon the occurrence of any Event of Default, Lessor may, at its option, declare this Lease to be in default, and so long as the default shall be continuing, Lessor may exercise one or more of the following remedies, as Lessor in its sole discretion (or at the discretion of the Lenders) shall elect, except that the remedies described in paragraph (c) and (d) of this Section 18 are mutually exclusive:

(a)   proceed by appropriate court action, either at law or in equity, to enforce performance by Lessee of the applicable covenants of this Lease or to recover damages for the breach thereof;

(b)   by notice in writing, terminate this Lease, whereupon all rights of Lessee to the use of the Equipment shall absolutely cease and terminate but Lessee shall remain liable as hereinafter provided; and thereupon Lessee shall, without further demand, forthwith pay to Lessor an amount equal to any unpaid Rent due and payable for Rental Periods up to and including the Rental Period during which Lessor shall have declared this Lease to be in default;

(c)   by notice in writing, cause Lessee, at Lessee's expense, promptly to return the Equipment to the possession of Lessor at the location where the Equipment is in last use and in the condition required upon the return thereof pursuant to and in accordance with the terms of Section 6 hereof, or Lessor, at its option, may enter upon the premises where the Equipment is located and take immediate possession of and remove the same by summary proceedings, or Lessor, at its option, may keep and store the Equipment on the premises of Lessee for a period not to exceed 60 days and dispose of the Equipment as hereinafter provided, and no such action shall be construed as a surrender of the Equipment by the Lessor or a failure of Lessor to take possession of the Equipment. If Lessor shall elect to proceed pursuant to this paragraph (c), Lessee shall, without further demand, forthwith pay to Lessor, as liquidated damages for loss of a bargain and not as a penalty, an amount equal to the Termination Value of the Equipment, computed as of the next Basic Rent Date following the date upon which Lessor has declared this Lease to be in default. Following the return of the Equipment to Lessor pursuant to this paragraph (c), Lessor shall proceed to sell the Equipment in such manner as it shall in good faith deem appropriate. The proceeds of such sale shall be applied by Lessor to reimburse Lessee for the Termintion Value previously paid by Lessee as liquidated damages; and any surplus shall be retained by Lessor. Lessee shall forthwith pay to

Lessor any deficiency between the proceeds from such sale and the Termination Value (to the extent not previously paid by Lessee), together with interest at the Overdue Rate from the date the Termination Value is payable until paid by Lessee; or

(d) by notice in writing, cause Lessee, at Lessee's expense, promptly to return the Equipment to the possession of Lessor at the location where the Equipment is in last use and in the condition required upon the return thereof pursuant to and in accordance with the terms of Section 6 hereof, or Lessor, at its option, may enter upon the premises where the Equipment is located and take immediate possession of and remove the same by summary proceedings, or Lessor, at its option may keep and store the Equipment on the premises of Lessee for a period not to exceed 60 days and no such action shall be construed as a surrender of the Equipment by Lessor, or a failure of Lessor to take possession of the Equipment. If Lessor shall elect to proceed pursuant to this paragraph (d), Lessee shall, without further demand, forthwith pay to Lessor, as liquidated damages for loss of a bargain and not as a penalty, an amount which represents the excess of the present worth, as of the next Basic Rent Date following the date upon which Lessor has declared this Lease to be in default, of all Rents for the Equipment which would otherwise have accrued hereunder after the Rental Period during which Lessor has declared this Lease to be in default to the end of the term of this Lease over the then present worth of the then fair rental value of the Equipment for such period computed by discounting from the end of such term to the Basic Rent Date next following the date upon which Lessor has declared this Lease to be in default, rentals which Lessor in good faith reasonably estimates to be obtainable for the use of the Equipment during such period, such present worth to be computed in each case on an actuarial rate basis of 0.795% per annum, compounded from the respective dates upon which Rents would have been payable hereunder had this Lease not been terminated.

No remedy referred to in this Section 18 is intended to be exclusive, but each (other than the remedies described in paragraph (c) and (d) which are mutually exclusive) shall be cumulative and in addition to any other remedy referred to above or otherwise available to Lessor at law or in equity. No express or implied waiver by Lessor of any default or Event of Default hereunder shall in any way be, or be construed to be, a waiver of any future or subsequent default or Event of Default. The failure or delay of Lessor in exercising any rights granted it hereunder upon any occurrence of any of the contingencies set forth herein shall not constitute a waiver of any such right upon the continuation or recurrence of any such contingencies or similar contingencies and any single or partial exercise of any particular right by Lessor shall not exhaust the same or constitute a waiver of any other right provided herein.

Lessor shall make all reasonable efforts to mitigate any damages suffered by it. Lessee shall be liable for any costs and expenses, including reasonable attorneys' fees and disbursements, incurred by Lessor, the Lenders or any other party by reason of the occurrence of any Event of Default or the exercise of Lessor's remedies with respect thereto. In no event shall Lessee be liable for any indirect, special or consequential damages of any kind under this Lease.

Section 19. Assignment and Sublease.

(a) Without the prior written consent of Lessor, which shall not be unreasonably withheld, Lessee shall not assign this Lease or its interest hereunder or sublet the Equipment, except that, upon written notice to Lessor (i) Lessee may sublet the Equipment, or any part thereof, or assign this Lease or its interest hereunder to a subsidiary, affiliate or parent of Lessee and (ii) Lessee may assign and transfer its leasehold interest in the Equipment and possession of the Equipment to any subsidiary or affiliate of Lessee then duly organized and validly existing in the United States of America and empowered and authorized to own Lessee's properties and to carry on its business as then conducted, which corporation shall have assumed all of the obligations hereunder of Lessee and shall have acquired by merger, consolidation or purchase all or substantially all of the property of Lessee. In the event that Lessee is a party to any consolidation or merger in which Lessee is the surviving entity, no consent to such merger or consolidation by Lessor shall be required. In no event shall Lessee sublease the Equipment or any part thereof if such sublease is not expressly made subject and subordinate to this Lease. No sublease of the Equipment by Lessee or assignment of this Lease or Lessee's interest hereunder shall relieve Lessee of any of its obligations hereunder, which shall be and remain those of a principal and not a guarantor, until termination thereof in accordance with the terms of this Lease, except in the case of an assignment pursuant to clause (ii) of this paragraph.

(b) This Lease and all rights of Lessor hereunder shall be assignable by Lessor to the Lenders or, with the prior written consent of Lessee, which shall not be unreasonably withheld, to any third party, provided, however, that Lessor shall not be required to obtain Lessee's approval for any assignment by Lessor of this Lease and all the rights of Lessor hereunder to any parent, subsidiary or affiliated company of Lessor, or to any corporation then duly organized and validly existing in the United States of America and empowered and authorized to own

Lessor's properties and to carry on its business as then conducted, which corporation shall have assumed all of the obligations hereunder of Lessor and shall have acquired by merger, consolidation or purchase all or substantially all of the property of Lessor.

(c)   No assignee for collateral purposes shall be obligated to perform any duty, covenant or condition required to be performed by Lessor under any of the terms hereof, but on the contrary, Lessee by its execution hereof acknowledges and agrees that notwithstanding any such assignment, each and all such covenants, agreements, representations and warranties of Lessor shall survive any such assignment and shall be and remain the sole liability of Lessor and of every person, firm or corporation succeeding (by merger, consolidation, purchase of assets or otherwise) to all or substantially all of the business, assets or goodwill of Lessor. Without limiting the foregoing, Lessee further acknowledges and agrees that from and after the receipt by Lessee of written notice of an assignment from Lessor or from an assignee making any subsequent assignment: (i) all rents and other sums which are the subject matter of the assignment shall be paid to the assignee thereof at the place of payment designated in the notice; (ii) if such assignment was made for collateral purposes, the rights of any such assignee in and to the rents and other sums payable by Lessee under any provisions of this Lease and so assigned shall be absolute and unconditional and shall not be subject to any abatement whatsoever, or to any defense, set-off, counterclaim or recoupment whatsoever by reason of (A) any damage to or loss or destruction of the Equipment (except as otherwise provided in Section 12 hereof), or (B) any defect in or failure of title of Lessor to the Equipment or any interruption from whatsoever cause (other than from the wrongful act of such assignee) in the use, operation or possession of the Equipment, or (C) by reason of any indebtedness or liability howsoever and whenever arising of Lessor to Lessee or to any other person firm, corporation or governmental agency or taxing authority or for any other reason, or (D) by reason of any willful misconduct or gross negligence of Lessor; and (iii) to the extent provided in such assignment, the assignee shall have the right to exercise all rights, privileges and remedies (either in its own name or in the name of the Lessor for the use and benefit of the assignee) which by the terms of the Lease or by applicable law are permitted or provided to be exercised by Lessor.

Section 20.   Lessee's Right of First Refusal;
Option of Lessee to Renew.

(a)   *Right of First Refusal.* Unless an Event of Default, or any event or condition which, upon notice or lapse of time, would constitute an Event of Default, shall have occurred and be continuing,

Lessor shall not, at the end of the primary term or a Renewal Period, sell, transfer or otherwise dispose of the Equipment unless:

(i) Lessor shall have received from a responsible purchaser a bona fide offer in writing to purchase the Equipment;

(ii) Lessor shall have given Lessee notice (A) setting forth in detail the identity of such purchaser, the propsed purchase price, the proposed date of purchase and all other material terms and conditions of such purchase, including, without limitation, any arrangements for the financing of such purchase known to Lessor and (B) offering to sell the Equipment to Lessee upon the same terms and conditions as those set forth in such notice; and

(iii) Lessee shall not have notified Lessor, within 20 days following receipt of such notice, of its election to purchase the Equipment upon such terms and conditions.

If Lessee shall not have so elected to purchase the Equipment, Lessor may sell the Equipment at a price and upon other terms and conditions no less favorable to Lessor than those specified in such notice, provided Lessor shall have completed such sale by the later of (x) the date 90 days after the end of the primary term (or the Renewal Period, as the case may be) or (y) the date 200 days after the date of such notice to Lessee. Notwithstanding the foregoing provisions of this Section 20(a), Lessor may, if Lessee has not renewed this Lease pursuant to Section 20(c), lease the Equipment at any time after the end of the primary term (or, if Lessee has renewed this Lease for a Renewal Period, at the end of such Renewal Period) without first offering to lease the Equipment to Lessee.

(b) *Sale Without Recourse or Warranty.* Any sale of the Equipment by Lessor to Lessee pursuant to this Section 20 shall be made without any recourse to or warranty of Lessor whatsoever, except as to its own acts.

(c) *Renewal Option.* If no Event of Default or any event or condition which after lapse of time or the giving of notice or both would constitute an Event of Default shall have occurred or be continuing, upon the expiration of the primary term, Lessee shall have the option to renew this Lease with respect to all, but not less than all, of the Equipment for a period of one year (such period being herein called a "Renewal Period"); provided, however, that in order to exercise such right to renew this Lease, Lessee shall give Lessor not less than 180 days' written notice prior to the expiration of the primary term of its election to exercise such option. Except as otherwise provided in this paragraph (c), the rights and obligations of Lessor and Lessee hereunder during the Renewal Period shall be upon the same terms and conditions provided in this Lease for the primary term. The monthly rent payable to Lessor by Lessee during the Renewal Period shall be the "Fair Rental Value" of the Equipment for the Renewal Period as determined by an appraisal mutually agreed to by two recognized independent computer equipment appraisers, one chosen by Lessor and one chosen by Lessee, or, if such appraisers cannot agree on the amount of such appraisal, as arrived at by a third independent appraiser chosen by the mutual consent of such two appraisers. If either party shall fail to appoint an appraiser within 30 days after Lessee shall have given notice of its election to exercise its renewal option hereunder or if such two appraisers cannot agree on the amount of such appraisal and fail to appoint a third appraiser within 30 days of such notice, then either party may apply to any court having jurisdiction to make such appointment. The costs and expenses of such appriasal shall be shared equally by Lessor and Lessee. Lessee shall have the right to extend the term of this Lease for successive one year Renewal Periods on the same basis as set forth above during the first and any succeeding Renewal Period or Periods hereof. The Fair Rental Value described in this Section 20(c) shall be determined on the basis of, and shall be equal in amount to, the value which would be obtained in an arm's-length transaction between an informed and willing lessee (other than a lessee currently in possession or a used equipment or scrap dealer) and an informed and willing lessor under no compulsion to lease. Any such determination shall be made without regard to the cost of dismantling and delivering possession of the Equipment to Lessor, which costs shall be borne by Lessee pursuant to Section 6 hereof.

Section 21. Early Termination.

(a)   Provided no Event of Default under this Lease shall have occurred and be continuing, Lessee shall have the right at its option at any time on or after three (3) years from the commencement of the primary term of this Lease, on at least 90 days' prior written notice to Lessor and the Lenders and subject to the conditions herein set forth, to terminate this Lease on a day specified in such notice during the primary term of this Lease when a Basic Rent payment is due (the "Termination Date"), provided that Lessee shall have made a good faith determination that the Equipment is obsolete or surplus to Lessee's requirements. During the period from the giving of such notice until the Termination Date Lessee, as agent for Lessor, shall use its best efforts to obtain bids for the purchase of the Equipment by a person other than Lessee or an affiliate thereof. Lessee shall promptly certify in writing to Lessor the amount and terms of each bid received by Lessee and the name and address of the party submitting such bid. Subject to Lessor's right to retain the Equipment as provided in Section 21(b), on the Termination Date Lessor shall transfer title to the Equipment to a purchaser solicited by Lessee without recourse or warranty of condition except that Lessor shall warrant title and sell the Equipment for cash to the bidder who shall have submitted the highest bid prior to such date. The total sale price realized at such sale shall be retained by Lessor and, in addition, on the Termination Date, Lessee shall pay to Lessor, together with the Basic Rent and all Supplemental Rent then due, the amount, if any, by which the Termination Value of the Equipment, computed as of the Termination Date, exceeds the proceeds of such sale (after deducting all reasonable expenses incurred by Lessor in selling the Equipment), whereupon this Lease shall terminate, except as herein otherwise expressly provided. Subject to the provisions of Section 21(c), in the event no bids are received by Lessee, Lessee shall pay to Lessor together with the Basic Rent and all Supplemental Rent then due, the Termination Value of the Equipment, computed as of the Termination Date, and deliver the Equipment to the Lessor in accordance with the provisions of Section 6 hereof, whereupon this Lease shall terminate, except as herein otherwise expressly provided.

(b) Notwithstanding the provisions of Section 21(a), Lessor shall have the right at any time up to and including the proposed sale date, within its sole discretion, to elect not to sell any of the Equipment to any prospective purchaser secured by Lessee ("Third Party Purchaser"). In the event Lessor elects not to sell the Equipment to the Third Party Purchaser, Lessee shall return the Equipment to Lessor in the condition and manner required by Section 6 hereof, and Lessor thereupon may retain such Equipment for its own account without further obligation under this Lease. If no sale shall have occurred on or as of the Termination Date because the Third Party Purchaser fails to consummate a proposed sale and Lessor shall not have requested the return of the Equipment pursuant hereto, the Lease shall continue in full force and effect. In the event of any such sale or the return of the Equipment to Lessor pursuant hereto and provided Lessee is not in default with respect to any obligation under this Lease, the obligation of Lessee to pay rent with respect to the Equipment for the period subsequent to the Termination Date shall cease.

(c) If the Termination Value exceeds the highest bid or in the event no bids are received by Lessee, Lessee may, at its option, upon written notice given to Lessor not less than 15 days prior to the Termination Date, elect to rescind and cancel Lessee's notice of termination, whereupon this Lease shall not terminate pursuant to this Section 21, but the Lease shall continue in full force and effect as though no notice of termination had been given by Lessee; provided, however, if Lessor elects to retain the Equipment for its own account in accordance with the provisions of Section 21(b) and notifies Lessee of such election within 5 days after receipt by it of such notice of recision from Lessee, then such election of recision by Lessee shall be void and of no effect and Lessee shall return the Equipment to Lessor in accordance with the provisions of Section 21(b).

Section 22. Filings.

Lessee will, from time to time, at its expense, (including payment of filing, registration or recording fees, taxes or charges) do and perform any other act and will execute, acknowledge, deliver, file, register, record and deposit (and will refile, re-register, re-record or redeposit whenever required) any and all instruments reasonably requested by Lessor or the Lenders for the purpose of proper protection, to the satisfaction of Lessor or the Lenders, as the case may be, of their respective interests in the Equipment, this Lease and the Security Agreement or for the purpose of carrying out the intention of this Lease; and Lessee will promptly furnish to Lessor and the Lenders evidences of all such filings, registrations, recordings or deposits.

Section 23. Notices.

Any notice required or permitted to be given by either party hereto to the other party or to the Lenders or by the Lenders to the parties hereto shall be deemed to have been given when personally delivered or deposited in the United States certified mail, return receipt requested, postage prepaid, and addressed to such party or parties or the Lenders at the respective addresses thereof indicated below or such other address as such party or parties or the Lenders shall hereafter furnish to the other party or parties and the Lenders in writing in accordance with this Section 23; provided, however, that copies of all notices required or permitted to be given by either party hereto or the Lenders shall be given by such party and the Lenders to the other party or parties hereto and the Lenders:

If to Lessor: American Bank and Trust Company
233 South Plaza Drive
Chicago, Ilinois 60606
Attention: Mr. N. Paul

If to Lessee: The Manhattan Company
100 East 40th Street
New York, New York 10017
Attention: Treasurer

If to Lenders: Arlington National Bank and Trust Company
200 Green Drive
Baltimore, Maryland 21229
Attention: Mr. R. Peters

The Milford Bank
200 West Street
Washington, D.C. 02137
Attention: Mr. J. Donald

Section 24. Statement of Lease.

It is expressly understood and agreed by and between the parties hereto that this instrument constitutes a lease of the Equipment, and nothing herein shall be construed as conveying to Lessee any right, title or interest in the Equipment except as a lessee only. Neither the execution nor the filing of any financing statement with respect to the Equipment or the execution or filing of any financing statement with respect to this Lease or recording hereof shall in any manner imply that the relationship between Lessor and Lessee is anything other than lessor and lessee, respectively. Any such filing of financing statements or recordation of this lease is accomplished solely to protect the interests of Lessor, Lessee and the Lenders in the event of any unwarranted assertions by any person not a party to this lease transaction.

Section 25. Security Interest Subject to Lease.

Lessor agrees that if a security interest in the Equipment is granted to an assignee of the rents as additional security for indebtedness of the Lessor, the security agreement covering the Equipment shall expressly provide that the right, title and interest of the secured party thereunder is subject to the right, title and interest of the Lessee in and to the Equipment as provided in this Lease, providing that no Event of Default shall have occurred and be continuing.

Section 26. Financial Information.

Lessee agrees to cause Lessor to be added to the list of persons who or which receive all information mailed to the shareholders of Lessee forthwith after the Closing Date and to maintain Lessee's name on such list during the term of this Lease. In the event that Lessee does not receive any Annual Report or interim unaudited financial statements of Lessee within 30 days after the same have been mailed to Lessee's shareholders, Lessee shall deliver the same to Lessor within 30 days after Lessor's written request therefor.

Section 27. Severability; Effect and Modification
of Lease.

Any provision of this Lease which is prohibited or unenforceable in any jurisdiction shall be as to such jurisdiction ineffective to the extent of such prohibition or unenforceability without invalidating the remaining provisions hereof, and any such prohibition or unenforceability in any jurisdiction shall not invalidate or render unenforceable such provision in any other jurisdiction.

This Lease, including the Annexes and Schedules hereto, exclusively and completely states the rights of Lessor and Lessee with respect to the Equipment and supersedes all other agreements, oral or written, with respect to the Equipment. No variation or modification of this Lease and no waiver of any of its provisions or conditions shall be valid unless in writing and signed by duly authorized officers of Lessor, Lessee and the Lenders.

Section 28. Execution in Counterparts.

The single executed original of this Lease marked "Original" shall be the "Original" and all other counterparts hereof shall be marked and be "Duplicates." To the extent, if any, that this Lease constitutes chattel paper (as such term is defined in the Uniform Commercial Code, as in effect in any applicable jurisdiction), no security interest in this Lease may be created through the transfer or possession of any counterpart other than the "Original." Although this Lease is dated as of the date first above written for convenience, the actual date or dates of execution hereof by Lessor and Lessee is, or are, respectively, the date or dates set forth opposite the signatures hereto and this Lease shall be effective on the latest of such dates.

Section 29. Successors and Assigns.

This Lease shall inure to the benefit of Lessor, Lessee, the Lenders and their respective successors and assigns.

Section 30. Governing Law.

This Lease shall be construed in accordance with and shall be governed by, the laws of the State of Illinois.

Section 31. Quiet Enjoyment.

Provided Lessee is not in default hereunder, Lessor will not take any action to hinder or molest Lessee's possession of the Equipment and the quiet enjoyment thereof.

IN WITNESS WHEREOF, Lessor and Lessee, each pursuant to due corporate authority, have caused this Lease to be signed in their respective names by duly authorized officers as of the date first above written.

Lessor: American Bank and Trust Company

Date: September 1, 19XX   By _____

Title _____

Lessee: The Manhattan Company

Date: September 1, 19XX By _____

Title _____

     NOTICE: THIS LEASE OF EQUIPMENT AND ALL RENT AND CERTAIN OTHER SUMS DUE AND TO BECOME DUE HEREUNDER ARE SUBJECT TO A SECURITY INTEREST IN FAVOR OF ARLINGTON NATIONAL BANK AND TRUST COMPANY AND THE MILFORD BANK, AS LENDERS, UNDER THE SECURITY AND LOAN AGREEMENT REFERRED TO HEREIN.

STATE OF   )

COUNTY OF   ) SS.

)

     Before me, _____, a Notary Public in and for said State, on this ____ day of September, 19XX, personally appeared _____, known to be the identical person who subscribed the name of the maker thereof to the foregoing instrument as _____ of American Bank and Trust Company, and acknowledged that he executed the same as his free and voluntary act and deed, and as the free and voluntary act and deed of such corporation for the uses and purposes therein setforth.

                /s/ _____

                        Notary Public

(NOTARIAL SEAL)

My Commission Expires:

_____

STATE OF   )

COUNTY OF   ) SS.

)

     Before me, _____, a Notary Public in and or said State, on this ____ day of September, 19XX, personally appeared

_____, known to be the identical person who subscribed the name of the maker thereof to the foregoing instrument as _____ _ of The Manhattan Company, and acknowledged that he executed the same as his free and voluntary act and deed, and as the free and voluntary act and deed of such corporation for the uses and purposes therein set forth.

/s/ _____
Notary Public

(NOTARIAL SEAL)

My Commission Expires:

_____

ANNEX A

CERTIFICATE OF LESSEE

This Certificate is delivered by the undersigned pursuant to the Equipment Lease (the "Lease") dated as of September 1, 19XX between American Bank and Trust Company (the "Lessor") and The Manhattan Company (the "Lessee").

The undersigned hereby certifies that:

1.   The representations and warranties contained in Section 5 of the Lease are true and accurate on and as of the date of this Certificate as though made on and as of such date and the Equipment has not been used prior to the date shown opposite the "Date of Acceptance" in Schedule A-I hereto.

2.   No Event of Default (as defined in the Lease) or event which, with the lapse of time or the giving of notice, or both, would become an Event of Default, has occurred and is continuing.

3.   The Equipment described in Schedule A-I hereto has been delivered to the Location of Equipment described in Schedule 2 to the Lease, has been inspected by authorized representative(s) of Lessee, has been fully and finally accepted by Lessee on behalf of Lessor under the Purchase Documents (as defined in the Lease) and on behalf of Lessee under the Lease on the date of acceptance indicated in Schedule A-I hereto and on said date has been found to be in good working order, new and unused, has been marked in accordance with Section 7 of the Lease and is Equipment described in such Schedule A-I.

Dated: September _____, 19XX

THE MANHATTAN COMPANY

By   _____

Title   _____

SCHEDULE A-1

Description of Equipment

Manufacturer: International Computer Manufacturer Corporation

Year: 19XX.

Mfr.	Type/Model	Qty.	Feature	Serial Number	Description	Invoice Price
ICM	3158/U36	1			4MB Processing Unit	$2,624,100
		1	1433		3rd Block Multi-plexer	16,160
		1	1434		4th Block Multi-plexer	15,040
		1	1435		5th Block Multi-plexer	7,565
		1	7840		3213 Printer Attachment	5,545
ICM	3213/1	1			Console Printer	7,635
		1	4450		Forms Stand	54
					TOTAL	$2,676,099

Date of Acceptance: September 1, 19XX

INCUMBENCY CERTIFICATE

This Certificate is delivered by the undersigned pursuant to the Equipment Lease (the "Lease") dated as of September 1, 19XX between American Bank and Trust Company (the "Lessor") and The Manhattan Company (the "Lessee").

The undersigned hereby certifies that the following persons are on the date hereof, and at all times since _____, 19XX have been, duly elected or appointed, qualified and acting officers of the Lessee holding the respective offices set opposite their names below and that the signatures set opposite their respective names and offices are their genuine signatures:

Names   *Title*   *Signature*

_____

_____

_____

_____

Dated: September ____, 19XX

THE MANHATTAN COMPANY

By_____

Title_____

OPINION OF LESSEE'S COUNSEL

Gentlemen:

As Counsel of The Manhattan Company ("Lessee"), I have examined the Equipment Lease dated as of September 1, 19XX (the "Lease"), between Lessee and American Bank and Trust Company ("Lessor"), the Purchase Documents (as defined in the Lease) entered into by Lessee and such other documents and corporate records as I have deemed relevant. Based on such examination, I am of the opinion that:

(i) Lessee is a corporation duly organized, validly existing and in good standing under the laws of the State of Delaware, with adequate corporate power to enter into the Lease and the Purchase Documents and is duly qualified to do business and in good standing in the jurisdiction where the Equipment (as defined in the Lease) will be located;

(ii) The Lease and the Purchase Documents executed by Lessee have been duly authorized, executed and delivered by Lessee and constitute valid, legal and binding agreements, enforceable in accordance with their terms, subject as to enforcement of remedies to applicable bankruptcy and insolvency laws;

(iii) No approval, consent or withholding of objection is required from any governmental authority with respect to the entering into or performance by Lessee of the Lease or the Purchase Documents;

(iv) To my knowledge, the entering into and performance by Lessee of the Lease and the Purchase Documents does not and will not violate any judgment, order, law or regulation applicable to Lessee or any provision of Lessee's certificate of incorporation or by-laws or result in any breach of, or constitute a default under, or result in the creation of any lien, charge, security interest or other encumbrance upon any assets of Lessee or on the Equipment pursuant to any indenture, mortgage, deed of trust, bank loan or credit agreement or other instrument to which Lessee is a party or by which it or its assets may be bound, other than the rights of Lessee under the Lease and the rights of the Lenders (as defined in the Lease) under the Security Agreement (as defined in the Lease);

(v) To my knowledge, there are no suits or proceedings pending or threatened in any court or before any regulatory commission, board or other governmental authority against or affecting Lessee, which will have a material adverse effect on the ability of Lessee to fulfill its obligations under the Lease;

(vi) Lessee is not in default in the payment of the principal of or interest on any indebtedness for borrowed money or in default under any instrument or instruments or agreements under and subject to which any indebtedness for borrowed money has been issued; and no event has occurred and is continuing under the provisions of any such instrument or agreement which with the lapse of time or the giving of notice, or both, would constitute an event of default thereunder; and

(vii) At the time Lessor becomes the owner of the Equipment, such Equipment will constitute "new section 38 property" within the meaning of Sections 46 and 48 of the Internal Revenue Code of 1954, as amended ("Code"), and will not have been used by any person so as to preclude "the original use of such property" within the meaning of Sections 48(b) and 167(c)(2) of the Code from commencing with Lessor.

ANNEX D

CERTIFICATE AS TO PRICE

This Certificate is delivered by the undersigned pursuant to the Equipment Lease (the "Lease") dated as of September 1, 19XX between American Bank and Trust Company (the "Lessor") and The Manhattan Company (the "Lessee").

The undersigned hereby certifies that the attached invoice(s) correctly set forth the full Lessor's Cost (as defined in the Lease) of the Equipment (as defined in the Lease) more particularly described below:

Mfr.	Type/Model	Qty.	Feature	Serial Number	Description	Invoice Price
ICM	3158/U36	1			4MB Processing Unit	$2,624,100
		1	1433		3rd Block Multiplexer	16,160
		1	1434		4th Block Multiplexer	15,040
		1	1435		5th Block Multiplexer	7,565
		1	7840		3213 Printer Attachment	5,545
ICM	3213/1	1			Console Printer	7,635
		1	4450		Forms Stand	54
					TOTAL	$2,676,099

The undersigned hereby confirms its understanding that the Basic Lease Rate Factor, the Casualty Values and the Termination Values (as such terms are defined in the Lease) with respect to the above-described computer equipment for which payment is to be made on the Closing Date are as set forth in Attachments A, B and C of Schedule 2 to the Lease, copies of which Attachments are attached hereto.

Very truly yours,

Dated: September _____, 19XX

THE MANHATTAN COMPANY

By _____

Title _____

SCHEDULE 1

Equipment Lease

Dated as of September 1, 19XX

between

American Bank and Trust Company ("Lessor")

and

The Manhattan Company ("Lessee")

Description of Equipment

Manufacturer: International Computer Manufacturer Corporation

Year: 19XX

Mfr.	Type/Model	Qty.	Feature	Serial Number	Description	Invoice Price
ICM	3158/U36	1			4MB Processing Unit	$2,624,100
		1	1433		3rd Block Multiplexer	16,160
		1	1434		4th Block Multiplexer	15,040
		1	1435		5th Block Multiplexer	7,565
		1	7840		3213 Printer Attachment	5,545
ICM	3213/1	1			Console Printer	7,635
		1	4450		Forms Stand	54
					TOTAL	$2,676,099

SCHEDULE 2

Basic Terms of Lease

Investment Tax Credit: 10%
Expiration Date: 7 years after Closing Date
Cut-Off Date: September 1, 19XX
First Early Termination Date: September 1, 19XX
First Basic Rent Date: September 1, 19XX

Basic Rent Dates:*   The 1st day of each month commencing
                             September 19XX to and including
                             August 19XX

Last Basic Rent Date: August 1, 19XX
Overdue Rate: the Lender's Interest Rate plus 1 3/4%
Depreciable Life: 7 years
Depreciation Method: 200% DDB/SYD
Salvage Value: 0%

Agent's Address: The Milford Bank
                             200 West Street
                             Baltimore, Maryland 21229

Lenders' Interest Rate: 9%

Location of Equipment: The Manhattan Company
                             Cleveland, Ohio

Basic Rent: The Basic Rent payable on each Basic Rent Date for the
             Equipment subject to this Lease shall be an amount equal to
             the Basic Rate Factor applicable to the Equipment as set
             forth in Attachment A to this Schedule 2 multiplied by the
             Lessor's Cost of the Equipment.

---

*If the Lease is renewed pursuant to Section 20(c) thereof, Basic Rent Dates shall continue to
be the 1st day of each month during the renewal term(s).

Attachment A to Schedule 2

Basic Lease Rate Factor Shall be:	1.22350%
Basic Rent (per month) Shall Be:	$32,742.07

Attachment B to Schedule 2

Attachment B to Schedule 2

SCHEDULE OF CASUALTY VALUES

The Casualty Value of any Unit to be paid on any Basic Rent Date pursuant to Section 12 of the Lease shall be an amount equal to the percentage of Lessor's Cost of the Unit set forth opposite the number of such Basic Rent Date in the following schedule; provided, however, that in the event Lessee is liable to make payments pursuant to Section 9 of the Lease to reflect a Loss of Investment Credit or Loss of Depreciation Deduction (as such terms are defined therein) such percentage of Lessor's Cost shall be redetermined and adjusted in a manner which, after taking into account such payments, will provide the Lessor the same pre-tax yield and after-tax cash flow as contemplated by the Lease except that no such adjustment shall decrease Casualty Value below the amount required to redeem, on any Basic Rent Date, the Notes (as defined in the Security Agreement) then outstanding at a price equal to the principal amount thereof plus accrued interest thereon to such date and premium, if any, thereon.

Basic Rent Payment Date No.	Percentage of Lessor's Cost
1	107.214
2	106.840
3	106.462
4	106.082
5	105.606
6	105.126
7	104.643
8	104.156
9	103.642
10	103.123
11	102.578
12	102.029
13	101.476
14	100.896
15	100.311
16	99.721
17	99.104
18	98.482
19	97.855
20	97.224
21	96.575
22	95.921

Basic Rent Payment Date No.	Percentage of Lessor's Cost
23	95.249
24	94.571
25	93.887
26	93.186
27	92.480
28	91.768
29	91.037
30	90.302
31	89.559
32	88.812
33	88.053
34	87.287
35	86.508
36	85.724
37	84.934
38	77.720
39	76.911
40	76.120
41	75.361
42	74.592
43	73.814
44	73.027
45	72.230
46	71.422
47	70.605
48	69.779
49	68.942
50	68.095
51	67.239
52	66.372
53	65.494
54	64.606
55	63.709
56	62.801
57	61.890
58	60.967
59	60.041
60	59.104
61	58.158
62	50.795
63	49.833
64	48.861
65	47.884

Basic Rent Payment Date No.	Percentage of Lessor's Cost
66	46.895
67	45.893
68	44.877
69	43.861
70	42.832
71	41.803
72	40.761
73	39.706
74	38.650
75	37.580
76	36.498
77	35.415
78	34.317
79	33.203
80	32.074
81	30.957
82	29.824
83	28.701
84	27.564
After 84th Basic Rent payment up to end of primary lease term	26.410
Thereafter	20.000

Attachment C to Schedule 2

SCHEDULE OF TERMINATION VALUES

The Termination Value of the Equipment to be paid on the thirty-seventh Basic Rent Date or any succeeding Basic Rent Date during the primary term of the Lease pursuant to Section 21 of the Lease shall be an amount equal to the percentage of Lessor's Cost of the Equipment set forth opposite the number of such Basic Rent date in the following schedule; provided, however, that in the event Lessee is liable to make payments pursuant to Section 9 of the Lease to reflect a Loss of Investment Credit or Loss of Depreciation Deduction (as such terms are defined therein) such percentage of Lessor's Cost shall be redetermined and adjusted in a manner which, after taking into account such payments, will provide the Lessor the same pre-tax yield and after-tax cash flow as contemplated by the Lease except that no such adjustment shall decrease Termination Value below the amount required to redeem, on any Basic Rent Date, the Notes (as defined in the Security Agreement) then outstanding at a price equal to the principal amount thereof plus accrued interest to such date and premium, if any, thereon.

Basic Rent Payment Date No.	Percentage of Lessor's Cost
37	71.498
38	70.643
39	69.781
40	68.913
41	68.032
42	67.144
43	66.249
44	65.347
45	64.438
46	63.522
47	62.599
48	61.669
49	60.731
50	59.787
51	58.835
52	57.875
53	56.908
54	55.934
55	54.952
56	53.963
57	52.973

Basic Rent Payment Date No.	Percentage of Lessor's Cost
58	51.975
59	50.975
60	49.968
61	42.543
62	41.526
63	40.502
64	39.470
65	38.437
66	37.393
67	36.340
68	35.276
69	34.214
70	33.143
71	32.074
72	30.994
73	29.904
74	28.817
75	27.719
76	26.610
77	25.504
78	24.385
79	23.254
80	22.110
81	20.980
82	19.837
83	18.707
84	17.565
Thereafter	Not Applicable

Appendix E

CERTIFICATE OF NON-USE

The American Company ("Lessee"), a Delaware corporation, does hereby represent and warrant to the Able Leasing Corporation ("Lessor") that the equipment described in Acceptance Supplement No. ____, dated _____, 19X9 (attached hereto as Exhibit A and made a part hereof) which the Lessee desires the Lessor to purchase and lease to the Lessee, in accordance with the terms of a lease dated January 3, 19X9 by and between Lessee and Lessor has not been used by any person so as to preclude "the original use of such property" (within the meaning of Section 167(c)(2) of the Internal Revenue Code of 1954, as amended to the date hereof) from commencing with the Lessor as of _____, 19X9.

Dated: _____, 19X9

The American Company

By _____

Title _____

INDEX